D1236823

SOCIAL COMPETENCE

SOCIAL COMPETENCE

Edited by
Jeri Dawn Wine

The Ontario Institute for Studies in Education

and
Marti Diane Smye

Jackson Smith Ltd., Toronto

The Guilford Press
New York   London

© 1981 The Guilford Press, New York
A Division of Guilford Publications, Inc.
200 Park Avenue South, New York, N.Y. 10003

Printed in the United States of America

Library of Congress Cataloging in Publication Data

Main entry under title:
Social competence.
  Bibliography: p.
  Includes indexes.
    1. Social interaction—Therapeutic use.   2. Social interaction.   3. Psychology,
Pathological—Philosophy.   4. Psychotherapy.   I. Wine, Jeri Dawn.
II. Smye, Marti Diane.
ISBN 0-89862-607-2   AACR1

To our friends, daughters, mothers, sisters—
the women in our lives

CONTRIBUTORS

Michael Argyle, DSc, Department of Experimental Psychology, Oxford University, Oxford, England

Steven R. Asher, PhD, Department of Educational Psychology, University of Illinois, Urbana–Champaign, Illinois

Lorna Smith Benjamin, PhD, Department of Psychiatry, University of Wisconsin Medical School, and Wisconsin Psychiatric Institute, Madison, Wisconsin

Patricia Benner, RNMS, School of Education, University of California, Berkeley, California

Lynda Butler, MA, Department of Psychology, University of Waterloo, Waterloo, Ontario, Canada

John P. Galassi, PhD, Department of Counseling Psychology, University of North Carolina at Chapel Hill, Chapel Hill, North Carolina

Merna Dee Galassi, EdD, Department of Counselor Education, North Carolina State University, Raleigh, North Carolina

Linda Gruson, PhD, Department of Psychology, University of Waterloo, Waterloo, Ontario, Canada

Shelley Hymel, MA, Department of Educational Psychology, University of Illinois, Urbana–Champaign, Illinois

Sharon E. Kahn, PhD, Department of Counseling Psychology, University of British Columbia, Vancouver, British Columbia, Canada

Richard S. Lazarus, PhD, Department of Psychology, University of California, Berkeley, California

Donald Meichenbaum, PhD, Department of Psychology, University of Waterloo, Waterloo, Ontario, Canada

Gordon L. Paul, PhD, Department of Psychology, University of Houston, Houston, Texas

Barbara R. Sarason, PhD, Department of Psychology, University of Washington, Seattle, Washington

Myrna B. Shure, PhD, Department of Mental Health Sciences, The Hahnemann Medical College and Hospital, Philadelphia, Pennsylvania

Marilyn J. Vedder, BA, Department of Counseling Psychology, University of North Carolina at Chapel Hill, Chapel Hill, North Carolina

Jeri Dawn Wine, PhD, Department of Applied Psychology, The Ontario Institute for Studies in Education, Toronto, Ontario, Canada

Judith Wrubel, MA, Human Development Program, University of California, San Francisco, California

PREFACE

The quality of interpersonal interactions as an essential ingredient in effective human functioning is becoming an increasingly focal issue among practitioners and researchers. The growth of social competence approaches has followed in the wake of several decades of assaults on the traditional medical model of mental illness and mental health. While the medical model defines mental health as the absence of defects, competence approaches focus on a much fuller range of human functioning. Identification and development of social skills, social problem-solving capacities, and strategies for coping with interpersonal stress are among the areas emphasized in social competence models, reflecting the view that humans are capable of functioning effectively beyond the avoidance of psychological disturbance.

The literature in the social competence area is rapidly mushrooming, at least partially as a function of our increasingly complex social milieu. Community psychologists frequently include educational programs designed to enhance interpersonal skills in their community-based programs. Practitioners are increasingly providing people with opportunities to improve their abilities to deal with others in rewarding, mutually satisfactory ways. There are a variety of extant concepts of social competence, associated assessment methodologies, and approaches to enhancing social competence available to the interested practitioner and researcher. The present volume presents a broad sample of the most influential and well researched of these approaches.

The volume grew out of the efforts and interests of a group of individuals in the Department of Applied Psychology at The Ontario Institute for Studies in Education in Toronto, Ontario. Jeri Wine joined the Applied Psychology faculty in counseling psychology in 1975, where she found a number of students and staff, under the stimulation of Clifford M. Christensen, conducting research and counseling practica in a program labeled the Interpersonal Coping Skills (ICS) approach. The ICS program is a synthesis of social learning theory, cognitive interpretations of emotion, and social problem-solving models of human interaction. Thus those who were exposed to the ICS program were exposed to a range of related social competence literature and approaches. Marti Smye was a student in the doctoral counseling program at that time and was strongly influenced by her exposure to the social competence counseling practicum and literature.

Jeri Wine moved from interest in evaluation anxiety, a negative or defect intrapersonal variable that interferes with competent performance, to an interest in nonevaluative description of social behaviors and cognitions, to her current focus on feminist analyses of social interactions. The latter shift was largely occasioned by the literature review involved in the editing of this volume. It became clear that as social competence is becoming popularized and institutionalized, its defining characteristics have been masculinized, a development that has unfortunate implications for the welfare of human beings. Marti Smye completed her doctoral dissertation work with Jeri Wine on a detailed examination of the social behaviors and cognitions of adolescent females and males. Wine and Smye have coauthored publications on their social-competence-related work in *Sex Roles: A Journal of Research* and in C. Stark-Adamec (Ed.), *Sex Roles: Origins, Influences, and Implications for Women* (1980).

The variety of competing, sometimes contradictory, concepts and approaches currently popular in the social competence area stimulated us to organize a conference, with a view to assembling some of the spokespersons in this area for idea presentation and exchange. With a small committee of doctoral students, who included Sandra Daley, Bernadette Lalonde, Randy Cole, Fernando Ferreira, and John Johnston, we organized a highly successful and stimulating 2-day conference entitled "The Identification and Enhancement of Social Competence" in August 1978 at The Ontario Institute for Studies in Education. The conference included symposia and multiple workshops, with participants from Canada, the United States, and Great Britain, including Donald Meichenbaum, Myrna Shure, George Albee, Richard Lazarus, Steven Asher, Michael Argyle, Pat Jakubowski, Irwin Sarason, Clifford Christensen, and Michel Hersen.

We asked some of the conference participants to contribute chapters to a volume; updated versions of their conference presentations appear here. These include the chapters by Meichenbaum, Butler, and Gruson (Chapter 2), Wrubel, Benner, and Lazarus (Chapter 3),

Asher and Hymel (Chapter 5), Shure (Chapter 6), Paul (Chapter 8), and Argyle (Chapter 9). We solicited additional chapters from other leading contributors to the social competence area, in an effort to assemble a broadly representative sample of the most influential work in the area. Part I of the book presents broad perspectives on the social competence construct, including historical background, conceptual models, and critical reviews. Part II presents work on the assessment and enhancement of social competence in children, while Part III focuses on institutionalized psychiatric populations. In Part IV a British social interaction approach to social skills training is contrasted with the popularized North American assertiveness model. The approaches presented in the book vary in their target populations and settings and in their concepts of social competence from those that focus on packages of specific overt behavioral skills to those primarily concerned with cognitive structures. They all share an emphasis on the effectiveness of interpersonal interaction.

We wish to extend our gratitude to Clifford M. Christensen, who provided the initial stimulation for examination of social competence constructs, and to that small band of hard-working graduate students, most of whom have now earned their doctorates, who helped us organize the conference on the identification and enhancement of social competence. Jeri Wine wishes to offer special thanks to her fine friend, Anneke Steenbeek, who sustained her with constant good humor, interest, and encouragement through the long and sometimes painful process of editing this volume.

Jeri Dawn Wine
Marti Diane Smye

CONTENTS

I

PERSPECTIVES ON SOCIAL COMPETENCE: BACKGROUND, CRITICAL ISSUES, AND CONCEPTUAL MODELS

FROM DEFECT
TO COMPETENCE MODELS

JERI DAWN WINE

JERI DAWN WINE is Associate Professor in the Department of Applied Psychology at The Ontario Institute for Studies in Education (OISE), Toronto, Ontario, Canada. She is perhaps best known for her work in cognitive–attentional interpretations of evaluation anxiety. Since 1975 she and her research team at OISE, including the coeditor of this volume, Marti Diane Smye, have explored cognitive–behavioral assessment of the social behavior of adolescents. Her more recent interests lie in feminist analysis of social interaction, work that is represented by three coauthored chapters in C. Stark-Adamec (1980), *Sex Roles: Origins, Influences, and Implications for Women.*

The present chapter is a critical overview of models of human functioning spanning several centuries. Defect models, particularly the demonological and medical models, are examined in the context of their service of social ideologies, and their many deficiencies—from inaccuracies through gross injustices—are noted. These deficiencies are demonstrated to be inherent in the basic assumptions of defect models, independent of their content. The rise of competence models is sketched with cautious optimism; it is noted that investigators and helping professionals must remain cognizant of the values inherent in the models they espouse.

Work in social competence is one of the most rapidly growing areas in the current psychological literature. The breadth and diversity of this literature is well represented by the chapters in the present volume, each of them authored by psychologists who are active contributors to the literature. These contributions vary in their conceptual frameworks from those that heavily emphasize the importance of cognitive processes in social competence to those that are almost solely concerned with specified overt behaviors. Represented are theoretical, assessment, and intervention focuses whose target populations range from children and adolescents to "normal" and institutionalized adults. Their concern in common is the understanding and enhancement of human effectiveness in social environments.

The advent of competence approaches is a fairly late development in the human service professions. Until recent years, these professions have been dominated by defect approaches, the medical and psychoanalytic models their best known examples. Adherents of defect approaches assume that pathological, socially deviant behavior is the most important feature to observe about human functioning. Deviant behavior is attributed to stable states inside the person, the cause of which occurred at some time removed from the present. In contrast, competence models are concerned with a fuller range of human functioning, stressing positive capacities. The ongoing interaction between individual and environment is emphasized; the two are regarded as mutually influencing, and the relationships between them as fluid and changeable. The person–environment relationship has been described as interdependent or transactional.

In the present chapter, I examine some of the trends that contributed to the recent burgeoning of interest in social competence, with particular attention to the shift from preoccupation with pathology to a focus on positive, effective functioning. In the post-World War II years the defect approaches that had long held sway in the mental health professions came under increasingly vociferous attack from a variety of quarters, resulting in their widespread rejection by many helping professionals. Though defect models are far from dead, many practitioners and researchers are presently likely to espouse competence approaches that accentuate positive capacities. Psychologists of this ilk often have a community orientation, and are concerned with identifying and enhancing the competencies of as many people as possible through educational and community-based programs. If their work is with individuals they are likely to view therapeutic change as the function of an educational process, and to be highly sensitized to environmental influences. Competency workers are attempting to generate vocabulary and associated concepts that are not simply translations of but qualitatively differing alternatives to defect model terminology and constructs. The growing literature in social competence is representative of the conviction of many psychologists that the most important features of human environments are other people, and among the most essential human competencies are those that contribute to mutually satisfying, rewarding interpersonal relationships.

In this chapter, I have assumed the prerogative of an editor, that of having both the first and last word—first, because it literally is the first chapter; last, because I, unlike the other authors, have had the privilege of reading and drawing on their contributions. I have not overviewed the literature on social competence; the other contributors herein have done so quite adequately. What I have attempted to do in this chapter is to provide a background and context for understanding the recent burgeoning of interest in social competence. Such a venture invariably exposes an author's prejudices and predilections whether such self-exposure is intentional or not. In this chapter, I have made an effort to be quite explicit about my biases. In addition, I have carried this process a step further in an attempt to explicate the values implicit in the models of human functioning under discussion here.

THE NATURE AND PURPOSES OF MODELS

Models of human functioning have no reality in and of themselves. Rather, "the basic character of a model is that it is a conceptual analogy that allows us to construe behavior in terms that are more familiar" (Heller & Monahan, 1977, p. 12).

> When we are confronted with a set of events or a structure we do not understand, we may attempt to give an account of the events or structure that relies upon an analogy. Thus we may conceive of the brain *as if* it were a computer, or may think of the heart *as if* if were a pump. In each case we attempt to understand the puzzling events or structures that confront us by thinking of them as if they were other events or structures with which we are more familiar. Of course, we may use analogies to help us understand events that are much more broadly conceived or problems that are less well defined than our examples of the heart or brain. For example, we may think of abnormal or deviant behavior as if it were an illness or disease. In using illness as an analogue or model, we are attempting to understand a set of events and behaviors which are puzzling to us (that is, abnormal behavior) by assuming that it is analogous to events we understand in more detail (that is, disease or illness). (Price, 1972, p. 3)

In addition to allowing us to construe puzzling aspects of reality in familiar terms, models direct their user's attention to particular aspects of the phenomena they are intended to explain, concomitantly deemphasizing aspects not considered of importance.[1] As well, they provide ready-made categories for sorting the phenomena. Perhaps their most important function is to provide dimensions, criteria on which phenomena may be evaluated; for example, the best computer, and thus the best brain, is the most efficient one, one that can handle speedily large amounts of data with little sign of overload. In descriptions of human functioning, the model propounded by any particular expert is, at the least, a statement of that individual's value system regarding what is good and bad in human experiencing, those aspects that should be fostered and encouraged, those that should be discouraged or eliminated. In the case of models of human functioning that are generally accepted at any given point in time, the values embodied in the model are those of the dominant social order. Levine and Levine (1970) have documented the shifts in the models underlying helping services in the United States as a function of prevailing social climate, noting that

> when the predominant ethos favors social change, people will be viewed as essentially good and the cause of problems seen in their living conditions. Helping forms will try to modify existing social institutions toward greater relevance for the immediate conditions of life and will try to develop new social institutions to provide for personal growth and development. When the predominant social ethos is essentially conservative, when the way of life is considered good and the institutions viable, the causes of problems will be located in the individual's personal weaknesses and deficiencies. Since he [or she] is an inadequate being, he [or she] will be able to take advantage of existing opportunities only when he [or she] is brought up to par. The helping form will arise as a separate community facility whose purpose is to help individuals to adapt themselves to existing social conditions. . . . In the language of contemporary social theory, such a mental health facility is primarily an agent of deviance control. (p. 279)

I would add to these observations that societies are essentially conservative, that is, their primary function is to maintain themselves. Their institutions are created for the perpetuation of the dominant social order. Defect models, those that flourish in a conservative social ethos, those designed to identify socially deviant individuals, to explain and correct or eliminate their deviance are, to the

---

[1]For example, I have attempted to avoid trivializing the full range of human experiencing with the generic label "behavior." To do so expands in importance a term whose original referent was overt, observable actions, removing the meaningfulness and descriptive utility of the term. Its use concomitantly reduces in importance many other aspects of human experience, such as thought, fantasy, feeling, intuition.

extent that they exert influence in the delivery of "helping" services, direct reflections of societal values. When models are adopted as expressions of the dominant social ethos they lose their "as if" quality and become reified as immutable statements of reality. Though no one seriously believes that the brain is a computer, many people, lay and professional alike, believe that the *mind* is a substantive entity that is subject to illness. Widely accepted models of positive functioning—in the past these were typically religious and, less often, secular philosophical models—describe socially preferred modes of behavior and experience. From the viewpoint of individuals within society, one of the major functions of models of human functioning are their provision of prescriptions for living. Thus, examination of the value system underlying such models is imperative, both for those who propound them and those who are their "beneficiaries."

Models, of course, vary in the adequacy of their fit to the phenomena they are intended to describe and explain. For example, the descriptive–explanatory powers of the computer–brain analogy is adequate only to a limited range of cognitive functions. It has no utility, for example, for an understanding of right/left brain functioning (or to the aspects of human experiencing to which the somewhat oversimplified right/left brain dichotomy applies) or to the processes involved in the uniquely human experiences of awe or love—the list could extend indefinitely.

In the following section, I describe and examine some of the value implications and the adequacy of fit to human experiencing of two kinds of defect models that have had considerable influence in the history of humanity. These are the demonological model and the medical model.

DEFECT MODELS IN PERSPECTIVE

Human beings have been fascinated throughout recorded history by deviations from socially expected modes of behavior, and have attempted to understand and control such deviations in a variety of ways. The defect models that have been wielded with the greatest influence in Western culture are those that attribute deviant functioning to either supernatural, physical, or psychic causes. These approaches have in common three defining assumptions of defect models: (1) the aspects of human functioning that are most important to observe are those that are deviant and abnormal; (2) these deviant characteristics are assumed to be manifestations of a pathological state located within the individual; (3) the cause of the intraindividual state, whether supernatural, physical, or psychic, occurred at some time in the past. Though traces of the original cause may continue to be operative in the present (e.g., continued consorting with the devil, imbalances in biochemical substrata, an unresolved Oedipal complex), its original and major impact occurred at a time in the fixed, unalterable past.

These basic assumptions serve the function of maintenance of societal value systems and the existing social structure in a very direct fashion. First, they define the limits of societally unacceptable human functioning. In addition, by locating the present impetus for deviance within the person the defect model precludes attention to social-environmental influences, concomitantly defining that individual as a member of a category of persons qualitatively different than persons who are normal, healthy, good. Identified deviants are held to be directly responsible for their own deviance; simultaneously their testimony regarding their deviance is held to be worthless due to their defective classification. They are neither free to challenge the existing value system and defend their behavior from the perspective of their own value system, nor are they—should they accept the prevailing value system—free to challenge the evidence that classified them as deviant within it. To do the former is to provide further evidence of pathology; to attempt the latter is useless, as the accused defective is not a credible witness except in her or his own prosecution. Locating the original cause of the deviance in the unchangeable past eliminates the possibility of genuine change, further locking the identified person into the category of deviant. Given these assumptions the logical means of dealing with persons so identified is either to help them reduce the overt manifestations of their deviance, or to remove the person from society by placing them in the custody of the state, or to eliminate them.

The Demonological Model

Throughout the medieval era satanic influence was considered to be the cause of any form of deviant human functioning. The prevailing value system was that of the established Christian church, which was at first Roman Catholic, later joined and matched in fervor and brutality by the Protestant churches. Within the value system of the dominant social order controlled by the Church the limits of acceptable behavior were extremely narrow; those for unacceptable behavior were wide and elastic. Many of the sins for which persons were condemned to torture and death were in the imaginations of their accusers and inquisitors. For some people the range of acceptability was defined as permanently inaccessible. In the early centuries of the European inquisitions many people were executed who were labeled heretics; most often they were suspected Jews or secret practitioners of the ancient matriarchal religions. Conversion to Christianity typically did not protect these persons; they were considered permanently tainted and defective. If one lived in a Catholic country and was Protestant or vice versa, one was automatically heretic and subject to condemnation to death. A large scale condemnation of this sort occurred in 1568 during the Spanish Inquisition of the Catholic church when the entire, predominantly Protestant, population of the Netherlands was pronounced heretic and condemned to death.

The prominent thrust of the later European Inquisitions, Catholic and Protestant alike, was the identification, torture, and execution of witches. Persecution of people identified as witches had been carried out sporadically throughout the inquisitions; the publication of two documents in the late 15th century launched a greatly intensified witch craze. In 1484, Pope Innocent VIII issued a bull calling for renewed efforts to identify and eliminate witches. Two years later, the two Dominican monks, Sprenger and Krämer, who had solicited the papal bull, published the *Malleus Maleficarum.* This infamous *Hammer of Witches* quickly became the official inquisitor's manual and remained so for the next 300 years.

The vast majority of the people who were convicted of witchcraft were women. The *Malleus* explained that the reason that witches were usually women is that "all witchcraft comes from carnal lust which is in women insatiable" (Sprenger & Krämer, 1486/1948, p. 46). Men were usually immune, according to the *Malleus,* because Jesus was a man and men were created in his image. Typically, the women who were accused were ones who lived independent of men's domination, either spinsters or widows. They were frequently midwives and natural healers: "midwives . . . surpass all others in wickedness" (Sprenger & Krämer, 1486/1948, p. 41). These "white witches" ministered to the illnesses and delivered the babies of the poor, challenging directly the authority of the Church: "For they who resort to such witches are thinking more of their bodily health than of God, and besides that, God cuts short their lives to punish them for taking into their own hands the vengeance for their wrongs" (Sprenger & Krämer, 1486/1948, p. 150).

The crude misogyny of established religion unbridled the sexual fantasies of accusers, inquisitors, and judges. Men were encouraged to see evidence of witchcraft in events as varied as temporary impotence, illness, violent weather, poor crops, death of livestock, ill temper. Inquisitors were directed to use as much torture as necessary to extract confessions. "Huge numbers of women were tortured to such an extreme degree that they confessed to anything and everything their tormentors lewdly desired and thus they became living proof of these fantasies" (Daly, 1978, p. 18). Judges were given license to interpret the evidence presented by inquisitors in the broadest manner possible as long as such interpretation was in favor of the verdict of witchcraft.

Physicians often played a major role in the witch identification process, distinguishing between persons suffering from natural illnesses and those who were genuine witches. In reality there was no escape for anyone accused. A definite diagnostic sign was the witch's mark. The physician subjected the skin to minute examination after all hair was shaved from the suspected witch's body. Any birthmark, mole, scar, or blemish, however small, constituted certain evidence. If there were no visible marks, the pricker, also often a physician, searched for an invisible witch's mark, a spot identifiable because when pricked deeply with a long sharp needle there was no pain or bleeding. Needless to say, there was a good deal of pain and bleeding before such an invisible mark might be found. Should the search for a witch's mark fail, the accused was tortured until a confession was elicited. Indeed, interrogation under torture was routine regardless of whether a mark had been located.

Estimates of the number of witches killed, the great majority burned alive slowly, range from hundreds of thousands to 9 million. The massacre reached its peak in the first half of the 17th century, then dwindled out over the next 100 years—not because of attacks on the demonological defect model itself but rather because the witch craze reached such a high pitch that too many ordinary people were being identified as witches.

The demonological defect model was a simple and highly effective one from the perspective of perpetuation of societal ideology. It was invoked as an explanation for any unexpected event, human or nonhuman. Blame was fixed on a proximal individual who fell outside of the value framework of the Church. The intraindividual state to which blame was fixed was that of witchcraft, a result of a past pact with the devil, rendering the accused woman a witch, member of a less-than-human category. Her only hope for salvation (though not from death) lay in complete capitulation to the authority of the Church through confession and repentance, after which she was executed anyway. All untoward events were thus explained to the satisfaction of most people, virtually all persons considered deviant were eliminated, and the authority of the Church and the values it propounded were absolutely upheld.

The European witch craze was an undeniable example of the maintenance of an existing social order through application of a defect model. It was impossible for any individual within these societies to openly dissent without the probability of themselves being declared witches. According to the *Malleus* anyone who either denied the existence of witchcraft or defended witches were themselves witches. It was not fear, however, that prevented most people from protesting, but genuine belief. There are no surviving documents from the centuries of the witch burnings in which the existence of witches is seriously questioned. The perpetrators of the system were the learned, professional men in these societies: "It [the craze] was forwarded by the cultivated Popes of the Renaissance, by the great Protestant Reformers, by the saints of the Counter-Reformation, by the scholars, lawyers, and the churchmen of the age of Scaliger and Lipsius, Bacon and Grotius, Berulle and Pascal" (Trevor-Roper, 1969, p. 91). The great thinkers and reformers of the Renaissance, the Reformation, and the Counter-Reformation not only did nothing to refute the demonological model, they were frequently likely to add fuel to the witch-burning fires. Those few individuals who were vocal critics did not criticize the demonological model but rather its application—too many nonwitches were diagnosed as witches! For the individuals in these societies the prevailing value system was a matter of self-evident truth—an omnipresent, unquestionable ground for the figure of its proper or improper application.

The Medical Model

The defect approach that gained ascendance after the prolonged reign of demonology was the medical model. The medical model has in 20th century practice combined two kinds of defect approaches, the physical and the psychic. According to the physical approaches disturbed behavior is symptomatic of underlying physically disordered states in biochemical substrata, toxicological substances, physical lesions, genetic imbalances, and the like. In the psychic defect approaches—psychoanalysis and its derivatives have been the most influential of these—human conduct disturbances are attributed to disturbed mental states in the psychic apparatus of the mind. These mental states are themselves attributable to events in the early social history of the individual. Medical terminology permeates the vocabulary of both the physical and psychic approaches (e.g., "mental illness," "mental health," "diagnosis," "pathology," "prognosis," "treatment," "therapy," "remission," "cure").

The physical and psychic approaches have been amalgamated in the practice of psychiatry during this century. Psychiatric diagnostic classifications recognize both physical or organic and psychic or functional origins of disturbed behavior; psychiatric interventions include both physical and psychic modes. Medical training is required for the practice of psychiatry; in North America the practice of psychoanalysis has required a medical degree. This amalgamation of physical and psychic defect approaches has proven a powerful combination, seemingly including the full range of possible explanations for deviant behaviors. The possibilities that classification of individuals in terms of defective behaviors may be a limited and inaccurate view, that the diagnosed behaviors may not be defective, or that their explanation may lie in another realm altogether than the intraindividual one are not options allowed by the medical model.

In the following sections I've sketched in very broad strokes some of the historical events and trends that led to the widespread adoption of the medical model in this century, concluding with an overview of the assaults that have been launched on this approach in recent decades.

ORIGINS OF THE MEDICAL MODEL

The origins of psychiatry and the medical model have been traced by psychiatric historians to the writings of men in the 15th and 16th centuries (Mora, 1967; Schneck, 1960; Zilboorg & Henry, 1941). The Dutch physician Johann Weyer (1563/1960) in particular has been credited with being an outstanding forerunner of modern psychiatry, with the views propounded in his book *De Praestigiis Daemonum* [*The Deceptions of the Devil*]. In this book he developed the position that many women convicted of witchcraft were actually insane. He objected to the brutality of the interrogation that resulted in inaccurate classification, believing that many women so identified were victims of overactive imaginations—their *own*! He did not refute the witchcraft theory, indeed claiming to know the exact number of witches, which was "seven million, four hundred nine thousand, one hundred and twenty-seven, and all of them were controlled by seventy-nine princes" (Szasz, 1970, p. 11). In point of fact, Weyer's position was not a novel one; madness had been a nominally legitimate, though not often effective, defense against the accusation of witch-craft throughout the Middle Ages. Madness was not considered an illness, however, but rather was a label for disturbed behavior that could not be attributed to natural physical causes or to witchcraft.

Sarbin (1967) traced one of the early uses of mental illness and re-lated disease concepts to Teresa of Avila, a prominent figure in the Counter-Reformation of the 16th century. She described a group of nuns exhibiting behaviors that would now be diagnosed as conver-sion hysteria as behaving "as if" they were physically ill in order to protect them from the Inquisition. "If a person's conduct could be ac-counted for by such natural causes, it was to be regarded not as evil, but comas enfermas, 'as if sick' " (Sarbin, 1967, p. 448). Initially the mental illness metaphor was just that, a metaphor, and not intended as a description of reality. The mental illness model differed from the demoniacal model of the Inquisition only in its implication that phy-sicians rather than clergymen should be the responsible social practi-tioners.

In their transition from the Middle Ages to modern versions mental illness concepts also made a transition from metaphor to myth, from the model as an analogy to its acceptance as a direct re-flection of reality. This transition coincided with the decline in power of the Church and the rise of science. Or as Szasz has stated: "The metamorphosis of the medieval into the modern mind entailed a vast ideological conversion from the perspective of theology to that of science" (Szasz, 1970, p. 137). Science replaced theology as the source of explanation for all events, both human and physical in nature.

As the power of the Church declined in the late Middle Ages other means for controlling societal deviants were required. In initial response mammoth "hospital" systems were erected throughout Europe, beginning in 1656 with the Hôpital Général in Paris. These madhouses were not intended as places for treatment or cure, but rather were prisons for incarcerating the insane, who included the poor, the chronically ill, the aged, the indigent, pregnant women and girls, children who "used their parents badly or who refused to work through laziness, or in the case of girls, who were debauched or in evi-dent danger of being debauched" (Rosen, 1963, p. 233). Conditions in these madhouses were deplorable; unruly inmates were routinely chained; brutal physical punishment was common; filth, overcrowd-ing, and near-starvation were commonplace. It was into these condi-tions that the physician Phillippe Pinel introduced reforms in the late 18th century, releasing patients at the Bicetre Hospital in Paris from their chains and taking a stance regarding their care that had far-reaching influence: "It is my conviction that these *mentally ill* are intractable only because they are deprived of fresh air and their liberty" (italics added, quoted in Ullmann & Krasner, 1969, p. 126). Pinel was one of the founders of the French school of psychiatry, and of psychiatry as a medical discipline. His practices were adopted in England and the United States and came to be labeled "moral treatment," a loosely connected set of approaches that were widely used in institutions for the insane during the period 1800–1860.

Moral treatment has been recently rediscovered and is widely touted as a humane, supportive, and highly effective approach to the care of the diagnosed mentally ill (Bockoven, 1963; Dain, 1964; Ullmann & Krasner, 1969). Moral treatment *was* more humane than previous practices but it was no less predicated on the desire to maintain authority and control over persons identified as insane. Pinel's (1801, 1806/1962) *Treatise on Insanity,* the primer text for moral treatment, is a treatise on the effective exercise of coercion. For example: "If met, however, by a force evidently and convincingly superior he (the madman) submits without opposition or violence. . . . In the preceding cases of insanity, we trace the happy effects of intimidation, without severity; of oppression, without violence; and of triumph, without outrage" (Pinel, 1801, 1906/1962, pp. 27, 63).

Benjamin Rush, an American moral therapist, is generally regarded as "the Father of American Psychiatry"; indeed, his portrait appears on the seal of the American Psychiatric Association. Rush was the single individual to establish mental illness concepts as scientific statements of truth in North America. As a medical practitioner, Rush was a proponent of heroic medicine, an approach labeled for its drastic measures. "The point was to produce the strongest possible effect on the patient, of any kind, as if the physician were competing with the disease to see which—the disease or the physician—could produce the most outrageous symptoms" (Ehrenreich & English, 1979, p. 45). Among the procedures used by practitioners of heroic medicine were blistering, vomiting, laxatives, enemas, and bloodletting. Rush was an enthusiastic practitioner of heroic methods; for example, during the yellow fever epidemic of 1793, he drew between 70 and 115 ounces of blood from each of several fever victims over a period of 5 days (Binger, 1966, p. 217).

Rush carried his enthusiasm for the powers of medicine into the diagnosis and care of the insane, recasting all aspects of human functioning in terms of sickness and health. He viewed any deviation from his definition of normal to be evidence of mental illness. Such deviations included opposition to the American Revolution (diagnosed as anarchia); failure to believe in medicine; any criminal act; the use of alcohol; smoking; lying; feelings of chagrin, shame, fear, or anger were all evidence of madness. He strongly believed in the use of terror as a cure for madness, inventing several ingeniously inquisitorial devices for inducing terror, and propounding the use of any and all psychiatric manipulations, however deceptive, that might play on the fear of the diagnosed insane patient. Loss of liberty was considered an essential ingredient to manipulating terror.

Rush's status and influence were considerable. He was one of the signers of the Declaration of Independence and counted among his circle of friends many of the founding fathers of the Confederation, including Thomas Jefferson. He lectured widely throughout North America and Europe. His opus, *Medical Inquiries and Observations upon the Diseases of the Mind* (1812/1962), went through a number of editions and translations into several languages and helped establish psychiatry as a medical speciality. Though Rush made no discoveries as a medical scientist, his claims that medicine *was* a science were widely accepted. His position that there was no difference between mental and bodily illnesses and that all human behavior could be classified as healthy or sick met society's need for scientifically linked explanations of social deviance and for control of deviance.

The methods of moral treatment can hardly be described as overflowing with the milk of human kindness, with respect for the individuality and human rights of the insane. Proponents of this approach did, however, assume that insanity was curable and invested "heroic" efforts in rendering the mad sane, reporting very high cure rates. Though they generally considered disturbed behavior to be the result of defects in the brain they also considered the brain to be highly malleable in response to environmental variations. In the mid-19th century another view gained in prominence, a strictly physical defect approach that eventuated in the demise of moral treatment. John P. Gray, physician and superintendent of Utica State Hospital in New York and editor of the *American Journal of Insanity*, is credited with being the most influential opponent of moral treatment and the most effective early proponent of the strictly organic version of the medical model. Gray's position was that insanity was due to defective brains in constitutionally inferior bodies (Albee, 1978).

General acceptance of these views among medical practitioners coincided with a period of great social unrest in North America—a period of rapid industrialization, of the rise of the robber barons, of the worship of rugged individualism, and of the intensified embracing of scientism as a social ideology, with its values of impersonal mechanistic objectivity. The United States became the recipient of a huge influx of immigrants from other countries. A number of these impoverished, bewildered, non-English-speaking peasants found themselves incarcerated in insane asylums. It was widely believed as a matter of informed psychiatric opinion that these immigrants were constitutionally inferior and hopelessly incurable, and should be housed in separate institutions from native-born Yankees. Herbert Spencer's (1873) formulation of Social Darwinism—that society, like nature, evolved according to the laws of survival of the fittest—provided an unshakable scientific rationale for these positions and for maintenance of the dominant social order. This was the period of the growth of the huge, sprawling, impersonal insane asylums whose purpose was solely the custodial care of the insane. In 1844, the powerful physicians who administered these asylums founded the Association of Medical Superintendents of American Institutions for the Insane, an organization that became the American Psychiatric Association in 1922.

As all insanity was considered to be due to defective brains, psychological or environmental approaches to treatment were seen as superficial, at best alleviating symptoms, leaving the root causes unchanged. Genuine treatment had to await medical research breakthroughs into the organic causes of insanity. The discovery of the linkage between syphilis and general paresis in the late 19th century provided timely grist for the medical model mill and further blocked the possibility of insights appropriate to other problems in human adaptation. The scientific approach grounded in the beliefs that human differences were a function of genetics and evolution was firmly established. A leading American psychiatrist of the 1880s exemplified the impersonal scientific approach by stating in all sincerity that the insane do not suffer unhappiness, and that depressed patients go through the motions of acting sad in a machinelike fashion without feeling genuine sadness (Bockoven, 1963).

PSYCHOANALYTIC CONTRIBUTIONS

In the years following the turn of the century, Sigmund Freud and his followers generated most of the remaining ingredients for the 20th-century version of the medical model. Freud was no less committed to the scientific approach and its language than were his contemporaries. As a physician and neurologist he had been conducting research on human functioning for some years, and was especially interested in explanation and cure of the puzzling conversion hysterias that mimicked physical afflictions but were anatomically impossible. His theories were initially advanced to account for hysteria, and they bear a close resemblance to the medieval theories of demon possession. He acknowledged this similarity on several occasions (e.g., "Do you remember how I always said that the medieval theory of possession . . . was identical with our theory of a foreign body and a splitting of consciousness?") (Freud, correspondence, 17 January 1897/1966, p. 20).[2]

Psychoanalysis, expanded and elaborated until Freud's death in 1939, and enriched by recurring controversies with his followers and their derivative theories, provided the perfect addition to the otherwise arid and limited organic defect version of the medical model. Freud created, then reified, a vast complex psychic machinery couched in scientifically respectable biological terminology. The explanation for any disturbance in human functioning could be found in defects, imbalances in the dynamically interlocking components of this psychic equipment. In its focus solely on intraindividual states as causes for current functioning, states themselves caused by distant, usually unverifiable, typically sexual, events in the individual's early childhood, the psychoanalytic approach was no less a defect model than the organic medical model. It was, however, infinitely more interesting and exciting. Psychoanalysis contained its own combination of physical—"biological destiny"—and psychic defect components. As an example, Freud's position regarding the female orgasm is instructive. That Freud was a committed misogynist has been amply documented (de Beauvoir, 1949; Chesler, 1972; Freidan, 1965; Millett, 1970); the supposed inferiority of women and the appropriateness of their subjection to men were constructs built into the fabric of his theoretical framework. His views on the immature clitoral (defective) orgasm and the mature vaginal orgasm demonstrate the power of the psychoanalytic approach in generating and explaining defective functioning. Physiological research has demonstrated that all female orgasms are clitoral, that the vaginal orgasm is nonexistent (Masters & Johnson, 1966). However, the vaginal orgasm is such a well-learned "fact" that even a self-proclaimed feminist psychologist has argued that though it does not exist physiologically it exists "psychologically" (Bardwick, 1971). Clearly, it is very difficult to bring data to bear in a decisive fashion on propositions generated from psychoanalytic

[2]As Ehrenreich and English (1979) have noted, Freud might have found a more accurate explanation for the hysterical symptoms of these upper-class women had he examined their stultifying existences as the useless appendages of Victorian husbands.

theory. Psychoanalysis in combination with the more strictly organic defect approaches forms an unassailable theoretical position for labeling and explaining deviance.

The medical model has been discussed here as exemplary of defect models in this century because of its widespread acceptance and undeniable impact in the service of the social order, especially in the hands of the psychiatric profession. In focusing on the medical model, I don't wish to contribute to an attitude of smug complacency regarding the role of psychology. Psychologists too have widely embraced both the physical and psychic defect versions of the medical model and have added their own unique ingredients to defect approaches. Ehrenreich and English (1979) note that psychology was born in the late 19th century as a full-blown science complete with its own laboratories. Pronouncements on the human condition made by the men running these laboratories were accepted as scientific truths. "The laboratory bench metamorphosed itself into the speakers' podium, from which the psychologist could hold forth on sexuality, criminology, ethnic differences in intelligence, industrial productivity, child raising, labour unrest—to give just a few of the areas to which early twentieth century American psychologists lent their expertise" (Ehrenreich & English, 1979, p. 198). Kamin (1974) has documented the role that the intelligence-testing movement has played in establishing social policy by demonstrating the defective mentality of various racial groups in support of restrictive immigration policies. Early psychologists who contributed heavily to the establishment of racist government policy include such notables as Lewis Terman, Robert Yerkes, and E. L. Thorndike. Intelligence-based defect models survive in only slightly altered form in the writings of contemporary social scientists such as Moynihan (1965) and Jensen (1969).

DEFECT MODEL ASSAULTS

The medical model was predominant with only sporadic dissent until the post-World War II era when, in North America, defect models in general, and the medical model in particular, came under increasingly vociferous attack from a variety of quarters. The intellectual and social climate of those decades was disenchantment with the scientific establishment in the wake of the scientific horrors perpetrated by Nazi Germany, and the holocausts of Nagasaki and Hiroshima attendant upon American nuclear discoveries. Clearly, objective science was unable to provide answers to the significant value-laden questions of human existence. Indeed, it had become obvious that science was a depersonalized powerful machinery that could be put to the service of any value system. The medical model, whose scientific status was highly doubtful in any event, but whose service of the social order was readily documented, was an obvious target. Thoughtful individuals in a number of disciplines, including renegade psychiatrists, sociologists, lawyers, and psychologists, as well as members of abused groups, such as feminists and homosexuals, all voiced criticisms of defect models. These criticisms focused simultaneously on the inaccuracies and incongruities inherent in these models and on the injustices perpetrated in their name. A position that gained wide currency is the one advanced in this chapter, that the medical model, as a socially accepted defect model, serves to label and control social deviants in the service of the dominant social order (Albee, 1978; Goffman, 1961; Scheff, 1966; Wooton, 1959).[3] Szasz, whose *The Manufacture of Madness* (1970) has been a major source for this paper, was one of the leading critics of this genre.

A major criticism of the medical model has been that mental *illness* is simply inaccurate.

> The basic referent for illness and for synonyms such as sickness and disease is a stable one, extending over centuries. The referent is discomfort of some kind, such as aches, pains, cramps, chills, paralyses, and so on. The discomfort is a self-appraisal through attention to unusual proximal stimuli, that is, stimuli located "inside" the organism. These proximal stimuli, when they occur simultaneously with dysfunction of bodily organs, are the so-called symptoms of illness. (Sarbin, 1967, p. 448)

In contrast, the criterion for diagnosis of *mental* illness is gross misconduct, disordered overt behaviors that are socially unacceptable. Wooton (1959) documented this position in detail, noting that mental illness is both inferred from antisocial behavior, and is then invoked as an explanation for it. The severity of mental illness is determined as a function of the degree of social failure it involves, a fundamentally different criterion than that used for physical illnesses, which are diagnosed through symptoms independent of social norms.

Ignorance or avoidance of environmental events, especially those in the social system, is a frequently cited shortcoming of defect models. Consistent with the position that defect models serve to control social deviance, it may well be that one of their major functions is

---

[3]One need not adhere to a strict labeling hypothesis, that is, that disturbed behavior exists only in the eye of the beholder, to favor the social deviance control position.

to divert attention from deficiencies in the social order. Through defining behavior disorders as symptoms of underlying causes located within the individual, causes which are rooted in the early history or biological equipment of the person, attention is diverted from those current events, persons, and dehumanizing social practices that are significant in precipitating and maintaining the socially deviant behavior of persons diagnosed as mentally ill.

The labeling process itself in the form of psychiatric diagnosis is one fraught with difficulties. Scheff (1966) has presented cogent evidence that psychiatric classification is heavily dependent on contextual factors, with psychiatrists highly prone to assume the sickness of individuals presented for psychiatric examination, the question not being whether they are mentally ill but what the diagnosis should be. With regard to specific diagnosis, the first requirement for a classification system to be useful is that it be reliable, yielding consistent results when used by trained observers. Psychiatric diagnosis has been demonstrated repeatedly to be appallingly unreliable (see Begelman, 1976, for review). In addition, diagnosis is pathology-laden, with the diagnostic decision being which defect label to apply; observation of strengths is precluded, and classification is based on the most extremely pathological of observed behaviors. In the case of physical illnesses, the major functions of diagnosis are to provide directives for treatment and prognosis of the illness. This is not the case with psychiatric diagnosis, specific diagnostic labels bearing little relationship to particular treatments administered or to prediction of future behaviors.

The third edition of the American Psychiatric Association's (1980) *Diagnostic and Statistical Manual of Mental Disorders* (DSM-III) has attempted to deal with some of the most glaring deficiencies of its predecessors. Patients are placed in a diagnostic category but are also referenced according to five other features that direct attention to, among other things, current environmental precipitants as well as to level of competence. McLemore and Benjamin (1979) have presented concerns regarding the DSM-III: "As in the past, diagnosis still rests partly on impressionistic clinical judgment, including for example, global ratings of the severity of psychosocial stresses and the patient's highest level of adaptive functioning during the past year. Second, the system still categorizes human beings in terms of illness very broadly defined. Finally, and most importantly, DSM-III shows near total neglect of social psychological variables and interpersonal behavior" (p. 18). DSM-III was in its first year of general use in 1980; therefore, evidence regarding its effectiveness will not be available for some time. It seems unlikely that it will escape the major criticisms of previous practices, being based on many of the same flawed assumptions.[4]

The nature of the interventions based on defect models are consistent with their basic assumptions. Since intervention is appropriate only when a problem has been identified, it tends to be initiated late in the development of the problem. Whether the intervention is of a physical or psychic nature it focuses on altering the defect, the site of which is placed within the individual. The prototypical physical treatments of drugs, electroconvulsive therapy (ECT), and psychosurgery, attempt to medically fix the individual's biological equipment so that it will function more normally. The traditional one-to-one psychotherapy seeks to tinker with the individual's psychic equipment to repair the psychic imbalance. In practice, mental health treatment of the psychic sort is very expensive, relying on highly educated professionals who are in chronically short supply. It is thus available exclusively to the affluent, and is typically administered on a voluntary outpatient basis. The poor are overrepresented among institutionalized populations who have more severe problems and who are the patients to whom the physical treatments are administered. In any case, neither the physical nor the psychic treatments are particularly effective (see Paul, Chapter 8, this volume).

Labeling through defect models does violence to the rights and integrity of the individual so labeled. With regard to the most extreme of defect labels, that of the diagnosis of mental illness, the identified deviant is deprived of civil rights, liberty, the capacity for self-determination. If accused of a criminal act and diagnosed as mentally ill, the individual is subject to indefinite incarceration without trial. Scheff's (1966) and Szasz's (1961) work has shown that psychiatrists assume persons presented for psychiatric examination to be guilty of mental illness, reversing the "innocent until proven guilty" basic tenet of the North American system of justice. Persons so labeled are stigmatized, placed in a special nonhuman class to be scorned and feared. There is a prevailing belief that this special kind of sickness is permanent; if the person at some later time shows normal behavior, the illness is "in remission"—it is not cured (Sarbin, 1967). Such stigmatization and loss of human dignity have profound effects on the self-esteem of individuals so labeled. The nonhuman status of the person cast in the role of patient is best served by passive, compliant ac-

[4]Benjamin has developed an alternative to the DSM-III based on interpersonal behavior that avoids many of these criticisms. See Chapter 7 of this volume.

ceptance of the requirements of the role—requirements that are antithetical to competent, autonomous adult functioning (Goffman, 1961).

Defect models have been used throughout history to eliminate entire groups of persons considered threatening to the social order, such as witches and heretics in medieval Europe, or to control groups whose subordination is essential to maintenance of the social order, such as women, the poor, or racial minorities. The role that the psychological as well as the psychiatric professions have played and continue to play in using defect models for racist, classist, ageist means of social control has been well documented (Albee, 1969; Kamin, 1974; Ryan, 1971; Szasz, 1970). A growing feminist literature is examining the use of defect models in the justification of men's subordination of women (Chesler, 1972; Daly, 1978; Smith & David, 1975). Ehrenreich and English's *For Her Own Good: 150 Years of the Experts' Advice to Women* (1979) is a recent, thoroughly documented and highly readable example of this genre. It's important to note that though the precise content of defect models may vary, they each have inherent within them the same problems; their application serves essentially the same purposes. As an example, proving the sexual inadequacy of women through their inability to achieve the physiologically impossible vaginal orgasm is parallel to proving the constitutional inferiority of the poor by their greater numbers in mental institutions—both are Catch-22 dilemmas for their victims. There is no more effective social-control device to maintain the subservience of specified groups or to defuse the attacks of social critics than the accusation of psychological inferiority. One need not appeal to the example of Soviet political dissidents incarcerated in mental institutions to make this point, as any vocal feminist accused of arrested psychosexual development or any militant black labeled as intellectually inferior can attest.

THE ADVENT OF COMPETENCE MODELS

Concomitant with the growing disillusionment with and attacks on defect models were a number of developments in the human areas of psychology. These changes reflected a movement away from the negative, intensely individual focus of defect approaches to more broadly based models that demonstrated greater concern with environmental influences on individual behavior, and emphasized positive aspects of functioning. Clinical psychology, whose practical training has traditionally taken place in psychiatric institutions under the supervision and tutelage of psychiatrists, began to move slowly under the prodding of spokespersons like George Albee (1969) toward a position of greater autonomy. There was a growing concern with prevention of human distress in contrast to delayed treatment of full-blown pathology. The postwar mental health movement became the community mental health movement and, at the Swampscott Conference in 1965, community psychology. The major hallmarks of these developments were shifts from a focus on pathology to one on effective functioning, and from the individual to the social environment, accompanied by an attempt to move away from medical concepts and terminology. The growth of community psychology has been described (Levine & Levine, 1970) as a revolution in the delivery of psychological helping services.

Other psychological revolutions were occurring simultaneously. The "third force" in psychology, humanism (the first two being psychoanalysis and behaviorism), was assuming the proportions of a social movement under the leadership of persons such as Maslow and Rogers. The associated development of counseling psychology as a discipline distinct from clinical psychology was characterized by its focus on providing help, often through growth and educational experiences, for essentially normal individuals in dealing with problems of daily living.

In experimental psychology there were parallel developments in the models underlying research on and understanding of human beings. Behaviorists had rejected the medical model, as well as all intra-individual defect approaches, in favor of an environmental control of behavior position (Ullmann & Krasner, 1969). The behavioral model of human functioning was, however, a limited and incomplete one. In the last decade, behavioristic, mechanistic, "empty organism" views have given way to what has been described as the "cognitive revolution" in psychology (Mahoney, 1977). Social learning theorists have developed complex models that highlight cognitive structures and capacities, and the mutually interdependent relationship between the individual and the environment (Bandura, 1977; Mischel, 1973). Theoretical models and research in child development, especially in the cognitive and social areas, have exemplified the shift to positive capacities and the individual–environment interplay (*American Psychologist*, 1979).

The subdiscipline of social psychology, launched by Lewin before and during the World War II era, developed into experimental social psychology, the purpose of which has been to examine uniquely human psychological processes as a function of social–environmental variations. Much of the research in this area has ignored individual variations and has employed contrived, impoverished laboratory situations bearing little or no resemblance to circumstances in the real world. In spite of this average organism–artificial environment combination, experimental social psychology has provided theoretical models and impetus to the cognitive revolution and to the shift to concern with environmental variables.

The single concept that best encapsulates the model of human functioning underlying these developments in psychology is *competence*. We have become accustomed to competence being associated with individuals and groups of human beings, ranging from the competent infant (Goldberg, 1977; Lewis & Rosenblum, 1974) to the competent community (Iscoe, 1974). As Bloom (1977) has stated, "Of all the concepts that have been introduced to link individual problems to characteristics of the social system, the most compelling have been the concepts of competence and competence building" (p. 250).

The defining characteristic of competence approaches is a concern with the effectiveness of the individual's interactions with the environment. These models deal explicitly with the individual's impact on the environment as well as with the impact of the environment on the individual; thus, they generally take a transactional view of the individual–environment relationship. In terms of individual differences, they usually emphasize, in combination with the effectiveness of overt behaviors, cognitive capacities such as response repertoires, coping skills, problem-solving abilities, the capacity to generate appropriate matches between behaviors and situational requirements. Though competence definitions share some basic characteristics they differ in emphasis, some defining competence as possession of intraindividual traits and dispositions (Doll, 1953; Smith, 1966), or as primarily a property of motivation (White, 1959), or in terms of a simple listing of accomplishments (Zigler & Phillips, 1961); others focus on specific overt behavioral coping skills (Hamburg & Adams, 1967), yet others on cognitive capacities (Goldfried & D'Zurilla, 1969).

The shift to competence models has encouraged more broadly based, optimistic views of the nature of human beings. In contrast to defect models, humans are seen as growing, changing, learning, and in continuous interaction with their environments. While defect models tune their users to the observation of pathology, the users of competence models are more likely to be alert to positive behaviors and capacities in individuals. In intervention, helping professionals who espouse competence models are likely to generate broadly based programs intended to be widely helpful to a number of people in a community. When used in individual work, these models lend themselves to helping individuals build skills and competencies for dealing with their world, rather than to the identification, understanding, and elimination of defects. People are seen as at least potentially capable of setting goals, identifying needs, and developing skills that will allow them to cope more effectively with stress, to interact more effectively with others, as well as to lead fuller, more productive lives. These models, at their best, also encourage their adherents to an acute awareness of individual environments and, more broadly, social structures.

In light of these very positive features, competence models appear to have not only avoided the problems associated with defect approaches, but to have no problems that are peculiar to them. They are, indeed, much less restrictive than defect models in allowing for individual variation, change, and environmental influence. However, as in all models of human functioning, whether negative or positive, there are implicit values that bear examination in competence models. Whereas defect models serve the prescriptive function of specifying aspects of human functioning that should be avoided and eliminated, competence models prescribe positive modes of functioning—how individuals may lead "the good life"; they provide professionals with templates for determining which individuals and groups are leading the good life. Competence models are beginning to enjoy widespread popularity and institutional acceptance. As Seymour Sarason (1970) has noted, "when a new, creative, and productive combination of ideas and practice become professionalized and institutionalized, the chances are very good that both the form and substance of this combination of ideas and practice become changed beyond recognition. In the end there is the word, whereas at the beginning there was the idea" (p. xiii). I would add that in the end there is also a gross magnification of the major value implications of any institutionalized model. The widespread forensic use of behavioral technologies is a case in point, often resulting in monstrous extremes of lack of individual freedom and excessive environmental control.

In examination of the values implicit in any model, it's helpful to search for an image, a metaphor, that seems to convey the essence of that model. It appears to me that the metaphorical image that best captures the essence of the competence model is that of "man against his environment" (masculine referents intended). Stated most strongly, it is the flip side of the image conveyed in the defect model associated with Social Darwinism, that is, the rugged individualist actively shaping his environment—in the case of social competence, other people—to his own needs and purposes, a masculinized image closely associated with the growth of industrialized, technological society. The values conveyed by such a metaphor are antithetical, for example, to the Eastern philosophical or North American native peoples' values of living in total harmony and communion with one's environment, and to the related female subcultural values of sensitivity to and concern for people and responsiveness to the needs of others.

Assertiveness: A Case Study

The assertiveness literature is overviewed very thoroughly in Chapter 10, this volume, by Galassi, Galassi, and Vedder, who provide an excellent overview of definitional issues, concluding that perhaps assertiveness should be abandoned in favor of a more broadly based social competence approach. In Chapter 11, this volume, Kahn examines problems involved in application of the assertiveness construct to women. I wish to use an influential piece of research generated from the assertiveness model as a case study to illustrate some of the problems associated with the "man against the environment" metaphor in relation to social interaction.[5] I have selected assertiveness as a focal construct since it conveys this metaphorical image most clearly of available social competence definitions. Though there are a number of competing definitions of assertion in the literature, they all suggest the image of the rugged individualist unswervingly propelled toward his own goals in social situations, actively asserting his rights, expressing his emotions, perhaps even shedding a tear occasionally—all in the service of his own needs (masculine pronouns deliberate).

The study that I will be examining in some detail is one reported by Schwartz and Gottman (1976) that has become a widely cited reference in the cognitive theory and intervention literature (e.g., see Meichenbaum, Butler, & Gruson, Chapter 2, this volume), as well as

[5]Many individuals doing research and intervention in the social competence area may object to the use of assertion as representative of the social competence construct. I submit that it is especially in examination of the most popularized and institutionalized examples of particular models that metaphorical images and their associated values most clearly emerge. Assertiveness, the subject of numerous pop psych books, publicized through the public media, and widely available through established institutions throughout North America, qualifies on these criteria as the most appropriate example of a North American social skills model.

the assertion literature (e.g., see Galassi, Galassi, & Vedder, Chapter 10, and Kahn, Chapter 11). The Schwartz and Gottman article presents a well-reasoned, indeed elegant, analysis of cognitive and behavioral components of assertiveness.

In the Schwartz and Gottman study the accepted definition of assertiveness was the narrowest and most problematic, from a broad social competence perspective, of the available definitions—that of refusal of unreasonable requests. College students were sorted into low-, moderate-, and high-assertive groups on the basis of their scores on the Conflict Resolution Inventory (CRI), a self-report measure of request refusal (McFall & Lillesand, 1971). The dependent measures were also subsets of items from the CRI: in one set presented in writing, the students were to select a model refusal response; that is, they were instructed to refuse. Not surprisingly, there were no differences among the groups on this measure. In the second set, six CRI items were presented on tape. The students were told to "imagine that a friend had given in to the unreasonable request because *the friend did not know how to refuse.* The subjects were asked to imagine that *a friend wanted to know* what to say at the time" (italics added, p. 914). Again, there were no differences in the refusal advice of the students' role-played oral response to their friend. The third set of items was intended to simulate real situations. The students were instructed to imagine that they were actually being confronted by the person making each request and to respond orally as they naturally would in that situation. On this set of items, the students who had been classified low-assertive proved less likely to refuse requests than did those classified as high-assertive. Moreover, in their self-report of thoughts during these situations the low-assertive students reported markedly more "negative" self-statements than did the moderate- or high-assertive students, while the high-assertives reported more "positive" self-statements than the lows. Cognitions were reported on a 34-item questionnaire with equal numbers of previously classified negative self-statements—ones that would make it harder to refuse a request—and positive self-statements—ones that would facilitate request refusal.

In their discussion of these results, the authors compare them to findings in other research "that a variety of *patients* had thought patterns characterized by negative and *maladaptive* self-statements" (italics added, p. 919). This observation is followed by discussion of suggestions for cognitive treatment of nonassertive persons designed to restructure their purported negative and maladaptive thought patterns. The value orientation of these authors, though not explicitly stated, is not difficult to detect: It is obviously better, more adaptive, to assertively refuse an unreasonable request than to concur with it; and, it is, of course, preferable to have positive thoughts than negative ones. An examination of the content of so-called positive versus negative self-statements is instructive from a value perspective. Examples of the positive self-statements are: "I was thinking that it doesn't matter what the person thinks of me. I was thinking that I am perfectly free to say no." Examples of the negative self-statements are: "I was thinking that it is better to help others than to be self-centered. I was thinking that the other person might be hurt or insulted if I refused." These sets of items, rather than reflecting adaptive versus maladaptive thought content, reflect markedly differing value orientations regarding interpersonal interaction. The so-called positive self-statements reflect a self-centered focus on autonomous pursuit of one's own desires. The negative self-statements reflect sensitivity to and concern for the person making the request, an altruistic, nurturant orientation. There is nothing inherently bad or wrong in the latter orientation; it simply embodies different priorities about what is important in interpersonal interaction. The response data demonstrate the altruistically oriented students to be no less competent and able than the assertive students; they could refuse requests when instructed to do so. When advising a hypothetical friend who "did not know how to refuse . . . [and] wanted to know what to say" (p. 914), their helping orientation was engaged and they gave refusal advice. When, however, they were allowed to express their *personal* preference for behavior in these situations, the altruistically inclined students chose not to refuse, explaining the rationale for their choice in their reported thoughts. That the differences in reported thoughts between the low- and high-assertive groups reflect stable differences in values regarding what is important in interpersonal situations is supported by the authors' observation "that not one low assertive subject in the present investigation had cognitive self-statement scores that were similar to those of the high assertive group" (p. 919). These marked differences in thought content undoubtedly reflect what Wrubel, Benner, and Lazarus (see Chapter 3, this volume) describe as the commitment aspect of values; commitments "integrate the individual into the world, particularly the social world, and *determine what is meaningful and salient* in any encounter" (p. 75).

I've discussed the Schwartz and Gottman study in such detail largely because it is a sophisticated one methodologically and conceptually and its impact on thinking and research in cognitive intervention and assertion has been considerable. This example demonstrates the importance of explicit examination of the values embedded in the research questions, methodology, and interpretations in investigations of human prescriptive constructs.

Women and Interpersonal Functioning

Traditionally, the interpersonal realm has been the domain of women. Largely as a result of their reproductive functions, women throughout history have been the nurturers, the caretakers, the tenders of the interpersonal needs of others, while men have busied themselves doing the "real work" of the world. Women's greater investment in interpersonal concerns has been consistently recognized in the psychological literature, though this investment has not always been viewed positively. For example, women's greater affiliation motivation has been cited in explanation for their supposedly inferior intellectual achievement strivings and behaviors (Hoffman, 1972). Stein and Bailey (1973) elaborated on this analysis, suggesting that females tend to invest their major achievement strivings in interpersonal areas rather than intellectual ones.

A recent review reported by myself and my colleagues (Wine, Moses, & Smye, 1980) suggests that the greater investment of women than of men in interpersonal concerns is reflected in greater social competencies. We examined the sex differences research literature on nonverbal behavior in social interaction, communication styles and speech patterns, proxemics, influence and power tactics, eye contact, and differences in specific social behaviors. We organized the evidence under rubrics loosely generated from an information-processing theoretical framework. In addition, we attempted a definition of socially competent behavior that would avoid the implications of much theory and research that reaching one's own self-defined goals and serving one's own needs are the most important yardsticks of social competence. It was our view that social competence definitions should reflect the female subcultural values of interpersonal sensitivity, altruism, and concern for communal good. We took an explicitly evaluative position, defining some behaviors as more socially "good," prosocial or competent, other behaviors as clearly more socially "bad," antisocial or incompetent, equating goodness and competence. A highly competent prosocial behavior was defined as one that results in positive consequences for its instigator *and* for any recipient of that behavior. An incompetent antisocial behavior is one that results in negative, unpleasant consequences for its instigator and/or its recipient(s). The literature reviewed suggested that females surpass males in: (1) being more attentive to social stimuli; (2) being more accurate decoders of social stimuli; (3) being effective encoders of social messages; (4) being more responsive to variations in social input; (5) having language and speech patterns that indicate greater complexity and interpersonal sensitivity; and (6) showing prosocial patterns as opposed to antisocial patterns of social behavior.

The definition of socially competent behavior that we used in the review is an unusual but a defensible one; it brings to the fore issues regarding the value implications of models of social competence. I submit that it is especially important that we examine models of interpersonal effectiveness for their emphasis on the needs of others as well as one's own goals. Stated differently, I suggest that we attend to women's greater historical and individual experience in the interpersonal realm and explicitly adopt female values in our definitions of social competence.

CONCLUSIONS AND CAUTIONS

The primary functions of models are to render a complex set of events manageable, to provide templates to lay over selected aspects of reality in order to organize, explain, and evaluate that chunk of reality. The development of models of human functioning is the essence and purpose of the discipline of psychology. I've described some of the deficiencies associated with defect models, one major type of model. The problems associated with defect approaches are independent of their specific content, and are inherent in their common focus on defects, the individual, and the unalterable past. I've also sketched the growth of competence models, which are more broadly based, and more positively oriented in their description of human functioning. These models show promise of capturing a fuller range of human experience, of fostering individual variation, of providing a much broader view of influences on human functioning and of human beings as agents of their own experience than do defect approaches. It is important to reiterate, however, that models, whether negatively or positively stated, serve a prescriptive function for the individuals who adopt them. For the professional the functioning of human beings is ordered, described, and evaluated on the basis of his or her model. The nature of helping services provided, the research conducted, the data that is collected, and how that data is interpreted are all dependent on the model adopted by the professional, whether it is implicit or explicit. For the layperson, the extent to which a model is generally accepted is the extent to which it is seen as a prescription for daily living, for screening, categorizing, and evaluating one's own and others' behaviors. It is clearly important to examine the values underlying such models.

The reader, shoud she or he be in general agreement with the position presented here regarding the deficiencies of defect models, may have come to the conclusions that those professionals who have been proponents of defect models have been deliberate servants of social ideology and have consciously employed their knowledge in the control of social deviants. Such a view is erroneous. Helping professionals are, typically, dedicated people who have invested many years gaining knowledge in the pursuit of understanding and helping people in distress. That this knowledge is generated from the context of existing models, and that these models are themselves intimately associated with social ideologies are typically not issues that are explicitly acknowledged. As noted earlier, the dominant social ethos at any point in time is, for most persons in a society, an unquestioned ground for the figure of its proper or improper application. In medieval society, everyone—peasant and scholar alike—knew of the existence and evil of witches, just as everyone—lay and professional alike—in the 19th and 20th centuries has known of the reality of mental illness and the importance of eliminating and avoiding it at all costs. It is only in periods when social ideology and thus the ideology of disciplines are in flux that the values embedded in models begin to surface. The process can be hastened by individuals deliberately undertaking the sometimes painful process of examining the values inherent in the models they employ.

THE PRESENT VOLUME

The remaining chapters in this volume convincingly present views regarding the contributions of social competence models. I share much of the optimism and enthusiasm of these authors. It seems essential that psychology in particular and the helping professions in general be oriented to the quality of human relationships, to the nature of interpersonal interactions, and to enhancing the satisfaction and effectiveness of people in social environments. I am convinced, as are many other psychologists, that it is the social nature of human beings that is their most uniquely human feature.

The remaining chapters in Part I, "Perspectives on Social Competence," present conceptual models and literature reviews important to the developing concepts of social competence. In Chapter 2, Meichenbaum, Butler, and Gruson present a conceptual model of social competence that draws extensively on recent theoretical work and is highly cognitive in its dimensions. In Chapter 3, Wrubel, Benner, and Lazarus examine the implications for social competence of the model generated from their extensive research on stress and coping. Sarason, in Chapter 4, reviews findings from a number of research areas that have contributed to concepts of social effectiveness.

Part II contains contributions regarding social competence in childhood. Asher and Hymel's chapter is a thoughtful review of the assessment literature, with particular emphasis on sociometric measures. Shure, in Chapter 6, describes in some detail a major piece of the intervention research derived from the problem-solving model of social competence.

The chapters in Part III examine the application of interpersonal interaction models in the assessment and treatment of institutionalized psychiatric patients. Benjamin's SASB model, which she describes and illustrates in Chapter 7, promises to be an excellent alternative to psychiatric diagnosis, avoiding many of the problems associated with such diagnosis. Paul's chapter summarizes the results of an impressive research program that assessed the effectiveness of training in interpersonal skills for long-term psychiatric patients.

Part IV presents literature reviews on two contrasting social competence models. In Chapter 9, Argyle discusses his social interaction research model as applied to social skills training. The model is one that focuses on a component behavioral analysis; the skill considered most central to a definition of social competence is that of rewardingness. The final two chapters are focused on assertiveness as a social competence model. Galassi, Galassi, and Vedder provide an extensive and comprehensive review of the recent assertiveness literature, while Kahn examines issues specific to the assessment and training of assertiveness in women.

In brief, the volume provides a broad sample of the recent theory, research, assessment, classification, and intervention literature in social competence. It is obviously not the final statement, as this is one of the most rapidly growing areas in the psychological literature, but it is an excellent beginning. I suggest that as social competence models gain in popularity those of us who espouse them maintain an acute awareness of their implications for the welfare of individuals and for humanity.

REFERENCES

Albee, G. W. Emerging conceptions of mental illness and models of treatment: The psychological point of view. *American Journal of Psychiatry*, 1969, *7*, 870–876.

Albee, G. W. *A competency model to replace the defect model.* Paper presented at conference on the Identification and Enhancement of Social Competence, Toronto, August 1978.

American Psychiatric Association. *Diagnostic and statistical manual of mental disorders* (3rd ed.). Washington, DC: Author, 1980.

American Psychologist. Special issue—Psychology and children: Current research and practice. October 1979, *34*, 809–1046.

Bandura, A. *Social learning theory.* Englewood Cliffs, NJ: Prentice-Hall, 1977.

Bardwick, J. *Psychology of women: A bio-cultural conflict.* New York: Harper & Row, 1971.

Beauvoir, S. de. *The second sex* (H. M. Parshley, Ed. and trans.). New York: Knopf, 1949.

Begelman, D. A. Behavioral classification. In M. Hersen & A. E. Bellack (Eds.), *Behavioral assessment: A practical handbook.* New York: Pergamon, 1976.

Binger, C. A. *Revolutionary doctor, Benjamin Rush.* New York: Norton, 1966.

Bloom, B. L. *Community mental health.* Monterey, CA: Brooks/Cole, 1977.

Bockoven, J. S. *Moral treatment in American psychiatry.* New York: Springer, 1963.

Chesler, P. *Women and madness.* New York: Avon, 1972.

Dain, N. *Concepts of insanity in the United States, 1789–1865.* New Brunswick, NJ: Rutgers University Press, 1964.

Daly, M. *Gyn ecology: The metaethics of radical feminism.* Boston: Beacon, 1978.

Doll, E. A. *Measurement of social competence.* Minneapolis: Educational Test Bureau, 1953.

Ehrenreich, B., & English, D. *For her own good: 150 years of the experts' advice to women.* New York: Doubleday, 1979.

Freidan, B. *The feminine mystique.* New York: Dell, 1963.

Freud, S. Letter 56 (to Wilhelm Fliess, 17 January 1897). In *The standard edition of the complete psychological works of Sigmund Freud* (Vol. 3). London: Hogarth, 1966.

Goffman, E. *Asylums: Essays on the social situation of mental patients and other inmates.* Garden City, NY: Anchor, 1961.

Goldberg, S. Social competence in infancy: A model of parent–infant interaction. *Merrill-Palmer Quarterly,* 1977, *23,* 163–177.

Goldfried, M. R., & D'Zurilla, T. J. A behavioral–analytic model for assessing competence. In C. D. Spielberger (Ed.), *Current topics in clinical and community psychology* (Vol. 1). New York: Academic Press, 1969.

Hamburg, D. A., & Adams, J. E. A perspective on coping behavior. *Archives of General Psychiatry,* 1967, *17,* 277–284.

Heller, K., & Monahan, J. *Psychology and community change.* Homewood, IL: Dorsey, 1977.

Hoffman, L. W. Early childhood experiences and women's achievement motives. Journal of Social Issues, 1972, *28,* 129–155.

Iscoe, I. Community psychology and the competent community. *American Psychologist,* 1974, *29,* 607–613.

Jensen, A. How much can we boost IQ and scholastic achievement? *Harvard Educational Review,* 1969, *39,* 1–123.

Kamin. L. *The science and politics of IQ.* Potomac, MD: Erlbaum, 1974.

Levine, M., & Levine, A. *A social history of helping services: Clinic, court, school and community.* New York: Appleton-Century-Crofts, 1970.

Lewis, M., & Rosenblum, L. *The effect of the infant on its caregiver.* New York: Wiley, 1974.

Mahoney, J. J. Reflections on the cognitive-learning trend in psychotherapy. *American Psychologist,* 1977, *32,* 5–13.

Masters, W. H., & Johnson, V. E. *Human sexual response.* Boston: Little, Brown, 1966.

McFall, R. M., & Lillesand, D. B. Behavior rehearsal with modeling and coaching in assertion training. *Journal of Abnormal Psychology,* 1971, *77,* 313–323.

McLemore, C. W., & Benjamin, L. S. Whatever happened to interpersonal diagnosis? A psychosocial alternative to DSM-III. *American Psychologist,* 1979, *34,* 17–34.

Millett, K. *Sexual politics.* New York: Doubleday, 1970.

Mischel, W. Toward a cognitive social learning reconceptualization of personality. *Psychological Review,* 1973, *80,* 252–283.

Mora, G. From demonology to the narrenturm. In I. Galdston (Ed.), *Historic derivations of modern psychiatry.* New York: McGraw-Hill, 1967.

Moynihan, D. P. *The Negro family: The case for national action.* Washington, DC: U.S. Government Printing Office, 1965.

Pinel, P. *Treatise on insanity* (D. D. Davis, trans.). New York: Hafner, 1962. (Originally published, 1801/1806.)

Price, R. H. *Abnormal psychology: Perspectives in conflict.* New York: Holt, Rinehart & Winston, 1972.

Rosen, G. Social attitudes to irrationality and madness in 17th and 18th century Europe. *Journal of the History of Medicine and Allied Sciences,* 1963, *18,* 220–240.

Rush, B. *Medical inquiries and observations upon the diseases of the mind.* New York: Hafner, 1962. (Originally published, 1812.)

Ryan, W. *Blaming the victim.* New York: Vintage, 1971.

Sarason, S. Preface. In M. Levine & A. Levine, *A social history of helping services: Clinic, court, school and community.* New York: Appleton-Century-Crofts, 1970.

Sarbin, T. R. On the futility of the proposition that some people be labelled "mentally ill." *Journal of Consulting Psychology,* 1967, *31,* 447–453.

Scheff, T. J. *Being mentally ill: A sociological theory.* Chicago: Aldine, 1966.

Schneck, J. *A history of psychiatry.* Springfield, IL: Charles C Thomas, 1960.

Schwartz, R. M., & Gottman, J. M. Toward a task analysis of assertive behavior. *Journal of Consulting and Clinical Psychology,* 1976, *44,* 910–920.

Smith, D. E., & David, S. J. *Women look at psychiatry: I'm not mad, I'm angry.* Vancouver, B.C.: Press Gang, 1975.

Smith, M. B. Competence and socialization. In J. A. Clausen (Ed.), *Socialization and society.* Boston: Little, Brown, 1966.

Spencer, H. *Recent discussions in science, philosophy, and morals.* New York: Appleton, 1873.

Sprenger, J., & Krämer, H. *Malleus Maleficarum* (M. Summers, Ed. and trans.). London: Pushkin, 1948. (Originally published, 1486.)

Stein, A. H., & Bailey, M. M. The socialization of achievement orientation in females. *Psychological Bulletin,* 1973, *86,* 345–366.

Szasz, T. S. *The myth of mental illness: Foundations of a theory of personal conduct.* New York: Hoeber-Harper, 1961.

Szasz, T. S. *The manufacture of madness: A comparative study of the inquisition and the mental health movement.* New York: Harper & Row, 1970.

Trevor-Roper, H. R. *The European witch-craze of the sixteenth and seventeenth centuries and other essays.* New York: Harper & Row, 1969.

Ullmann, L. P., & Krasner, L. *A psychological approach to abnormal behavior.* Englewood Cliffs, NJ: Prentice-Hall, 1969.

Weyer, J. *De praestigiis daemonum* [The deceptions of the devil]. In J. M. Schneck, *A history of psychiatry.* Springfield, IL: Charles C Thomas, 1960. (Originally published, 1563.)

White, R. W. Motivation reconsidered: The concept of competence. *Psychological Review,* 1959, *66,* 297–333.

Wine, J. D., Moses, B., & Smye, M. D. Female superiority in sex difference competence comparisons: A review of the literature. In C. Stark-Adamec (Ed.), *Sex roles: Origins, influences, and implications for women.* Montreal: Eden Press Women's Publications, 1980.

Wooton, B. *Social science and social pathology.* London: George Allen & Unwin, 1959.

Zigler, E., & Phillips, L. Social competence and outcome in psychiatric disorder. *Journal of Abnormal and Social Psychology,* 1961, *63,* 264–271.

Zilboorg, G., & Henry, G. *A history of medical psychology.* New York: Norton, 1941.

2

TOWARD A CONCEPTUAL MODEL OF SOCIAL COMPETENCE

DONALD MEICHENBAUM
LYNDA BUTLER
LINDA GRUSON

DONALD MEICHENBAUM is Professor of Psychology at the University of Waterloo, Waterloo, Ontario, Canada, where he has been conducting cognitive–behavioral research for a number of years. Meichenbaum is perhaps best known for his work in self-instructional training. Much of his work is summarized in his book, *Cognitive-Behavior Modification: An Integrative Approach.* Lynda Butler and Linda Gruson, members of the Waterloo cognitive–behavioral research team, are clinical doctoral students who are researching the development of competence. Butler's focus of attention is the development of interpersonal problem-solving skills in school children, while Gruson's research focuses on the development of competence in novice and expert pianists. These are two of several areas of competence being researched at Waterloo. The juxtaposition of diverse areas provides an interesting basis for comparison.

Meichenbaum, Butler, and Gruson make a significant contribution to the social competence area by providing a broad conceptual framework that heavily emphasizes cognitive factors. The import and content of specific overt behavior are minimized as compared to their *meaning* to the actor and recipient. This approach is in marked contrast to other authors in this volume, such as Argyle and Paul. A large body of literature on cognitive theory and research is reviewed and brought to bear on a conceptual framework for social competence. Of particular interest is their emphasis on higher-level cognitive structures.

In recent years the literature on social competence has been burgeoning. Evidence for this growth has been offered by Garmezy, Masten, Nordstrom, and Ferrarese (1980), who searched the *Psychological Abstracts* for the last 50 years and noted a recent exponential increase in research on this topic. A persistent theme in this literature concerns the definition and identification of social competence. A number of different research paradigms have been employed in the study of social competence. Each perspective seems to identify one aspect of social competence to the exclusion of other aspects. One would readily compare attempts to define social competence to the proverbial tale about the blind men who study the elephant, each only having one piece of the elephant's anatomy in hand, but none stepping back to grasp a perspective of the entire pachyderm.

The present chapter is designed to work toward a model of social competence that may help to clarify and integrate the various definitions and paradigms employed in the study of social competence. It is our hope that the proposed model will provide a framework for conceptualizing and integrating many different approaches to the study of social competence.

COMPONENTS OF THE MODEL

The components of the model we are proposing include: (1) overt behaviors; (2) cognitive processes; and (3) cognitive structures. Overt behaviors refer to directly observable behaviors, or what the individual does both verbally and nonverbally in an interpersonal context. Cognitive processes, as we use the term, refer to the thoughts and images (self-statements, expectancies, appraisals, etc.) that precede, accompany, and follow overt behaviors, as well as the thinking skills and styles of information processing that the individual employs in social situations. Cognitive structures is a more elusive concept, but refers in the present model to the individual's meaning system, which provides motivation and direction for both thought and behavior. We shall examine each of these components of the model in some detail, and then consider how they can be employed in conceptualizing social competence. Even though these components are described separately, it is important to appreciate that they are considered in the proposed model to be highly interdependent as they interweave in contributing to social competence.

Overt Behaviors

An examination of the social competence literature (O'Malley, 1977; Sundberg, Snowden, & Reynolds, 1978) indicates that much of the research has focused on the nature of the individual's overt behaviors. As O'Malley (1977) notes, the nature and frequency of behavior patterns is often used to *define* social competence. For example, the Harvard Preschool Project (White, Kaban, Marmor, & Shapiro, 1972) suggested that social competence was reflected in the manner in which children secured adult attention and how they utilized adults as resources. Other behaviors found to reflect children's social competence were the ability to express hostility and affection toward peers, to lead and follow peers, to imitate both adults and peers, and to show pride in accomplishment.

In a series of studies of social competence, Gottman and his colleagues investigated the peer interactions of children in their homes (Gottman & Parkhurst, 1977) and in school (Gottman, 1977; Gottman, Gonso, & Rasmussen, 1975), focusing upon the frequency of social contacts and the sequence of communications within these interactions. Ratings of children's behavior were found to relate positively to peer ratings of popularity (one way of operationalizing social competence.) Similarly, Hymel and Asher (1977) and Singleton and Asher (1977) assessed children's social skills by examining the frequency and quality of their social interactions (see also Asher & Hymel, Chapter 5, this volume). Specifically, the amount of time spent alone, observing peers, and interacting with peers and teachers was recorded, and the interactions were also coded as involving cooperative, affectionate, noncompliant, derogatory, or attacking behavior. Once again, behavioral ratings were significantly related to sociometric ratings. In an investigation of the social interactions of omega children (i.e., children chosen last for athletic teams during play periods at school), Ginsberg, Wauson, and Easley (1977) examined the following aspects of the behavior of these children: (1) their spatial proximity to other children; (2) the amount of physical contact with others; (3) the frequency of aggressive episodes; and (4) the children's location in relation to the rest of the group. The results indicated that omega children were generally peripheral to the stream of ongoing activity. Not only were they isolated in location, but they also engaged in fewer physical and agonistic encounters as compared with higher ranking children.

Trower, Bryant, and Argyle (1978) have microscopically examined the elements of socially competent behavior in adults (see Argyle, Chapter 9, this volume, for an overview of this work). Nonverbal behaviors (such as facial expressions, gestures, gaze, spatial behavior, nonverbal aspects of speech, bodily contact and appearance), as well as verbal acts (e.g., instructions, questions, comments, informal chatting, performance utterances, social routines, and the expression of emotional states, attitudes, and latent messages) have come under study by these authors.

The foregoing are but a few of the examples that could be offered of studies that have focused on what a competent person does while interacting with others. The ability to draw upon a varied repertoire of socially appropriate behaviors pursuant to goal attainment may be considered to be an important feature of social competence. It is the contention, however, of the present paper that a focus on overt behaviors per se is a necessary, but not sufficient, defining characteristic of social competence. We must also take into account the role of the individual's thoughts and cognitions in any definition of social competence. It is to these cognitive processes that we now turn.

Cognitive Processes

The proposed model includes under the rubric of cognitive processes the diversity of thoughts and styles of information processing that occur when an individual is confronted with a social situation. These include the internal dialogue that accompanies behavior and reflects the individual's thoughts and feelings *about* the situation and/or himself or herself, the expectancies with which the individual approaches the situation and his or her appraisal of situational or personal outcomes, as well as the amount and nature of the social information that the individual possesses about the situation. The proposed model suggests that some form of cognitive processing takes place in all social situations. The individual may be highly aware of these cognitive processes on occasion (as, for example, in the case of an anxious, self-deprecating internal dialogue with which the individual is preoccupied to the detriment of social behavior, or in the case of intentional impression management). It may frequently be the case, however, that cognitive processing operates in a highly automatic, thoughtless, or scripted fashion (see Abelson, 1978; Gagnon & Simon, 1973; Langer, 1978; Schank & Abelson, 1978; and Thorngate, 1976, for a more complete discussion of cognitive and behavioral scripts). In this case, the expectancies or thoughts that subtly control behavior are not particularly salient for the individual at the time, but can be brought into awareness and captured by a variety of cognitive assessment techniques.

The present section highlights aspects of cognitive processing that we think important for the competent handling of social situations. We discuss, first, factors that may *interfere with* social competence (negative internal dialogue, negative expectancies, etc.), then turn to cognitive factors (thought content and style) that may *facilitate* positive social interaction. In each instance, we discuss briefly illustrative findings from the social competence literature, as well as potential assessment methodologies.

COGNITIONS THAT INTERFERE WITH SOCIAL COMPETENCE

INTERNAL DIALOGUE

Perhaps the most dramatic illustration of the impact of a negative internal dialogue on social behavior is offered by Greenburg and Jacobs (1966), whose humorous book, *How to Make Yourself Miserable,* provides innumerable examples of negative self-referent ideation that can interfere with the socially competence handling of interpersonal situations. We particularly liked one cartoon of a couple who, while being intimate in an idyllic country scene, entertained the following set of hazardous thoughts: a passing bird could soil their heads; a passing airline could jettison its septic tank on their car or persons; a rabid herring could leap out of the stream and attack their toes; their companion could suddenly realize how boring they were; and so forth. This rather far-fetched account of a romantic afternoon undoubtedly gone awry contains, nevertheless, more than an element of truth. Recent evidence on thinking processes indicates that such negative, self-referent ideation contributes to inadequate performance in a variety of situations. Consider, for example, the following inter- and intrapersonal tasks where the individual is required to be competent: (1) taking an examination (Deffenbacher, 1978; Heckhausen, in press; Hollandsworth, Glazeski, Kirkland, Jones, & Van Norman, 1978; Holroyd, Westbrook, Wolf, & Badhorn, 1978; Houston, in press; Sarason & Stoops, 1977); (2) responding to social challenges (Schwartz & Gottman, 1976; Smye, 1977); (3) undergoing catheterization procedures (Kendall, Williams, Pechacek, Graham, Shisslak, & Herzoff, 1979); (4) tolerating pain (Genest, Turk, & Meichenbaum, 1977); (5) performing in athletic competition (Mahoney & Avener, 1977; O'Hara, 1977); and (6) producing creative cartoon captions and creative responses on tests of divergent thinking (Goor &

Sommerfeld, 1975; Henshaw, 1978). In each of these situations, a common pattern of self-referent negative ideation preceded, accompanied, and followed behavioral acts and contributed to inadequate performance. The nature of the negative ideation was not perhaps as colorful as that offered by Greenburg and Jacobs (1966), but the consequences were likely the same. Meichenbaum, Henshaw, and Himel (in press) have even gone so far as to speculate that a common pattern of thinking processes (which they characterize as a failure to adopt a problem-solving set) contributes to inadequate performance on a variety of tasks. Illustrative of this line of research is a recent study by Schwartz and Gottman (1976).

In trying to understand the nature of social anxiety, Schwartz and Gottman conducted a task analysis of the cognitive and behavioral deficits of individuals who were low in social assertiveness. They identified groups of low-assertive and high-assertive individuals and conducted multiple assessments in order to discern the role cognitive factors might play in the behavioral deficit. They found that low-assertive individuals did not differ from their more assertive counterparts with regard to knowledge of what was an appropriate response on an assertiveness questionnaire, nor did the two groups differ in the behavioral expression of assertion in a safe role-playing situation (i.e., showing a friend how to handle specific assertive situations). If both groups knew *what* to do and, moreover, *could* do it in certain circumstances, then what was the nature of the low-assertive individuals' deficit? The answer was provided by a third condition, in which Schwartz and Gottman asked their subjects to role-play assertive behavior in a situation approximating real life (the subject was to imagine being personally confronted with an unreasonable request). In this condition, the low-assertive group manifested deficient assertive behavior.

In an attempt to understand why high- and low-assertive subjects differed in the real-life role-playing situation, Schwartz and Gottman asked subjects to indicate on a self-statement questionnaire how frequently "positive" as opposed to "negative" self-statements had characterized their thought processes during the preceding assertiveness situations. Positive self-statements were defined as thoughts that would make it easier to refuse an unreasonable request; negative self-statements were those that would make it harder to refuse. They found that moderate- and high-assertive subjects had experienced significantly more positive than negative self-statements in the role-playing situations; whereas low-assertive subjects did not differ in the number of positive and negative self-statements. It appeared that while high-assertive individuals had a positive orientation and usually little doubt in their minds as to the appropriateness of their actions, low-assertive subjects, in contrast, could be characterized as experiencing an internal dialogue of conflict in which positive and negative self-statements competed against one another and interfered with interpersonal behavior. That negative cognitions may play such a directive role in social anxiety was underscored by a study conducted by Glass, Gottman, and Schmurak (1976), who found that cognitive modeling therapy in the form of alteration of self-statements was most effective in reducing underassertive behavior.

The postperformance questionnaire format developed by Schwartz and Gottman has been successfully employed by Kendall *et al.* (1979) with hospitalized cardiac patients and by Henshaw (1978) in the study of creative problem solving. Such an assessment procedure is only one of a variety of means to tap an individual's internal dialogue. We have argued elsewhere (Meichenbaum, 1977; Meichenbaum & Butler, in press) for the development of a *cognitive ethology* that will help us describe the content, frequency, and most important, patterning of self-statements, thoughts, and images that accompany behavior and contribute to individual differences in performance in a variety of situations. It is our suggestion that the cognitive ethologist search the cognitive domain for evidence of explanatory constructs in much the same way that ethologists describe sequences of overt behaviors, looking for evidence of fixed-action patterns, releasing stimuli, and so forth. Such a task requires the development of an armamentarium of techniques (interviews, questionnaires, think-aloud protocols, videotape reconstruction, thought sampling, etc.) to assess more adequately the individual's cognitive processes. These procedures are not without problems (see the recent papers by Cacioppo & Petty, 1978; Ericsson & Simon, 1978; Kendall & Korgeski, in press; Meichenbaum & Butler, in press; Nisbett & Wilson, 1977; Smith & Miller, 1978; and the recent book edited by Pope & Singer, 1978, for a discussion of the advantages and pitfalls of various cognitive assessment procedures). At the same time, it is our contention that any definition of social competence must be broadened to consider the important impact of the individual's internal dialogue on his or her social behavior.

EXPECTANCIES AND APPRAISALS

One aspect of cognitive processes that we would like to highlight is the interaction between the expectancies that an individual brings to a social situation and his or her appraisal of social outcomes, as well as the impact of both on social behavior. "Expectancies" represent the individual's personal prediction (whether from previous experience or the affective meaning that the situation holds for him or her) about what will happen in a given social situation. Expectancies may be reflected in elements of the internal dialogue in which the individual engages in a given situation, as in the case of the person who pauses at the threshold of a party and says to himself or herself: "Here I am, anxious again. I'll probably freeze up. I hate parties." Expectancies may also, in some individuals or in some circumstances, operate without the individual's awareness of specific thought, as in the case of the person whose general sense is that social approaches typically turn out badly for him or her.

"Social outcomes" represent the wide range of events to which an individual may have some cognitive or behavioral reaction. These may include tangible results (e.g., another person's verbal or nonverbal response), as well as internal events (such as physiological reactions, mood states, etc.). We would suggest that it is not the social outcome per se that is important, but the individual's appraisal of this outcome. For example, physiological arousal may be interpreted as debilitating social anxiety, or as nervous excitement in anticipation of positive social experiences. A conversational partner's momentary lapse of attention may be interpreted as disinterest or boredom with oneself, or as the result of the partner's fatigue, social unease, his or her recognition of a familiar voice across the room, or a host of other factors.

The proposed model suggests that expectancies and appraisals of social outcomes interact in complex ways with one another and with social behavior. Expectancies may operate to constrain the social cues that one processes, as well as the evaluation one places upon them. This, in turn, has an important impact upon the social behavior emitted in the situation. Appraisals of behavioral outcomes can in turn so constrain attention and behavior as to set up or confirm expectancies in current or future social situations. An illustration of research findings that are supportive of this view of social competence is a recent study by Fiedler and Beach (1978). Fiedler and Beach, using a decision–expectancy model, secured ratings from adult women on the likelihood of various behavioral alternatives in specific hypothetical assertive situations. They found that expectancies about consequences following a proposed behavioral act more adequately explained unassertiveness and social incompetence than did the subject's behavioral repertoire. Fiedler and Beach conclude that the focus of competence training should be on changing the participant's expectations about the results of his or her behavior, rather than focusing on either values or on specific behaviors. These results are consistent with the data and arguments put forth by Bandura (1977) about the important role of expectancies in influencing interpersonal competence.

An important corollary of this view of social competence is the notion that individuals actively create their environments by their choice of social situations and partners, by their processing of social information in these situations, and by their interpersonal behavior. This is very much a *transactional* view of the person–environment exchange. This view has been presented in some variation by Bowers (1973), Lazarus and Launier (1979; see also Wrubel, Benner, & Lazarus, Chapter 3, this volume), Meichenbaum (1977), Mischel (1973), Moos (1976), Wachtel (1973), and others. In effect, we are suggesting that any definition of social competence must include not only the individual's cognitive or behavioral response to a social situation, but his or her active engendering of a *changing* social environment. It may be that one key ingredient of social competence is the individual's ability to create and maintain positive and supportive social environments. Socially incompetent behavior, on the other hand, may result from distorted or constrained processing of social information, even when the individual has a wide variety of social and behavioral skills in his or her repertoire.

COGNITIONS THAT FACILITATE
SOCIAL COMPETENCE

The focus of the discussion thus far has been on the characteristics of cognitive processes that seem to interfere with social competence. It is much more difficult to specify what elements of thinking facilitate or enhance socially competent behavior. One area of interest in recent years has been *social cognition,* which Shantz (1975) describes as "the child's intuitive or logical representation of others, that is, how he (or she) characterizes others and makes inferences about their covert inner psychological experience" (p. 258). The ability to infer accurately what other people are like and what they are seeing, feeling, thinking, and intending, appears to be an important prerequisite for effective social interaction (Shantz, 1975).

INTERPERSONAL PROBLEM-SOLVING SKILLS

One aspect of social cognition, which has been proposed by Spivack, Shure, and their colleagues at Hahnemann Medical College and Hospital as an important mediator of behavioral and social adjustment at a variety of age levels, is social problem-solving thinking (see Shure, Chapter 6, this volume). Spivack and his colleagues have identified the following interpersonal cognitive problem-solving (ICPS) skills: (1) sensitivity to interpersonal problem situations; (2) generation of alternative solutions to a problem situation; (3) means-ends thinking (the ability to plan, step-by-step, toward attainment of an intra- or interpersonal goal); (4) the tendency to weigh consequences in terms of their probable effectiveness and social acceptability; and (5) the ability to perceive cause-and-effect relations in interpersonal events.

In a series of investigations Shure, Spivack and their collaborators have provided evidence that deficiencies in various ICPS skills are associated with social and behavioral maladjustment. Deficits in problem-solving cognition as assessed by performance on interview- and projectivelike tasks, for example, have been found among diverse socially incompetent populations: poorly adjusted preschool children from disadvantaged environments (Shure, Spivack, & Jaeger, 1971); emotionally disturbed 10- to 12-year-old children (Shure & Spivack, 1972); impulsive teenagers institutionalized for remedial purposes (Spivack & Levine, 1963); adolescent psychiatric patients (Platt, Altman, & Altman, 1973); youthful incarcerated heroin addicts (Platt, Scura, & Hannon, 1973); and adult psychiatric patients (Platt & Spivack, 1972a, 1972b; 1974). More direct evidence that social cognitive problem-solving skills mediate social and behavioral adjustment in children comes from educational intervention programs where ICPS skills were taught to preschool children (Shure, Spivack, & Gordon, 1972; Spivack & Shure, 1974). These programs significantly improved certain dimensions of problem-solving thinking in children with behavioral difficulties (i.e., impulsive and overinhibited preschoolers), with subsequent improvement in the teacher-rated social adjustment of these children at posttraining assessment and 6 months later. While much of the social problem-solving research has methodological limitations that restrict the kind of conclusions that may be drawn from these studies (Allen, Chinsky, Larcen, Lochman, & Selinger, 1976; Butler, 1979; Krasnor & Rubin, 1978; Sharp, 1978), social problem-solving thinking may yet prove to be a useful conceptualization of some of the social cognitive skills that underlie social competence.

ROLE-TAKING SKILLS

A related social cognitive skill that has received considerable attention, particularly in the developmental literature, has been the ability to take the perspective of another person, a process referred to as role taking. Role taking, it has been suggested, underlies a variety of social cognitive skills, such as person perception (the characterization of what an individual is like), empathy (the ability to perceive and feel another's affective state), and referential communication (the ability to effectively communicate with another person).

Piaget (1954) underscored the importance of role taking in the development of reciprocal social behavior. In the present section, we shall review briefly some of the research that has attempted to examine the relationship between role taking and social behavior. In a correlational study, Rubin and Schneider (1973) found a positive relationship between referential communication (a communicative role-taking situation in which the subjects must take the perspective of the other into account as they describe an object available only to themselves), and various measures of prosocial behavior, such as altruism, generosity, and helpfulness. A number of studies investigating the relationship between role-taking skill and various indices of social competence have found role-taking abilities to be related to positive behavior in social interactions rather than to popularity as measured by sociometric ratings (Deutsch, 1974; Rothenberg, 1970; Rubin, 1972). Gottman et al. (1975), however, found referential communication accuracy to be significantly related to sociometric popularity. Chandler (1973) found that chronically delinquent boys were deficient in role-taking skills compared to nondelinquent boys. Similarly, Feshbach and Feshbach (1969) found an inverse relationship between empathy and aggression in boys over the age of 5.

A number of studies have attempted to improve social behavior through training social cognitive skills. Staub (1971) trained children in prosocial role playing and found resultant increases in helping behavior for girls, and in sharing behavior for boys. Chandler (1973) found reductions in delinquent behavior in chronically delinquent boys following training in role-taking skills, behavioral changes that persisted through an 18-month follow-up period. In a similar study, Chandler, Greenspan, and Barenboim (1974) gave institutionalized emotionally disturbed children training in role taking and referential communication that resulted in improvements in social adjustment over a 12-month follow-up period.

Although the evidence is far from conclusive and further research is needed in this area, it would appear that social cognitive skills such as role-taking ability and related skills (e.g., empathy, person perception, and referential communication) are potentially important cognitive components of social competence.

INFORMATION-PROCESSING STYLES

The focus of attention thus far in considering cognitive processes has been on the content of the individual's cognitive processes. We have briefly noted the role of the internal dialogue, expectancies and appraisals, social problem-solving ability, and role taking and related skills. This list of topics reads like a litany of social cognition research. Although we share the belief that each of these processes and abilities must be considered in any comprehensive model of social competence, there is still another way to view the role of cognitive processes in the development and expression of social competence. We are referring to the style and manner of information processing that individuals bring to bear in social situations.

CHUNKING OF INFORMATION

What aspects of information-processing styles may be relevant to social competence? Cognitive psychology has presented a good deal of evidence in support of the view that people learn and remember information by a process of actively categorizing, chunking, or coding input according to conceptual schemata (Bransford & Johnson, 1973; Flavell, 1979; Meichenbaum & Asarnow, 1980; Minsky, 1975; Posner & Keele, 1968; Schank & Abelson, 1978). The essential observation is that the way information is chunked has important effects on the individual's proficiency in the performance of an act. If one considers competence in such skills areas as chess playing, or playing a musical instrument, or even typing, the changing role of cognitive processes is quite evident. For example, in their work on chess players, Chase and Simon (1973) found that when briefly presented with meaningful chess placements, the master chess player was able to recall about four times as many pieces as the novice player, a superiority that disappeared when random chess positions were presented. Chase and Simon concluded that the experienced player could store meaningful information more efficiently in a few chunks in short-term memory. Specifically, the chunks of the experienced chess player were structured in terms of relationships (e.g., attack and defense) or in terms of coded games (e.g., Spassky–Fisher, game 2), whereas the chunks of the novice player failed to show structured organization. Similarly, in the areas of musical sight reading (Bean, 1938; Sloboda, 1976; Wolf, 1976), and piano practicing (Joseph, 1978), the ability to organize a series of musical notes into informational chunks was found to be related to competence in the performance of these tasks.

From the viewpoint of social competence, we may ask what is the equivalent to a categorization such as "Spassky–Fisher, game 2" How often do we, in social situations, appraise, attribute, label, or read social situations in ways that in turn guide and control our behavior? How is proficiency, in terms of social competence, reflected in differences in the chunks we impose? How does individuals' chunking of social information change as they gain proficiency in various kinds of social situations? We would argue that the answer to these questions may contribute to our understanding of social competence. Research in the area of "person perception" represents one attempt to answer such questions. For example, Campbell and Yarrow (1961) found that children's social effectance was related to the level of organization and the use of inferences in their descriptions of others. In relation to cognitions concerning the self, Markus (1977) distinguished subjects who had formed or had not formed "self-schemata" (Markus's term for domain-specific cognitive generalizations about the self derived from past experience). Markus demonstrated that subjects who possessed self-schemata more easily and rapidly processed information about themselves, more readily retrieved relevant behavioral evidence, more confidently predicted new responses, and showed greater resistance to contradictory information.

In investigating the role of cognitive processes in competence, one must not overlook the potential influence of individual differences in information processing. Examples from cognitive psychology indicate that individual differences in the style of chunking correspond with different types of proficiencies. It is not the ability to chunk per se that is important for effective behavior, but the fit between the task and the information-processing strategy employed. For example, Wolf (1976) distinguished between good and poor sight readers among professional pianists. Although all subjects were competent musical artists, Wolf found that poor sight readers reported reading music note-by-note, while good sight readers employed a pattern recognition approach (the abstraction of familiar patterns of notes) as the basis of their performance. The poor sight readers, on the other hand, were found to be superior at memorizing music compared to the good sight readers, and all musicians reported using a note-by-note approach in their practicing. We describe the Wolf study to underscore the need for sensitivity to individual differences in defining competence, whether in the situation of piano playing or in social situations. A tone that often pervades the social competence literature is that there are correct ways of being competent (good guys vs. bad guys), instead of an appreciation of *different* ways of being competent and a recognition that each approach has its benefits as well as its costs.

An alternative way of conceptualizing social competence might be in terms of a problem-solving process in which the problem to be solved is the selection of the most appropriate information-processing style for the task demands. Whether processing style is a variable that is a function of familiarity with a task or is a characteristic of the subject remains to be investigated. Whether an individual can shift processing strategies in response to differing environmental demands is also a question for future research. The Wolf study on musical sight-reading suggests that there may be some people who can flexibly shift strategies to suit the demands of the situation, while others are locked into one way of processing information. Although the latter individuals may be able to perform a particular task with high proficiency, they lack the flexibility required to perform effectively in a variety of situations. Examples in the area of social competence come easily to mind. Imagine, for instance, the individual who is effective in a one-to-one social situation with a close friend but feels lost and uncomfortable in an ocean of acquaintances at a cocktail party or when introduced to a stranger.

AUTOMATICITY OR MINDLESSNESS

Another aspect of information processing that may be important to an understanding of social competence concerns the automaticity with which an act is performed—that is, the degree to which a behavior will be enacted "mindlessly," or without intentional cognitive activity. The cognitive psychology literature indicates that the automaticity with which an act is performed will have important effects on the level of performance of that act. Depending upon the state reached in the skill-acquisition process, conscious cognitive processing may enhance or hinder performance. Shiffrin and Schneider (1977) have proposed two information-processing modes: a conscious, controlled process that produces slow but accurate performance, and an automatic process that allows the rapid execution of highly stereotyped response sequences without the necessity of conscious control. With the acquisition of skill and the establishment of associative connections there is a switch from controlled to automatic processing (see Gal'perin, 1969; Kimble & Perlmutter, 1970; and Meichenbaum, 1977, for similar discussions of changes in the mental act that accompany proficiency). Specific tasks may differ in their information-processing demands—this applies to both cognitive tasks and social situations. We would suggest that any definition of social competence might well include the assessment of the individual's ability, not only to recognize the information-processing demands of the situation, but also to adjust appropriately between automatic and controlled modes of operating.

The question may now arise as to what in a social situation leads an individual to shift from the automatic, mindless, stereotyped responses that constitute much of our social behavior to conscious control. We would argue that one important determining factor is interruption of automatic behavioral sequences and plans. Any one of a variety of factors may cause this interruption. It may be externally based—something the other person says or does, or it may be internally generated due to affective experiences, etc. In a social situation the evidence that one has shifted from an automatic interpersonal mode of operating to a controlled mode may be the act of taking a *metaperspective*. As Heider (1958) noted some time ago, "a person reacts to what he thinks the other person is perceiving, feeling and thinking, in addition to what the other person may be doing." Moreover, a metaperspective aspect of behavior may also be evident with individuals responding to what he or she thinks the other person is thinking that they are thinking. If confused, recall the subtitled scripts in Woody Allen's movie *Annie Hall*, or consider the following example, offered by a young, attractive, female psychologist.

When engaged in a professional conversation with a male psychologist, this individual reported having observed nonverbal cues that suggested to her that the male psychologist had a hidden (seductive) agenda in the interaction. This perception of discordant information (professional and sexual) stimulated attentive and conscious processing of subsequent social cues, which in turn affected the direction and outcome of the interaction. This attentive and conscious processing (metaperspective taking) could be expected to facilitate the competent handling of ambiguous social situations in most instances. It is important to note, however, that metaperspective taking may on occasion hinder socially competent behavior in situations where it is evoked by inaccurate perception of social cues, negative response to external cues that one's own behavior has in fact subtly provoked, or where it reflects intense negative concerns that engender anxiety, which interferes with competent social behavior.

In summary, it is clear from the preceding discussion of various cognitive processes that every social situation includes a number of elements over and above what would be observed in a videotape replay of the interaction. Any definition of social competence must include such cognitive factors as the role of the individual's internal dialogue, his or her expectancies and appraisals of outcomes, the social cognitive skills in his or her repertoire, and the style of organizing and processing social information that he or she employs—as well as the impact of all of these on the interpersonal behavior emitted in social situations.

We would argue, however, that social competence is *more* than the sum of all of these factors. This brings us to our conceptualization of cognitive structures and the role that such structures may play in influencing socially competent behavior.

Cognitive Structures

The term "cognitive structures" was first made familiar by Tolman (1932) and Lewin (1935). Since then, under the banner of cognitive structures have fallen such concepts as Bandura's (1978) self-system; Bartlett's (1932) schema; Hilgard's (1976) control systems; Kelly's (1955) personal constructs; Miller, Galanter, and Pribram's (1960) images and plans; Morris's (1975) structures of meaning; Parkes's (1971) and Frank's (1961) assumptive worlds; Piaget's (1954) schemata; and Sarbin's roles (Sarbin & Coe, 1972). As varied as the terminology is, however, Averill (1979) has pointed out that the basic idea behind cognitive structures is the same: "Events are only meaningful to the extent that they can be assimilated into some existing cognitive model or structure; and if they cannot be assimilated, then the relevant cognitive structures must be altered to accommodate the environmental input" (p. 24).

The distinction between cognitive structures and cognitive processes is a difficult task and one that we shall not attempt to develop fully in the present paper. Whereas we have discussed earlier under cognitive processes social cognitive skills, expectancies, and information-processing styles, we believe they imply underlying structures of organized information. The conceptualization of cognitive structures that we have chosen to focus upon in this section is somewhat different in emphasis from what was covered under cognitive processes. This conceptualization focuses upon the broader motivational or affective structures that may underlie cognitive processes or overt behavior in social and other situations.

As we use the term "cognitive structures" in the proposed model of social competence, we are trying to account for the motivation, direction, and organization of social behavior. We want to use such a construct in order to understand why individuals differ in their response to the same environmental stimuli (i.e., in their expectancies, appraisals of outcomes, and in their social behavior). We also wish to use this concept to explain why a particular individual may show the same type of response to apparently dissimilar events. Thus far, in our discussion of the other components of the proposed model (overt behavior and cognitive processes), we have in effect been suggesting *how* individuals may differ in aspects of their social competence. By invoking the present conceptualization of cognitive structures, we are seeking to understand *why* such individual differences may occur.

The conception of cognitive structure that we have chosen to focus upon is what we call the individual's "meaning system" (a concept somewhat akin to Klinger's, 1977, concept of current concerns). As we have hinted earlier, it is our suggestion that any given social situation may hold a somewhat different meaning for each individual. For example, a party for some individuals may be a pleasant social event, an opportunity to meet new people or to "let loose." For others, it may be a chance to impress others with one's brilliance or social repartee. For yet others, a party may be a trial where every aspect of one's person or behavior is judged, or a situation where one is inevitably alone in a crowd, or a setting where one's main concern is attractiveness to members of the opposite sex.

The meaning that individuals attach to general social settings (like parties), as well as to specific social interactions within those settings, we see as part of a broader network of concerns or goals that determines what are important issues in the individual's life and the position he or she takes in relation to them. These concerns may vary in intensity (how important or central they are) and in valence (positive or negative). An individual will normally have a multiplicity of concerns, some of which support and others that compete with one another, in situations that the individual encounters. In any given situation with which the individual is confronted (e.g., a social situation), the overall meaning that he or she attaches to the situation will determine whether he or she will participate, what aspects of the situation he or she will attend and respond to, how intense the involvement will be, and the general positive or negative orientation of thought and behavior in that situation.

In short, we see the individual's meaning system as a kind of executive processor that holds the blueprints for both thinking and behavior. The meaning system functions to set behavior in motion, to guide the choice and direction of particular sequences of thought and behavior, and to determine their continuation, interruption, or change of direction. In a complex chain of events, the meaning that an individual attaches to a social situation functions to influence his or her expectancies and appraisals of outcomes, to set in motion the internal dialogue that reflects the individual's feelings about the situation or his or her attempts to cope, to determine the employment or nonemployment of social cognitive skills such as problem solving or role taking, and to influence the social behavior that the individual emits in any social interaction.

Let us briefly consider some of the ramifications of this point of view for a model of social competence. The individual for whom a given social situation or situations provokes an intense negative concern or a multiplicity of negative concerns may find himself or herself in a position where the cognitive or behavioral skills in his or her repertoire are swamped by an internal dialogue that focuses on negative affect and expectancies. The reader may be reminded here of Schwartz and Gottman's (1976) low-assertive subjects who, when faced with a situation that presumably evoked real-life concerns, failed to employ the assertive skills that they understood and were able to use in other situations. Instead, their internal dialogue focused on a variety of negative concerns, which, by definition, made the performance of an assertive response difficult.

It may also be the case that individuals may have a range of social skills, but be so limited in terms of their meaning system or current concerns that they may be viewed as socially incompetent. Consider, for example, colleagues who are so preoccupied with their place in psychology that they impose their concern inappropriately in social situations. It is unlikely, for example, that you would want to be seated next to such people at dinner. In fact, do we not try to read each others' concerns in choosing individuals with whom to interact? Perhaps the accurate perception of others' concerns and the choice of individuals whose concerns are compatible is another hallmark of social competence, part of the process of engendering positive or supportive social environments to which we referred earlier.

It is also important to note that the environment changes in defining the appropriateness of an individual's current concern. The individual's ability to recognize this shift in situational demands and adjust accordingly also may contribute to social competence. The point simply is that any definition of social competence must be in flux, for it reflects not only the characteristics of the individual but also the characteristics of a changing environment (Meichenbaum, 1980).

Finally, the nature and number of an individual's concerns about social situations should be predictive of the magnitude of anxiety in social situations, and thus the potential for distortion of social information and/or interference with socially competent behavior. From the point of view of treatment, the prognosis for an individual with a large number of intensely negative concerns would be less favorable than that for a person who has either a relatively limited negative concern or intense positive concerns that override the negative meaning he or she attaches to social situations. The nature of an individual's concerns should also be predictive of the generality of social anxiety across situations (parties, informal small gatherings, interviews, dates, casual conversations, etc.) and the particular situations in which it might occur. The individual whose concern is attractiveness to members of the opposite sex, for example, may have more difficulty on dates or at parties where he or she perceives this factor as a salient feature of the social setting. What we are proposing is consistent with Bem and Allen's (1974) conclusion that cross-situational consistency of behavior depends upon the individual's perception of similarity in situations. It is our contention that the individual's meaning system influences his or her perception of such similarity, and thus the range of social situations in which cognitive or behavioral difficulties will be manifest.

Thus we are proposing that any assessment of social competence must include a careful analysis of the meanings that individuals attach to social situations. These meanings influence the internal dialogue, expectancies and appraisals of outcomes, and styles of information processing, as well as the employment of cognitive and behavioral social skills in the individual's repertoire. We must not impose a uniformity myth (Keisler, 1966) on either socially competent or socially incompetent individuals. Different meanings may underlie many of the same cognitive or overt behaviors. Any definition of social competence, we would suggest, must include a conceptualization not only of *how* individuals differ in the competent handling of social situations but of *why* they may do so.

SUMMARY

The present model proposes that social competence can best be conceptualized as consisting of several interacting components that operate on one another to produce a kind of self-perpetuating cycle, elements of which may be operating at a very automatic stereotyped level. Social competence includes the individual's meaning system or current concerns (what we have called cognitive structures), which change with experience and with the demands of the situation. The nature of the individual's concerns will influence both cognitive processing of information and the behavioral acts emitted by the individual in a given situation. The elements of cognitive processing that we suggest may have implications for defining social competence include: the internal dialogue, appraisals, expectancies, problem-solving and other social cognitive skills, and information-processing styles (chunking, metaperspective taking, etc.). The nature of the cognitive processes actively called into play in a social situation depends upon the individual's information-processing proficiency, the demands of the situation, the individual's current concerns, and the responses of other participants. The overt behavior, or what the individual does in the situation, represents only one element (albeit an important element) of social competence. But overt behavior takes on particular meaning because it leads to consequences, both intra- and interpersonal, and the nature of the cognitive processes surrounding those consequences will further affect the self-perpetuating cycle. It is also important to recognize that individuals are active in selecting and engendering such cycles (both intra- and interpersonal), and in this sense actively create their social environment.

Finally, the model of social competence that is proposed in the present paper encompasses the individual's meaning system, overt behavior, and cognitive processes in continuous interaction with one another and the social environment. In this framework, social competence should not merely be equated with observable behaviors, or cognitive processes or cognitive structures. Instead *social competence is a construct that summarizes this entire chain of events.* Such a view is consistent with the recent reciprocal determinism system offered by Bandura (1978). Bandura suggests that psychological functioning involves continuous reciprocal interaction between behavioral, cognitive, and environmental influences. When we come to appreciate the complexity of the nature of these processes, then we will begin to more adequately define social competence.

REFERENCES

Abelson, R. *Scripts.* Paper presented at the meeting of the Midwestern Psychological Association, Chicago, 1978.

Allen, G., Chinsky, J., Larcen, S., Lochman, J., & Selinger, W. *Community psychology and the schools: A behaviorally oriented multi-level preventive approach.* Hillsdale, NJ: Erlbaum, 1976.

Averill, J. A selective review of cognitive and behavioral factors involved in the regulation of stress. In R. Depue (Ed.), *The psychobiology of depressive disorders: Implications for the effects of stress.* New York: Academic Press, 1979.

Bandura, A. Self-efficacy: Toward a unifying theory of behavioral change. *Psychological Review,* 1977, *84,* 191–215.

Bandura, A. The self-system in reciprocal determinism. *American Psychologist,* 1978, *33,* 344–358.

Bartlett, F. *Remembering.* Cambridge, England: Cambridge University Press, 1932.

Bean, K. An approach to the reading of music. *Psychological Monographs,* 1938, *226,* 1–80.

Bem, D. S., & Allen, A. On predicting some of the people some of the time: the search for cross-situational consistencies in behavior. *Psychological Review,* 1974, *81,* 506–520.

Bowers, K. Situationism in psychology: An analysis and critique. *Psychological Review,* 1973, *80,* 307–336.

Bransford, J., & Johnson, M. Considerations of some problems of comprehension. In W. Chase (Ed.), *Visual information processing.* New York: Academic Press, 1973.

Butler, L. *Interpersonal problem-solving skills, peer acceptance, and social behavior in children.* Unpublished master's thesis, University of Waterloo, Waterloo, Ontario, Canada, 1979.

Cacioppo, J., & Petty, R. *Inductive techniques for the assessment of cognitive response.* Unpublished manuscript, University of Notre Dame, 1978.

Campbell, J. D., & Yarrow, M. R. Perceptual and behavioral correlates of social effectiveness. *Sociometry,* 1961, *24*(1), 1–20.

Chandler, M. J., Egocentrism and antisocial behavior: The assessment and training of social perspective-taking skills. *Developmental Psychology,* 1973, *9*(3), 326–332.

Chandler, M. J., Greenspan, S., & Barenboim, C. Assessment and training of role-taking and referential communication skills in institutionalized emotionally-disturbed children. *Developmental Psychology,* 1974, *10*(4), 546–553.

Chase, W., & Simon, H. The mind's eye in chess. In W. Chase (Ed.), *Visual information processing.* New York: Academic Press, 1973.

Deffenbacher, J. Worry, emotionality and interference in test anxiety. An empirical test of attentional theory. *Journal of Educational Psychology,* 1978, *70,* 248–254.

Deutsch, F. Observational and sociometric measures of peer popularity and their relationship to egocentric communication in female preschoolers. *Developmental Psychology,* 1974, *10,* 745–747.

Ericsson, K., & Simon, H. *Retrospective verbal reports as data* (C.I.P. Working Paper). Pittsburgh: Carnegie-Mellon University, 1978.

Feshbach, W. D., & Feshbach, S. The relationship between empathy and aggression in two age groups. *Developmental Psychology,* 1969, *1,* 102–107.

Fiedler, D., & Beach, L. R. On the decision to be assertive. *Journal of Consulting and Clinical Psychology,* 1978, *46,* 537–546.

Flavell, J. Metacognitive development. In J. Scandura & C. Brainerd (Eds.), *Structural-process theories of complex human behavior.* Leyden, the Netherlands: Sigthoff, 1979.

Frank, J. *Persuasion and healing.* Baltimore: Johns Hopkins Press, 1961.

Gagnon, J., & Simon, W. *Sexual conduct: The social sources of human sexuality.* Chicago: Aldine, 1973.

Gal'perin, P. Stages in the development of mental acts. In M. Cole & I. Maltzman (Eds.), *A handbook of contemporary Soviet psychology.* New York: Basic Books, 1969.

Garmezy, N., Masten, A., Nordstrom, L., & Ferrarese, M. The nature of competence in normal and deviant children. In M. Kent & J. Rolf (Eds.), *The primary prevention of psychopathology: Promoting social competence and coping in children* (Vol. 3). Hanover, NH: University Press of New England, 1980.

Genest, M., Turk, D., & Meichenbaum, D. *A cognitive behavioral approach to the management of pain.* Paper presented at the meeting of the Association for the Advancement of Behavior Therapy, Atlanta, 1977.

Ginsberg, H. J., Wauson, M. S., & Easley, M. *Omega children: A study of lowest ranking members of the children's play group hierarchy.* Paper presented at the Biennial Meeting of the Society for Research in Child Development, New Orleans, March 1977.

Glass, C., Gottman, J., & Schmurak, S. Response acquisition and cognitive self-statement modification approaches to dating-skills-training. *Journal of Counseling Psychology,* 1976, *23,* 520–526.

Goor, A., & Sommerfeld, R. A comparison of problem-solving processes of creative students and non-creative students. *Journal of Educational Psychology,* 1975, *67,* 495–505.

Gottman, J. M. Toward a definition of social isolation in children. *Child Development,* 1977, *48,* 513–517.

Gottman, J. M., Gonso, J., & Rasmussen, B. Social interaction, social competence and friendship in children. *Child Development,* 1975, *46,* 709–718.

Gottman, J. M., & Parkhurst, J. T. *Developing may not always be improving: A developmental study of children's best friendships.* Paper presented at the Biennial Meeting of the Society for Research in Child Development, New Orleans, March 1977.

Greenburg, D., & Jacobs, M. *How to make yourself miserable.* New York: Random House, 1966.

Heckhausen, H. Task-irrelevant cognitions during an exam: Incidence and effects. In H. Krohne & L. Laux (Eds.), *Achievement stress and anxiety.* Washington, DC: Hemisphere, in press.

Heider, F. *The psychology of interpersonal relations.* New York: Wiley, 1958.

Henshaw, D. *A cognitive analysis of creative problem-solving.* Unpublished doctoral dissertation, University of Waterloo, Waterloo, Ontario, Canada, 1978.

Hilgard, E. Neodissociation theory of multiple cognitive control systems. In G. Schwartz & D. Shapiro (Eds.), *Consciousness and self-regulation* (Vol. 1). New York: Plenum Press, 1976.

Hollandsworth, J., Glazeski, R., Kirkland, K., Jones, G., & Van Norman, L. *An analysis of the nature and effects of test anxiety: Cognitive, behavioral and physiological components.* Unpublished manuscript, University of Southern Mississippi, 1978.

Holroyd, K., Westbrook, T., Wolf, M., & Badhorn, E. *Performance, cognition and physiological responding in test anxiety.* Unpublished manuscript, Ohio University, 1978.

Houston, K. Trait anxiety and cognitive coping behavior. In H. Krohne & L. Laux (Eds.), *Achievement stress and anxiety.* Washington, DC: Hemisphere, in press.

Hymel, S., & Asher, S. R. *Assessment and training of isolated children's social skills.* Paper presented at the Biennial Meeting of the Society for Research in Child Development, New Orleans, March 1977.

Joseph, L. *An observational study of the acquisition of musical skills.* Unpublished master's thesis, University of Waterloo, Waterloo, Ontario, Canada, 1978.

Keisler, D. Some myths of psychotherapy research and the search for a paradigm. *Psychological Bulletin,* 1966, *65,* 110–136.

Kelly, G. *The psychology of personal constructs* (2 vols.). New York: Norton, 1955.

Kendall, P., & Korgeski, G. Assessment and cognitive–behavioral interventions. *Cognitive Therapy and Research,* in press.

Kendall, P., Williams, L., Pechacek, T., Graham, L., Shisslak, C., & Herzoff, N. Cognitive–behavioral and patient education in catheterization procedures. *Journal of Consulting and Clinical Psychology,* 1979, *47,* 49–58.

Kimble, G., & Perlmutter, L. The problem of volition. *Psychological Review,* 1970, *77,* 361–384.

Klinger, E. *Meaning and void: Inner experience and the incentives in people's lives.* Minneapolis: University of Minnesota Press, 1977.

Krasnor, L., & Rubin, K. *Preschoolers' verbal and behavioral solutions to social problems.* Paper presented at the meeting of the Canadian Psychological Association, Ottawa, June 1978.

Langer, E. Rethinking the role of thought in social interaction. In J. Harvey, W. Ickes, & R. Kidd (Eds.), *New directions in attribution research* (Vol. 2). Hillsdale, NJ: Erlbaum, 1978.

Lazarus, R., & Launier, R. Stress-related transactions between person and environment. In L. Pervin & M. Lewis (Eds.), *Interaction between internal and external determinants of behavior.* New York: Plenum Press, 1979.

Lewin, K. *A dynamic theory of personality.* New York: McGraw-Hill, 1935.

Mahoney, M., & Avener, M. Psychology of the elite athlete: An explanatory study. *Cognitive Therapy and Research,* 1977, *1,* 135–142.

Markus, H. Self-schemata and processing information about the self. *Journal of Personality and Social Psychology,* 1977, *2,* 63–78.

Meichenbaum, D. *Cognitive-behavior modification: An integrative approach.* New York: Plenum Press, 1977.

Meichenbaum, D. Stability of personality, change and psychotherapy. In E. Staub (Ed.), *Personality: Basic issues and current research.* Englewood Cliffs, NJ: Prentice-Hall, 1980.

Meichenbaum, D., & Asarnow, J. Cognitive-behavior modification and metacognitive development: Implications for the classroom. In P. Kendall & S. Hollon (Eds.), *Cognitive–behavioral interventions: Theory research and procedures.* New York: Academic Press, 1980.

Meichenbaum, D., & Butler, L. Cognitive ethology: Assessing the streams of cognition and emotion. In K. Blankstein, P. Pliner, & J. Polivy (Eds.), *Advances in the study of emotion communication and affect: Assessment and modification of emotional behavior* (Vol. 6). New York: Plenum Press, in press.

Meichenbaum, D., Henshaw, D., & Himel, N. Coping with stress as a problem-solving process. In W. Krohne & L. Laux (Eds.), *Achievement stress and anxiety.* Washington, DC: Hemisphere, in press.

Miller, G., Galanter, E., & Pribram, K. *Plans and the structure of behavior.* New York: Holt, Rinehart & Winston, 1960.

Minsky, M. A framework for representing knowledge. In P. Winston (Ed.), *The psychology of computer vision.* New York: McGraw-Hill, 1975.

Mischel, W. Toward a cognitive social learning reconceptualization of personality. *Psychological Review,* 1973, *80,* 252–283.

Moos, R. *The human context: Environmental determinants of behavior.* New York: Wiley, 1976.

Morris, P. *Loss and change.* Garden City, NY: Doubleday, 1975.

Nisbett, R., & Wilson, T. Telling more than we can know: Verbal report on mental processes. *Psychological Review,* 1977, *84,* 231–259.

O'Hara, T. *A demonstration of the relationship between cognitive experience and performance debilitation in high evaluation conditions.* Paper presented at the 9th Canadian Psycho-motor Learning and Sport Symposium, Banff, October 1977.

O'Malley, J. Research perspective on social competence. *Merrill-Palmer Quarterly,* 1977, *23,* 29–44.

Parkes, C. Psychosocial transitions: A field for study. *Social Science and Medicine,* 1971, *5,* 101–115.

Piaget, J. *The moral judgment of the child.* New York: Free Press, 1954.

Platt, J., Altman, N., & Altman, D. *Dimensions of interpersonal problem-solving thinking in adolescent psychiatric patients.* Paper presented at the meeting of the Eastern Psychological Association, Washington, DC, May 1973.

Platt, J., Scura, W., & Hannon, J. Problem-solving thinking of youthful incarcerated heroin addicts. *Journal of Community Psychology,* 1973, *1,* 278–281.

Platt, J., & Spivack, G. Problem-solving thinking of psychiatric patients. *Journal of Consulting and Clinical Psychology,* 1972, *39,* 148–151.(a)

Platt, J., & Spivack, G. Social competence and effective problem-solving thinking in psychiatric patients. *Journal of Clinical Psychology,* 1972, *28,* 3–5.(b)

Platt, J., & Spivack, G. *Means–ends problem-solving procedure (MEPS): Manual and tentative norms.* Philadelphia: Department of Mental Health Sciences, Hahnemann Medical College and Hospital, 1974.

Pope, K., & Singer, J. (Eds.). *The stream of consciousness.* New York: Plenum Press, 1978.

Posner, M., & Keele, S. On the genesis of abstract ideas. *Journal of Experimental Psychology,* 1968, *77,* 353–363.

Rothenberg, B. Children's social sensitivity and the relationship to interpersonal competence, intrapersonal comfort, and intellectual level. *Developmental Psychology,* 1970, *2,* 225–350.

Rubin, K. H. Relationship between egocentric communication and popularity among peers. *Developmental Psychology,* 1972, *7,* 364.

Rubin, K. H., & Schneider, F. W. The relationship between moral judgment, egocentrism, and altruistic behavior. *Child Development,* 1973, *44,* 661–665.

Sarason, I., & Stoops, R. Test anxiety and the passage of time. *Journal of Consulting and Clinical Psychology,* 1977, *46,* 102–109.

Sarbin, T., & Coe, W. *Hypnosis: A social psychological analysis of influence communication.* New York: Holt, Rinehart & Winston, 1972.

Schank, R., & Abelson, R. *Scripts, plans, goals, and understanding.* Hillsdale, NJ: Erlbaum, 1978.

Schwartz, R., & Gottman, J. Toward a task analysis of assertive behavior. *Journal of Consulting and Clinical Psychology,* 1976, *44,* 910–920.

Shantz, C. V. The development of social cognition. In E. M. Hetherington (Ed.), *Review of child development research* (Vol. 5). Chicago: University of Chicago Press, 1975.

Sharp, K. C. *Interpersonal problem-solving capacity and behavioral adjustment in preschool children.* Paper presented at the meeting of the American Psychological Association, Toronto, August 1978.

Shiffrin, R., & Schneider, W. Controlled and automatic human information processing: I. Detection, search, and attention. *Psychological Review,* 1977, *84,* 1–66.

Shure, M., & Spivack, G. Means–ends thinking, adjustment and social class among elementary school-aged children. *Journal of Consulting and Clinical Psychology,* 1972, *38,* 348–353.

Shure, M., Spivack, G., & Gordon, R. Problem-solving thinking: A preventive mental health program for preschool children. *Reading World,* 1972, *11,* 259–274.

Shure, M., Spivack, G., & Jaeger, M. Problem-solving thinking and adjustment among disadvantaged preschool children. *Child Development,* 1971, *42,* 1791–1803.

Singleton, L. C., & Asher, S. R. Peer preferences and social interaction among third-grade children in an integrated school district. *Journal of Educational Psychology,* 1977, *69,* 330–336.

Sloboda, J. Visual perception of musical notation: Registering pitch symbols in memory. *Quarterly Journal of Experimental Psychology,* 1976, *28,* 1–16.

Smith, E., & Miller, F. Limits on perception of cognitive processes: A reply to Nisbett and Wilson. *Psychological Review,* 1978, *85,* 355–362.

Smye, M. *Verbal, cognitive and behavioral correlates of social anxiety.* Unpublished doctoral dissertation, Ontario Institute for Studies in Education, University of Toronto, 1977.

Spivack, G., & Levine, M. *Self-regulation in acting out and normal adolescents* (Report M-4531). Washington, DC: National Institutes of Health, 1963.

Spivack, G., & Shure, M. *Social adjustment of young children: A cognitive approach to solving real-life problems.* San Francisco: Jossey-Bass, 1974.

Staub, E. The use of role playing and induction in children's learning of helping and sharing behavior. *Child Development,* 1971, *42,* 805–816.

Sundberg, N., Snowden, L., & Reynolds, W. Toward assessment of personal competence and incompetence in life situations. *Annual Review of Psychology,* 1978, *29,* 179–222.

Thorngate, W. Must we always think before we act? *Personality and Social Psychology Bulletin,* 1976, *2,* 31–35.

Tolman, E. *Purposive behavior in animals and men.* New York: Century, 1932.

Trower, P., Bryant, B., & Argyle, M. *Social skills and mental health.* London: Methuen 1978.

Wachtel, P. Psychodynamics, behavior therapy, and the implacable experimenter: An inquiry into consistency of personality. *Journal of Abnormal Psychology,* 1973, *82,* 324–334.

White, B., Kaban, B., Marmor, J., & Shapiro, B. *Child rearing practices and the development of competence.* Cambridge, MA: Laboratory of Human Development, Harvard University, 1972.

Wolf, T. A cognitive model of musical sight-reading. *Journal of Psycholinguistic Research,* 1976, *5,* 143–172.

3

SOCIAL COMPETENCE FROM THE PERSPECTIVE OF STRESS AND COPING

JUDITH WRUBEL
PATRICIA BENNER
RICHARD S. LAZARUS

THE AUTHORS of Chapter 3 have worked together on the Stress and Coping in Aging Project since 1976, with Richard S. Lazarus as principal investigator, Judith Wrubel and Patricia Benner as advanced graduate students, and the National Institute of Aging providing support. The research provides an unusual opportunity to document the daily life stresses, coping efforts, and adaptational outcomes of a little studied group—middle-aged, community-dwelling men and women. Judith Wrubel is completing her doctoral dissertation in the Human Development Program at the University of California, San Francisco, on stress and coping processes relevant to life events. Patricia Benner's doctoral research is being done within the School of Education of the University of California, Berkeley, and concerns stress and coping and the meaning of work in daily life. The research and theoretical writing of Richard Lazarus, Professor of Psychology at the University of California, Berkeley, on stress and coping is widely known, and his book in 1966, *Psychological Stress and the Coping Process,* has become a classic in the field.

Wrubel, Benner, and Lazarus's work in stress and coping has yielded a number of theoretical constructs that are highly appropriate to an understanding of social competence. In this chapter, they explore the implications of the conceptual framework and findings developed in their research on stress and coping in their implications for a model of social competence.

The concept of *social competence* has special importance for the study of adaptive functioning in humans. Efforts to define psychological health in positive terms during the 1950s (Jahoda, 1958; Joint Commission of Mental Illness and Health, 1961), and a growing concern with the effects of poverty and social inequality on the potential for psychological health, stimulated interest in social competence because of its clear emphasis on the full range of human functioning rather than merely the avoidance of pathology. Implicit in the notion is the assumption that humankind is not solely concerned with adaptation and, hence, survival, but is capable of flourishing in many diverse ways.

Social competence usually refers to the effective participation of the person in the activities of his or her society. For example, Foote and Cottrell (1955) spoke of interpersonal competence as involving little-understood social skills that give the individual control over his or her social affairs and increase the likelihood of optimal development along self-chosen lines. These skills were said to depend on the uniquely human cognitive processes of suspended action, abstract memory, reverie, foresight, reflection, and imagination. The competent person is better able to become sufficiently detached from the present situation to develop independent values and to declare an adult identity of his or her own. Variants of this view can be found in the writings of Adler (1924), Erikson (1950/1963), Fromm (1941), Horney (1937), Maslow (1954), Sullivan (1953), and others. Thus, the dominant view of social competence is that the competent individual actively defines what he or she wants in a social situation, and, furthermore, possesses the skills to actualize the individually defined goals in the context of specific social situations (Weinstein, 1969). Often, the social situation is defined as being at odds with individual goals; the task of the self-possessed, self-defined individual is then to overcome these odds through social competence, thereby becoming liberated from lines of action that are not self-chosen.

Recent writers, including Inkeles (1966), Gladwin (1967), Phillips (1968), and Tyler and Gatz (1977), have continued in this vein, attempting to name or describe the personality traits, behavioral patterns, and social skills that, taken together, constitute social competence. From their perspective, social competence refers to a set of human characteristics that, in combination, comprise a generalized disposition to function effectively across the full range of human social contexts.

The social competence approach to human functioning avoids some of the pitfalls of stereotypical labeling of persons as pathological and of overgeneralizing human deficits. Zubin and Spring (1977) address this issue in their discussion of work competence among schizophrenics. Studies of patients' employment patterns revealed that people who are highly vulnerable to schizophrenia have still demonstrated work competence before and after hospitalization and, in some cases, even during their illness.

Perhaps more important though, the social competence concept turns us toward questions about how to promote the development of competence and, where it is lacking, how to assist people to be more effective in managing problems of living. In our view, the key problem for researchers and those who hope to inculcate social competence educationally, or through treatment or prevention, is that social competence is usually viewed as a set of resources residing *within* the person, which the person can draw upon in relevant social situations. This is a frankly *trait* or structural conception, and as such it overlooks the possibility that the possession of a potentially useful set of skills and personal characteristics does not guarantee that they will be used in a given social encounter. For example, Horner (1972) suggests that women who are competent may choose not to use their skills when they are in competition with a man. Moreover, the trait approach tends to reify social competence as a set of desirable traits or dispositions that guarantees the "good life," or guarantees effective handling of social situations. Although this is probably a less destructive error than the pathology stereotype that has been dominant, it still can lead to the currently popular but mistaken notion that healthy or competent people are always or usually happy and self-actualized.

As an alternative to the dispositional approach, the environment has also been studied structurally by social scientists (Klausner, 1971) as a set of resources, constraints, and demands to be used or responded to. This idea is reflected in research focusing on environmental press (Lawton, 1972; Moos, 1975), and on therapeutic or preventive interventions directed toward ecological units (Hobbs, as reviewed by Gladwin, 1967). In the case of research by Scheidt and Schaie (1978), to cite another example, assessing competence in the elderly requires a taxonomy of attributes of environmental situations that the elderly might be expected to encounter. In this same vein, one can easily conceive of a person who is highly competent in a particular kind of social or cultural environment, such as an inner-city ghetto or in an elementary schoolroom, but whose competencies are irrelevant in another setting or another time of life. However, if social competence is understood in terms of environmental demands, the assessment of competence must lose its global, dispositional, or trait character and become increasingly fractionated according to specific situational characteristics. Thus, neither the environmental nor the dispositional view is able to render a coherent picture of the person across contexts, nor explicate the modes or direction of influence between the person and the environment.

A third conception of social competence, which would avoid the pitfalls of both the dispositional and the environmental approaches, would require an understanding of the person *and* the situation as factors that mutually influence each other. For example, the physical and emotional exhaustion commonly understood by the term "burnout" contributes to low morale and poor performance among health service professionals (Maslach & Pines, 1978; Pines & Maslach, 1978). Such persons were once highly competent and involved. The temporary poor functioning—incompetence, if you like—is the result of overload conditions that affect, over a time, competent and committed workers, some of whom are possibly more vulnerable than others.

In this chapter we draw upon our conceptualizations of stress and coping in addressing the problem we have touched on above in order to clarify and modify the notion of social competence as it is used in theory and practice. Although social competence can be manifest outside the context of stress, and can even reduce the extent of stress in a person's life through anticipatory and preventive coping, stress can also damage effective functioning or force the person to develop new or rarely used skills. Moreover, social competence overlaps stress-related concepts such as coping, coping effectiveness, and coping competence.

We shall develop the thesis that social competence should be viewed as we view coping, that is, as a transactional concept viewed from a cognitive–phenomenological perspective. This means that one searches neither for determinant traits in the person, nor for inescapable forces in the environment, but for the ways individuals and their particular historical environments mutually influence one another. When social competence is considered from a transactional perspective, it is readily understood as a global summation of an individual's many and specific encounters with the social environment. When this global summation is broken down into its additive bits, it reveals the person as sometimes successful, and sometimes unsuccessful, in his or her dealings with the social world. We shall attempt to expand this thesis. We shall begin with a brief statement of our theoretical perspective, including some conceptually based defini-

tions of competence and coping. Then we shall discuss specific features of the person and the environment, which function transactionally in specific encounters and can greatly affect the expression of
competence.

THE THEORY OF PSYCHOLOGICAL
STRESS AND COPING

Our cognitive–phenomenological approach to psychological stress,
and to coping, which is an integral part of it, is transactional. A good
sample of citations for this theoretical treatment, both early and recent ones, include Lazarus (1966, 1968, 1981), Lazarus, Averill, and
Opton (1970), Lazarus and Cohen (1977), Lazarus and Launier (1978),
Lazarus, Kanner, and Folkman (1980), and Folkman, Schaefer, and
Lazarus (1979). In our analysis, transaction refers to the dynamic relationship between a person and an environment. Drawing on the
work of Dewey and Bentley (1949), Pervin (1968; Pervin & Lewis,
1978) has defined the essential features of transactionalism as
follows:

1. Each part of the system has no independence outside of the
other parts of the system, or the system as a whole.

2. One part of the system is not acted upon by another part, but
instead there is a constant reciprocal relationship.

3. Action in any part of the system has consequences for other
parts of the system.

We would also more strongly and explicitly emphasize a concept
that is only implicit in Pervin's analysis, namely, that the relationship between the person and the environment is *constantly changing*
from one moment to the next. This is exactly the way emotions behave; they ebb and flow and change in quality as the person–environment transaction proceeds. Psychological stress, and how it is coped
with, is also constantly changing over time, as, for example, in grief
work. With recognition of this dynamic quality comes an alteration
in one's conception of and research on coping and social competence.
Observation and documentation of these changes across time and
across situations must precede an overall evaluation of level of functioning.

Pervin's three points correspond well to a theme we have addressed elsewhere (Lazarus, 1981; Lazarus & Launier, 1978), namely,

that the relationship between the person and the environment can on-ly be understood when the separate sets of variables of person and environment are translated into a new, higher-level interpretive concept. In sociology, the concept of alienation or anomie (Durkheim, 1951) is just such a transactional concept. Durkheim (1951) wrote, for example, about what happens (anomie) when environmental conditions change faster than the person's adaptational response: "In the case of economic disasters, indeed, something like a declassification occurs which suddenly casts *certain individuals* into a lower state than their previous one. . . . But society cannot adjust them instantaneously to this new life and teach them to practice the increased self-repression to which they are unaccustomed" (p. 253, italics ours).

Notice in the above quotation the use of the expression "certain individuals," which points up the transactional nature of this event: The outcome depends on the combination of environmental change and the incapacity of certain individuals to deal with it. The central theme of a transactional approach is that adaptational outcomes depend on both person and environment, and reflect a new and special relationship that is given an interpretive term—for example, anomie. To assign the term either to the person (trait) or to the environment (external demand) is to misapply the concept.

In the cognitive–phenomenological theory of coping, cognitive appraisal is an interpretive process representing a transaction as it is construed by the person; appraisal fuses the situational encounter with its meaning for the person. In our analysis of psychological stress, three kinds of transaction are possible, each reflecting different primary cognitive appraisals of the person–environment relationship: *irrelevant,* meaning that the transaction is judged as having no bearing on the person's well-being; *benign–positive,* which means that the transaction has a noninjurious or positive significance; and *stressful,* which means that the actual or potential outcome is construed as either already harmful, threatening (future harm), or challenging. From this cognitive–phenomenological perspective, the emotional reaction depends on how the person construes (appraises) the significance of any encounter for well-being. Presumably, an appraisal of an event as irrelevant will generate little or no emotional reaction; a benign–positive appraisal will generate neutral or positively toned emotions, and a stressful appraisal will generate negatively toned emotions, except in the special case of challenge (Lazarus *et al.,* 1980).

All troubled or stressful encounters also require coping; that is, something must be done either to alter the troubled person–environment relationship, to regulate the emotion (and perhaps distress) associated with it, or both. Considerations relevant to coping are the concern of "secondary" cognitive appraisal, a process in which coping resources and options are evaluated. Depending on the situation and the person, this process may involve thoughtful consideration of alternatives for action, resources, and consequences, or, just as often, it involves rapid, nonreflective decisions that result nonetheless in explicit action (Folkman *et al.*, 1979; Janis & Mann, 1977). Primary and secondary appraisals are constantly taking place in all adaptational encounters. They represent evaluative perceptions of what is happening, about to happen, or could happen. As coping efforts change the person–environment relationship, appraisals are altered too, bringing shifts in the intensity and quality of the emotional response.

Coping has been classified into four modes (Lazarus & Launier, 1978). The first of these is *information seeking*, on which reappraisal of the harm, threat, or challenge, or some form of action may depend. The second mode is *direct action* to change the environment or oneself in some way in order to undo the injury, prevent the harm, or meet the challenge. In the third mode, *inhibition of action*, the person resists acting because it is poorly grounded, dangerous, embarrassing, or morally reprehensible. Finally, there is a complex class of intrapsychic forms of coping, or what might be better called *cognitive coping*, in which the person manipulates his or her attention or changes the way events are apprehended in order to reduce the sense of injury or threat. In other contexts we have referred to this as "palliation" because such self-generated cognitive coping makes the person feel better about things even though the objective situation has not changed. Cognitive coping includes denial, avoidance, intellectualized detachment, and other intrapsychic processes.

When we think of coping effectiveness and competence, we must remember that coping has two main functions: changing the troubled person–environment relationship and regulating the emotional distress. Palliation does not do the former, but it can help with the latter, mainly by altering harm or threat appraisal. Despite the standard clinical wisdom that reality distortion, avoidance, and intellectualization defenses are always pathological and bound to lead to trouble (Ellis, 1962), we think that these defenses are used liberally by most well-functioning persons in their management of life stress, though individuals appear to differ greatly in the patterns of thoughts and acts involved in their coping (Lazarus, in press). Clearly there are times when palliative coping is damaging, as in observations of women who denied the potentially serious implications of a breast lump and delayed getting medical attention (Katz, Weiner, Gallagher, & Hellman, 1970), and of men who engaged in vigorous physical exertion during a heart attack in order to convince themselves that nothing was seriously wrong (Hackett & Cassem, 1975). On the other hand, in situations in which nothing constructive can be done through direct actions, as in postsurgery (Cohen & Lazarus, 1973), denial and avoidant modes of coping could have positive adaptational outcomes. In effect, the relationship between the two main functions of coping, problem solving and palliation, can be either mutually facilitative or contradictory, depending on the conditions of stress encountered.

Most coping is a complex constellation of acts and thoughts taking place and changing over time as the person encounters diverse, stressful aspects of living. A good model for what we mean is bereavement, in which the grief process is altered as time passes, and as the events with which the person must deal change too. At the outset there may be shock and numbness, refusal to believe the loss, and recurrent attempts to bring the lost person back in thought and action. The tasks and meanings of early grief are different from later grief, not only in the details of daily living, but in the direction of effort. The loss must ultimately be fully believed and accepted. The struggle involved in this process may produce compulsive action patterns, anger, social withdrawal, and depression, simultaneously or at different times or stages. In the long run, the person must reinvest in new commitments, and the lost relationship and pattern of living must be given up in favor of new ways of living. The person is not confronting a single presenting demand or problem, as in a laboratory stress experiment, but must encounter many situations covered by the loss, some special and unique (as in the funeral and the financial arrangements) and some continuing over a long time (such as going to bed alone, taking care of the household, managing outside work, maintaining the car, caring for the children, etc.). The process is best seen as a complex, ongoing struggle taking place and changing over time. Coping cannot be understood as a single, static response to a single demand, but can only be properly understood in a transactional sense as a changing constellation of processes.

DEFINITION OF TERMS

Having briefly outlined our theoretical approach to stress and coping, we are now ready to return to the key concepts with which we began and, from our perspective, to define them and indicate their relationships. We must focus on two major generic terms, coping and competence, each of which includes several subvarieties: coping includes process, style, effectiveness, and coping competence; social competence includes the parallel concepts of process, style, effectiveness, and competence.

As we have said, a "coping process" refers to the transaction over time between person and environment. In coping, unlike much adaptational behavior, an automatic solution to a demand is unavailable and one must mobilize in some way to deal with the transaction (White, 1974). The term "process" indicates that coping occurs in specific encounters and each encounter occurs over time. Thus, in order to observe and do research on coping processes, it is necessary to inquire, for example, about the specific stressful encounters an individual has faced in a work situation, and what exactly transpired during those events, rather than asking in general how a person copes with work.

Although coping is best regarded as a process involving change, there is still room for "coping styles," that is, stable ways of managing various stressful encounters. The identification of coping styles, for us, is first an empirical question that can best be settled for a given individual or group by observing stability and change across encounters and over time. Only then can the conceptual leap to a style be made. To determine such stability—itself variable from person to person—requires that the configuration or pattern of coping in one kind of stressful encounter be compared with that displayed by the same person in other encounters. For example, within our research project one study (Folkman, 1979) attempted to examine stability and variablity of coping across numerous stressful encounters. Coping patterns were assessed with two subscales of a coping questionnaire, one dealing with problem-focused modes of coping, the other with emotion-focused modes. Looking at the relative use of these two modes by subjects across various types of social contexts (e.g., work-, family- or health-related), only a small number of people (5% of the sample of 100) were highly stable in their coping pattern; most people were quite variable, depending on the stressful context. Although this provides little support for coping styles, which must rest on a pattern of stability, we think nonetheless that such styles will ultimately be identified, albeit at perhaps a more molar level of behavior analysis. Coping style, after all, has to do with a general life-stance, including ways of conceiving and dealing with the world (e.g., the tendency to ward off anticipated stressful encounters or to fail to think ahead), processes that were not tapped in the above study.

"Coping effectiveness," in our view, is best regarded as the adaptational outcome of specific stressful transactions. That is, we say that in each encounter the person was highly effective or ineffective. There are at least three sets of values inherent in such a judgment: morale, social functioning, and somatic health. One of the problems in evaluating coping effectiveness in any given transaction is that, although there is overlap among the three main outcome values, there also may be considerable independence and even conflict. For example, effective social functioning is sometimes bought at the expense of morale or somatic health, as in the highly publicized tendency for Type A personalities to have a greater risk of cardiovascular disease (Friedman, Byers, Diamant, & Rosenman, 1975). Conversely, a benign affective state can be bought at the expense of full utilization of a person's social or occupational resources.

Whereas coping effectiveness refers to the outcomes of specific stressful encounters, "coping competence" refers to the presence of *generalized* skills and resources for coping. Coping effectiveness is known from the outcome of a particular stressful transaction, but coping competence is known from a history—often extensive—of coping effectiveness over a range of stressful transactions, and over a period of time. Coping competence is thus, empirically, a kind of *summation* of outcomes, the inference about skills and resources for coping (coping competence) being based on observations about how well the person has managed a few or many stressful episodes over a limited or extended period. The more such person observations exist, the surer the inference becomes, and the better basis there is to evaluate the types of encounters in which the person copes well or poorly; or, stated differently, the more that is known about coping competence, the more that is known about his or her areas of personal strength and vulnerability. In this sense, then, coping competence (as opposed to coping effectiveness) is a trait or disposition whose limits are set by the variability of adaptive outcomes from one life context to another.

"Social competence" is also a summation of how well the person functions (social effectiveness) in a variety of social settings. As in the case of coping competence, social competence is known best from actual knowledge about how the person manages a variety of social situations. It differs from coping competence only in the arena of management. That is, coping refers to the management of stressful transactions, which include not only social encounters, but physical, physiological, and impersonal demands as well. Social competence, in turn, refers to the management of any social encounter, whether stressful or not. However, since the most important, persistent, and troubling encounters in human existence are often social in nature (Lazarus & Cohen, 1977; Pearlin & Lieberman, 1977) there is a large area of overlap between the two concepts. Within the area of overlap it is possible to view social competence as a high level of coping competence, and indeed, the ability to deal with others with minimal levels of stress may be one of its criteria. "Competence" is thus the generic term here, coping and social competence being highly overlapping subvarieties.

It is important to make these diverse terms clear and distinct, both for the generation of theory and for the practical needs of research related to education, prevention, and treatment. For us, the important research considerations lie in being able to describe ongoing coping and social processes, a step that precedes the development of broad abstractions such as competence, which spans many types of encounters or periods in a person's life. A great weakness in traditional research on coping and social competence is the absence of appropriate assessment methods for the description and interpretation of processes. In short, before we can speak knowledgeably about competence, we must be able to assess the ongoing processes underlying these abstractions as they occur in specific encounters, and we must extend such assessment to how the same persons manage diverse types of stressful or social transactions over time (Lazarus, 1981; Lazarus, Cohen, Folkman, Kanner, & Schaefer, 1980).

With the preceding set of definitions of the concepts most relevant to coping and social competence, we are ready to address some of the personal and situational features that affect coping and social effectiveness in specific transactions.

PERSON QUALITIES THAT OPERATE
TRANSACTIONALLY

Because the impact of unique demands is such that people do not always behave congruently with their dispositional profiles, some writers have questioned the existence of stable or generalized person qualities, arguing that people change, chameleonlike, according to the characteristics of each situation. Although a transactional approach to human functioning does credit situational–environmental forces with playing a major role in transactions, it gives equal weight to person characteristics that influence the meaning of a situation for an individual and, thus, guide choice and action. But one of the stumbling blocks to research examining transactions between the person and the environment has been the absence of cognitive–phenomeno-logical conceptualizations that identify the personal meanings that operate in the transactional process. Traits, as they are usually conceptualized and measured, seem not to work well in predicting what happens in specific person–situation transactions (Cohen & Lazarus, 1973).

In this section we shall consider two important person characteristics that operate transactionally, values and beliefs. Since we think of these characteristics as relatively stable, they are personality dispositions; as such they are likely to be activated by situational encounters and shape responses to those encounters.

A person characteristic is capable of affecting social effectiveness and social competence when it influences the social process, the transaction between the person and the social environment, and hence the adaptational outcome of the transaction. Values and beliefs can influence the transaction and its adaptational outcome in a number of ways. First, these dispositional variables operate primarily in the appraisal of the meaning and salience of any encounter for the person's well-being. The person will interpret any encounter that involves a strongly held value as meaningful and salient to the extent that the outcome harms or threatens the value, or facilitates its expression and makes possible positive feelings such as joy, love, exhilaration, relief, and so on. Values are thus involved in the mobilization of social or coping efforts, and in the evaluation of the consequences of these efforts.

Second, the impact of values is not limited to shaping reactions to situations that chance brings, but they also guide people into and away from situations that can challenge or threaten, benefit or harm them (Liberty, Burnstein, & Moulton, 1966). An example is the association between Type A behavior and increased risk of cardiovascular disease, which is attributed to an intense commitment on the part of Type A's to the social value of achievement (Glass, 1977). In short, by determining meaningfulness and salience and directing purposive activity, values are central to social transactions and the appraisal of their outcomes. Beliefs operate in an analogous way by providing part of the basis for the appraisal of the outcome of an encounter, as well as by influencing the meanings and expectations on which such appraisals are based, including expectations about how effectively the person can expect to achieve a value commitment in the face of social demands, constraints, and resources. Below we shall more closely examine the individual role of values and beliefs in social transactions.

Values

Values find expression in the person at three different levels, each reflecting increased involvement with choice and action. First, they are expressed as *ideals,* that is, as concrete or abstract preferences independent of a situation requiring choice or activity. Second, values sometimes operate as *goals,* desired future outcomes. Finally, they operate as motives or *commitments.* Dreyfus (1972) has summed up the interrelationship of these three levels by noting that "man's ultimate concern is not just to achieve some goal which is the end of a series; rather, interest in the goal is present at each moment structuring the whole of experience and guiding our activity as we constantly select what is relevant in terms of its significance to the situation at hand" (p. 187).

We can illustrate the transition of values from one level to another with parenthood. The parental ideal may become the goal of having one's own children, but the possibility of commitment does not fully arise until one has one's own particular child. We can also see by this example that the expression of a value in choice and action does not necessarily require its expression on either of the two other levels. Many parents have had neither the ideal nor the goal of parenthood, but nevertheless have found themselves deeply committed to their accidental offspring. Even in the case of the long-awaited child, the ideals espoused by an expectant parent about being a parent are not always transformed into commitments. The contingencies and particularities of being the real-life parent to a specific child give rise to completely unanticipated commitments that operate in the daily transactions between parent and child.

Of the three levels of expression, commitments are of greater interest to coping theory. They represent the person's pattern of values expressed in long-range behavior, thus providing an index of what is of concern to a person (Klinger, 1975). An appreciation of a person's commitments helps explain ineffective coping and overall failure to demonstrate coping and social competence. For example, Mr. A, a participant in our research, is a man who has translated the common cultural ideal of independence and autonomy into a personal commitment. Mr. A ran a successful one-man business in which he performed all functions, from major decision making to duplicating. During our study he was put in charge of a small organization. The appointment carried with it a certain amount of prestige and a lot of responsibility. That Mr. A was chosen for this position indicated how much his peers respected his competence. However, shortly after he took up the new job he went into a deep depression. The organization was not running smoothly; his office staff was disgruntled. His commitment to autonomy prevented him from dealing effectively with the demands of a responsible position because the very nature of the job required delegation of reponsibility and dependence on others to get the work done. His depression was a clear indicator of the inadequacy of his coping efforts in the face of the demands of his new position, but his commitment to autonomy prevented him from using his many personal resources effectively, from seeking information, or from learning the skills needed in his new position.

Mr. A may be an unusual example; probably few people have one such powerful, overriding commitment. Commitments—that is, the things that matter to a person—are usually plural, and form a *network of concerns* (Klinger, 1975) in a more or less loose organization. They might be taken as a reflection of a person's social competence, for they reveal a person's ability to assume role responsibility, to form and maintain relationships, to pursue job or career, and, in general, to function in an expectable fashion. The extreme condition of being unable to care about anything, to form any commitments, represents an ultimate in social incompetence.

To the extent that we are able to draw a picture of a person's network of concerns, we are able to see that person's relatedness to the world. While we might deduce from this a person's ability to function effectively in the social world, from the point of view of stress theory it is more revealing that a person's network of concerns provides an image of what might threaten or harm that person. Commitments reveal what might constitute either possibilities for or barriers to the expression of competence.

Commitments shape *cue sensitivity,* directing attention to what is relevant to the self in any person–situation encounter. While we do not altogether understand the underlying mechanisms, a person, often on a tacit or nonconscious level, responds to cues in the environment related to commitment. An example drawn from common experience is found in the sleeping mother's sensitivity to her own infant's cries.

This ability to respond to cues tacitly (Polanyi, 1966) has been demonstrated in laboratory experiments (Lazarus & McCleary, 1951) in which subjects were shown a series of nonsense syllables in rapid succession; upon being shown certain syllables, subjects were given an electric shock. The subjects soon showed signs of anticipating the shock (as evidenced by galvanic skin responses) when the syllables associated with the shocks appeared, but they were unable to name them. Heightened cue sensitivity—even without full conscious-ness—enhances the highly adaptive capability of appraising a situation as threatening without having to identify logically each aspect of the stimulus configuration that makes it threatening. Thus, by guiding attention to what is relevant (either positively or negatively) to the self in any situation, commitments influence both environmental responsivity and self-directed activity.

Klinger (1975) has elaborated on the cue-sensitivity aspect of commitments in showing how they operate as motives. In his view, depression is a normal result of disengaging from commitments when they have become overpowering or untenable. Successful disengagement from a commitment entails loss of that sense of meaning with which relevant environmental aspects are infused by means of tacit awareness and cue sensitivity. In the interim between this disengagement and engagement with a new commitment, a person may experience "apathy, reduced instrumental striving, loss of concentration, and increased preoccupation with momentary cues" (p. 8), or, in brief, depression.

Commitments, then, are the expression of individual values of greatest use in studying coping. They integrate the individual into the world, particularly the social world, and *determine what is meaningful and salient* in any encounter. They often function in a nonexplicit fashion, so that it is only possible to identify an individual's commitments or network of concerns by documenting the course of his or her thoughts and actions.

Beliefs

We think of beliefs as personally formed or culturally shared cognitive configurations that can be rationally or irrationally derived. Beliefs concern what one thinks is true, whether or not one likes it or approves of it, while values reflect what one wants or prefers. Beliefs and commitments differ in their cognitive–emotional quality. Although beliefs are said not to contain an emotional component, that is, they are affectively neutral (Feather, 1975), in actual psychological events in nature beliefs can fuse with emotion (Folkman *et al.*, 1979). In general, beliefs do have an important relation to emotion; they can give rise to emotion, as in the case of a belief that underlies a threat appraisal (e.g., that the world is hostile or dangerous, or that one is inadequate). They can also serve to dampen or regulate an emotional response, as in the case of a belief used as a coping resource (e.g., that supportive others exist).

Implicitly held beliefs provide a "conceptual framework [that] determines what counts as a fact" (Dreyfus, 1972, p. 190). This kind of belief is a preexisting notion concerning reality that can determine primary appraisal and hence the emotional response. For example, chronic anxiety can result from a primary appraisal of threat based on the implicitly held belief that the world is a hostile place (Lazarus, 1966). That these kinds of beliefs are very deep-rooted and difficult to change is illustrated by the story of the man who believed he was a corpse. The doctor, wishing to dissuade the man from his delusion, asked him, "Well, tell me one thing, sir; do corpses bleed?" "No, of course not," he answered, whereupon the doctor pricked the man's finger and drew a drop of blood. The man was amazed. "What do you know, corpses do bleed!"

Implicitly held beliefs act like a perceptual lens, or a "set," to use the term preferred by perception psychologists. In Gestaltlike terms, they serve as advance organizers of a situation. One of our participants illustrates how a world view can shape stress experiences. A middle-aged woman, married and with children, Mrs. M has never experienced any major losses in her life. Even her parents, now in their 90s, are in good health and live nearby. And yet Mrs. M has come to view the world as a dangerous, risky place, and herself as vulnerable and in need of protection.

> Death or serious illness of myself or my family members is so painful to think about and I am a chicken. I don't like to be hurt and I can't stand physical pain. I don't mind working long and hard, or being imposed upon, but I just don't like pain. [I: Do you feel you have a lot?] No, I think I have built up a kind of fear . . . whoever taught me about it did a good job. My mother is a first-class worrier, and we were overly taken care of as children. I just built up a general fear of anything that is a little bit risky.

Although Mrs. M has been subjected to a minimum of stressful external experiences, she nonetheless appraises benign circumstances as potentially threatening and consequently suffers constantly from subjective stress.

From a developmental perspective, we are reminded here of the research of Levy (1943), which describes overprotecting mothers who cared for their children as they would a baby far beyond the age at which such care would be appropriate. Such overprotection also included oversolicitude such that the child was forced to stay within sight or call and was continually warned against danger ("Don't cross the street, you might get hurt." "Don't run so much, you might get sick."). It is not surprising that these children came to perceive the world as dangerous and frightening, felt mistrust of others, and failed to develop the interpersonal skills that underlie social competence. Recent research along these lines has also been reported by Baumrind (1975), which sharpens and extends Levy's earlier findings.

In this paper we have not emphasized the developmental experiences that might be important in coping and social competence. But it is important to recognize that some stressful events in childhood or adulthood appear to favor the growth of coping and social competence (Murphy, 1974; Murphy & associates, 1962; Murphy & Moriarty, 1976), while others produce a constriction of exploration with a consequent curtailment of the establishment of social and coping skills. Stressful encounters in which the person is overwhelmed, traditionally referred to as trauma, have many of the same constricting effects as the overprotective mothers in Levy's and Baumrind's research. Perhaps they harm the person by generating a persistent belief that the world is highly dangerous and the person wholly incapable of dealing with it (Benner, Roskies, & Lazarus, 1980).

Negative beliefs about the world and the self can result in similar primary appraisals across situations. The holders of such views are unable to discriminate threatening situations from benign ones. Although such a pattern represents an extreme, it is likely to give rise to the persistent experience of distressing emotions such as anxiety (Lazarus, 1966) and to be resistent to coping efforts by the individual because of negative expectations about what might be done. More common are those implicitly held beliefs that apply to a single class of situation, such as meeting strangers, being evaluated (test anxiety), speaking in front of an audience, or flying in an airplane.

Beliefs about self are as important in appraisal and competence as are beliefs about the external world. For example, persons who believe in their general self-efficacy (Bandura, 1977) are likely to have a very different orientation to social encounters than those who have doubts about themselves or are certain that they will be inept. The former will probably approach many situations feeling more competent, and hence less stressed and uncomfortable, than persons whose belief in their self-efficacy is less well developed. As such, they will have less difficulty too with the disrupting effects of anxiety in pressing and even ordinary social situations, and thereby have a greater chance of functioning effectively. Other beliefs about self, such as about physical or social attractiveness, intelligence, or sexuality, are also clearly related to coping and social competence.

Beliefs function in the coping process in two different ways. First, they operate as an *interpretive system* when one is attempting to understand some troubling event that has already occurred. An interpretive system enables one to manage a difficult emotional response by changing how it is construed, after the fact. Although beliefs can function rapidly and on a prerational basis (primary appraisal), they can also be used in a deliberate way to reinterpret or transform one's definition of a situation (reappraisal), especially when such beliefs are formal and explicit, as in religion (Pearlin & Schooler, 1978). For example, a woman in our study, a fundamentalist Christian, at first experienced anxiety over having told the interviewer personal details of her life. However, she typically analyzed all pleasant and unpleasant experiences in terms of how they might express divine purposes. In this case, she concluded that God wanted her to have someone in whom to confide. In effect, she erased the source of her anxiety by reforming the meaning of the situation. She was no longer speaking intimately with a comparative stranger but was enjoying a blessing.

Many clinical intervention programs rely on the use of explicitly held beliefs as interpretive systems in reappraisal of past events in order to change a person's behavior in future encounters. For example, in assertiveness training a person is taught to reevaluate situations with newly acquired beliefs about their personal power and interactional possibilities. An entire therapeutic system, rational–emotive therapy (Ellis, 1962), one that has had a major impact on cognitive-behavior therapy in general, is based on the concept that irrational beliefs or assumptions underlie distressing and disruptive emotional reactions. An example, cited by Ellis, is the belief that "one should be thoroughly competent, adequate, and achieving in all possible respects, if one is to consider oneself worthwhile" (p. 63). The therapeutic program consists of efforts to change such irrational beliefs because these result in threat even in transactions in which threat appraisals are unreasonable and counterproductive.

Explicitly held beliefs also function as a *resource for coping* with situations whose real-world qualities do not lend themselves easily to reappraisal. Functioning in this way, beliefs do not transform totally one's view of actual reality. The event may still be considered threatening or harmful, and the person may still have little or no hope for mitigating the harm or mastering the situation, but he or she can be reassured, comforted, or strengthened by beliefs. When direct action is possible, but anxiety or some other distressing emotion interferes with it, beliefs can still help alleviate distress and allow the person to get on with direct action aimed at the problem. For example, Mechanic (1962) used the term "comforting cognitions" to describe the supportive beliefs and reappraisals that students facing a crucial examination relied on to dampen the threat and regulate their emotional distress. One could, for example, assume that one's history of past success in dealing with difficult tasks was a valuable asset, or that even if one failed there were other rewarding career directions in which to go, or other styles of life that would be worthwhile, perhaps even superior to the one that was endangered.

However, even when there is no option for direct action, favorable beliefs can support one in the face of harm. For example, a woman who was 20 years old at the time of her internment in a Nazi concentration camp reported later: "I had a belief, a religious belief. I was convinced that all the wrong things had to change and we would be free. My mother put in me the belief that if someone is doing right, he will not always suffer. . . . I knew to survive [in Auschwitz] I had to believe, believe that such a bad thing cannot win" (Dimsdale, 1974, p. 793). This woman's belief system served as a countervailing force against the inescapable horror of the Holocaust. She used a belief in the ultimate triumph of good to strengthen herself against persecution, and to reassure herself of ultimate survival, thus lessening the threat somewhat.

Values and beliefs are person qualities that operate transactionally because they are the basis for determining the meaning of situational encounters in relation to oneself. They tie a person on a large scale to a culture and on a small scale to a personal network of concerns; they provide the person with a social context, and the meaning that operates within it. In spite of the broad cultural basis of shared meanings, values and beliefs also operate in highly individual ways that help explain the tremendous individual variation in the transactional processes that underlie emotions, coping, and social competence. Individual differences in values and beliefs mean that people will be threatened or sustained by different types of encounter, will cope with them differently, and will display divergent areas and degrees of competence and incompetence.

SITUATIONAL DEMAND CHARACTERISTICS

While an examination of values and beliefs can show us how people engage with the world and thereby enter into transactions, these person qualities cannot by themselves explain the various adaptational outcomes that result from such encounters. Every transaction involves a set of real environmental demands, constraints and resources with which to cope. Murray's (1938) distinction between the environment as it is (alpha press), and as it is perceived (appraised) by the individual (beta press), helps us remember that environmental contingencies operate despite efforts to cope, legislating for or against the success of such coping efforts, or placing such heavy demands on the person that the success of coping is bought only at high personal cost (see also Lewin's, 1935, 1936, concept of the "foreign hull of the life space").

The situational demand characteristics discussed in this section are offered as examples of how situational forces operate in the transactional process. It must be remembered that a prerequisite of engaging in a coping process is that the situation has meaning and salience for the person in terms of well-being. From our perspective, one cannot abstract these situational features from their meaning context and predict their stress-producing quality or prescribe coping strategies. This is the approach of the environmentalists, and its limitation is that it no longer considers situation in process terms. We have separated person and situational features of the transaction in order to illustrate how both aspects of the transaction, when considered in process terms, can affect the expression of competence. We offer the caveat that the four examples of situational demand—uniqueness, duration–frequency, pervasiveness, and ambiguity—should not be used as abstractions outside of the transactional context.

Uniqueness

It is the nature of life to present us with unique demands that have never been encountered before. Even in political crisis management, political scientists are often ambivalent about what can be learned from previous crisis experiences, believing that decision groups must guard against seeing in a current crisis (e.g., Soviet cold war acts) the same process and coping response that applied in earlier instances (e.g., Nazi actions before World War II). In some way each new stressful encounter is different from the last, and in important respects perhaps unique, calling for different appraisals and coping responses. Most stressful encounters present some factors that are different from previous ones within the same family, making the precise constellation of factors different despite striking similarities. Yet, in both individual stress and social stress, we tend to believe, whether correctly or not, that present encounters can repeat the themes of the past. The issue is a difficult one to evalute before the fact.

The most general characteristic of the unique situation is that the person has no previous experiences or cultural practices to provide the knowledge and skills with which to respond. Sometimes it is possible to anticipate a new situation and, by analytic thought and rehearsal, neutralize the threat before the confrontation. Neugarten, Wood, Kraines, and Loomis (1968) have proposed that women deal with menopause by such anticipation. Socialization experiences normally help to short-circuit stress appraisals by providing adaptive skills and attitudes that are serviceable in new but predictable life situations. For example, school trains children to recognize the requirements of occupation and political participation (Dreeben, 1968), thus reducing the uniqueness of some of the demands of adult life.

However, socialization can help only in the case of predictable experiences, and to be human is to be beset by novel and unanticipated situations. These arise partly because of intentional exposure to the new and different (Zuckerman, Kalin, Price, & Zoob's sensation-seeking scale, 1964, 1979), and because of the pursuit of goals and commitments. People involved in unique situations can be vulnerable to severe stress and even the breakdown of functioning. The person gets into trouble either through the lack of requisite coping resources or through the use of coping strategies that are inappropriate because of the failure to recognize the uniqueness of the adaptational requirements.

Culture shock is a common example of the loss of social competence as a result of the uniqueness of demands. In a foreign culture not only can the more obvious customs and practices be different, but subtle nonverbal communication and deeply held implicit views and beliefs about the world (Merton, 1957) are apt to isolate the foreigner from the familiar social and meaning contexts.

Duration–Frequency

"Duration" refers to the length of time a demand is present. For example, it was the long duration of overload conditions that led to burn-out in mental health professionals (Maslach & Pines, 1978; Pines & Maslach, 1978) cited earlier. "Frequency," on the other hand, refers to the repetition of a discrete demand. Commuting or having noisy neighbors are typical examples of demands characterized by frequency. We call these time-limited, but regularly repeated demands, daily hassles as distinguished from major life events, and are currently examining how they fit into the overall patterns of stress and coping of the participants in our study. We are typically offered two contradictory perspectives on hassles. One view is that people get used to them; the other is that people are worn down by them. We believe that it is the overall context of demands (i.e., their importance, significance, and potential for mastery) that determines the impact of frequency.

A demand that combines long duration and frequency has a particular potential for undermining coping efforts. Chronic illnesses (e.g., diabetes, kidney failure) involve this double demand. The person may adapt successfully to the chronic aspect of the illness and integrate the management of it into his or her life-style to such an extent that there is little or no perceived stress when things are going well. But, there is a limit to the effective control of chronic illnesses that require constant watchfulness, so that, despite continuing coping and active management, the person will from time to time fall ill. This makes such illnesses special in their impact on the sustained coping required to survive and flourish in spite of them.

Extended duration and frequency can also combine with uniqueness to create another kind of stressful demand. For example, the duration of a demand and the possibility of mastery, which is reduced by uniqueness, will influence the individual's decision about whether to tolerate the stress or mount extensive efforts to cope through direct actions. Becker (1964) predicts that a person will make few adaptive sacrifices where high demands are seen as temporary. The interaction of duration and uniqueness is illustrated by the distinction between culture shock and culture fatigue. With culture fatigue, it is the repeated demand that the person perform in novel situations that takes its toll (Textor, 1966).

> Culture fatigue is the physical and emotional exhaustion that almost invariably results from the infinite series of minute adjustments required for long-term survival in an alien culture. Living and working overseas generally requires that one must suspend his automatic evaluations and judgments; that he must supply new interpretations to seemingly familiar behavior; and that he must demand of himself constant alterations in the style and content of his activity. (sic, pp. 48–49)

The duration of a stressful situation is particularly significant where the person sees little possibility of changing either the self or the environment. If the duration appears to be indefinite or interminable, and change appears impossible, the person may succumb to a feeling of hopelessness, a position consistent with great vulnerability, anxiety, and depression (Stotland, 1969). On the other hand, the person may come to accept the damage or loss by relinquishing the commitments on which it is based (Kubler-Ross, 1969; Lindemann, 1944).

Pervasiveness

Situational demands become pervasive when they permeate every corner of experience or when one demand inevitably entails a whole series of additional demands. Pierce (1974, pp. 110–119) compared the stress experienced in the extreme environment of the South Pole scientific expeditions and the daily stress of life in the inner-city and found them similar in the pervasiveness of demands. For example, falling ill for the poverty-level resident of the inner-city entails not just the distressing effects of the illness itself, but also the uncomfortable experience of seeking care in overcrowded hospitals where one must wait a long time for attention. In addition, crowded living conditions and limited food supply may then offer little in the way of a comfortable, supportive environment for recuperation.

Bereavement is another life stress in which the situational demands for social readjustment are most pervasive. The bereaved person must reorganize most or all previously patterned activities. The extensive and continuing situational demands for change and readjustment in one's responsibilities and social roles leave virtually no part of life untouched.

Bereavement is not unique in this regard. Ilfeld (1977) investigated the relationship between socioenvironmental stress and anxiety by examining the impact of five current social stressors (marriage, finance, parenthood, job, and neighborhood). He found that anxiety increased with the number of stressors experienced. The group highest in anxiety experienced three or more current social stressors. A partialing of the variance showed that no one current stress accounted for the increase in anxiety. There appeared to be a cumulative effect of the stressors as shown by the increase in anxiety. But more pertinently, there also appeared to be a patterning of the stressors themselves, with the most vulnerable group experiencing stressors that were linked to one another, (e.g., being separated, having financial problems, and having parenting problems).

Life experiences commonly involve us in chains and networks of stressful encounters, making the stressful encounters seem pervasive. While separate demands can possibly be met and dealt with, pervasiveness itself changes the experience. One has the sense that every aspect of one's life is threatened or disturbed, and that there is no refuge.

Ambiguity

Some situations are highly explicit and structured (or institutionalized); their demands can be characterized as having great clarity. School represents one kind of institutionalized situation that is designed to achieve such clarity, although it can often fail in this. But the majority of life situations are not institutionalized, nor clear.

By their very nature social situations are often ambiguous, although they are not always experienced as such (see discussion below regarding personal control). Ambiguity in role relationships may be a source of damaging conflict and stress (Kahn, Wolfe, Quinn, & Snoek, 1964). But in extreme situations—for example, when dealing with a life-threatening illness—the ambiguity of implications and outcomes may actually be a resource offering hope and choices for living despite the presence of extreme threat (Folkman *et al.*, 1979).

Mr. C in our sample was a person for whom ambiguity presented a major demand in an already-threatening situation. Mr. C experienced little stress in his life; he sought and secured rapid closure on all problems. But when his wife developed symptoms associated with colorectal cancer, none of his usual coping strategies was applicable. His wife consulted a physician soon after the onset of symptoms, but had to wait a week before being admitted to the hospital for diagnostic tests, During this time Mr. C couldn't eat, sleep, or concentrate on work. His wife, experiencing severe anxiety herself, finally told him, "You're not helping, you know." Fortunately for Mr. and Mrs. C, the illness proved nonmalignant, and Mr. C was left with only the memory of the time when he, in his own words, "fell apart." What he would have done to cope if there had been a cancer is an unanswered question.

COPING AND SOCIAL EFFECTIVENESS IN THE TRANSACTION

Having emphasized some of the person and environment factors that operate transactionally in stressful encounters and influence coping and social effectiveness, we now turn to the transactional process itself, remembering that the judgment about coping and social competence is made, ideally, by creating a portrait of effectiveness and in-effectiveness over many encounters. In coping theory, effectiveness must be judged not only on the basis of the quality of problem solving but also on the quality of the emotional experience, the somatic costs of the effort, and how the person feels about him or herself in the world (morale). We suggest that social competence too rests on being effective, not only in many specific social relationships, but also in enhancing or maintaining these other values, which also define adap-tationally desirable outcomes.

Moreover, if we take the transactional perspective seriously, it is clearly a mistake to assign responsibility for coping and social effec-tiveness solely to the person *or* the environment, although this mistake is often made. Most commonly, this error occurs when a transactional concept is used either as a personality or environmen-tal variable. For example, Durkheim's (1951) notion of anomie (see earlier discussion) has been used sometimes to describe alienated peo-ple and sometimes an alienating society. When a transactional con-cept is thus wrongly applied, the basis for evaluating effectiveness (and hence competence) is incorrect.

For those interested in concepts such as coping and social com-petence, and the effectiveness of transactions on which such abstrac-tions depend, two important theoretical and research directions have recently emerged as particularly salient, namely, the personal con-trol of events, and the role of social groups and networks in the main-tenance of somatic and mental health.

Personal Control

The issue of personal control is relevant to our thesis because such control is widely regarded as prerequisite for social competence and ineffective social functioning is often attributed to its lack. And yet, as we have shown in the last section, people can be engaged in mean-ingful transactions with the environment in which control is not the source of effective functioning. Indeed, in the extreme demand condi-tions described above, taking personal control would require disen-gaging from the transaction—for the diabetic not to care whether he were healthy or ill, for the widow not to care whether her husband had lived or died. And such disengagement has high costs in terms of adaptation.

In addition, the notion of personal control fits ideally with our thesis because the research on locus of control (Rotter, 1966) il-lustrates well the mistaken attribution of transactional concepts to either person or situation. There are two main errors. First, belief in the internal versus the external locus of control is studied typically as a personality trait. Nevertheless, neither Rotter nor Lefcourt (1973) seem willing to regard them as such theoretically, but prefer to treat them as a product of social learning in which both person and environmental variables play an equally important role. In effect, the actual research on these variables is seldom transactional despite a theoretical underpinning that is quite compatible with a transactional perspective.

Second, a superficial review of the experimental, laboratory-based research on control might lead the reader to conclude that control, or the illusion of control, is always stress-reducing. Although in Western culture control is usually preferred, the preference does not hold for all people and all circumstances (Averill, 1973; Averill, DeWitt, & Zimmer, 1978; Gal & Lazarus, 1975), nor is control always a more comfortable state of being. And there is evidence that persons with an external locus of control are less anxious in situations in which they are not in control (Joe, 1971). Averill (1973) has helped clarify the various meanings of personal control, as well as the situations in which such control might reduce stress, by distinguishing between behavioral control and decisional control.

"Behavioral control" refers to direct actions that might make a threatening event less threatening. The ability to have an impact on, change, or modify an impending threat is typically believed to be in itself stress-reducing; however, experimental findings by Weiss (1968) show that stress is in part a function of the number of coping responses. Even in the case where the behavior is effective, the greater the number of responses, the higher the stress.

Averill (1973) has suggested that the reduction of stress supposedly resulting from behavioral control can most often be attributed to the reduction of uncertainty (the subjective side of ambiguity). Furthermore, uncertainty may either reflect ambiguous conditions or arise because of insufficient or delayed evidence about coping effectiveness. Under experimental conditions, behavioral control is usually preferred by human subjects, probably because it reduces uncertainty, yet subjects still experience stress in terms of galvanic skin response, anxiety, and pain (Haggard, 1943; Pervin, 1963). Such findings lead Averill (1973) to conclude that behavioral control over uncertainty may be preferred by people, but may not be stress-reducing in the short term. However, it may be highly effective in doing so over the long run.

"Decisional control" is experienced in the process of making choices. Averill (1973) notes that "a person will experience choice when he is acting according to his beliefs or doing that with which he agrees" (p. 299). This view matches our own about the role of beliefs and commitments in guiding choice and determining cue-sensitivity in any transaction.

Finally, "the illusion of control" (Langer, 1975; Lefcourt, 1973) extends the concept of decisional control by showing how the person can be misled by situational cues. It has been shown experimentally that people will react as if they have control over situations governed by chance if these situations resemble those previously associated with such control. This tendency to misjudge one's control over situations has been taken advantage of in therapeutic interventions. For example, allowing elderly nursing home patients to make decisions on relatively small matters creates in them the sense of having greater control over their lives than they do in fact have, with a resultant improvement in morale (Rodin & Langer, 1977). Any activity, particularly when it *seems* related to the control of threat, can be quite effective in reducing anxiety (Gal & Lazarus, 1975). Nevertheless, it is not particularly adaptive to continue to make effortful responses in a situation where outcomes are not related to effort. The cultural or personal baggage of a strong need for control may cause people to struggle counterproductively in circumstances where control is not possible (Averill, O'Brien, & DeWitt, 1977).

A further example of this is Seligman's (1975) research on learned helplessness, in which dogs exposed to shock in a no-escape situation gave up, and became apathetic and inactive. This giving-up behavior continued even after the no-escape situation was changed. What is often overlooked in studies of learned helplessness is that decreased effort and disengagement can often be adaptive. For the dog (or person) to continue to try to escape, after discovering that no escape is possible, would be a less effective coping strategy than simply giving up and thus, appropriately, conserving energy. The response is maladaptive only under the special circumstances in which changed conditions make escape once again possible.

In each form of personal control—behavioral, decisional, or illusory—a dynamic relationship exists between the person and the situation. To attribute the variable of control solely to the person or to the situation obscures this (dynamic) transaction, and misleads us in understanding competence. Effective functioning, which should be the basis for judgments of competence, is based on the ability both to stop trying when effort is pointless and to recognize a new situation in which effort would pay off. But under the learned helplessness model, giving up is viewed as rigid or pathological, while continuing instrumental striving is automatically regarded as competent. By wrongly assigning the transactional variable, control, solely to the person we can, ironically, be led to propose models of effective functioning that are actually maladaptive.

Social Groups and Networks

Just as the concept of personal control tends to be treated as a person variable, a trait, rather than being viewed transactionally, so social groups and social networks are treated as features of the environment having the characteristics of demands, constraints, or resources. And because personal control is often viewed as a major component of social competence, social groups and networks and the individual's highly complex relations to them are frequently overlooked. Yet to understand coping and social competence, we need to grasp the transactional process created when a particular individual is in a social group or network, and has encounters within and outside the group. We can better understand how social groups and networks can operate simultaneously as a demand, a constraint, *and* as a resource from a transactional standpoint.

There is a growing interest in the role of social networks and social supports in coping with stress (Antonovsky, 1972; Cassel, 1976; Cobb, 1976; Kaplan, Cassel, & Gore, 1977; Nuckolls, Cassel, & Kaplan, 1972). Close, positive, supportive relationships appear to facilitate good health and morale despite personal crises, and persons characterized as having elaborate social networks at their disposal generally live longer than isolates (Berkman, 1977). Although mere social ties (networks) are not uniformly supportive (Friedman, Chodoff, Mason, & Hamburg, 1963; Mechanic, 1962), social relations that are supportive appear central to most coping activity.

No one seems to question that social and relational skills as well as their product, social networks or support systems, can be major resources in coping effectiveness. Little is known, however, about how they work. In a review of coping with stress, Hamburg and Adams (1967) concluded that in general, "individuals cope more effectively with disability problems when they have a firm sense of belonging in highly valued groups" (p. 279). But we don't know why this is so. A provocative study by Stack (1974) illustrates concretely the adaptational value of social networks for poverty-level blacks living in the flatlands of Oakland. These people would have been considered highly incompetent, or at least uninterpretable, if studied as single individuals outside the context of their group. For example, as soon as they got any money, furniture, clothes, or food, they gave it away. A welfare check intended to pay the recipient's rent went to pay for shoes for her daughter's children and a payment on a friend's furniture. What Stack discovered, however, was the existence of a highly complex system of swapping. While no one was ever able to accumulate money or goods, or plan ahead for any contingency, this system made it possible for everyone in the group to survive from day to day. If one person in the swapping network was asked by another for her new chair, she would give it knowing that she could some day, in turn, call on that person for money or clothes or milk for her own children. Given the scarcity of resources, the swapping system actually provided a wider range of resources and more adaptational possibilities than would be available on an individual level.

When competence is viewed as a relational concept, it is possible to see that ineffective coping can both lessen the available environmental resources and/or increase the situational demands, as well as vice versa for effective coping. Coyne's interactive approach to depression illustrates this kind of transactional effect. Coyne (1976) notes, in essence, that the depressed person counterproductively creates particular patterns of response from the social network, which extend and exacerbate the depression:

> Irritated, yet inhibited and increasingly guilt-ridden, members of the social environment [of the depressed person] continue to give verbal assurance of support and acceptance. However, a growing discrepancy between the verbal content and the affective quality of these responses proves validation for the depressive's suspicions that he is not really being accepted and that further interaction cannot be assured. To maintain his increasingly uncertain security, the depressive displays more symptoms. (p. 34)

In this way, the depressive's transactions with the social environment have the effect of decreasing social supports and increasing the number of social reactions the depressive will appraise as threatening. The result is a downward spiral of coping and social competence.

Kobler and Stotland (1964) have accounted for an epidemic of suicide in a mental hospital by observing just such a transactional process. When changes in treatment and management procedures were not successful with a patient, the staff indirectly communicated to the other patients their sense of hopelessness about providing effective treatment. An epidemic of suicide resulted and was attributed to the lack of a sense of support in the social environment. Along the same line, Hamburg and Adams (1967) concluded that burned patients and patients with severe poliomyelitis make "efforts toward testing of key figures in their personal environment in order to determine whether they would still be regarded with positive feelings in spite of their damaged condition, whether they could still win affection and respect in ways that had proved effective in the past, and whether new patterns of interaction would be required" (p. 279).

The research literature is replete with examples of the mutual influence of social networks and supports on social competence, morale, and health. What is needed is more naturalistic studies of how these transactions unfold over time. Such research would increase our ability to look beyond the individual level to the person's transactions with others and with the larger social network. A better understanding of the coping functions of social supports could correct the past error of the context-free study of the person.

Some of the most enlightening research on the coping functions served by social groups has been done on groups formed by stressful circumstances. Few situations have illustrated the importance of the group more dramatically than Grinker and Spiegel's (1945a) studies of men in air combat. Commitment to and trust in the combat crew was thought to be a necessary condition for managing the threat of combat. Grinker and Spiegel (1945b) state:

> Many factors contribute to this inability to "take it." Loss of morale within the combat outfit is one of the principal forces destroying the resistance of the individual. In time of victory, morale is usually high. When the fighting is uncertain or defeat imminent, the morale of the group assumes great importance for the individual, sustaining him if it is good, further weakening his resistance if it is low. (p. 69)

Moreover, those men who had poor social adjustment prior to entering the combat situation added to the stress experienced by the group, and were also likely candidates for combat neuroses.

In a study of less extreme circumstances, Mechanic (1962) found that students studying for doctoral examinations both used and misused the social group in coping. In some cases the group increased the individual's sense of discomfort, but nevertheless propelled the students to information search, shaped study tactics, and contributed to shared tension-relief strategies. An increase in tension generated by the group sometimes facilitated effective coping tactics, that is, encouraged appropriate study activity; at other times, however, the increased tension blocked the student from being able to study.

In short, the individual's coping effectiveness was highly dependent on group influences.

In a study of men who were trapped in a coal mine, Lucas (1969) has also argued that social influence and acceptability were crucial to the emergence of effective survival behavior. Management of the emotion of disgust, and the ability to engage in the abhorrent behavior of drinking their own urine, were facilitated by social influence as well as personal (intrapsychic) cognitive strategies. The group's favorable response to the idea of drinking their own urine was vital to the individual's own acceptance of the idea. However, the miner still had to manage his own emotions on an individual level before drinking urine was possible. To do this he might, for example, try to imagine it was something else, or suck it through a piece of charred wood.

Group structure and decision-making processes also change with situational demands (Brenner, 1974; Lawrence & Lorsch, 1967). Janis and Mann (1977) present an extensive analysis of group decision making under stressful conditions. They describe collective coping strategies within groups and provide criteria for predicting the effectiveness of decision making based upon the group's coping strategies. Earlier, Janis (1972) had described the phenomenon of "group think" as a collective pattern of defensive avoidance. A highly stressed cohesive group, with little hope for finding a solution other than the one proffered by an influential person in the group, will tend to discourage all disagreement and seek conformity of opinion. As a group they make bad decisions by creating the mutual illusion of invulnerability and a strong belief in their inherent morality, while stereotyping outsiders as inferior.

In sum, small group research has shown that a person is subject to forces of conformity in a group because appraisal is altered just by the commitment to the group and to group social processes. In this way, groups can expand or limit an individual's coping effectiveness. Stress can transform a loose collection of people into a group that is integrated by its joint coping efforts. Under extreme circumstances these coping efforts determine, for better or worse, individual and group survival and the long-term effects of the experience. Groups develop coping responses that are community-oriented and cannot be understood if they are reduced solely to the individual level. Just as individual identity may change as a result of coping, so does the group process and identity. In some ways, therefore, social competence is not only an individual achievement. In a transactional perspective, the person is always viewed in a context; for social competence theory, that context is always peopled. Understanding how different social contexts operate to facilitate or impair the effective functioning of the individual, and the group, is crucial for the theory and assessment of social competence.

APPLICATION TO RESEARCH

The thrust of this chapter has been to direct attention to the ways the ongoing encounter between person and situation, which we call transaction, can determine effective functioning. If, as we have argued, coping and social competence are summative inferences about how effectively a person functions in specific social and/or stressful encounters, then those interested in the assessment and enhancement of competence should turn their interest to the transactional process and its components. This means that we must study adequately functioning people in depth and across numerous adaptationally relevant encounters.

The brief vignettes we have given throughout of the people in our study represent part of a systematic study of stress and coping in selected people living in the community. More than 100 such persons were studied over a period of 1 year, using in-depth interviews in their homes on a monthly basis. In addition, other measures, often presented as homework each month and constructed to emphasize process, permit descriptions of emotional patterns, the social environment and social supports, values and commitments, beliefs and outlooks, sources of stress (including major life changes and daily hassles), sources of satisfaction, and patterns of coping. Still other measures tackle adaptational outcomes, including morale, social and work functioning, and somatic and mental health.

To examine process, which implies change, our research design is ipsative–normative in style (Broverman, 1962; Marceil, 1977), which means that measures of emotional patterns, daily hassles, and coping are obtained repeatedly for the same persons across diverse encounters over the period of the year. This provides us with two complementary research perspectives: (1) interindividual (normative), in which participants can be compared with each other on any variable, and (2) intraindividual (ipsative), in which the person can be compared with himself or herself under different circumstances. The basic rationale for this type of research design has been thoroughly outlined elsewhere (Lazarus, 1981; Lazarus & Cohen, 1976), and need not be belabored here.

In this way, we will ultimately be in a position to say something about many of the issues raised earlier in this chapter. For example, we can describe the coping process as it unfolds in various types of stressful encounters; thus, not only can we evaluate the stability of the coping process for each person, but we can also attempt to identify the role of the type of encounter and other social and personal factors as influences on the coping process. In addition, we can assess the part played by commitments and beliefs in the coping process, evaluate the effectiveness of each coping episode, and assay coping competence (which often overlaps with social competence) by examining any individual's overall pattern of effectiveness. Finally, this description and evaluation of coping can also be related to the various categories of adaptational outcome.

We expect this naturalistic, process-oriented, multileveled, and ipsative–normative style of research to add significantly to our understanding of coping and social competence. Indeed, we believe that only in this way can the major theoretical issues we have addressed above be effectively examined. Ultimately, such observations should clarify what works and what fails in coping and social transactions, helping us to use better the possibilities and limitations inherent in therapeutic interventions, in prevention, and in education for coping and social competence.

CONCLUSION

The current concept of social competence has promoted a view of humans as active and self-regulating, rather than passive and merely reactive, and in so doing has spurred efforts of intervention directed at promoting a sense of autonomy, feelings of self-efficacy, and social skills. But this notion of the socially competent person as being active and self-regulating and in charge of his or her own life raises two major questions. Why is it that some people appear not to strive for competence, or seem as if they cannot be taught to be competent in some social situations? In our quotidian existence we are presented with the mysterious fact that people often possess the requisite social skills, but seem unable to draw on those skills in particular social situations or at particular times.

Secondly, how can a position that values autonomy and self-determination, as the social competence concept has, account for the highly complex ways people belong to, identify with, and are influenced by social groups? To participate in group life requires that one be able to partake of the group's shared understandings and meanings as well as introduce one's own positions and interpretations. In other words, to be socially competent requires that in addition to freely expressing one's own values through lines of action, one must be able to understand and participate in the values of others.

We have offered a cognitive–phenomenological theory of coping that emphasizes the person–situation transactional process as a perspective from which answers to these questions might be found. We have rejected both the environmentalists' position that the individual is a passive recipient of social pressures (i.e., merely reactive), as well as the trait conception that the responsibility for the expression of social competence resides solely within the person.

We hold that persons come to social situations with a background of shared assumptions about their meaning. Being reared in a culture allows people to experience social situations as already imbued with meaning. The individual's *particular* concerns and commitments shape his or her particular relationship to specific social situations in a transactional fashion. The individual cannot arbitrarily choose to appropriate just any view or position. Some positions are outside one's group or culture's practices or understanding. More importantly, some positions are untenable given the person's commitments, ideals, and beliefs.

This position has been presented earlier in an interpretation of stress and coping among survivors of the Holocaust (Brenner *et al.*, 1980). Survivors were not free to choose a new understanding of their world without incorporating their personal knowledge that the worst had happened, and therefore, could possibly happen again. They were not free to pick up their faith in the order and predictability of their world in the same way as before, when they had taken it for granted.

Active choice does not mean unlimited choice, or choice without respect for one's history, understanding, commitments, ideals, and beliefs. Active choice is best understood as made possible by being situated in a network of concerns and human relationships. There is no perfect environment, though environments may be improved. There is no way to make oneself competent for all circumstances, though one's range of possibilities and abilities to function in new circumstances can be enhanced. Both extreme notions, the perfect environment, and the omnicompetent individual, preclude change and growth and puts one outside the realm of human discourse and experience. Solutions that invite change must come to terms with the two-way process of engagement between person and environment. In short, approaches to social competence and coping competence must ultimately be transactional in outlook.

ACKNOWLEDGMENTS

This study was supported in part by a research grant from the National Institute of Aging (AG 00799).

REFERENCES

Adler, A. *The practice and theory of individual psychology* (P. Radin, trans.). New York: Harcourt, Brace, 1924.

Antonovsky, A. Breakdown: A needed fourth step in the conceptual armamentarium of modern medicine. *Social Science and Medicine,* 1972, *6,* 537–544.

Averill, J. R. Personal control over aversive stimuli and its relationship to stress. *Psychological Bulletin,* 1973, *80,* 286–303.

Averill, J. R., DeWitt, G. W., & Zimmer, M. The self-attribution of emotion as a function of success and failure. *Journal of Personality,* 1978, *46,* 323–347.

Averill, J. R., O'Brien, L., & DeWitt, G. W. The influence of response effectiveness on the preference for warning and on psychophysiological stress reactions. *Journal of Personality,* 1977, *45,* 395–418.

Bandura, A. Self-efficacy: Toward a unifying theory of behavioral change. *Psychological Review,* 1977, *84,* 191–215.

Baumrind, D. Early socialization and the discipline controversy. In I. Spence (Ed.), *University programs modular studies.* Morristown, NJ: General Learning Press, 1975.

Becker, H. Personal change in adult life. *Sociometry,* 1964, *27,* 40–53.

Benner, P., Roskies, E., & Lazarus, R. S. Stress and coping under extreme conditions. In J. E. Dimsdale (Ed.), *Survivors, victims, perpetrators: Essays on the Nazi holocaust.* Washington, DC: Hemisphere, 1980.

Benner, R. *The strategy and structure of change in the university: Theory and research on decision making in complex organizations.* Unpublished doctoral dissertation, Stanford University, May 1974.

Berkman, L. *Social networks, host resistance and morality.* Unpublished doctoral dissertation, University of California, Berkeley, 1977.

Broverman, D. M. Normative and ipsative measurement in psychology. *Psychological Review,* 1962, *4,* 295–305.

Cassel, J. The contribution of the social environment to host resistance. *American Journal of Epidemiology,* 1976, *104,* 107–123.

Cobb, S. Social support as moderator of life stresses. *Psychosomatic Medicine,* 1976, *38,* 300–314.

Cohen, F., & Lazarus, R. S. Active coping processes, coping dispositions and recovery from surgery. *Psychosomatic Medicine,* 1973, *35,* 375–389.

Coyne, J. C. Towards an interactional description of depression. *Psychiatry,* 1976, *39,* 28–40.

Dewey, J., & Bentley, A. F. *Knowing and the known.* Boston: Beacon, 1949.

Dimsdale, J. E. The coping behavior of Nazi concentration camp survivors. *American Journal of Psychiatry,* 1974, *131,* 792–797.

Dreeben, R. *On what is learned in school.* Reading, MA: Addison-Wesley, 1968.

Dreyfus, H. L. *What computors can't do: A critique of artifical reason.* New York: Harper & Row, 1972.

Durkheim, E. *Suicide: A study in sociology* (J. A. Spaulding & G. Simpson, trans.). New York: Free Press, 1951.

Ellis, A. *Reason and emotion in psychotherapy.* New York: Lyle Stuart, 1962.

Erikson, E. H. *Childhood and society* (1st & 2nd eds.). New York: Norton, 1950, 1963.

Feather, N. T. *Values in education and society.* New York: Free Press, 1975.

Folkman, S. K. *An analysis of coping in an adequately functioning middle-aged population.* Unpublished doctoral dissertation, University of California, Berkeley, 1979.

Folkman, S., Schaefer, C., & Lazarus, R. S. Cognitive processes as mediators of stress and coping, In V. Hamilton & D. M. Warburton (Eds.), *Human stress and cognition: An information-processing approach.* London: Wiley, 1979.

Foote, N. N., & Cottrell, L. S. *Identity and interpersonal competence.* Chicago: University of Chicago Press, 1955.

Friedman, M., Byers, S. D., Diamant, J., & Rosenman, R. H. Plasma catecholamine response of coronary-prone subjects (Type A) to a specific challenge. *Metabolism,* 1975, *24,* 205–210.

Friedman, S. B., Chodoff, P., Mason, J. W., & Hamburg, D. A. Behavioral observations on parents anticipating the death of a child. *Pediatrics,* 1963, *32,* 610–625.

Fromm, E. *Escape from freedom.* New York: Rinehart & Winston, 1941.

Gal, R., & Lazarus, R. S. The role of activity in anticipating and confronting stressful situations. *Journal of Human Stress,* 1975, *1,* 4–20.

Gladwin, T. Social competence and clinical practice. *Psychiatry,* 1967, *30,* 30–43.

Glass, D. C. Stress, behavior patterns and coronary disease. *American Scientist,* 1977, *65,* 177–187.

Grinker, R. R., & Spiegel, J. P. *War neuroses.* Philadelphia: Blakiston, 1945. (a)

Grinker, R. R., & Spiegel, J. P. *Men under stress.* New York: McGraw-Hill, 1945. (b)

Hackett, T. P., & Cassem, H. Psychological management of myocardial infarction patient. *Journal of Human Stress,* 1975, *1,* 25–38.

Haggard, E. A. Experimental studies in affective processes: I. Some effects of cognitive structure and active participation on certain autonomic reactions during and following experimentally induced stress. *Journal of Experimental Psychology,* 1943, *33,* 257–284.

Hamburg, D. A., & Adams, J. E. A perspective on coping: Seeking and utilizing information in major transitions. *Archives of General Psychiatry,* 1967, *17,* 277–284.

Horner, M. S. Toward an understanding of achievement-related conflicts in women. *Journal of Social Issues,* 1972, *28,* 157–175.

Horney, K. *The neurotic personality of our time.* New York: Norton, 1937.

Ilfeld, F. W. *Persons at high risk for symptoms of anxiety.* Paper presented at Excerpta Medica Symposium, "Clinical Anxiety/Tension in Primary Medicine," Washington, DC, September 1977.

Inkeles, A. Social structure and the socialization of competence. *Harvard Educational Review,* 1966, *36,* 265–283.

Jahoda, M. *Current conceptions of positive mental health.* New York: Basic Books, 1958.

Janis, I. L. *Victims of groupthink.* Boston: Houghton Mifflin, 1972.

Janis, I. L., & Mann, L. *Decision making: A psychological analysis of conflict, choice, and commitment.* New York: Free Press, 1977.

Joe, V. C. Review of the internal-external control construct as a personality variable. *Psychological Reports,* 1971, *28,* 619–640.

Joint Commission of Mental Illness and Health. *Action for mental health.* New York: Science Editions, 1961.

Kahn, R. L., Wolfe, D. M., Quinn, R. P., & Snoek, J. D. *Organizational stress: Studies in role conflict and ambiguity.* New York: Wiley, 1964.

Kaplan, B., Cassel, J., & Gore, S. Social support and health. *Medical Care,* 1977, *15*(5), 47–58.

Katz, J. L., Weiner, H., Gallagher, T. G., & Hellman, L. Stress, distress and ego defenses. *Archives of General Psychiatry,* 1970, *23,* 131–142.

Klausner, S. Z. *On man and his environment.* San Francisco: Jossey-Bass, 1971.

Klinger, E. Consequences of commitment to and disengagement from incentives. *Psychological Review,* 1975, *82,* 1–25.

Kobler, A. L., & Stotland, E. *The end of hope: A social-clinical study of suicide.* New York: Free Press, 1964.

Kubler-Ross, E. *On death and dying.* New York: Macmillan, 1969.

Langer, E. J. The illusion of control. *Journal of Personality and Social Psychology,* 1975, *32,* 311–328.

Lawrence, P. R., & Lorsch, J. W. *Organization and environment.* Boston: Division of Research, Graduate School of Business Administration, Harvard University, 1967.

Lawton, M. P. Some beginnings of an ecological psychology of old age. In J. F. Wohlwill & D. H. Carson (Eds.), *Environment and the social sciences: Perspectives and applications.* Washington, DC: American Psychological Association, 1972.

Lazarus, R. S. *Psychological stress and the coping process.* New York: McGraw-Hill, 1966.

Lazarus, R. S. Emotions and adaptation: Conceptual and empirical relations. In W. J. Arnold (Ed.), *Nebraska Symposium on Motivation.* Lincoln: University of Nebraska Press, 1968.

Lazarus, R. S. The stress and coping paradigm. In C. Eisdorfer, D. Cohen, A. Kleinman, & P. Maxim (Eds.), *Theoretical bases for psychopathology.* New York: Spectrum, 1981.

Lazarus, R. S. *The costs and benefits of denial.* In S. Breznitz (Ed.), *Denial of stress.* New York: International Universities Press, in press.

Lazarus, R. S., Averill, J. R., & Opton, E. M., Jr. Toward a cognitive theory of emotion. In M. Arnold (Ed.), *Feelings and emotion.* New York: Academic Press, 1970.

Lazarus, R. S. & Cohen, J. B. *Theory and method in the study of stress and coping.* Paper presented at the 5th W.H.O. Conference on Society, Stress and Disease: Aging and Old Age, Stockholm, Sweden, June 1976.

Lazarus, R. S., & Cohen, J. B. Environmental stress. In I. Altman & J. F. Wohlwill (Eds.), *Human behavior and environment* (Vol. 1). New York: Plenum, 1977.

Lazarus, R. S., Cohen, J. B., Folkman, S., Kanner, A., & Schaefer, C. Psychological stress and adaptation: Some unresolved issues. In H. Selye (Ed.), *Selye's guide to stress research* (Vol. 1). New York: Van Nostrand Reinhold, 1980.

Lazarus, R. S., Kanner, A., & Folkman, S. Emotions: A cognitive–phenomenological analysis. In R. Plutchik & H. Kellerman (Eds.), *Theories of emotion.* New York: Academic Press, 1980.

Lazarus, R. S., & Launier, R. Stress-related transactions between person and environment. In L. A. Pervin & M. Lewis (Eds.), *Perspectives in interactional psychology*. New York: Plenum, 1978.

Lazarus, R. S., & McCleary, R. A. Autonomic discrimination without awareness: A study of subception. *Psychological Review*, 1951, *58*, 113-122.

Lefcourt, H. M. The function of the illusions of control and freedom. *American Psychologist*, 1973, *28*, 417-425.

Levy, D. M. *Maternal overprotection*. New York: Columbia University Press, 1943.

Lewin, K. A. *A dynamic theory of personality* (K. E. Zener & D. K. Adams, trans.). New York: McGraw-Hill, 1935.

Lewin, K. A. *Principles of topological psychology* (F. Heider & G. Heider, trans.). New York: McGraw-Hill, 1936.

Liberty, P. G., Burnstein, E., & Moulton, R. W. Concern with mastery and occupational attraction. *Journal of Personality*, 1966, *34*, 105-117.

Lindemann, E. Symptomatology and management of acute grief. *American Journal of Psychiatry*, 1944, *101*, 141-148.

Lucas, R. A. *Men in crisis*. New York: Basic Books, 1969.

Marceil, J. C. Implicit dimensions of idiography and nomothesis: A reformulation. *American Psychologist*, 1977, *32*, 1046-1055.

Maslach, C., & Pines, A. Burn-out: The loss of human caring. In A. Pines & C. Maslach (Eds.), *Experiencing social psychology*. New York: Random House, 1978.

Maslow, A. H. *Motivation and personality*. New York: Harper & Row, 1954.

Mechanic, D. *Students under stress*. New York: Free Press, 1962.

Merton, R. K. *Social structure*. Glencoe, IL: Free Press, 1957.

Moos, R. H. Assessment and impact of social climate. In P. McReynolds (Ed.), *Advances in psychological assessment* (Vol. 3). San Francisco: Jossey-Bass, 1975.

Murphy, L. B. Coping, vulnerability and resilience in childhood. In C. V. Coelho, D. A. Hamburg, & J. E. Adams (Eds.), *Coping and adaptation*. New York: Basic Books, 1974.

Murphy, L. B., & associates. *The widening world of childhood: Paths toward mastery*. New York: Basic Books, 1962.

Murphy, L. B., & Moriarty, A. E. *Vulnerability, coping, and growth*. New Haven: Yale University Press, 1976.

Murray, H. A. *Explorations in personality*. New York: Oxford University Press, 1938.

Neugarten, B. L., Wood, V., Kraines, R. J., & Loomis, B. Women's attitudes toward menopause. In B. L. Neugarten (Ed.), *Middle age and aging*. Chicago: University of Chicago Press, 1968.

Nuckolls, K. B., Cassel, J., & Kaplan, B. H. Psychosocial assets, life crisis and the prognosis of pregnancy. *American Journal of Epidemiology*, 1972, *95*, 431-441.

Pearlin, L. I., & Lieberman, M. A. Social sources of emotional distress. In R. Simmons (Ed.), *Research in community and mental health*. Greenwich, CT: JAI Press, 1977.

Pearlin, L. I., & Schooler, C. The structure of coping. *Journal of Health and Social Behavior*, 1978, *19*, 2-21.

Pervin, L. A. The need to predict and control under conditions of threat. *Journal of Personality*, 1963, *31*, 570-587.

Pervin, L. A. Performance and satisfaction as a function of individual-environment fit. *Psychological Bulletin*, 1968, *29*, 56-68.

Pervin, L. A., & Lewis, M. Overview of the internal-external issue. In L. A. Pervin & M. Lewis (Eds.), *Perspectives in interactional psychology*. New York: Plenum, 1978.

Phillips, L. *Human adaptation and its failures*. New York: Academic Press, 1968.

Pierce, C. The mundane extreme environment and its effect on learning. In S. G. Brainard (Ed.), *Learning disabilities: Issues and recommendations for research.* Washington, DC: National Institute of Education, U.S. Department of Health, Education and Welfare, July 1974.

Pines, A., & Maslach, C. Characteristics of staff burnout in mental health settings. *Hospital and Community Psychiatry,* 1978, *29,* 233–237.

Polanyi, M. *The tacit dimension.* Garden City, NY: Anchor, 1966.

Rodin, J., & Langer, E. J. Long-term effects of a control relevant intervention with the institutionalized aged. *Journal of Personality and Social Psychology,* 1977, *35,* 897–902.

Rotter, J. B. *Generalized expectancies for internal versus external control of reinforcement.* Washington, DC: American Psychological Association, 1966.

Scheidt, R. J., & Schaie, K. W. A taxonomy of situations for elderly population: Generating situational criteria. *Journal of Gerontology,* 1978, *33,* 848–857.

Seligman, M. E. *Helplessness.* San Francisco: Freeman, 1975.

Stack, C. *All our kin: Strategies for survival in a black community.* San Francisco: Harper & Row, 1974.

Stotland, E. *The psychology of hope.* San Francisco: Jossey-Bass, 1969.

Sullivan, H. S. *Conceptions of modern psychiatry.* New York: Norton, 1953.

Textor, R. B. *Cultural frontiers of the peace corps.* Cambridge, MA: Massachusetts Institute of Technology Press, 1966.

Tyler, F. B., & Gatz, M. Development of individual psychosocial competence in a high school setting. *Journal of Counseling and Clinical Psychology,* 1977, *45,* 441–449.

Weinstein, E. A. The development of interpersonal competence. In D. A. Goslin (Eds.), *Handbook of socialization theory and research.* Chicago: Rand-McNally, 1969.

Weiss, J. M. Effects of coping response on stress. *Journal of Comparative and Physiological Psychology,* 1968, *65,* 251–260.

White, R. Strategies of adaptation: An attempt at systematic description. In C. V. Coelho, D. A. Hamburg, & J. E. Adams (Eds.), *Coping and adaptation.* New York: Basic Books, 1974.

Zubin, J., & Spring, B. Vulnerability—A new view of schizophrenia. *Journal of Abnormal Psychology,* 1977, *86,* 103–126.

Zuckerman, M., Kalin, E., Price, L., & Zoob, I. Development of a sensation-seeking scale. *Journal of Consulting Psychology,* 1964, *28,* 477–482.

Zuckerman, M. *Sensation seeking: Beyond the optimal level of arousal.* Hillsdale, NJ: Erlbaum Associates, 1979.

4

THE DIMENSIONS
OF SOCIAL COMPETENCE:
CONTRIBUTIONS FROM
A VARIETY OF
RESEARCH AREAS

BARBARA R. SARASON

BARBARA R. SARASON is Senior Research Associate at the University of Washington. One of her primary interests is the use of cognitive techniques taught through modeling as a vehicle for behavior change. She has published on the roles of cognitions and moderator variables in stress and on modeling as a practical classroom technique for teachers and is involved currently in several projects that are directed toward increasing social competence and stress coping skills in high school students and military recruits. She is coauthor of two textbooks: *Psychology: The Frontiers of Behavior* (with R. E. Smith and I. G. Sarason) and *Abnormal Psychology*, third edition (with I. G. Sarason).

Sarason brings to bear on the social competence area a wide range of cognitive and behavioral change research. Her selection reflects her long-term interest in cognitive techniques as vehicles for behavioral change. Her applied focus distinguishes this chapter from Chapters 2 and 3 in that she uses findings to develop a systematic approach for examining specific techniques and interventions for the enhancement of social competence.

"Social competence" means possession of and ability to use appropriate social skills. Psychologists usually view these skills as acquired by some combination of the developmental process and learning. Personality factors and the role of motivation also must be considered.

At any given developmental level, social incompetence may be viewed as caused by attentional, informational, and motivational defects.

From a learning theory viewpoint, ineffective behavior occurs because an individual has never had an opportunity to learn effective responses appropriate for a particular type of situation. This view suggests that someone who behaves effectively has developed his or her competencies through trial and error in an operant situation, through receiving instruction and social reinforcement for correct responses, or by observing effective problem solving that results in reinforcement for someone else.

Traditional behavior modification has been based on the idea that programmed reinforcement of desired behaviors will produce an increased frequency of the desired behavior. If the individual does not possess the desired response in his or her repertoire, then a shaping program may be instituted. From this viewpoint, the situation has a strong positive pulling force that will elicit the appropriate response if it is available. Once these appropriate responses have been learned, and adequate reinforcement is available, effective behavior should occur. One obvious problem with such a formulation is the complexity of social behavior and the difficulty an individual may have in developing a set of useful rules about what is appropriate and when. Perhaps it is because of this complexity of social behavior that many attempts to teach social skills have failed to produce behavior that generalizes enduringly to other situations or even transfers from the laboratory to other behavior settings in the individual's life (Mc-Combs, Filipczak, Friedman, & Wodarsi, 1978). There is, however, evidence that modeling could be an effective long-term agent in changing the behavior of delinquents and criminals (Bornstein, Winegardner, Rychtarik, Paul, Naifeh, Sweeney, & Justman, 1979; Goldstein, Sherman, Gershaw, Sprafkin, & Glick, 1978; Sarason, 1968, 1978; Sarason & Ganzer, 1973). The cognitive elements of social skills are of special interest because of recent positive evidence concerning cognitive training offered by several researchers (Snyder & White, 1979; Spence & Marzillier, 1979; Williams & Akamatsu, 1978).

Among the topics that must be considered in building a social competence program are problem solving, empathy, impulsive behavior, and building social skills. Work on methods by which to utilize research findings on this topic must also be considered—in particular, methods focused primarily on behavior such as traditional modeling and cognitive approaches that emphasize self-instruction through self-talk. To cover each of these areas exhaustively is not the intention of this chapter. Rather, a few examples of each approach will be cited in an attempt to show how knowledge gained from widely separated areas can contribute to programs constructed for use in applied settings.

RESEARCH AREAS PERTINENT TO SOCIAL SKILLS TRAINING

Problem-Solving Behavior

In a widely cited article, D'Zurilla and Goldfried (1971) defined problem solving as a "behavioral process, whether overt or cognitive in nature, which (a) makes available a variety of potentially effective response alternatives for dealing with a problematic situation and, (b) increases the probability of selecting the most effective response among these various alternatives" (p. 108). Thus, both a facility in generating alternatives and the ability to evaluate and select the most effective ones are necessary for efficient problem-solving behavior.

Traditionally, most problem-solving research has been targeted toward intellectual tasks such as water jar problems, arithmetic tasks, and puzzles (Simon & Newell, 1971). One characteristic that seems to differentiate successful and unsuccessful problem solvers is skill at stating the problem in nonambiguous behavioral terms (Bloom & Broder, 1950; Crutchfield, 1969; Skinner, 1953). This step is a necessary preliminary to the next step in problem solving, the generation of alternatives. Much of the work on alternative generation derives from Osborn's method of brainstorming (1963). Both Osborn and later Parnes and others (Meadow & Parnes, 1959; Parnes, 1967) concluded that the quantity of responses was positively related to their quality. Learning to produce a large number of alternatives then becomes a desirable skill.

Once the alternatives are listed, identification of the best, most effective of them becomes necessary. Individuals are not always able to identify this best idea (Johnson, Parrott, & Stratton, 1968). One way decision makers may improve their choice among alternatives is through a consideration of the consequences of the choice or decision. In their review of the decision-making process, Janis and Mann (1977) suggest a number of criteria for evaluating the quality of decision making. Several of these criteria relate to the generation of as wide a range of alternatives as possible, a careful weighing of costs and risks, and a search for new information relevant to these risks.

Research on decision making and managerial skills in business or other large institutional settings has helped move the focus of problem-solving behavior from intellectual tasks toward interpersonal problem solving. Until very recently, the problem solving approach as it relates to interpersonal relations in everyday life, but not in institutional settings, has had scant attention. Adherents of cognitively oriented psychotherapy have emphasized, however, the need for the individual to consider alternatives and consequences (Kelly, 1955; Rotter, 1954). One early study did attempt to assess the effect of discussing alternative behaviors and consequences using Thematic Apperception Test (TAT) stories as a starting point and produced results suggestive of the utility of this approach (Morton, 1955). Morton asked each client to discuss what problems were faced by the main character in each TAT story and what alternative responses might have been chosen other than the one selected. Compared to a control group, the clients using this approach responded to attitude scales with answers showing increased confidence in various types of social relations.

ALTERNATIVE CREATION AND ADJUSTMENT

The research of Spivack and his coworkers has emphasized the importance of the generation of alternatives as a problem-solving skill. One finding of interest to those attempting to construct programs for improving social skills is that competent individuals produce more relevant alternatives than do less competent subjects when they are asked to generate solutions to interpersonal problems (Platt & Spivack, 1972; Shure & Spivack, 1972; Shure, Chapter 6, this volume). The inability to generate options or alternatives is found in poorly adjusted children from preschool through adolescence (Platt, Spivack, Altman, Allman, & Peizer, 1974; Shure & Spivack, 1970a, 1970b). This research supports the teaching of thinking about alternatives as a useful avenue in improving problem solving in social behavior. Spivack's group has developed a program for training young children to generate alternative solutions in simple peer conflict situations. These solutions are accepted uncritically by the group leader. The children are then encouraged to consider the likely consequences for each of the alternatives (Spivack & Shure, 1974).

There is much evidence that maladjusted adolescents show poor problem-solving ability in various kinds of social situations (Freedman, Rosenthal, Donahoe, Schlundt, & McFall, 1978; Platt, Scura, & Hannon, 1973; Platt et al., 1974). Low correlations between general intelligence and certain cognitive problem-solving skills have been reported (Spivack, Platt, & Shure, 1976). This suggests that differential learning experiences, not merely intellectual level, may be the pertinent variable in problem-solving performance.

PROBLEM SOLVING AND DEVELOPMENT

A videotaped program and a game approach were used by Stone, Hinds, and Schmidt (1975) to train elementary school students in problem-solving skills. Although the program produced changes in problem-solving behavior, the three school class levels involved were affected differently. This result suggests the strength of the developmental process in its interaction with a learning situation. In another research effort, a combination of videotaped programs and practice in problem-solving skills produced a change in the number of alternatives generated by sixth-grade students but did not change other aspects of their problem-solving behavior (Poitras-Martin & Stone, 1977).

Empathy and Perspective Taking

Another factor involved in social skills has emerged from work on empathy and perspective taking. Piaget refers to young children's egocentrism and their inability to perceive a situation from another person's point of view (Piaget, 1926). He believed that decentration, or the ability to view a situation from another's perspective, was part of a developmental process. However, even though basically developmental, this process is not an automatic one; experience with peers seems to be an essential ingredient. Decentration must take place, according to Piaget, before mature thought can occur. The importance of this ability to adopt an alternate perspective was also emphasized by Mead (1934). He used the term "empathy" to describe the increased social sensitivity that allows an individual to look at a situation from the viewpoint of the other person as well as his or her own view.

ROLE TAKING

Piaget's original conception of role-taking ability has been investigated and elaborated by a number of researchers, including Flavell (1963, 1974; Flavell, Botkin, Fry, Wright, & Jarvis, 1968) and Chandler (1970, 1973). The emphasis in most of this research has been on the cognitive aspects of role taking. Picture sequences devised by Flavell et al. (1968) and cartoon series devised by Chandler (1973) were both directed at this aspect of role-taking behavior. A number of investigators (Chandler, 1973; Feffer, 1970; Neale, 1966) have observed marked developmental delays in role taking in institutionalized emotionally disturbed children. Further, programs designed to facilitate acquisition of decentering skills have improved the performance of these children (Chandler, Greenspan, & Barenboim, 1974). This improvement was associated with improved social adjustment 12 months later.

A number of writers have differentiated the affective from the cognitive aspects of role taking. Cognitive role taking was defined by Rotenberg (1974, p. 180) as "the intuitive ability to put oneself in another's shoes and predict his [or her] responses" without being involved with the other's feelings. Affective role taking, defined as "a behavioral disposition to relive the distress of others" (Rotenberg, 1974, p. 180) was found to differentiate juvenile delinquents from other adolescents. The nondelinquents, while no different in cognitive role taking, were significantly superior to delinquents in affective role taking. Writers as different in their theoretical perspectives as McDougall (1908), Fenichel (1945), and Sullivan (1953) have all discussed empathy, defined as a form of emotional communication.

Feshbach (1975) has argued for more clearly defined terminology in the discussion of empathy. She considers both affective and cognitive elements to be present in an empathetic response, but argues that these parameters must be carefully specified in order to make discussions of research findings meaningful.

PERSON PERCEPTION

Aspects of the person-perception literature are also relevant to understanding and strengthening adaptive social behavior. Piaget believed that the decrease of egocentric thought as the child grew older was related, not to cues actually perceived, but to an increased awareness of the cultural meanings usually associated with them. Much experimental work on social awareness is concerned simply with the relationship between age and the awareness of socially relevant changes in voice, posture, and expression in others. An interpretation of a developmental factor in person perception is handicapped by the fact that the child's verbal ability, as well as other characteristics, also increases with age. It is difficult to separate the effects of the various simultaneous developmental processes that take place in people. There are a few studies that have used nonverbal measures (Borke, 1979, 1973; Gilbert, 1969) that have reported age-related changes. In addition, a number of studies using verbalizations as measures have reported an age-related increase in the number of references to internal psychological states in others (Gilbert, 1969; Livesley & Bromley, 1973; Peevers & Secord, 1973). This may be interpreted as a greater awareness of the reactions of others to one's behavior.

Impulsive Behavior

Impulsive behavior is a feature of many behavior problems that arise during childhood. Two main lines of investigation within the area of impulsive behavior have been (1) the acquisition of cognitive styles, and (2) the variable ability of young children to delay gratification.

COGNITIVE STYLE

Impulsivity has been conceptualized by Kagan (1966) as one extreme on the impulsivity–reflectivity continuum. The Matching Familiar Figures (MFF) Test (Kagan, Rosman, Day, Albert, & Phillips, 1964) has been the commonly used assessment instrument to measure impulsivity defined in this way. Impulsivity is often considered to be a personality characteristic (Buss & Plomin, 1975; Murray, 1938). However, there is little evidence for its stability throughout development (Buss & Plomin, 1975) and considerable evidence for its modifiability (Kendall & Finch, 1979). Methods to decrease impulsive behavior have included required delay of response, the teaching of strategies such as searching and scanning, response-cost contingencies, and self-instructional training. Perhaps one of the most interesting and influential methods is the utilization of self-instruction through a think-aloud program of self-talk that includes definition of the problem, focusing of attention, self-reinforcement, and self-evaluation (Meichenbaum & Goodman, 1971; see also Meichenbaum, Butler, & Gruson, Chapter 2, this volume). Using this method with emotionally disturbed children averaging 10 years in age, Kendall and Finch (1978) found that although self-report measures did not change, both performance and latency of the MFF increased and, even more significantly, teacher ratings of impulsive behavior indicated positive treatment effects.

DELAY OF GRATIFICATION

Another approach to impulsive behavior has emphasized delay of gratification. Mischel and his coworkers have carried out an extensive program of investigation of the relevant variables that enable young children to postpone an immediate gratification for a later and larger reward (Mischel, 1974; Mischel & Mischel, 1976). This research has shown the usefulness of cognitions in extending the delay period and also has emphasized the many relevant situational factors that combine to determine what type of cognitions are most effective. In one of the few studies with older subjects, Fry (1972) used modeling to increase self-imposed delay of gratification in high school dropouts and high school graduates in an actual job choice situation.

Kanfer and his associates have focused on resistance to temptation and devised self-instructional strategies for use by young children (Hartig & Kanfer, 1973; Kanfer & Zich, 1974). Their programs, which focused on consequences, positive or negative, proved effective in enabling children to wait longer before giving in to an experimenter-produced temptation.

Mischel and Patterson (1976) investigated cognitive plans as an aid to resisting distraction. Their findings indicate that such plans may be effective but that both the content and the structure of the plans are important in their success.

Social Skills Training

An increasingly influential viewpoint on inappropriate or ineffective behavior is simply that the individual has, for some reason, never learned the adaptive or appropriate responses necessary. Unpopular children have been shown to be deficient in a variety of social skills, such as communicating emotions and needs accurately, or responding to peers with appropriate affection or help (Gottman, Gonso, & Rasmussen, 1975).

A low level of social skills in a child may generate future social failure. Children deficient in the basic skills may have difficulty in learning the complex skills needed in adulthood and may have an increased vulnerability for maladaptive behavior (Bornstein, Bellack, & Hersen, 1977).

Social skills training has been approached in two general ways. Some researchers have concentrated on a situational approach, the appropriate sequence of actions needed to solve a particular kind of problem situation. Others have attempted to study the elements of a variety of situations in order to specify the discrete behavior elements that make up overall behavior rated as socially skilled and adaptive.

THE SITUATIONAL APPROACH

The situational approach is characterized by research based on modeling. Many studies have shown modeling to be effective in improving the personal interaction skills of preschool children (Hart,

Reynolds, Baer, Brawley, & Harris, 1968; Keller & Carlson, 1974). Evidence concerning older children and adolescents is somewhat more limited. The most effective programs deal with both peer and adult relations. Some programs are geared to special populations. For example, Sarason (1968, 1978; Sarason & Ganzer, 1973) has worked with juvenile delinquents using a program that dealt mainly with behavioral skills related to a specific task (e.g., how to apply for a job, how to resist peer pressure). Other research has shown that teaching the component skills involved in interviewing for a job improves actual job interview performance of employable psychiatric patients (Furman, Geller, Simon, & Kelly, 1979).

THE BEHAVIOR ELEMENTS APPROACH

Argyle (see Chapter 9, this volume) has been a leader in the study of the elements of social interactions. His work has produced several ideas of value to those who wish to help others improve their social skills. He is particularly concerned with the rules that govern behavior in interpersonal situations. Many of these rules vary from culture to culture. In order to function adequately in a new cultural setting, whether it represents that of a different nation or simply a social subgroup, an individual must attend to a variety of subtle behaviors, from facial expressions, to clothing choices, to the observance of complex rules of personal distance (Argyle, 1972, 1981). This knowledge of rules is essential to the mobile person in job, social class, or nationality change. The appropriate sequence of behaviors in specific types of personal interactions has also been studied by Argyle.

Argyle and his coworkers have been able to make use of their behavior-elements approach in interpreting various types of social behavior. For example, they found that neurotic individuals often had problems that related to very specific behavior sequences. Trower and others (Trower, Yardley, Bryant, & Shaw, 1978) have found that social skills training is as effective a method of helping phobic patients as is desensitization. Argyle (1972) has also used the approach in designing intervention strategies (e.g., helping personnel managers to become more effective through modeling, video feedback, and verbal comments on their performance).

Another approach to social skills training that also breaks down behaviors into small components is the applied behavior analysis approach. This method has been used in a variety of situations. Hersen and Bellack (1976) demonstrated in two studies using single-subject designs that it was possible to use this procedure to increase overall assertive behavior and also specific behaviors related to assertiveness in hospitalized chronic schizophrenics. Minkin and others (Minkin, Braukmann, Minkin, Timbers, Timbers, Fixsen, Phillips, & Wolf, 1976) demonstrated that conversational skills could be broken down into specific components and that using the components in an instruction program produced improvement in the conversational skills of several adolescent girls.

Assertiveness as a Social Skill

When the social skills of a well-adjusted person are described, appropriate assertiveness is often part of the picture. Appropriate assertiveness is an area of social skills in which children are often judged to be deficient. Many writers have stressed the need to train children to stand up for their rights and to express anger and positive feelings in a manner both acceptable to others and effective in changing their behavior.

Complicating the study of assertiveness is the fact that, however desirable in adult life or children's social interaction, it does not seem valued in all phases of a child's life. For example, within the classroom, where children spend a good proportion of their time, teachers attach less value to interpersonal assertive skills than to characteristics such as obedience and responsibility (Cartledge & Milburn, 1978). Further, this type of conformity—attending, remaining on the task, and complying with teacher requests—has been shown to be positively related to success in learning (Cobb, 1970).

Some studies with young children (Charlesworth & Hartup, 1967; Hartup, Glazer, & Charlesworth, 1967) have found low assertiveness or submissiveness to be a positive reinforcement between peers. On the other hand, submissiveness has been shown in some research to function as a reinforcement to aggression (Patterson, Littmar, & Bricker, 1967). Children encounter many situations in which assertive behavior may be facilitating. Bornstein and his associates (Bornstein et al., 1977) showed that the use of behavioral rehearsal, a common procedure in adult assertiveness training, can also be used effectively with children. Assertive behavior in adults consists of both commendatory and oppositional skills. It appears that these two aspects of assertiveness must be trained separately because skill gained in one does not appear to generalize to the other (Kelly, Frederiksen, Fitts, & Phillips, 1978). Difficulties in obtaining generalization of assertive behavior even within the same aspect has been found for psychiatric patients (Hersen, Eisler, & Miller, 1974).

Training Methods

MODELING

Since Bandura's early work on social learning (Bandura, 1969, 1971; Bandura & Walters, 1963) demonstrated that modeling was an effective technique to promote learning, the technique has been used in a wide variety of situations, and some of the important parameters have been fairly well specified.

Modeling has been used both to (1) increase or introduce desirable behavior and (2) decrease the frequency of maladaptive behavior. It has been shown to be an effective vehicle for modifying a variety of behaviors, including impulsiveness, food preferences, and goal setting. Problem-solving strategies can be learned by observing models. Rule induction, such as the learning of grammatical rules, can also occur from observing models' behavior.

While modeling is often used to increase response rates, it can also be used successfully in reducing the occurrence of certain behaviors. For example, it is well known that treatment of fearful behavior or phobic responses through modeling is effective. This can be shown with such object-focused fears as those of snakes or dogs (Bandura, Blanchard, & Ritter, 1969; Bandura & Menlove, 1968) or in the rather diffuse fears engendered by test-taking situations (Mann & Rosenthal, 1969; Sarason, 1978). Withdrawn behavior can be decreased in young children by modeling the use of social reinforcers (smiles, laughing, and imitation) that attract reinforcements from others (Keller & Carlson, 1974). Aggressive behavior in young children can also be decreased by modeling cooperative solutions to peer conflict situations (Liebert, Neale, & Davidson, 1973).

Considerable effort has been devoted to determining the effective elements within the modeling situation. Although the characteristics of the model, such as status, attractiveness, and similarity to the observer, have been shown to be important in some research, a recent review (Zimmerman, 1977) suggests that these differences are both small and inconsistent. Observer characteristics have been studied relatively infrequently. Findings relating to sex, personality, and demographic characteristics of the observer are also inconsistent. Perhaps the most consistently found observer characteristic is age. Modeling more effectively influences the behavior of older children than younger ones, particularly if the modeled task is complex (Zimmerman, 1977).

The verbal accompaniment to the modeling presentation also seems to be an important variable. Certain kinds of verbal accompaniment are effective in improving observer learning. These verbalizations or scripts may be presented by the model, the observer, or the experimenter. All can be effective. The important factor appears to be the form of the verbalization. A description of the rule covered by the modeled behavior or other coded presentation of the material is much more effective in promoting retention and transfer than a detailed description of the modeled scene (Gerst, 1971; Rosenthal, Alford, & Rasp, 1972; Zimmerman & Rosenthal, 1972).

Modeling can be an effective tool in applied settings. The Sarason studies previously referred to are one example (Sarason, 1968, 1978; Sarason & Ganzer, 1973). Another modeling program was used with potential high school dropouts by Harris (1973). She used occupational models, all under 30, and minority group members. They appeared either in live discussion sessions or videotape. Compared to the control group, the experimental subjects showed higher vocational aspirations, more internal locus of control, less intention to drop out of school, and improved teacher ratings on follow-up 3 months later.

SELF-INSTRUCTION THROUGH PRIVATE SPEECH

Piaget (1926) was one of the first researchers to comment about the characteristic speech of the young child, much of which was neither designed for nor adapted to the listener. Piaget observed this private speech to reach its maximum at about age 5 or 6 and to decline thereafter as the child, becoming less egocentric, shifted to social as opposed to private speech. Russian researchers interested in the function of language, such as Vygotsky and Luria, also investigated private speech. Luria (1961) thought speech development moved from overt to covert expression as the child progressed in its ability to guide its own actions and to plan them rather than act only on the directions of others. Vygotsky (1962) emphasized the control aspect of this speech, which he thought functioned as a form of self-guidance in problem-solving situations.

One reasonable hypothesis is that the child uses private speech because it is initially facilitative in developing new behaviors and then drops it (or internalizes it) as the behavior becomes well learned (Gal'perin, 1969). However, observation indicates that many well-functioning adults also use private speech. It seems to function as a kind of control and directing mechanism when they are alone or engaged in a new or difficult task (e.g., saying to oneself, "I better not lose my temper").

Meichenbaum (1974) has likened private speech to a "cognitive prosthesis" used in overcoming inadequate performance. He believes the procedure facilitates behavior in several ways: in organizing the material, in generating alternative solutions, and in helping evaluation feedback. It also promotes positive task orientation and aids in maintaining task-relevant behaviors. In addition, it may provide self-reinforcement or offer a method of coping with failure (Meichenbaum & Asarnow, 1979).

The series of studies emanating from Meichenbaum's laboratories have greatly increased the awareness of self-talk as an important behavior control mechanism. In an early study, Meichenbaum and Goodman (1971) demonstrated that the use of verbal self-instruction improved the performance of impulsive children on a variety of tasks. Meichenbaum (1975) called attention to the uses of self-instruction in dealing with stressful situations. Camp and her coworkers (Camp, Zimet, Van Doorninck, & Dahlem, 1977) found that aggressive boys of kindergarten through second-grade level showed a deficit in mediational use of verbal ability rather than a deficiency in test-measured verbal skills.

Many applications of the self-instruction model have been made with children. For example, hyperactive children trained in modeling, self-verbalization, and self-reinforcement techniques showed significant improvement over controls at follow-up (Douglas, Parry, Marton, & Gasson, 1976). This procedure is superior to reinforcement techniques that may actually serve as distractors for hyperactive children (Parry, 1973).

Much of the work utilizing self-instruction as a tool for improved performance has been done with children. However, a variety of studies are now applying it to adult programs. Sarason (1973) showed that utilization of self-instructions could improve test performance of highly anxious college students. Glass and her coworkers (Glass, Gottman, & Shmurak, 1976) improved the dating skills behavior of college men through a cognitive self-statement modification program. Institutionalized adolescents were able to reduce impulsive behaviors (such as aggression, property destruction, and improved school attendance) through following a self-instructional program that highlighted private speech (Snyder & White, 1979).

RECENT PROGRAMS

A number of applied research programs have attempted to utilize some of these past research efforts in skill training programs. Most of these have focused on children under age 12. One of the most successful has been that of the Hahnemann group (Shure & Spivack, 1979, pp. 201–219; Spivack, Platt, & Shure, 1976). Working with groups ranging from preschool through the early elementary years, they have implemented a problem-solving skills approach with considerable success. Larcen and the Connecticut group (McClure, Chinsky, & Larcen, 1978) have used problem solving with third- and fourth-graders. While their approach is promising, these researchers point out that "ability to solve hypothetical problems does not necessarily transfer to real-life problem-solving skills" (p. 512). Project AWARE, based on cognitive role-taking and problem-solving skills, has demonstrated improved adjustment in fourth- and fifth-grade children (Elardo & Cooper, 1977). Early encouraging reports are available on a program based at the University of Rochester (Gersten, de Apodaca, Rains, Weissberg, & Cowen, 1979) that utilizes overt and covert self-verbalization and the Spivack and Shure problem-solving approach in third-grade classrooms. In one of the few studies with adolescents, a cognitive self-instruction program has been used with institutionalized adolescents (Snyder & White, 1979). It produced a decrease in impulsive behavior and improvement in performance of daily living requirements at a 6-week follow-up.

Although some results have been encouraging, more work on applied programs stressing cognitive skills involved in social skill acquisition is clearly indicated. The programs that stress problem-solving thinking in younger children have in many cases found the generalization of the trained skills to be weak. Very little such work has been done with adolescents, particularly noninstitutionalized adolescents.

A PROGRAM FOR ADOLESCENTS ILLUSTRATING THE INTEGRATION OF LABORATORY- AND FIELD-BASED RESEARCH

One attempt to remedy this lack of data, an ongoing project by the author and I. G. Sarason, was designed to build on the research in problem solving, empathy, inhibition of impulsivity, and acquisition of social skills, but added a cognitive control element. The study emphasizes the cognitive processing involved in modeling in order to facilitate generalization of the modeled behaviors to new situations.

Taking the focus from earlier work with institutionalized delinquents (Sarason, 1968, 1978; Sarason & Ganzer, 1973), the project, designed to increase social competence in low-achieving high school students, has been in progress for some time. The aim of the study is to determine whether methods effective with an institutionalized population can be extended to the community and used as a preventive measure. During pilot work, extensive interviewing of students, teachers, and student employers revealed a consistent picture of lack of social competence. For example, students said they often avoided contacts with nonpeers because they felt unsure of how to behave. The students also showed little concern about the consequences of their present behavior choices for the future. Employers and teachers focused on students' low frustration tolerance and lack of problem-solving skills. Students appeared to these groups to have a lack of awareness both of their effect on others and of others' points of view.

Based on these data, role-play scripts were written that emphasized

1. the consequences of an action
2. the alternatives available in a situation
3. the effects of the individual's behavior on others and the importance of understanding of others' points of view
4. communication skills

The role-play scripts covered some of the same material as those in the delinquency study. They also added scenes relevant to high school life. The role plays differed most from the earlier work in that not only behavior *but also cognitions* were modeled. The role plays were presented live to some groups and videotaped to others.

A number of long- and short-term measures are being used in this study. On a long-term basis, students will be followed throughout their remaining high school years in regard to grades, attendance records, disciplinary records, and whether they complete the requirements for graduation. Short-term indices include a measure of means–ends thinking adapted from the Means–Ends Problem-Solving (MEPS) procedure (Platt & Spivack, 1975), a measure of the ability to produce alternatives in a problem situation, and voluntary performance in an authentic job interview situation.

Only short-term data from the first experimental phase comparing live models, video models, and a control group are reported here. The three MEPS-type stories showed highly significant differences in the total number of means produced ($p < .008$) and in the number of responses involving introspection, problem solving, and understanding the other person's point of view ($p < .001$ for each of these measures).

The problem situations produced highly significant differences not only in number of alternatives ($p < .002$), but in their overall quality ($p < .015$) and in the quality of the best alternative ($p < .002$).

The interview measure was constructed as an actual job interview opportunity to be perceived by the student as unconnected with the experimental program. A significantly higher proportion of students who had been in the experimental groups signed up for the interviews as compared to the controls ($p < .001$). The interview results show significant differences among the groups for rating of overall performance made by the interviewer ($p < .03$) and by raters viewing a videotape of the interview ($p < .001$) and for amount of eye contact, one of the behaviors specifically taught in the modeling scripts ($p < .0001$). The interviewee's statement of personal qualifications was also superior for the modeling groups ($p < .001$).

The results from this program are encouraging. Measures obtained so far indicate that social and cognitive skills can be taught to low-achieving high school students through a role-play format, can be learned in a short time period, and can be applied to other problems.

THE CONTRIBUTION OF LABORATORY RESEARCH TO SOCIAL COMPETENCE TRAINING

One of the greatest challenges to the researcher in applied settings is the effective integration of findings from laboratory work into a research plan for the applied work. Often the global nature of applied interventions seems to have little in common with the precise focus of much laboratory research. The many variables that are beyond the control of even the most careful worker in applied settings also serve to widen the apparent gap between the two types of research. Probably, however, the most effective deterrent to a wider utilization of laboratory findings in the field is the lack of communication between these two groups of researchers.

Many topics of research that may not seem immediately relevant either in their subject matter or in their focus, may, on closer examination, be of value to someone constructing an intervention program.

Many recent and current social competency programs have reported difficulties in two areas, generalization of results and maintenance of gains in the posttreatment period. These problems, of course not confined to this area of work, suggest that perhaps at this stage in our knowledge the most appropriate intervention is the one that is most multifaceted. Once training has reached the requisite level of effectiveness, then an effort may be made to identify the relevant change factors.

In this chapter an attempt has been made to identify some of the variables that may combine to yield increased social competence behavior and to highlight the insights available from that research.

Problem-solving behavior has rarely been dealt with except in solution of thought problems of an academic nature or the dynamic process of problem solving in a group setting. However, the research data do reveal several points of interest for social competence research. First, there are several important steps in the problem-solving process: stating the problem, generating alternative solutions, and selecting the best alternative through consideration of the consequences of each. Broken down in this way, the process has become much more accessible to training efforts. Further, there is a fair amount of data suggesting that teaching these component processes improves performance. Work on problem solving further suggests that these skills are correlated not so much with intelligence as with adjustment, another insight important to the social competence researcher.

Another field of investigation that is relevant is work on the topic of empathy. Although the decentering process seems to have a developmental component, results show that decentering behavior can be improved by practice. Another important contribution in this area is the differentiation of affective and cognitive aspects of empathy and the suggestion that they may have different sources. Impulsivity has been characterized as a response style, but laboratory work suggests that it is modifiable. Impulsivity can be reflected not only in quick responses often based on inadequate information, but also by the inability to delay gratification. Extensive work in this area has shown that cognitive factors can be utilized to increase the delay tolerated, but that the particular cognitive factors that are effective depend on the precise situational factors present.

Social skills training has demonstrated that by analyzing why some people are more socially effective than others many specific elements of style can be identified and that these factors may be relevant only to certain settings and certainly vary in different settings. Again, by breaking down the social interchange into elements, much more effective interventions are possible.

The work on assertiveness has indicated a discrepancy between descriptions of effectively assertive behavior and adaptive classroom behavior. In addition to these subject matter categories, a great deal of current research activity has addressed itself to techniques useful in modifying behavior either in the laboratory or in a clinical setting. Work in modeling involving modeling of cognitive behavior and in the use of self-instruction through private speech has emphasized the effectiveness of cognitive control mechanisms in behavior change.

These cognitive techniques hold promise of greatly increasing the effectiveness of social competence training by aiding both in its generalization to other tasks and in its long-term effectiveness. However exciting their contribution, a much more solid basis for their possible efficacy can be achieved by first, a careful analysis of the situation in which the skills are to be used, an analysis that includes information from as many viewpoints as possible, and, second, a careful scrutiny of this information for relationships to specific and perhaps highly specialized areas of laboratory research, which can give leads to unravel some of the complexities present in any research project in an area as multifaceted as that of social competence.

ACKNOWLEDGMENTS

Preparation of this chapter and the research project described were under grant support from the National Institute of Mental Health (Grant No. R01-MH24823).

REFERENCES

Argyle, M. *Social interaction.* London: Methuen, 1972.

Argyle, M. The experimental study of the basic features of situations. In D. Magnusson (Ed.), *Toward a psychology of situations: An interactional perspective.* Hillsdale, NJ: Erlbaum, 1981.

Bandura, A. *Principles of behavior modification.* New York: Holt, Rinehart, & Winston, 1969.

Bandura, A. *Social learning theory.* New York: General Learning Press, 1971.

Bandura, A., Blanchard, E. B., & Ritter, B. The relative efficacy of desensitization and modeling approaches for inducing behavioral, affective, and attitudinal changes. *Journal of Personality and Social Psychology,* 1969, *13,* 173–199.

Bandura, A., & Menlove, F. L. Factors determining vicarious extinction of avoidance behavior through symbolic modeling. *Journal of Personality and Social Psychology,* 1968, *8,* 99–108.

Bandura, A., & Walters, R. H. *Social learning and personality development.* New York: Holt, Rinehart, & Winston, 1963.

Bloom, B. S., & Broder, L. J. *Problem solving processes of college students.* Chicago: University of Chicago Press, 1950.

Borke, H. Interpersonal perception of young children: Egocentrism or empathy. *Developmental Psychology,* 1971, *5,* 263–269.

Borke, H. The development of empathy in Chinese and American children between 3 and 6 years of age: A cross-cultural study. *Developmental Psychology,* 1973, *9,* 102–108.

Bornstein, M. R., Bellack, A.˙S., & Hersen, M. Social skills training for unassertive children: A multiple baseline analysis. *Journal of Applied Behavior Analysis,* 1977, *10,* 183–195.

Bornstein, P. H., Winegardner, J., Rychtarik, R. G., Paul, W. P., Naifeh, S. J., Sweeney, T. M., & Justman, A. Interpersonal skills training: Evaluation of a program with adult male offenders. *Criminal Justice and Behavior,* 1979, *6,* 119–132.

Buss, A. H., & Plomin, R. *A temperament theory of personality development.* New York: Wiley, 1975.

Camp, B., Zimet, S., Van Doorninck, W., & Dahlem, N. Verbal abilities in young aggressive boys. *Journal of Educational Psychology,* 1977, *69,* 129–135.

Cartledge, G., & Milburn, J. F. The case for teaching social skills in the classroom: A review. *Review of Educational Research,* 1978, *1,* 133–156.

Chandler, M. J. Egocentrism in normal and pathological child development. In F. Monks, W. Hartup, & J. DeWitt (Eds.), *Determinants of behavioral development.* New York: Academic Press, 1970.

Chandler, M. J. Egocentrism and antisocial behavior: The assessment and training of social perspective taking skills. *Developmental Psychology,* 1973, *93,* 326–332.

Chandler, M. J., Greenspan, S., & Barenboim, C. Assessment and training of role taking and referential communication skills in institutionalized emotionally disturbed children. *Developmental Psychology,* 1974, *10,* 546–553.

Charlesworth, R., & Hartup, W. Positive social reinforcement in the nursery school peer group. *Child Development,* 1967, *38,* 993–1002.

Cobb, J. A. *Survival skills and first grade academic achievement* (Report No. 1, University of Oregon, Contract No. NPECE-70-005, OEC 0-70-4512, 607). Eugene, OR: Oregon Research Institute, December 1970.

Crutchfield, R. S. Nurturing the cognitive skills of productive thinking. In L. J. Rubin (Ed.), *Life skills in school and society.* Washington, DC: Association for Supervision and Curriculum Development, 1969.

Douglas, V. I., Parry, P., Marton, P., & Gasson, C. Assessment of a cognitive training program for hyperactive children. *Journal of Abnormal Child Psychology,* 1976, *4,* 389–410.

D'Zurilla, T., & Goldfried, M. Problem solving and behavior modification. *Journal of Abnormal Psychology,* 1971, *78,* 107–126.

Elardo, P. T., & Cooper, M. *Project AWARE: A handbook for teachers.* Menlo Park, CA: Addison-Wesley, 1977.

Feffer, M. H. A developmental analysis of interpersonal behavior. *Psychological Review,* 1970, *77,* 197–214.

Fenichel, J. *The psychoanalytic theory of neurosis.* New York: Norton, 1945.

Feshbach, N. D. Empathy in children: Some theoretical and empirical considerations. *Counseling Psychologist,* 1975, *5,* 25–30.

Flavell, J. H. *The developmental psychology of Jean Piaget.* Princeton, NJ: Van Nostrand, 1963.

Flavell, J. H. The development of inferences about others. In T. Mischel (Ed.), *Under-*

standing other persons. Oxford, England: Blackwell, 1974.

Flavell, J. H., Botkin, P. T., Fry, C. L., Jr., Wright, J. W., & Jarvis, P. E. *The development of role taking and communication skills in children.* New York: Wiley, 1968.

Freedman, B. J., Rosenthal, L., Donahoe, C. P., Jr., Schlundt, D. G., & McFall, R. M. A social–behavioral analysis of skill deficits in delinquent and nondelinquent adolescent boys. *Journal of Consulting and Clinical Psychology,* 1978, *46,* 1448–1462.

Fry, P. S. Self-imposed delay of gratification as a function of modeling. *Journal of Counseling Psychology,* 1972, *19,* 234–237.

Furman, W., Geller, M., Simon, S. J., & Kelly, J. A. The use of a behavior rehearsal procedure for teaching job interviewing skills to psychiatric patients. *Behavior Therapy,* 1979, *10,* 157–167.

Gal'perin, P. Y. Stages in the development of mental acts. In M. Cole & I. Mallzmon (Eds.), *The handbook of contemporary Soviet psychology.* New York: Basic Books, 1969.

Gerst, M. D. Symbolic coding processes in observational learning. *Journal of Personality and Social Psychology,* 1971, *19,* 7–17.

Gersten, E. L., de Apodaca, R. F., Rains, M., Weissberg, R. P., & Cowen, E. L. Promoting peer-related social competence in schools. In M. W. Kent & J. E. Roff (Eds.), *The primary prevention of psychopathology* (Vol. 3). Hanover, NH: University Press of New England, 1979.

Gilbert, D. The young child's awareness of affect. *Child Development,* 1969, *39,* 619–636.

Glass, C. R., Gottman, J. M., & Shmurak, S. H. Response-acquisition and cognitive self-statement modification approaches to dating skills behavior. *Journal of Counseling Psychology,* 1976, *23,* 520–526.

Goldstein, A. P., Sherman, M., Gershaw, N. J., Sprafkin, R. P., & Glick, B. Training aggressive adolescents in prosocial behavior. *Journal of Youth and Adolescence,* 1978, *7,* 73–92.

Gottman, J., Gonso, J., & Rasmussen, B. Social interaction, social competence, and friendship in children. *Child Development,* 1975, *46,* 709–718.

Harris, G. G. The use of modeling procedures to modify vocational aspirations of potential high school dropouts. *Journal of Community Psychology,* 1973, *1,* 298–301.

Hart, B. M., Reynolds, N. J., Baer, D. M., Brawley, E. R., & Harris, F. R. Effect of contingent and noncontingent social reinforcement on the cooperative play of a preschool child. *Journal of Applied Behavior Analysis,* 1968, *1,* 73–76.

Hartig, M., & Kanfer, F. H. The role of verbal self-instructions in children's resistance to temptation. *Journal of Personality and Social Psychology,* 1973, *25,* 259–267.

Hartup, W., Glazer, J., & Charlesworth, R. Peer reinforcement and sociometric status. *Child Development,* 1967, *38,* 1017–1024.

Hersen, M., & Bellack, A. S. A multiple baseline analysis of social skills training in chronic schizophrenics. *Journal of Applied Behavior Analysis,* 1976, *9,* 239–245.

Hersen, M., Eisler, R. M., & Miller, P. M. An experimental analysis of generalization in assertive training. *Behaviour Research and Therapy,* 1974, *12,* 295–310.

Janis, I., & Mann, L. *Decision making: A psychological analysis of conflict, choice, and commitment.* New York: Free Press, 1977.

Johnson, D. M., Parrott, G. R., & Stratton, R. P. Production and judgement of solutions to five problems. *Journal of Educational Psychology Monograph Supplement*, 1968, *59*, (6, Pt. 2), 1–21.

Kagan, J. Reflection-impulsivity: The generality and dynamics of conceptual tempo. *Journal of Abnormal Psychology*, 1966, *71*, 17–24.

Kagan, J., Rosman, B. L., Day, D., Albert, J., & Phillips, W. Information processing in the child: Significance of analytic and reflective attitudes. *Psychological Monographs*, 1964, *78*, (1, Whole No. 578).

Kanfer, F., & Zich, J. Self-control training: The effects of external control on children's resistance to temptation. *Developmental Psychology*, 1974, *10*, 108–115.

Keller, M. F., & Carlson, P. M. The use of symbolic modeling to promote social skills in preschool children with low levels of social responsiveness. *Child Development*, 1974, *45*, 912–919.

Kelly, G. A. *The psychology of personal constructs: II. Clinical diagnosis and psychotherapy.* New York: Norton, 1955.

Kelly, J. A., Frederiksen, L. W., Fitts, H., & Phillips, J. Training and generalization of commendatory assertiveness: A controlled single subject experiment. *Journal of Behavior Therapy and Experimental Psychiatry*, 1978, *9*, 17–21.

Kendall, P. C., & Finch, A. J., Jr. A cognitive–behavioral treatment for impulsivity: A group comparison study. *Journal of Consulting and Clinical Psychology*, 1978, *46*, 110–118.

Kendall, P. C., & Finch, A. J., Jr. Developing nonimpulsive behavior in children: Cognitive–behavioral strategies for self-control. In P. C. Kendall & S. D. Hollon (Eds.), *Cognitive–behavioral interventions: Theory, research, and procedures.* New York: Academic Press, 1979.

Liebert, R. M., Neale, J. M., & Davidson, E. S. *The early window: Effects of television on children and youth.* New York: Pergamon Press, 1973.

Livesley, W. J., & Bromley, D. B. *Person perception in childhood and adolescence.* New York: Wiley, 1973.

Luria, A. R. *The role of speech in the regulation of normal and abnormal behavior.* New York: Liveright, 1961.

Mann, J., & Rosenthal, T. L. Vicarious and direct counter-conditioning of test anxiety through individual and group desensitization. *Behaviour Research and Therapy*, 1969, *7*, 359–367.

McClure, L. F., Chinsky, J. M., & Larcen, S. W. Enhancing social problem-solving performance in an elementary school setting. *Journal of Educational Psychology*, 1978, *70*, 504–513.

McCombs, D., Filipczak, J., Friedman, R. M., & Wodarsi, J. S. Long-term follow-up of behavior modification with high-risk adolescents. *Criminal Justice and Behavior*, 1978, *5*, 1–22.

McDougall, W. *An introduction to social psychology.* London: Methuen, 1908.

Mead, G. H. *Mind, self, and society.* Chicago: University of Chicago Press, 1934.

Meadow, A., & Parnes, S. J. Evaluation of training in creative problem-solving. *Journal of Applied Psychology*, 1959, *43*, 189–194.

Meichenbaum, D. Self-instructional training: A cognitive prosthesis for the aged. *Human Development*, 1974, *17*, 273–280.

Meichenbaum, D. A self-instructional approach to stress management: A proposal for stress inoculation training. In C. D. Spielberger & I. G. Sarason (Eds.), *Stress and anxiety* (Vol. 1). New York: Wiley, 1975.

Meichenbaum, D., & Asarnow, J. Cognitive-behavior modification and metacognitive development: Implications for the classroom. In P. C. Kendall & S. D. Hollon

(Eds.), *Cognitive-behavioral interventions: Theory, research, and procedures.* New York: Academic Press, 1979.

Meichenbaum, D., & Goodman, J. Training impulsive children to talk to themselves: A means of developing self-control. *Journal of Abnormal Psychology,* 1971, *77,* 115-126.

Minkin, N., Braukmann, C. J., Minkin, B. L., Timbers, G. D., Timbers, B. J., Fixsen, D. L., Phillips, E. L., & Wolf, M. M. The social validation and training of conversational skills. *Journal of Applied Behavior Analysis,* 1976, *9,* 127-139.

Mischel, W. Processes in delay of gratification. In L. Berkowitz (Ed.), *Advances in experimental social psychology* (Vol. 7). New York: Academic Press, 1974.

Mischel, W., & Mischel, H. A cognitive social learning approach to morality and self regulation. In T. Lickona (Ed.), *Moral development and behavior: Theory, research, and social issues.* New York: Holt, Rinehart, & Winston, 1976.

Mischel, W., & Patterson, C. J. Substantive and structural elements of effective plans for self-control. *Journal of Personality and Social Psychology,* 1976, *34,* 942-950.

Morton, R. B. An experiment in brief psychotherapy. *Psychological Monographs,* 1955, *69,* (1, Whole No. 386).

Murray, H. A. *Explorations in personality.* New York: Oxford, 1938.

Neale, J. M. Egocentrism in institutionalized and noninstitutionalized children. *Child Development,* 1966, *37,* 97-101.

Osborn, A. F. *Applied imagination: Principles and procedures of creative problem solving* (3rd ed.). New York: Scribners, 1963.

Parnes, S. J. *Creative behavior guidebook.* New York: Scribners, 1967.

Parry, P. *The effects of reward on the performance of hyperactive children.* Unpublished doctoral dissertation, McGill University, Montreal, 1973.

Patterson, G. R., Littmar, R. A., & Bricker, W. Assertive behavior in children: A step toward a theory of aggression. *Monographs of the Society for Research in Child Development,* 1967, *32,* 1-43.

Peevers, B. H., & Secord, P. F. Developmental changes in attribution of descriptive concepts to persons. *Journal of Personality and Social Psychology,* 1973, *27,* 120-218.

Piaget, J. *The language and thought of the child.* London: Routledge & Kegan Paul, 1926.

Platt, J. J., Scura, W., & Hannon, J. R. Problem-solving thinking of youthful incarcerated heroin addicts. *Journal of Community Psychology,* 1973, *1,* 278-281.

Platt, J. J., & Spivack, G. Social competence and effective problem solving in psychiatric patients. *Journal of Clinical Psychology,* 1972, *28,* 3-5.

Platt, J. J., & Spivack, G. *Manual for means-ends problem-solving procedure.* Philadelphia: Department of Mental Health Sciences, Hahnemann Community Mental Health/Mental Retardation Center, 1975.

Platt, J. J., Spivack, G., Allman, N., Allman, D., & Peizer; S. B. Adolescent problem-solving thinking. *Journal of Consulting and Clinical Psychology,* 1974, *42,* 787-793.

Poitras-Martin, D., & Stone, G. L. Psychological education: A skill-oriented approach. *Journal of Counseling Psychology,* 1977, *24,* 153-157.

Rosenthal, T. L., Alford, G. S., & Rasp, L. M. Concept attainment, generalization, and retention through observation and verbal coding. *Journal of Experimental Child Psychology,* 1972, *13,* 183-194.

Rotenberg, M. Conceptual and methodological notes in affective and cognitive role taking (sympathy and empathy): An illustrative experiment with delinquent and nondelinquent boys. *Journal of Genetic Psychology,* 1974, *125,* 177-185.

Rotter, J. B. *Social learning and clinical psychology.* Englewood Cliffs, NJ: Prentice-Hall, 1954.

Sarason, I. G. Verbal learning, modeling, and juvenile delinquency. *American Psychologist,* 1968, *23,* 245–266.

Sarason, I. G. Test anxiety and cognitive modeling. *Journal of Personality and Social Psychology,* 1973, *28,* 58–61.

Sarason, I. G. The test anxiety scale: Concept and research. In C. D. Spielberger & I. G. Sarason (Eds.), *Stress and anxiety* (Vol. 5). Washington, DC: Hemisphere, 1978.

Sarason, I. G., & Ganzer, V. J. Modeling and group discussion in the rehabilitation of delinquents. *Journal of Consulting Psychology,* 1973, *20,* 442–449.

Shure, M. B., & Spivack, G. *Cognitive problem-solving skills, adjustment, and social class* (Research and Evaluation Report No. 26). Philadelphia: Department of Mental Health Sciences, Hahnemann Community Mental Health/Mental Retardation Center, 1970. (a)

Shure, M. B., & Spivack, G. *Problem-solving capacity, social class, and adjustment among nursery school children.* Paper presented at Eastern Psychological Association, Atlantic City, 1970. (b)

Shure, M. B., & Spivack, G. Means–ends thinking, adjustment, and social class among elementary school-aged children. *Journal of Consulting and Clinical Psychology,* 1972, *38,* 348–353.

Shure, M. B., & Spivack, G. Interpersonal problem-solving thinking and adjustment in the mother–child dyad. In M. W. Whalen & J. E. Rolf (Eds.), *Primary prevention of psychopathology* (Vol. 3): *Social competence in childhood.* Hanover, NH: University Press of New England, 1979.

Simon, H. A., & Newell, A. Human problem solving: The state of the theory in 1970. *American Psychologist,* 1971, *26,* 145–159.

Skinner, B. F. *Science and human behavior.* New York: Macmillan, 1953.

Snyder, J. J., & White, M. J. The use of cognitive self-instruction in the treatment of behaviorally disturbed adolescents. *Behavior Therapy,* 1979, *10,* 227–235.

Spence, S. H., & Marzillier, J. S. Social skills training with adolescent male offenders: I. Short-term effects. *Behaviour Research and Therapy,* 1979, *17,* 7–16.

Spivack, G., Platt, J. J., & Shure, M. B. *The problem-solving approach to adjustment.* San Francisco: Jossey-Bass, 1976.

Spivack, G., & Shure, M. *Social adjustment of young children: A cognitive approach to solving real-life problems.* San Francisco: Jossey-Bass, 1974.

Stone, G., Hinds, W., & Schmidt, G. Teaching mental health behaviors to elementary school children. *Professional Psychology,* 1975, *6,* 34–40.

Sullivan, H. S. *The interpersonal theory of psychiatry.* New York: Norton, 1953.

Trower, P., Yardley, K., Bryant, B. M., & Shaw, P. The treatment of social failure: A comparison of anxiety-reduction and skills-acquisition procedures on two social problems. *Behavior Modification,* 1978, *2,* 41–60.

Vygotsky, L. *Thought and language.* Cambridge, MA: Massachusetts Institute of Technology Press, 1962.

Williams, D. Y., & Akamatsu, T. J. Cognitive self-guidance training with juvenile delinquents: Applicability and generalization. *Cognitive Therapy and Research,* 1978, *2,* 285–288.

Zimmerman, B. J. Modeling. In H. L. Hom, Jr., & P. A. Robinson (Eds.), *Psychological processes in early education.* New York: Academic Press, 1977.

Zimmerman, B. J., & Rosenthal, T. L. Concept attainment, transfer and retention observation and rule provision. *Journal of Experimental Child Psychology,* 1972, *14,* 139–150.

II

SOCIAL COMPETENCE IN CHILDHOOD: ASSESSMENT AND INTERVENTION

5

CHILDREN'S SOCIAL COMPETENCE IN PEER RELATIONS: SOCIOMETRIC AND BEHAVIORAL ASSESSMENT

STEVEN R. ASHER
SHELLEY HYMEL

STEVEN R. ASHER is Associate Professor of Educational Psychology and Psychology at the University of Illinois, Urbana–Champaign, and currently holds an appointment in the Bureau of Educational Research. His research interests within the area of children's social competence have focused on the development of referential communication skills and on the assessment and training of social skills relevant to friendship making. Shelley Hymel is a doctoral student in the Human Development Division of the Department of Educational Psychology at the University of Illinois, Urbana–Champaign. She has done research on both peer interaction and parent–child relations. Both authors are regular contributors to the literature on children's peer relations and social skills.

In examination of the construct of social competence one of the key questions concerns assessment for the purposes of observation, intervention, and evaluation. Asher and Hymel's chapter provides a rich methodology for the identification of social competence in children. The authors recognize the important role that one's impact on others plays as an index of social competence. Thus their review focuses on sociometric methods for gaining information on how children are viewed by others. Detailed consideration is also given to the correlates of sociometric status that have been identified with different methods of behavioral assessment. In this context, the strengths and limitations of various behavioral assessment strategies are noted. This chapter, then, represents a call for diversity in the methods used to study children's social competence.

Developmental psychologists traditionally have stressed the role of the family, especially parent–child relations, in describing the social development of the child. More recently, however, the role of peer relations has been increasingly recognized as providing unique contributions to the development of social competence (Asher, 1978; Hartup, 1978, 1980; Lewis & Schaeffer, 1981; Youniss, 1980). Children's relations with peers serve a variety of important functions. For example, children provide each other with emotional support in unfamiliar or threatening circumstances (Freud & Dann, 1951; Schwartz, 1972), facilitate complex forms of imaginary play (Gottman & Parkhurst, 1980), and provide direct instruction in various social, physical, and cognitive skills (Allen, 1976; Fine, 1981).

The importance of peer relations has been most clearly demonstrated in research examining the negative effects of inadequate peer relations. Deprivation studies with animals have shown that a lack of contact with age-mates during the first few months of life seriously alters subsequent relations with other animals (Harlow, 1969; Suomi & Harlow, 1975). Although such deprivation studies cannot for ethical reasons be carried out with humans, various correlational studies suggest that early problems in peer relations are related to adjustment problems in later life. These include mental health problems (Cowen, Pederson, Babigian, Izzo, & Trost, 1973; Kohn & Clausen 1955), "bad conduct" discharges from military service (Roff, 1961), suicide (Stengel, 1971), dropping out of school (Ullmann, 1957), and delinquency (Roff, Sells, & Golden, 1972).

Considering the significance of early peer relations, it becomes important to first establish methods of identifying children who have difficulties in relating to peers and then to develop methods for determining the reasons for such difficulties. This chapter is addressed to both of these issues. We will first discuss sociometric assessment as a valid and reliable methodology for identifying children as at risk in their peer relations. Next, we will examine alternative methods that are useful in assessing the behavioral competencies leading to peer acceptance and friendship and the deficits leading to social isolation and rejection. These assessment approaches vary considerably in their procedures, in the questions they are best suited to address, and in their limitations, but each has a contribution to make in helping to understand the dynamics of peer acceptance and rejection. It is our hope that this chapter will encourage enlightened diversity in the use of assessment strategies with socially isolated and rejected children.

SOCIOMETRIC ASSESSMENT

Sociometry is a procedure for measuring the attraction between individual members of a specified group. Several different types of sociometric measures have been developed, each of which is designed to measure how well children are liked or disliked by their peers. In discussing sociometric measures we do not include techniques such as the Guess Who technique (Hartshorne, May, & Maller, 1929) or the Class Play measure (Bower, 1960). Although these are often classified as sociometric measures, they require children to indicate certain characteristics, traits, or roles of their peers rather than to describe how much they like or dislike certain peers. As such, these techniques are better thought of as peer-assessment measures than as sociometric measures (Gronlund, 1959; Kane & Lawler, 1978), and will therefore be considered in the section on behavioral assessment.

The distinction between sociometric and peer-assessment measures is important. Failure to distinguish them can result in confusion in interpreting research findings concerning the behavioral correlates of sociometric status. Research on the behavioral correlates of acceptance requires that a measure of attraction be related to one or more measures of behavior. However, when a peer-assessment measure is used instead of a sociometric measure, peer descriptions of behavior are being related to other measures of behavior. Such studies would best be interpreted as studies of the validity of peer assessment rather than studies of the behavioral correlates of sociometric status.

Types of Sociometric Measures

In the following discussion, we first describe two major methods of sociometric assessment—nomination and rating-scale sociometric measures—and then consider some relevant issues in the identification and classification of children using these measures. The view advanced here is that sociometric methodology offers a reliable and valid index of children's effectiveness with peers and that different types of sociometric measures can be used to identify different dimensions of social status.

NOMINATION MEASURES

The most common sociometric technique is the peer-nomination measure, developed by Moreno (1934), in which children are asked to

nominate a certain number of classmates according to specified interpersonal criteria (e.g., best friend, especially liked). Although in the
majority of studies, the nomination sociometric measure has been
used with positive sociometric criteria (e.g., "Name three classmates
you especially like"), negative sociometric criteria (e.g., "Name three
classmates you don't like very much") have also been employed. In
both cases, a child's score is the number of nominations, either positive or negative, received from peers.

One of the primary virtues of the nomination sociometric technique is that nomination scores tend to be stable over time, at least
for elementary school children. Bonney (1943) examined the test–retest reliability of positive nomination scores with elementary school
students over a 1-year period and found the reliability of sociometric
scores to be comparable to that of achievement test scores. More recently, Busk, Ford, and Schulman (1973) reported test–retest correlations over an 8-week period for children's sociometric rank based on
positive nomination scores. The test–retest correlation across different classrooms averaged .76 for fourth-grade students and .84 for
sixth-grade students. Roff *et al.* (1972) reported that the test–retest
reliability for positive nomination scores received by elementary
school students was .52 over a 1-year period and .42 over a 2-year period. The test–retest reliability correlations for negative nomination
scores were .38 and .34, respectively.

Although nomination scores, especially positive nomination
scores, are stable over time for elementary school children, reliability
is only moderately high when preschool children are involved. In an
attempt to improve sociometric measures for preschool children, Mc-
Candless and Marshall (1957a) used a picture nomination technique
that allowed children to point to pictures of classmates in response to
sociometric questions rather than requiring them to remember other
children's names. Despite this innovation, the test–retest correlations for preschool children using picture sociometric measures still
have been much lower than those obtained with older children (Hartup, Glazer, & Charlesworth, 1967; McCandless & Marshall, 1957a;
Moore & Updegraff, 1964). For example, Moore and Updegraff (1964)
found test–retest correlations of .33 over a 3-week period.

RATING-SCALE MEASURES

The rating-scale measure (Roistacher, 1974; Singleton & Asher,
1977; Thompson & Powell, 1951) is a different type of sociometric
technique. Here children are provided with a list of all their class-

mates and asked to rate each classmate according to a specified criterion. In the version of the rating-scale measure we use with elementary school children (Hymel & Asher, 1977; Oden & Asher, 1977; Singleton & Asher, 1977), children circle a number from 1 to 5 that best describes how much they like to play with (or work with) each classmate at school. A low rating indicates that they "don't like to" and a high rating indicates that they "like to a lot." Faces ranging from a frown to a smile accompany the scale to help communicate the meaning of each of the numbers. A child's score on this measure is the average rating received from classmates.

The rating-scale technique has several attractive features. First, each child rates all classmates, thus providing an indication of the child's attitude toward each of the group members. A limitation of the nomination method is that one only learns about the child's view of those peers he or she nominates. Second, the rating-scale approach appears to be sensitive to subtle changes in scale criteria. For example, Singleton and Asher (1977) found that white children rated black classmates higher in response to the question "How much do you like to play with this person at school?" than in response to the question "How much do you like to work with this person at school?" In another study, Oden and Asher (1977) found that training low-accepted children in social skills in a play situation led to significant increases in the children's ratings by peers in response to a "play with" sociometric question but not in response to a "work with" sociometric question.

A third feature of the rating-scale technique is that the test–retest reliability of rating-scale scores is higher than that for nomination scores. Oden and Asher (1977) examined the test–retest correlations in 11 classes of third- and fourth-grade children. Over a 6-week period, the median correlation was .82 for a "play with" rating scale, .84 for a "work with" rating scale, and .69 for a positive nomination measure. Similarly, in a study of sixth-grade students, Thompson and Powell (1951) found that the test–retest reliability of rating-scale sociometric scores was higher than for positive nomination scores over intervals of 1 week, 4 weeks, and 5 weeks. The greater reliability of rating-scale scores is most likely due to the fact that a child's score on the rating-scale measure is the average rating received from a large number of peers and, as such, a change in the rating given by one or two peers would have relatively little effect. In contrast, on the nomination measures, children typically only receive a few positive or negative nominations and the gain or loss of a single nomination per child could have dramatic effects on the distribution of scores.

The superior reliability of the rating-scale method is particularly apparent with preschool children. In a study by Asher, Singleton, Tinsley, and Hymel (1979), 4-year-old children first responded to positive and negative nomination questions by pointing to photographs of three classmates with whom they liked to play, and three classmates with whom they did not like to play. Children then rated peers by assigning photographs of each of their classmates to one of three boxes according to how much the child liked to play with the classmate at school. The three boxes were distinguished by a happy, neutral, or sad face intended to help the child to remember the meaning of each point on the scale. With two classes of children, the test-retest correlation for the rating scale measure over a 4-week period was higher (.81, .74) than for a positive nomination measure (.56, .38), or for a negative nomination measure (.42; the negative nomination measure was not administered in the second classroom). Thus, the rating-scale technique provides a promising measure for research on peer acceptance in young children.[1]

Issues in Sociometric Testing

SEX BIASES IN CHILDREN'S SOCIOMETRIC PREFERENCES

One important issue to be considered in using sociometric measures is defining the peer group on which sociometric scores are based. Most researchers have calculated sociometric scores based on nominations or ratings from all peers in the group under consideration. However, elementary school children exhibit strong bias against opposite-sex peers (Criswell, 1939; Singleton & Asher, 1977). Since cross-sex nominations and ratings are often negative and children's primary membership group typically consists of same-sex peers, some researchers have selected children for participation in social skills training programs on the basis of sociometric scores from only same-sex peers (Hymel & Asher, 1977; Oden & Asher, 1977).

How does inclusion of cross-sex nominations and ratings affect children's sociometric scores? We examined this issue using socio-

---

[1]We have not included the paired-comparison sociometric technique (Koch, 1933) in our discussion of sociometric measures due to space limitations. This technique, however, is another highly reliable sociometric method used with young children. It may be particularly useful for studying attraction between particular pairs of children (see Cohen & VanTassel, 1978; Vaughn & Waters, 1980).

metric data obtained by Hymel and Asher (1977) from 205 third-through fifth-grade children. As would be expected from previous research, the majority of positive nominations were from same-sex peers. The mean number of positive nominations received from same-sex peers was 2.63 (SD = 2.01), whereas the average number received from opposite-sex peers was .37 (SD = .73). On the other hand, the majority of negative nominations were from opposite-sex peers. On the average, children received 1.95 (SD = 2.20) negative nominations from opposite-sex peers as compared with .93 (SD = 1.53) from same-sex peers. The tendency for negative scores to be obtained primarily from opposite-sex peers was also reflected in the rating-scale sociometric scores. Children received much lower ratings from cross-sex peers ($\bar{x}$ = 1.93, SD = .64) than from same-sex peers ($\bar{x}$ = 3.58, SD = .71).

How does this pattern influence the distribution of scores based on same-sex, cross-sex, and both-sex peers? The correlations between sociometric scores based on same-sex and cross-sex peer groups were only moderately high, $r(203)$ = .41, p < .01, for positive nominations; $r(203)$ = .54, p < .01, for negative nominations; $r(203)$ < .48, p < .01, for play ratings. This suggests that boys and girls are using somewhat different criteria when making their nominations and ratings. Still, inclusion of nominations and ratings by opposite-sex peers does not greatly alter the distribution of children's sociometric scores compared to the distribution of scores based on same-sex peers only. This can be demonstrated by the rather high correlations between sociometric scores based on same-sex peers and scores based on peers of both sexes: $r(203)$ = .96, p < .01, for positive nomination scores; $r(203)$ = .83, p < .01, for negative nomination scores; $r(203)$ = .84, p < .01, for rating-scale scores.

It appears, then, that the decision about whether to use scores based on same-sex or both-sex responses must be based on the particular purposes for which sociometric assessment is being used. When selecting elementary school children who have peer relationship problems it may be important to give more weight to same-sex scores since inclusion of opposite-sex data might lead to the selection of children who actually are fairly well liked by what is probably their primary membership group, same-sex peers. However, in studies of the behavioral correlates of sociometric status, it may be of interest to examine the behavioral correlates of being accepted by same-sex versus cross-sex peers, rather than correlating behavior only with both-sex scores as has been done in the past (e.g., Gottman, Gonso, & Rasmussen, 1975; Hartup et al., 1967).

CLASSIFYING LOW-STATUS CHILDREN BASED ON MULTIPLE SOCIOMETRIC MEASURES

Each of the sociometric measures described above provides a somewhat different index of a child's social status within a group. In this section, we will review evidence that low sociometric status is a multidimensional phenomenon and that there is a great deal of information to be gained by examining how children are classified according to various sociometric measures. We will first examine the relationship between positive nomination and rating-scale measures.

LIKABILITY VERSUS FRIENDSHIP

The positive nomination and rating-scale sociometric measures have been found to be fairly highly related, $r(203) = .63, p < .01$ (Hymel & Asher, 1977), suggesting that these two measures would yield similar results. However, examination of how children are classified according to these two measures indicates certain important differences. There are a number of children who have no best friends in class (receive no positive nominations), yet are rather well liked by their peers. For instance, in the Hymel and Asher (1977) data, of the 23 children who received no positive nominations from same sex peers, 11 received fairly high play ratings (above 3.00). How can a child who is nominated by no one as "especially liked" receive a relatively high average play rating? One possibility is that the positive nomination and rating-scale sociometric measures are actually tapping two different aspects of social status. Positive nomination measures may indicate how many peers regard a child as a best friend or high-priority playmate whereas the rating-scale measure may provide an index of a child's overall level of acceptability or likability among peers.

There are data to suggest the utility of the positive nomination and rating-scale measures for distinguishing between likability and best friendship. For example, the literature on cross-race peer relations indicates that elementary school black and white children accept or like one another as measured by a rating-scale measure (Singleton & Asher, 1977, 1979), even though they do not typically nominate each other as best friends or most preferred playmates (Shaw, 1973). The distinction between being liked or accepted and having best friends also helps in interpreting the findings from recent intervention efforts. Oden and Asher (1977) coached low-status children in play skills by instructing children in concepts such as participation, cooperation, communication, and being validating or supportive of others. Children made significant gains in how well they were liked according to a "play with" rating-scale measure but did not make significant gains in best friendships on a positive nomination measure. As Oden and Asher noted, it seems plausible that the skills involved in making a best friend go beyond those that were coached. For example, children may need to learn how to initiate after-school activities with other children in order to establish close friendships. Further research is needed regarding the utility of the nomination and rating-scale measures for studying this distinction between likability and friendship.

ACCEPTANCE VERSUS REJECTION

As described previously, the nomination sociometric measure has been used with both positive and negative criteria. Originally, the number of positive and negative sociometric nominations children received were thought to be unidimensional and thus highly negatively correlated. However, research has consistently found this not to be the case. Positive and negative nomination scores have been found to be only moderately negatively related (Gottman, 1977; Moore & Updegraff, 1964; Roff et al., 1972) or not related at all (Hartup et al., 1967; Hymel & Asher, 1977). Further support for the distinction between acceptance and rejection is obtained from studies of the behavioral correlates of sociometric status. Research has shown that the correlates of acceptance are different from the correlates of rejection (Gronlund & Anderson, 1957; Hartup et al., 1967). For example, Hartup et al. (1967) observed nursery school children and categorized their behavior as either positively or negatively reinforcing to peers. Positively reinforcing behaviors were found to correlate significantly with acceptance but not with rejection. On the other hand, negative reinforcing behaviors correlated significantly with rejection but not with acceptance.

The distinction between acceptance and rejection permits the identification of two different types of low-accepted children: those who are neglected by peers (i.e., receive few or no positive nominations and few or no negative nominations), and those who are rejected by peers (i.e., receive few or no positive nominations and several negative nominations). Most often this distinction is ignored. For example, it is common to refer to all children who are without friends in class as socially isolated, even though some of these children are openly rejected by their peers while others are indeed neglected.

What percentage of children who receive no positive nominations are neglected as opposed to rejected by their peers? Sociometric data obtained by Hymel and Asher (1977) indicated that 23 (11%) of the 205 third- through fifth-grade children in the sample received no nominations as "especially liked" from same-sex peers. These children could then be subclassified on the basis of the number of negative nominations received. Eleven of these children also received no negative nominations from same-sex peers. These neglected children fit the image associated with the term "socially isolated"; they are neither well-accepted nor rejected by same-sex peers, but instead are ignored. However, seven of the children who received no positive nominations received two or more negative nominations from same-sex peers. These children could be classified as rejected, and for them the term "socially isolated" would be misleading.

Although the distinction between rejected and neglected children cannot be made from positive nomination data alone, most of the research on social skill assessment and intervention with low-accepted children has typically employed only positive nomination measures. One reason for not using negative nomination measures is that some parents and teachers fear that such measures will implicitly signal to their children that saying negative things about others is sanctioned, or that in the process of having to name a specified number of disliked peers the children will actually come to view certain children more negatively than they already do. Even those researchers who employ negative sociometric criteria recognize the potential problems (Moore, 1973; Roff *et al.*, 1972).

Still, arguments in favor of the combined use of positive and negative criteria would seem to prevail. Past research demonstrates that rejection among children is a factor in classroom social structure, and studying the phenomenon is the first step toward preventing or ameliorating it. Furthermore, experience with young children, at least, suggests that having children respond to negative sociometric questions under experimental conditions does not result in increased interpersonal rancor (Moore, 1973). Still, there are no hard data on the issue of whether requesting negative nominations alters children's feelings or subsequent interactions in the classroom. Given the absence of such data, researchers and practitioners should proceed cautiously when considering inclusion of negative nomination criteria.

One important implication of the findings presented in this section is that the type of child who is identified as a low-status child may depend on the type of sociometric measures employed. Although there appears to be some consistency in status scores across sociometric measures, there are considerable differences in the number of children and type of children identified by each. Choice of a particular sociometric measure depends on how one defines a problem in peer relations; therefore, researchers should select a sociometric measure appropriate to the kind of peer relationship problem they wish to investigate. Furthermore, care should be taken when comparing studies that use different sociometric measures since different types of children may be involved.

Another implication is that sociometric assessment would typically be strengthened by using multiple measures. There is useful information to be gained by employing positive and negative nomination measures in addition to a rating-scale measure. Positive and negative nomination measures are needed to distinguish neglected and rejected children, and rating-scale positive nomination measures are necessary to distinguish a child's overall acceptability or likability within the group and the extent to which he or she has best friendships. Multiple sociometric measures would ensure a more complete description of research samples and could be used to select more homogeneous groups than have been studied in previous research.

METHODS OF BEHAVIORAL ASSESSMENT

Sociometric measures indicate the extent to which children have friends or are accepted or rejected by their peers, but they do not provide information about the behaviors that determine children's sociometric status. In this section, methods of studying the behavioral correlates of sociometric status will be discussed. Research on the behavioral correlates of sociometric status has a remarkably long history, yet given that history there are surprisingly few studies. Research on children's social behavior has waxed and waned over the past 50 years. Indeed, as Hartup (1970) has pointed out, the 1930s and early 1940s were far richer than the 1950s and early 1960s in their detailed attention to children's social behavior. However, in the past decade there has been a revitalization of interest in children's peer relations, and, with it, several new approaches to the assessment of children's social behavior have been explored. In the following sections, we will discuss various methods of behavioral assessment, with particular emphasis on the distinctive contributions and limitations of each method. Four methods will be discussed: naturalistic observation, observation in analogue situations, peer assessment, and simulation methods. Given that each measure has limitations, it is important to think of these as a family of complementary methods. No single measure will provide a complete picutre, but various measures used in combination can be extremely informative.

Naturalistic Observation

Naturalistic observation methods are perhaps the most face-valid of the behavioral assessment methods. How better to study the behavioral correlates of peer acceptance than to observe children's everyday interactions with peers? Naturalistic observation studies of children's peer relations have been of two major types. One set of studies has examined the children's interaction with peers, regardless of the features or content of the interaction. An example of this type of approach to behavioral observation is found in the literature on social withdrawal, where children who are observed to interact infrequently with peers are identified and targeted for intervention (Allen, Hart, Buell, Harris, & Wolf, 1964; Evers & Schwarz, 1973; Furman, Rahe, & Hartup, 1979; Greenwood, Walker, Todd, & Hops, 1977; O'Connor, 1969, 1972). Studies using this type of measure generally find little relationship between children's frequency or rate of interaction and how well they are liked (Deutsch, 1974; Gottman, 1977; Greenwood *et al.*, 1977; Jennings, 1975), and it has been suggested that the simple rate-of-interaction index is an inadequate measure of social competence (Asher, Markell, & Hymel, in press). A more fruitful approach is taken in research on qualitatively defined individual difference measures. Accordingly, we will devote detailed attention to this type of naturalistic observation method.

A number of studies have addressed the question of how qualitative aspects of children's behavior as observed in natural settings relate to sociometric status (Bonney & Powell, 1953; Clifford, 1963; Gottman *et al.*, 1975; Hartup *et al.*, 1967; Hymel & Asher, 1977; Hymel, Tinsley, Asher, & Geraci, 1981; Koch, 1933; Lippitt, 1941; Marshall, 1957; Marshall & McCandless, 1957a, 1957b; McCandless & Marshall, 1957b; McGuire, 1973; Moore & Updegraff, 1964). The Hartup *et al.* (1967) study is undoubtedly the most oft-cited in this area. These investigators found a significant positive relationship between sociometric acceptance and interacting positively with peers, while interacting negatively with peers was found to be significantly related to sociometric rejection. Similar results have been reported in other research. Marshall and McCandless (1957a) found that the amount of associative play and "friendly approach" behavior was significantly related to positive nomination sociometric scores.

Hymel *et al.* (1981) found that highly accepted children, as determined by a rating-scale sociometric, both initiated and received more positive initiations from peers, while less frequently accepted children received more negative initiations from peers. In addition, the number of negative nominations received from peers was significantly related to the number of negative initiations made toward peers and the number of negative initiations received from peers.

Not all studies, however, have demonstrated clear-cut relationships between sociometric status and behavior observed in naturalistic settings. Some studies have found relationships between sociometric status and only very few of the behaviors observed (e.g., Bonney & Powell, 1953; Gottman *et al.*, 1975; Koch, 1933), some studies have found that the relationship between status and behavior varied depending on the sex of the children observed (McCandless & Marshall, 1957b; McGuire, 1973), and other studies have failed to find any significant relationship between sociometric status and observed behavior (Clifford, 1963; Hymel & Asher, 1977; Lippitt, 1941).

Our examination of this literature suggests that significant relationships between observed behavior and sociometric status are more consistently obtained with preschool than with elementary school children. Several studies of preschool children (Hartup *et al.*, 1967; Hymel *et al.*, 1981; Marshall & McCandless, 1957a, 1957b; McCandless & Marshall, 1957b; McGuire, 1973; Moore & Updegraff, 1964) have found significant relationships between sociometric scores and observed behavior. Fewer studies have been conducted with elementary school children, but results from these studies are less compelling. Hymel and Asher (1977) found no behavioral differences between popular and unpopular third-, fourth-, and fifth-grade children. Somewhat stronger, although still modest relationships, were found by Gottman *et al.* (1975). Gottman *et al.* (1975) examined the relationship between status and observed behavior among third- and fourth-grade children but found only a few behaviors to be associated with sociometric status. They did find that children with many friends *received* significantly more positive reinforcement from peers than children with few friends, but the tendency for children with many friends to distribute more positive reinforcement to peers was not significant. An unpublished study by Benson and Gottman (reported in Putallaz & Gottman, 1981) with first-, third-, and fourth-grade children found no behavioral differences between popular and unpopular children in style of initiation toward peers. Interestingly, as in Gottman *et al.* (1975), there were differences in the type of interactions initiated by other children toward them.

Why might a discrepancy exist between studies conducted with older versus younger children? The limitations of naturalistic observation methodology as used to date in this area may help to explain the modest relationships obtained between sociometric status and observed behavior among older children. First, it seems possible that the types of friendship-making behaviors commonly observed in the preschool classroom may be less likely to occur in the more highly structured elementary school classroom. Even free time is much more regulated in the elementary school than in the nursery school classroom. This would result in far fewer opportunities for social interaction than would be observed during a preschool free-play period. Researchers should consider the possibility of conducting observations during recess, lunch periods, or after school, as well as during class periods. Such times may provide a more representative sample of social interaction among older children. It is suggestive that the elementary school studies with the strongest results (Benson & Gottman, reported in Putallaz & Gottman, 1981; Gottman et al., 1975) included observations outside the classroom (e.g., recess) as well as in the classroom.

Failure to demonstrate strong relationships between observed behavior and sociometric status may also be a function of developmental changes in the types of characteristics that mediate status. First, it should be recognized that many of the correlates of sociometric status are not behavioral characteristics per se. Indeed, it may be the case that older as compared to younger children's status is more influenced by a variety of nonbehavioral factors, such as race, gender, and physical attractiveness. Although this issue has not been examined directly, evidence does indicate that such nonbehavioral factors are related to social status (Asher, Oden, & Gottman, 1977). That these characteristics may become increasingly important determinants of peer status as children grow older is suggested by the finding that race assumes greater importance in children's friendship choices across age (Criswell, 1939; Singleton & Asher, 1979).

Furthermore, the behaviors that do contribute to sociometric status may change over age. Research on person perception and children's descriptions of liked and disliked peers suggests that older children focus more on behavioral dimensions that are less readily observable (Bigelow, 1977; Bigelow & LaGaipa, 1975; Livesley & Bromley, 1973; Peevers & Secord, 1973; Scarlett, Press, & Crockett, 1971). For example, Scarlett et al. (1971) found that younger children tended to use more personal and concrete constructs in describing their peers (e.g., "We play together," "He hits me," "She gives me things"), while older children were more likely to employ less personal and more abstract constructs in their peer descriptions (e.g., "She is intelligent" or "He is kind"). Another study, by Peevers and Secord (1973), found that older children were more likely than younger children to describe liked peers in terms of attitudes, belief, and interests as well as other general dispositional characteristics. Similarly, Damon (1977), based on the work of Selman (1976) and Youniss (1975), has suggested a three-stage developmental progression in children's friendships. Early on, friends are playmates or frequent associates, and friendship is affirmed through the sharing of material resources. At the next stage, friendship is no longer determined by frequency of contact or simple sharing of material goods, but by reciprocal interest. Friends are persons who assist one another and friendship is affirmed through concrete or material acts of kindness. At the third stage, friendship is affirmed through mutual sharing of thoughts, interests and feelings, and can only be terminated by a continual display of lack of understanding or loyalty.

Each of these authors has suggested that as children get older their conceptions of friendship changes and with it the behaviors or actions that define or affirm friendship. The physical, material, contact-oriented conceptions of friendship at younger ages give way to more abstract conceptions of friendship at older ages. In effect, we suspect that the typical behavioral observation scheme is better coordinated to the social world of the young child and not designed to reflect the more complex and perhaps idiosyncratic reasons older children have for liking and disliking one another. It may also be the case that the behaviors that contribute to friendship at older ages are less readily observable in daily classroom interaction.

Detection of relationships between sociometric status and behavior among older children also may be constrained by the way data are coded and analyzed. It could be that observational systems used with older children need to take into account the sequential nature of the interaction rather than simple frequencies of different types of behavior. For example, it is critical whether a child's hitting of another child is in response to another child's hostile overture or is unprovoked. Older children are probably more sensitive to the patterning and sequential aspects of social interaction than are younger children. Recently developed techniques for analyzing sequences of interaction (e.g., Sackett, 1978) may prove useful here.

In concluding our discussion of naturalistic observation, one final issue deserves comment. One potential limitation of this methodology for studying children of all ages is its capability to capture those low-frequency events that mediate attraction or rejection. For example, if a child receives help with an important school assignment, that child may value the helper for a long time afterward. On the other hand, a child who is hit by another child without provocation is likely to view the aggressor negatively for a long time to come. In each case, children's perceptions of one another are heavily weighted by distinctive low-frequency events. To capture infrequently occurring but psychologically significant events, it is imperative that observers sample behavior over extensive periods of time. The typical naturalistic observation study has observed each child for anywhere from 30 minutes to 2 hours over several school days. Although 1 to 2 hours per child is commendable in terms of the costs and practical constraints of observational research, it may be an inadequate amount of time for capturing low-frequency events. Also, observations are typically made in a restricted range of situations, thereby limiting opportunities to observe certain categories of behavior.

Clearly, more extensive observations are required to study the relationship between sociometric status and behavior in natural settings. For practical reasons these studies may need to be done with relatively small samples. At the same time, naturalistic observations should be supplemented with methods that may be better suited to studying the effects of low-frequency events. Among the advantages of the other assessment strategies to be discussed are their potential for measuring those behaviors that occur rarely but have considerable impact on children's feelings about one another.

Assessment in Analogue Situations

Behavioral observation research need not always be done in the everyday or natural environment of the child. For certain purposes it is useful to arrange special situations in order to observe behaviors that are of theoretical interest but difficult to study in natural settings. Analogue methodology, a strategy that has kept experimental social and developmental psychologists gainfully employed for years, is nonetheless a neglected method in studies of the behavioral correlates of sociometric status.

There are several reasons for studying behavior in specially designed, contrived environments. First, it faciliates research on infrequently occurring behaviors or events, since researchers can arrange the experimental setting to facilitate the occurrence of those events. Second, analogue situations allow for more complete control over potentially influential variables, such as group composition or the type of activity children are involved in. Third, analogue situations permit greater standardization across subjects, making comparisons easier. Fourth, analogue research makes it possible to use more complex coding systems and more sophisticated analyses of data. For example, videotape records can be made more easily in analogue settings such as specially equipped rooms or mobile research trailers. Videotape records, in turn, allow for more extensive coding of observed behavior and for the more complete coding of interactants' behavior that is required for sequential analysis of observational data.

Two recent studies have used analogue situations to study the relationship between behavior toward peers and sociometric status. One found strong evidence of behavioral differences between popular and unpopular children (Putallaz & Gottman, 1981), while the other did not (Oden & Asher, 1977). Speculation is possible about the features of each study that may be responsible for detecting or failing to detect differences in behavior that relate to sociometric status.

Putallaz and Gottman studied how popular and unpopular children enter a play group composed of either popular or unpopular children. The entry situation is a particularly interesting context in which to study differences between popular and unpopular children, since several social skills training studies (e.g., O'Connor, 1969, 1972) have assumed that withdrawn children are deficient in entry skills and have geared training to precisely those skills. The study of entry behavior lends itself to analogue research because entry situations occur infrequently in normal classroom situations and even when such situations do occur, many relevant variables, such as group composition and type of activity, are uncontrolled. Furthermore, the study of the success or failure of different types of entry strategies requires relatively fine-grained, sequential analyses of the content of children's speech, a task greatly facilitated by the availability of videotape records of the children's behavior in the entry situation.

Putallaz and Gottman classified second- and third-grade children as either popular or unpopular based on a positive nomination sociometric measure. Children were then observed as they attempted to gain entry into a dyad of either popular or unpopular children who were playing a board game. Children were videotaped from behind a one-way mirror and the videotapes later were transcribed and coded for specific entry strategies. Results indicated, first, that popular and unpopular dyads of children differed behaviorally prior to the arrival of the third child. Most notably, popular dyads agreed with each other more and disagreed less than did unpopular dyads. Second, there were interesting differences in the entry style of popular and unpopular children. Unpopular children made more entry bids but were more likely to be ignored and less likely to be accepted. Unpopular children were more likely to be disagreeable, to say something about themselves, to state their feelings, and to ask questions. These behaviors seem to have the effect of calling attention to the entering child rather than the ongoing activity. In contrast, popular children joined in the group's ongoing conversation, thus adopting the group's frame of reference, and so were more likely to gain group acceptance.

In another study that employed an analogue situation, Oden and Asher (1977) obtained their observational data as part of a social skills training study with third- and fourth-grade children. Before the low-status children received any training, baseline behavioral data were collected by pairing popular and unpopular children with a same-sex peer of average sociometric status. In each case, the pair of children played a game together for 12 minutes and an observer in the room coded whether children were participating in the activity or not, and what type of peer-oriented behavior the children exhibited. No differences were found between popular and unpopular children's degree of participation or in their style of interaction with peers.

Several factors may account for the lack of relationship between sociometric status and behavior in this study. First, popular and unpopular children played with a peer of average status, which may have had a leveling effect on the interactions. Second, the play situation may have been structured in a way that minimized individual differences; the games were low-conflict activities and children did not have to initiate interaction, since the session was structured by the experimenter. Third, the observer remained in the room with the children throughout the play session, which may have inhibited the children's interaction. Our experience suggests that the presence of an adult observer in a small experimental room is much more inhibiting of children's interaction with peers than is the presence of a video camera. Finally, the coding system used was rather global compared to the more detailed analysis of children's speech made by Putallaz and Gottman (1981).

To summarize, analogue research offers a neglected but potentially useful approach to behavioral assessment. The Putallaz and Gottman (1981) study illustrates the use of analogue situations to study low-frequency events that may be psychologically important. By contrasting this study with the Oden and Asher study, we have suggested several features of the assessment procedure that could influence the sensitivity of analogue methodology to individual differences in children's behavior.

Peer Assessment

The assessment methods discussed thus far involve observations by an outside observer, either in the natural setting or in an artificially created situation. Peer assessment, on the other hand, makes use of "inside observers," namely, the child's fellow group members. In general, two different types of research strategies have been employed. One is to elicit open-ended verbal or written descriptions of peers by asking children to indicate what other children are like or to give reasons why they like or dislike certain children. One particularly important aspect of this methodology is its hypothesis-generating function. By relating descriptions of children to how well these children are liked it is possible to develop hypotheses about the behaviors that mediate peer acceptance. Such open-ended descriptions can suggest dimensions that are considered important or psychologically relevant from the point of view of the children themselves, dimensions that may have been overlooked in other, more adult-directed assessment strategies.

A second approach to peer assessment involves more structured questionnaires or interview procedures to examine children's perceptions of peer behavior. Here, children are asked to nominate peers according to how well their behavior matches specific characteristics or descriptions that are provided. Like the open-ended peer-description procedure, these more structured peer-assessment techniques could serve a hypothesis-generating function. By including a wide variety of characteristics for children to respond to, one could identify the types of behaviors relevant to peer acceptance. In addition, these more structured peer-assessment procedures are perhaps better suited to testing more refined ideas about the interpersonal functions of specific behaviors or personality characteristics.

As Gronlund (1959) has pointed out, peer-assessment methodology developed independently of and prior to the sociometric movement. The first researchers to make systematic use of peer assessment were Hartshorne *et al.* (1929) in their classic studies of children's character. Hartshorne *et al.* created the Guess Who test, in which children indicated which of their classmates best fit a series of descriptions or word-pictures of different types of children. The Hartshorne *et al.* work gave rise to a line of investigations (MacFarlane, Honzik, & Davis, 1937; Tryon, 1939; Tuddenham, 1952; Walder, Abelson, Eron, Banta, & Laulicht, 1961) where children, as "conveniently placed observers" (Walder *et al.*, 1961), provided insight into the behavior of their peers. Thus from the beginning, the purpose of peer-assessment techniques was to assess the behavior of children being rated rather than children's attraction toward one another. In later years the peer-assessment and sociometric traditions became somewhat interwoven; nonetheless, the two methodologies remain distinct measures of children's peer relations.

Peer-assessment methods have several attractive features. Data can be collected easily with large groups of children, thereby facilitating research with different age groups. It thus becomes possible to identify the dimensions that are psychologically significant at different developmental levels. Furthermore, children's judgments of their peers are based on many more hours of observation in many more situations than could readily be observed by an outside researcher. In addition, children's assessments of one another's behavior undoubtedly take into account those low-frequency but psychologically significant behaviors that often elude the observer who devotes only a modest amount of time to watching each child.

In spite of the potential wealth of information available via peer assessment, it is a relatively neglected method within the literature on the behavioral basis of sociometric status. The strong behavioral influence in psychology has created suspicions about the objectivity of peer reports of behavior. It is true that peer-assessment methodology is vulnerable to halo effects (Yarrow & Campbell, 1963). Children may ascribe positive qualities to those they like, and negative qualities to those they dislike, partly because of their feelings, rather than because of an objective assessment they have made of the peer's behavior. Despite such effects, peers can provide valid sources of information. Furthermore, peer assessment reveals interesting and interpretable findings concerning the relationship between sociometric status and behavior that are not easily uncovered by other behavioral assessment strategies.

OPEN-ENDED PEER DESCRIPTION

Several studies have been conducted within the past decade in which children were asked to describe certain liked or disliked peers (Livesley & Bromley, 1973; Peevers & Secord, 1973; Scarlett *et al.,* 1971). The primary focus of these studies has been on cognitive or structural changes in the process of person perception over age rather than on the content of children's descriptions of liked and disliked peers. However, as noted earlier, these studies have provided some insight into the content of the behaviors valued by children and have demonstrated that the type of information obtained in children's peer descriptions varies as a function of the age of the children involved. In addition, there is an earlier set of studies on children's perceptions of peers in which the primary focus was on learning about what types of behavioral characteristics are associated with being liked or disliked by peers (Elkins, 1958; Feinberg, Smith, & Schmidt, 1958; Yarrow & Campbell, 1963). These studies have shown that children provide a wide array of reasons for liking or disliking other children, including both behavioral and nonbehavioral characteristics (Elkins, 1958). Moreover, these studies have shown that the reasons given for peer acceptance or rejection vary as a function of factors like social class (Feinberg *et al.,* 1958), and as a function of age, gender, and the length of time children are together (Yarrow & Campbell, 1963). It is therefore necessary to take into account these characteristics of the peer group in identifying the correlates of social status.

Although studies using open-ended descripions have provided interesting data, certain weaknesses in the procedure limit confidence in the findings. First, children are typically asked to name a liked or disliked peer and, at the same time, to provide reasons for these judgments. This close association between the peer-nomination process and the peer-assessment process undoubtedly increases pressure on children to rationalize their nominations. This in turn could magnify differences in children's descriptions of liked and disliked peers. A second problem has been the tendency to rely on the nomination sociometric method. Having children name liked and disliked peers and then describe those peers yields sociometric and behavioral information only on those children nominated. Even when behavioral information is received about a child, it is based only on those few children who happened to nominate the child. We learn nothing about how the child is perceived by other members of the group.

A procedure that avoids these two limitations is to obtain from children descriptions of each of their classmates and then at a different time, using a different experimenter, collect sociometric ratings of each of the group members. This procedure provides a complete and independent set of sociometric and peer-assessment data. A recent study by Dor and Asher (in preparation) used this procedure and also exploited the method's value for developmental inquiry. Third- and sixth-grade children were asked to describe each of their same-sex classmates. Sociometric ratings of each classmate were also obtained at a different time and by a different experimenter. Results indicated that about 54% of the descriptions children gave about their classmates referred to some aspect of interpersonal behavior. Within the interpersonal categories, reference to aggressive behavior declined over age, while reference to deviant behavior and quiet or withdrawn behavior increased. With respect to sociometric status, the deviant but nonaggressive behavior category (including dishonest, irritating, and immature behaviors) showed particularly large differences between high- and low-status children. These data illustrate the hypothesis-generating function of peer-description methodology. That older children describe low-status peers primarily in terms of a variety of deviant but nonaggressive behaviors suggests that the focus of behavioral observation methods must be broadened in order to develop an adequate account of the processes by which children are accepted or rejected by their peers.

STRUCTURED PEER ASSESSMENT

The most commonly used structured peer-assessment method is the Guess Who technique (Hartshorne et al., 1929). This technique has been used with children ranging from preschool age (Moore, 1967) to adolescence (Kuhlen & Lee, 1943) and has been used to study the way in which the behavioral correlates of sociometric status vary over age (e.g., Coppotelli & Coie, 1978). Peer judgments obtained from the Guess Who technique have been found to correlate with teacher ratings of the same children's behavior (Gottlieb, Semmel, & Veldman, 1978; Lesser, 1959; Pekarik, Prinz, Liebert, Weintraub, & Neale, 1976; Rothenberg, 1970), and with direct observations of children's behavior (Winder & Wiggins, 1964).

The Guess Who technique has been administered in two different ways. Originally researchers asked children to nominate a specific number of classmates in response to descriptions of behavior. Later, investigators modified this by presenting children with an items-by-peers matrix and having children check those items that described each classmate. This latter procedure has the advantage of ensuring that children consider each classmate with respect to each trait. The procedure could be modified and presumably further strengthened by asking children to rate each child on each dimension rather than simply making yes–no judgments. The time-consuming nature of this more complex rating task could be reduced somewhat by presenting each child with either a subsample of items or a subsample of classmates to be rated.

The Guess Who technique has been used to examine how variations in a particular category of behavior influence peer acceptance. For example, Lesser (1959) examined the relationship between different types of aggressive behavior and popularity. Low-income children were provided with written descriptions of five different types of aggressive behavior: (1) provoked physical aggression; (2) outburst aggression; (3) unprovoked physical aggression; (4) verbal aggression; and (5) indirect aggression (i.e., attacking or injuring someone indirectly by aggressing against another person or object). Children received five scores based on the number of times they were named for each of the five types of aggressive behavior. Interestingly, of all five types of aggression, indirect aggression was the most strongly related to popularity (in a negative direction). Unfortunately a status score (positive nominations minus negative nominations) was used to measure popularity. This type of score is likely to obscure important information, given that positive and negative nomination scores are largely independent of one another. A better strategy would be to take fuller advantage of the different types of sociometric measures and the various classifications of children they permit (Gronlund & Anderson, 1957).

A more recent study using the Guess Who technique was done by Gottlieb et al. (1978). They were interested in exploring why educable mentally retarded (EMR) children are rejected in classrooms with normal children (i.e., mainstreamed classrooms). Clearly, one possibility is that EMR children are perceived by their peers as intellectually unsuited to classroom tasks. Another possibility is that EMR children engage in various forms of classroom misconduct that lead to rejection. These alternatives were examined using the Guess Who technique—peers nominated classmates in response to requests for names of children who fit various "disruptive" descriptions (e.g., "Who is always bothering other children?" and "Who always wants their own way?'') and various "dull" items (e.g., "Who never knows the answers in class?" and "Who never gets their school work done on time?"). Results indicated that perceived academic competence correlated with a sociometric measure of acceptance but not rejection, and that perceived misbehavior correlated with rejection but only minimally with acceptance. It seems, then, from these peer-assessment data that rejection of EMR children in mainstreamed classrooms is more due to conduct problems than academic difficulties, but that the formation of positive relationships may be constrained by EMR children's more limited academic skills.

A variation of the Guess Who technique is the Class Play technique, developed by Bower (1960), in which the child is given a list of positive and negative descriptions and the child is asked to imagine that each of these descriptions refers to characters in a play. The child's task is to nominate classmates who best fit each description. Research indicates that the Class Play measure has predictive validity. Cowen *et al.* (1973) found that the number of nominations a child received, especially negative nominations, predicted to children's later life mental health adjustment better than a variety of other measures, including absenteeism from school, teacher ratings, grade-point average, IQ, school nurse referrals, self-concept scores, and anxiety scores.

Recent research also indicates that the Class Play measure has concurrent validity in that it relates to behavioral interaction as observed in analogue situations (Wagner, 1979) and in naturalistic classroom situations (Butler, 1979). Wagner used sequential analytic techniques to study dyadic interaction of children in third through sixth grade. Children low in reputation according to the Class Play were found to be more deferential to their partner and less likely to vie for dominance. Also, analysis of simple frequencies indicated that low-reputation children were more hostile–submissive in their style of interaction.

Butler (1979) studied fifth-grade children's interaction in the classroom using a more traditional time-sampling methodology. She found that children low in Class Play reputation were less task-oriented in noninteractive situations, less giving of positive reinforcement, and more giving of negative reinforcement. They also received less positive and more negative reinforcement from peers, and were more involved in negative interactions with the teacher. Additional data collected by Butler indicated that children's Class Play reputations correlated negatively with their academic achievement and classroom adjustment as evaluated by teachers.

Unfortunately, interpretation of these long-term adjustment and behavioral observation studies is made difficult by certain features of the measure and its use. Unlike the Guess Who technique, which is scored by summing the number of nominations each child receives on each behavioral dimension, the Class Play has been scored by summing nominations across items to create a total positive and a total negative nomination score. Given that different types of items comprise each score, it is not known what specific type of peer judgment relates to observed behavior or to later life adjustment. A second problem has to do with the wording of particular items. When, for example, a child nominates a classmate for the role of a class president, a true friend, or a school nurse or doctor, it isn't clear what behavioral characteristics the child has in mind. It would seem that more behaviorally defined items, analyzed separately from one another as in the Guess Who technique, do more to advance our understanding of the processes of peer acceptance and rejection.

Simulation Methods

Each of the behavioral assessment methods discussed thus far is designed to provide information about how a child typically behaves. When a significant relationship emerges between behavior and sociometric status, the assumption is usually made that a child's social skills deficits, as reflected in behavior, are causing his or her low sociometric status. There are two parts to this assumption that need careful testing. First, a child's behavior is not necessarily an indication of his or her competence. For example, a child might know how to behave in a given situation but be debilitated by excessive anxiety or lack of confidence. Another possibility is that the child may have alternative, nonsocial goals in a particular situation and simply choose not to exhibit certain behaviors. It is inappropriate, therefore, to conclude from the behavioral assessment methods previously discussed that a child exhibiting a certain ineffective interaction style lacks knowledge of how to interact.

A second aspect of the assumption that requires verification is that the child's interaction style is, indeed, the cause of low status. The reverse possibility can also be envisioned; that is, the child's low status in the peer group may cause certain styles of behavior to emerge. The most competent individual might begin to behave dysfunctionally if consistently ignored or treated harshly by a peer group. It is premature to infer causality from data correlating sociometric status with observed or reported behavior. All of the studies discussed thus far have assessed children's interaction style with the same peers who have completed the sociometric nominations or ratings on these children.

Given this analysis, we need assessment procedures that measure children's social knowledge independent of the pressures, constraints, and motivations of real-life performance situations. This can provide more direct information about what children *can* do, as opposed to what they *do* do. In addition, we need to assess children's interaction style outside of the group in which their sociometric status is assessed. Behavioral simulation methodology offers a way of meeting both of these requirements. In this type of methodology, children are individually presented with hypothetical situations and asked to respond by role playing their responses or by saying what someone could do in that situation. Because this assessment is made individually and independently of the group context it provides an indication of the child's performance apart from the group in which the sociometric assessment is made. Furthermore, the situation is relatively nonthreatening compared to more real-life performance settings.

Several studies have recently examined the relationship between sociometric status and behavior in simulated situations. Gottman *et al.* (1975) studied third- and fourth-grade children's ability to initiate relationships with peers. Each child was asked to pretend that he or she was meeting a child for the first time and wanted to make friends with that child. Children's responses to this situation were recorded and categorized. Results indicated that popular children were more likely than unpopular children to employ initiating strategies such as offering a greeting, giving information, requesting information, or extending inclusion (e.g. "Wanna come over to my house some time?").

A variation on simulation methodology involves presenting children with a hypothetical situation and asking what the protagonist could or should do. Ladd and Oden (1979) showed third- and fifth-grade children cartoons of situations that potentially called for giving help (e.g., a child being teased) and each child was asked how help might be offered. Ladd and Oden were interested in knowing whether there was a relationship between children's ideas about how to help and their sociometric status. Each idea was coded into one of 13 categories (e.g., console–comfort; solicit an adult). Results indicated that children of high sociometric status were more likely to give ideas that were also suggested by other children. This finding implies that there are rather standard categories of responses called for in particular situations and that unpopular children are less aware of these social conventions. These results also imply that it is important to analyze the content of children's responses to problematic situations.

One of the limitations of behavioral observation in natural or analogue settings is its cost. The amount of time required to obtain reliable amounts of data for each child tends to prohibit gathering data in more than a few contexts at most. By contrast, one of the virtues of simulation methodology is that it provides a practical way of assessing children's social knowledge across a wide variety of situations. Asher, Renshaw, Geraci, and Dor (1979) have presented some preliminary work in this direction. Sixty-five popular and unpopular preschool children were each shown nine hypothetical problematic social situations. Each of the nine items or story situations were presented to the child along with a picture. There were two versions of each story and picture, identical except for the sex of the characters. Children were shown one item at a time and asked what the protagonist could do.

There were three types of items: one concerned with the problem of getting to know a new group of children or a new child, one concerned with the maintenance of social relations as in carrying on a conversation or helping a friend, and a third concerned with the management of conflict, such as how to respond when another child tries to take away a toy. Although popular and unpopular children offered many of the same strategies, interesting differences existed as well. Unpopular children were more likely to suggest physically aggressive strategies in response to conflict and they seemed less resourceful in initiation and maintenance situations. When all categories of response were rated by judges in terms of how *assertive, relationship-enhancing,* and *effective* the response was, unpopular children's responses were found to be significantly less relationship-enhancing and significantly less effective. Thus, it appears that unpopular children do exhibit social skill deficits even when the assessment is made independently of their existing peer group.

In sum, the simulation methodology provides a means of assessing children's social knowledge across a variety of social situations. By examining children's responses it should be possible to gain a rather detailed picture of children's notions of how to cope in various problematic situations independently of how that child actually behaves in real-life situations. In this sense, simulation methods potentially differ from the other behavioral assessment methods discussed in this chapter. Whereas peer assessment and observations in natural and analogue settings measure children's actual behavior, simulation measures can be designed to assess children's social knowledge rather than their performance.

SUMMARY

A substantial number of children have been identified as having potentially serious difficulties in their relationships with peers. Furthermore, these children are more likely to experience long-term adjustment problems, which may result from early problems in social interaction. In this chapter, we have discussed a variety of sociometric measures that can be used to identify children having problems in peer relations. The combined use of various sociometric measures can help to distinguish between children with different kinds of problems in peer relations, including rejected versus neglected children and children who are generally well accepted but have no best friends within the classroom.

Although sociometric measures can provide a useful if not essential index of peer relations, more direct measures of social behavior are needed in order to identify the competencies that lead to peer acceptance and friendship and the deficits that lead to isolation and rejection. Accordingly, we have discussed a variety of behavioral assessment procedures designed to identify the correlates of status in the peer group. These behavioral assessment approaches vary considerably in their procedures, in the questions they are best suited to address, and in their limitations, yet each has a contribution to make in helping to understand the dynamics of children's peer relationships. Such understanding should in turn improve our chances of designing and implementing strategies for helping children gain acceptance and friends.

REFERENCES

Allen, K. E., Hart, B., Buell, J. S., Harris, F. R., & Wolf, M. M. Effects of social reinforcement on isolate behavior of a nursery school child. *Child Development*, 1964, *35*, 511–518.

Allen, V. L. (Ed.). *Children as teachers: Theory and research on tutoring.* New York: Academic Press, 1976.

Asher, S. R. Children's peer relations. In M. E. Lamb (Ed.), *Social and personality development.* New York: Holt, Rinehart & Winston, 1978.

Asher, S. R., Markell, R. A., & Hymel, S. Identifying children at risk in peer relations: A critique of the rate-of-interaction approach to assessment. *Child Development*, in press.

Asher, S. R., Oden, S. L., & Gottman, J. M. Children's friendships in school settings. In L. G. Katz (Ed.), *Current topics in early childhood education* (Vol. 1). Norwood, NJ: Ablex, 1977.

Asher, S. R., Renshaw, P. D., Geraci, R. L., & Dor, A. K. *Peer acceptance and social skill training: The selection of program content.* Paper presented at the biennial meeting of the Society for Research in Child Development, San Francisco, 1979.

Asher, S. R., Singleton, L. C., Tinsley, B. R., & Hymel, S. A reliable sociometric measure for preschool children. *Developmental Psychology*, 1979, *15*, 443–444.

Bigelow, B. J. Children's friendship expectations: A cognitive–developmental study. *Child Development*, 1977, *48*, 246–253.

Bigelow, B. J., & LaGaipa, J. J. Children's written descriptions of friendship: A multidimensional analysis. *Developmental Psychology*, 1975, *11*, 857–858.

Bonney, M. E. The relative stability of social, intellectual, and academic status in grades II to IV, and the interrelationships between these various forms of growth. *Journal of Educational Psychology*, 1943, *34*, 88–102.

Bonney, M. E., & Powell, J. Differences in social behavior between sociometrically high and sociometrically low children. *Journal of Educational Research*, 1953, *46*, 481–496.

Bower, E. M. *Early identification of emotionally handicapped children in school.* Springfield, IL: Charles C Thomas, 1960.

Busk, P. L., Ford, R. C., & Schulman, J. L. Stability of sociometric responses in classrooms. *Journal of Genetic Psychology*, 1973, *123*, 69–84.

Butler, L. J. *Social and behavioral correlates of peer reputation.* Paper presented at the biennial meeting of the Society for Research in Child Development, San Francisco, 1979.

Clifford, E. Social visibility. *Child Development*, 1963, *34*, 799–808.

Cohen, A. S., & VanTassel, E. A paired-comparison sociometric test for preschool groups. *Applied Psychological Measurement*, 1978, *2*, 31–40.

Coppotelli, H. A., & Coie, J. D. *Childhood deviance—A peer perspective.* Paper presented at the 5th Biennial Southeastern Conference on Human Development, Atlanta, 1978.

Cowen, E. L., Pederson, A., Babigian, H., Izzo, L. D., & Trost, M. A. Long-term follow-up of early detected vulnerable children. *Journal of Consulting and Clinical Psychology*, 1973, *41*, 438–446.

Criswell, J. H. A sociometric study of race cleavage in the classroom. *Archives of Psychology*, 1939, No. 235, 1–82.

Damon, W. *The social world of the child.* San Francisco: Jossey-Bass, 1977.

Deutsch, F. Observational and sociometric measures of peer popularity and their relationship to egocentric communication in female preschoolers. *Developmental Psychology*, 1974, *10*, 745–747.

Dor, A. K., & Asher, S. R. *Developmental changes in the correlates of sociometric status.* Unpublished manuscript, University of Illinois, in preparation.

Elkins, D. Some factors related to the choice status of ninety eighth-grade children in school society. *Genetic Psychology Monographs*, 1958, *58*, 202–272.

Evers, W. L., & Schwarz, J. C. Modifying social withdrawal in preschoolers: The effects of filmed modeling and teacher praise. *Journal of Abnormal Child Psychology*, 1973, *1*, 248–256.

Feinberg, M. R., Smith, M., & Schmidt, R. An analysis of expressions used by adolescents at varying economic levels to describe accepted and rejected peers. *Journal of Genetic Psychology*, 1958, *93*, 133–148.

Fine, G. A. Friends, impression management, and pre-adolescent behavior. In S. R. Asher & J. M. Gottman (Eds.), *The development of children's friendships.* New York: Cambridge University Press, 1981.

Freud, A., & Dann, S. An experiment in group upbringing. *Psychoanalytic Study of the Child*, 1951, *6*, 127–168.

Furman, W., Rahe, D. F., & Hartup, W. W. Rehabilitation of socially withdrawn children through mixed-age and same-age socialization. *Child Development,* 1979, *50,* 915–922.

Gottlieb, J., Semmel, M. I., & Veldman, D. J. Correlates of social status among mainstreamed mentally retarded children. *Journal of Educational Psychology,* 1978, *70,* 396–405.

Gottman, J. M. Toward a definition of social isolation in children. *Child Development,* 1977, *48,* 513–517.

Gottman, J., Gonso, J., & Rasmussen, B. Social interaction, social competence and friendship in children. *Child Development,* 1975, *46,* 709–718.

Gottman, J. M., & Parkhurst, J. T. A developmental theory of friendship and acquaintanceship processes. In A. Collins (Ed.), *Minnesota symposia on child psychology* (Vol. 13). Hillsdale, NJ: Erlbaum, 1980.

Greenwood, C. R., Walker, H. M., Todd, N. M., & Hops, H. *The utility of the peer nomination sociometric as a predictive variable in preschool social withdrawal* (Report No. 30). Eugene: Center at Oregon for Research in the Behavioral Education of the Handicapped, 1977.

Gronlund, N. E. *Sociometry in the classroom.* New York: Harper, 1959.

Gronlund, N. E., & Anderson, L. Personality characteristics of socially accepted, socially neglected, and socially rejected junior high school pupils. *Educational Administration and Supervision,* 1957, *43,* 329–338.

Harlow, H. F. Age-mate or peer affectional system. In D. S. Lehrman, R. A. Hinde, & E. Shaw (Eds.), *Advances in the study of behavior* (Vol. 2). New York: Academic Press, 1969.

Hartshorne, H., May, M. A., & Maller, J. B. *Studies in the nature of character: II. Studies in service and self-control.* New York: Macmillan, 1929.

Hartup, W. W. Peer interaction and social organization. In P. H. Mussen (Ed.), *Carmichael's manual of child psychology* (Vol. 2). New York: Wiley, 1970.

Hartup, W. W. Children and their friends. In H. McGurk (Ed.), *Issues in childhood social development.* London: Methuen, 1978.

Hartup, W. W. Peer relations and family relations: Two social worlds. In M. Rutter (Ed.), *Scientific foundations of developmental psychiatry.* London: Heinnemann Medical, 1980.

Hartup, W. W., Glazer, J. A., & Charlesworth, R. Peer reinforcement and sociometric status. *Child Development,* 1967, *38,* 1017–1024.

Hymel, S., & Asher, S. R. *Assessment and training of isolated children's social skills* (ERIC Document Service Reproduction Service No. ED 136 930). Paper presented at the biennial meeting of the Society for Research in Child Development, New Orleans, 1977.

Hymel, S., Tinsley, B. R., Asher, S. R., & Geraci, R. L. *Sociometric status and social skills: The initiating style of preschool children.* Unpublished manuscript, University of Illinois, 1981.

Jennings, K. D. People versus object orientation, social behavior, and intellectual abilities in children. *Developmental Psychology,* 1975, *11,* 511–519.

Kane, J. S., & Lawler, E. E., III., Methods of peer assessment, *Psychological Bulletin,* 1978, *85,* 555–586.

Koch, H. L. Popularity in preschool children: Some related factors and a technique for its measurement. *Child Development,* 1933, *4,* 164–175.

Kohn, M., & Clausen, J. Social isolation and schizophrenia. *American Sociological Review,* 1955, *20,* 265–273.

Kuhlen, R. G., & Lee, B. J. Personality characteristics and social acceptability in adolescence. *Journal of Educational Psychology,* 1943, *34,* 321–340.

Ladd, G. W., & Oden, S. The relationship between peer acceptance and children's ideas about helpfulness. *Child Development*, 1979, *50*, 402–408.

Lesser, G. S. The relationship between various forms of aggression and popularity among lower-class children. *Journal of Educational Psychology*, 1959, *50*, 20–25.

Lewis, M., & Schaeffer, S. Peer behavior and mother–infant interaction in maltreated children. In M. Lewis & L. Rosenblum (Eds.), *The uncommon child: The genesis of behavior* (Vol. 3). New York: Plenum, 1981.

Lippitt, R. Popularity among preschool children. *Child Development*, 1941, *12*, 305–332.

Livesley, W. J., & Bromley, D. B. *Person perception in childhood and adolescence.* London: Wiley, 1973.

MacFarlane, J. W., Honzik, M. P., & Davis, M. H. Reputation differences among young school children. *Journal of Educational Psychology*, 1937, *28*, 161–175.

Marshall, H. R. An evaluation of sociometric-social behavior research with preschool children. *Child Development*, 1957, *28*, 131–137.

Marshall, H. R., & McCandless, B. R. A study in prediction of social behavior of preschool children. *Child Development*, 1957, *28*, 149–159. (a)

Marshall, H. R., & McCandless, B. R. Relationships between dependence on adults and social acceptance by peers. *Child Development*, 1957, *28*, 413–419. (b)

McCandless, B. R., & Marshall, H. R. A picture sociometric technique for preschool children and its relation to teacher judgments of friendship. *Child Development*, 1957, *28*, 139–148. (a)

McCandless, B. R., & Marshall, H. R. Sex differences in social acceptance and participation of preschool children. *Child Development*, 1957, *28*, 421–425. (b)

McGuire, J. M. Aggression and sociometric status with preschool children. *Sociometry*, 1973, *36*, 542–549.

Moore, S. G. Correlates of peer acceptance in nursery school children. In W. W. Hartup & N. L. Smothergill (Eds.), *The young child*. Washington, DC: National Association for the Education of Young Children, 1967.

Moore, S. G. *A sociometric status test for young children: Manual of instructions.* Unpublished manuscript, University of Minnesota, 1973.

Moore, S. G., & Updegraff, R. Sociometric status of preschool children related to age, sex, nurturance giving, and dependency. *Child Development*, 1964, *35*, 519–524.

Moreno, J. L. *Who shall survive? A new approach to the problem of human interrelations.* Washington, DC: Nervous and Mental Disease Publishing, 1934.

O'Connor, R. D. Modification of social withdrawal through symbolic modeling. *Journal of Applied Behavior Analysis*, 1969, *2*, 15–22.

O'Connor, R. D. Relative efficacy of modeling, shaping, and the combined procedures for modification of social withdrawal. *Journal of Abnormal Psychology*, 1972, *79*, 327–334.

Oden, S., & Asher, S. R. Coaching children in social skills for friendship making. *Child Development*, 1977, *48*, 495–506.

Peevers, B. H., & Secord, P. F. Developmental changes in attribution of descriptive concepts to persons. *Journal of Personality and Social Psychology*, 1973, *27*, 120–128.

Pekarik, E. G., Prinz, R. J., Liebert, D. E., Weintraub, S., & Neale, J. M. The Pupil Evaluation Inventory: A sociometric technique for assessing children's social behavior. *Journal of Abnormal Child Psychology*, 1976, *4*, 83–97.

Putallaz, M., & Gottman, J. M. Social skills and group acceptance. In S. R. Asher & J. M. Gottman (Eds.), *The development of children's friendships*. New York: Cambridge University Press, 1981.

Roff, M. Childhood social interactions and young adult bad conduct. *Journal of Abnormal and Social Psychology*, 1961, *63*, 333–337.

Roff, M., Sells, S. B., & Golden, M. M. *Social adjustment and personality development in children*. Minneapolis: University of Minnesota Press, 1972.

Roistacher, R. C. A microeconomic model of sociometric choice. *Sociometry*, 1974, *37*, 219–238.

Rothenberg, B. B. Children's social sensitivity and the relationship to interpersonal competence, intrapersonal conflict, and intellectual level. *Developmental Psychology*, 1970, *2*, 335–350.

Sackett, G. P. (Ed.). *Observing behavior: Data collection and analysis*. Baltimore: University Park Press, 1978.

Scarlett, H. H., Press, A. N., & Crockett, W. H. Children's descriptions of peers: A Wernerian developmental analysis. *Child Development*, 1971, *42*, 439–453.

Schwarz, J. C. Effects of peer familiarity on the behavior of preschoolers in a novel situation. *Journal of Personality and Social Psychology*, 1972, *24*, 276–284.

Selman, R. The development of interpersonal reasoning. In A. Pick (Ed.), *Minnesota symposia on child psychology* (Vol. 10). Minneapolis: University of Minnesota Press, 1976.

Shaw, M. E. Changes in sociometric choices following forced integration of an elementary school. *Journal of Social Issues*, 1973, *29*(4), 143–157.

Singleton, L. C., & Asher, S. R. Peer preferences and social interaction among third-grade children in an integrated school district. *Journal of Educational Psychology*, 1977, *69*, 330–336.

Singleton, L. C., & Asher, S. R. Racial integration and children's peer preferences: An investigation of developmental and cohort differences. *Child Development*, 1979, *50*, 936–941.

Stengel, E. *Suicide and attempted suicide*. Middlesex: Penguin, 1971.

Suomi, S. J., & Harlow, H. F. The role and reason of peer relationships in rhesus monkeys. In M. Lewis & L. A. Rosenblum (Eds.), *Friendship and peer relations*. New York: Wiley, 1975.

Thompson, G. G., & Powell, M. An investigation of the rating-scale approach to the measurement of social status. *Educational and Psychological Measurement*, 1951, *11*, 440–455.

Tryon, C. M. Evaluations of adolescent personality by adolescents. *Monographs of the Society for Research in Child Development*, 1939, *4*, (4, Serial No. 23).

Tuddenham, R. D. Studies in reputation: I. Sex and grade differences in school children's evaluations of their peers. II. The diagnosis of social adjustment. *Psychological Monographs*, 1952, *66*, (1, Whole No. 333).

Ullmann, C. A. Teachers, peers and tests as predictors of adjustment. *Journal of Educational Psychology*, 1957, *48*, 257–267.

Vaughn, B. E., & Waters, E. *Attention structure, sociometric status and dominance: Interrelations, behavioral correlates and relationships to social competence*. Unpublished manuscript, University of California, Los Angeles, 1980.

Wagner, E. *Interpersonal behavior and peer status*. Paper presented at the biennial meeting of the Society for Research in Child Development, San Francisco, 1979.

Walder, L. O., Abelson, R. P., Eron, L. D., Banta, T. J., & Laulicht, J. H. Development of a peer-rating measure of aggression. *Psychological Reports*, 1961, *9*, 497–556.

Winder, C. L., & Wiggins, J. S. Social reputation and social behavior: A further validation of the Peer Nomination Inventory. *Journal of Abnormal and Social Psychology*, 1964, *68*, 681–684.

Yarrow, M. R., & Campbell, J. D. Person perception in children. *Merrill-Palmer Quarterly,* 1963, *9,* 57–72.

Youniss, J. Another perspective on social cognition. In A. Pick (Ed.), *Minnesota symposia on child psychology* (Vol. 9). Minneapolis: University of Minnesota Press, 1975.

Youniss, J. *Parents and peers in social development: A Sullivan–Piaget perspective.* Chicago: University of Chicago Press, 1980.

6

SOCIAL COMPETENCE AS A PROBLEM-SOLVING SKILL

MYRNA B. SHURE

MYRNA B. SHURE is Professor of Psychology in the Department of Mental Health Sciences, The Hahnemann Medical College and Hospital. Shure, Spivack, and their colleagues have done groundbreaking work in the area of social competence. Their research is cited frequently by investigators in the area, including many of the other authors in this volume. Shure has coauthored three books in the area of interpersonal cognitive problem solving, has created problem-solving training programs and tests to evaluate them, and has authored or coauthored numerous journal articles and book chapters in this area.

In the present chapter, Shure refers briefly to her previous work on social competence. The bulk of the contribution is, however, focused on a highly innovative and effective program using teachers and mothers in the development of social competence in children. This program is representative of the movement toward community-based educational programs for the enhancement of human competencies.

A PROBLEM-SOLVING VIEW OF SOCIAL COMPETENCE

What do we mean when we say a person is, or is not, socially competent? Are we referring to how that person *acts* when relating to others? We believe that social competence can also be viewed in light of how people *think,* because in the interpersonal world, how they think can dramatically affect what they do.

This chapter will highlight particular kinds of thought processes, those of how people think through and solve typical everyday problems that come up with others. To the extent that interpersonal cognitive processes precede action, and that good problem-solvers are better adjusted and more socially competent than poor ones, we can begin to envision social competence as a problem-solving skill, not just in adults, but as far as we can measure it, in children as young as 4 years of age.

According to Spivack (1973), an individual who plans his or her actions, can weigh the pros and cons, and consider the effects of interpersonal acts upon others is less likely to fail and make impulsive mistakes, and thereby suffers less frustration. If problem after problem should remain unresolved, and interpersonal needs remain consistently unsatisfied, maladaptive behavior and other social difficulties could subsequently ensue. Just as it seems reasonable to assume that one's ability to think is facilitated *by* emotional relief, it seems equally reasonable to assume that ability to think may facilitate emotional relief.

One process of thought, that of "means–ends" thinking, includes ability to plan, step-by-step, ways to reach an interpersonal goal. As part of this process, one considers potential obstacles that could interfere with reaching that goal, and also recognizes that problem resolution does not always occur immediately. Another process involves the spontaneous tendency to weigh the pros and cons of transgression, a form of consequential thinking. A series of studies have shown that means–ends thinking skills significantly distinguish normals from the diagnostically disturbed or behaviorally troubled beginning at about age 9, while a spontaneous tendency to weigh pros and cons of an act emerges as significant to behavior during the adolescent years. (A complete review of these and other social thinking skills is detailed in Spivack, Platt, & Shure, 1976.)

After an initial series of correlational studies with the above-mentioned age groups, we decided to test the assumption that problem-solving thinking skills were an antecedent to and not merely a result of social adjustment. An intervention program could test this assumption by altering problem-solving thinking ability, and then observing whether those who most improve in the trained cognitive skills would also be those who most improve in social adjustment and interpersonal competence. Recognizing the service value as well as the theoretical significance of such intervention, and that early training might yield optimal potential for primary prevention, we searched for the earliest age that such skills could distinguish normal youngsters displaying more than average amounts of behavioral difficult-ies from those who were not. We were able to identify such skills in children at age 4.

Four-year-olds could not plan sequential means to reach a goal, but they could conceive of alternative ways to solve problems by naming different types or categories of solutions. Spontaneous weighing of pros and cons to an act was beyond the developmental level of a 4-year-old, but if specifically asked, they could describe what might happen next or what another person might do or say if an act were carried out. We found that 4-year-olds who could generate al-ternative solutions to interpersonal peer- and authority-type prob-lems were likely to display relatively well-adjusted behaviors. Poor problem-solvers were likely to display behaviors characteristic of im-pulsivity or inhibition, to show little concern for or even awareness of others in distress, and were less liked by their peers.

Youngsters who actually carried out acts of impulsivity, such as hitting children or grabbing toys, were more deficient than their better-adjusted peers in their consequential thinking skills, but inter-estingly, could think of more potential consequences to such acts than could the socially inhibited (Shure, Newman, & Silver, 1973; Shure & Spivack, 1975a; Spivack & Shure, 1974). If impulsive chil-dren recognize that they might get hit back after hitting another to obtain a toy, they might might not let that stop them for one of two possible reasons: (1) they might be reacting emotionally to frustra-tion, or (2) they cannot, or do not, think of something else to do. Inhib-ited children may have experienced failure so often that they just need to withdraw from people and from problems they cannot solve. Perhaps these youngsters need not think about what to do or what might happen next because, other than to watch others play or to play by themselves, they rarely *do* anything at all.

Robin, a good problem-solver and well-adjusted child, was seen exercising *her* skills. She wanted Melissa to give her the water cup (containing plant seeds). When Melissa said, "No, I need them" (the seeds), Robin did not create a new problem by reacting impulsively. Her ability to think of other options led her to another tactic. "When I get the big bike, I'll let you ride it." Defiantly, Melissa shouted, "I said NO!" Robin then asked, "What are you going to do with those seeds?" and Melissa answered, "Grow them." A few minutes later, Robin returned with a sand shovel, and offered "I'll bury some and you bury some. Two of the flowers can be yours and two can be mine. How's that?" Melissa and Robin began to count the seeds, each bury-ing "their own" in the dirt. Like other good problem-solvers, Robin may have *thought* about hitting, or grabbing the cup from Melissa. She may also have been able to anticipate the consequences of such acts. But her ability to find out about the other child's motives and incorporate them into a solution that ended successfully prevented Robin from experiencing frustration and failure.

Having learned that alternative-solution thinking relates most strongly to social adjustment in young children, followed by consequential thinking, a series of questions were asked to test the efficacy of the problem-solving approach to social adjustment and interpersonal competence:

1. Can such thinking skills be taught?

2. Do such skills mediate adjustment?

3. Would the effects of such training last?

4. What is the optimal amount and timing of training?

5. What is the impact of the mother's thinking skills on the child?

6. Can mothers and teachers function as equally effective training agents?

How training by teachers and mothers affected the interpersonal cognitive problem-solving (ICPS) skills and subsequent behavior of young children will form the central focus of this chapter. We believe these skills will add to our understanding of the thinking processes that move a young child to act.

THE TRAINING PROGRAM

The format of the program is a script, first developed for use by nursery teachers (Shure & Spivack, 1971; Spivack & Shure, 1974), with the content upgraded in sophistication for use in kindergarten (Shure & Spivack, 1974a/1978), and modified for flexible use with a single child at home (Shure & Spivack, 1975c, 1978). The scripts are divided into daily 20-minute lessons that take about 3 months to complete. The goal is to teach children how (but not what) to think so that they can learn to solve their own problems, in their own way.

Formal Sequenced Games

To increase children's ICPS skills, games are sequenced, and begin with simple word concepts built in for later association with problem solving. For example, the word "not" is taught so children can later decide what and what *not* to do, and whether an idea is or is *not* a good one. The word "or" helps children understand that there is more than one way to solve a problem: "I can do this *or* I can do that." The word "different" helps to think of alternatives, that is, of *different* things to do. Identification of and sensitivity to people's feelings is vital in problem solving. Children learn that there is more than one way to find out what people like and how they feel—by watching what they do, hearing what they say, and asking if they are not sure. To help children understand the effect of their behavior on others, and of others' behavior on them, games focus on why children might feel as they do: "Peter's mad *because* I took his toy.'

After mastering these described skills, children are presented with pictures and puppets depicting interpersonal problem situations and asked for all the ways they can think of for the portrayed child to, for example, "have a turn to feed the animals." All solutions are accepted equally (e.g., forceful ones such as "hit" or "grab the food," and nonforceful ones such as "say please" or "I'll be your friend"). In subsequent games, the children evaluate for themselves why an idea is or is not a good one.

Informal Problem-Solving Communication (Dialoguing)

In addition to the formal sequenced games, teachers and parents are taught how to apply problem-solving techniques of communication when real problems come up. If, for example, a child grabs a toy from another, the adult is taught to elicit (1) the child's view of the problem; (2) how each child feels about it; (3) what happened when he or she grabbed the toy; and (4) what else the child can do so the problem can be resolved without negative consequences. As in the formal program, solutions are not suggested or demanded; the child is guided to define the problem, what might have led up to it, and to consider options and consequences. In this way, children can develop a style of thinking such that if their first idea fails, they will not give up too soon, but rather, will think again and try another solution before reacting with impulsivity, frustration, or withdrawal.

Before training, one teacher could not get Daniel to stop grabbing toys from children.

TEACHER: Daniel, why did you grab that shovel from Jamie?

CHILD: He never shares.

TEACHER: You can't grab toys. Jamie doesn't like that. You should ask.

CHILD: It's not fair. He won't give it to me.

TEACHER: If you grab like that, he won't play with you anymore.

CHILD: I don't care.

TEACHER: Daniel, I told you to ask him for it.

(Daniel asked, was refused, and either in frustration, or by decision, hit Jamie.)

Why did this teacher bother to ask why? No matter what Daniel had said, this teacher would no doubt have said what she said anyway: "You can't grab." A command was issued. "Jamie doesn't like that." Daniel didn't care. "You should ask." She told him what to do. When told the consequences, "He won't play with you anymore," Daniel didn't care about that either. The end result of Daniel's hitting Jamie now created a new problem, and the power play began all over again. If a child does comply, how often is it just a solution to another problem—how to get rid of the demanding adult?

After training, the same teacher handled a similar problem this way:

TEACHER: Shelly, what happened when you grabbed that doll from Tasha?

CHILD: She snatched it back.

TEACHER: And what else happened?

CHILD: She hit me.

(Teacher guides child to consider consequences.)

TEACHER: How did that make you feel?

CHILD: Mad.

TEACHER: How do you think Tasha feels?

CHILD: Mad.

(Teacher guides child to think of own and other's feelings.)

TEACHER: You're mad and Tasha's mad. Can you think of a *different* way to get Tasha to let you have that doll?

CHILD: But she said no. And I want it!

TEACHER: If you try real hard, I bet you can think of an idea.

(Teacher encouraging child not to give up.)

CHILD: *(to Tasha)* Let's have a puppet show. We can take turns holding it [the doll].

(Tasha agreed, if she could go first.)

This kind of communication, which we call "problem-solving dialoguing," led not only to satisfaction for both children, but their beaming expression suggested a sense of pride for having thought of their own solution.

In situations wherein children cannot have what they want, they are encouraged to think of something different to do that will satisfy their needs. Sherry asked her teacher if she could go outside, at what Sherry knew was an inconvenient time. When asked if she could think of something she could do inside for now, she thought for a moment (an important step in itself) and then said, "I'll play with Tammy." Had the teacher *suggested* she play with Tammy, Sherry would no doubt have whined, "I don't want to play with Tammy; I want to go outside." A child is much more likely to carry out his or her *own* idea than one suggested or demanded by an adult, making the otherwise inevitable power play unnecessary. Thus, our aim is to help children learn how to problem solve when the goal is obtainable, and how to cope with the frustration when it is not.

The impact of the formal training, used in combination with problem-solving techniques of communication (dialogues), was evaluated systematically over a 4-year period, 2 years of which training agents were teachers, and 2 of which they were mothers.

THE STUDY DESIGN

Children trained by teachers were followed throughout a 2-year period: in nursery (Project Year 1), and in kindergarten (Project Year 2). In Project Years 3 and 4, two different samples of nursery children were trained by their mothers at home. To evaluate the effect of mother-training, these children attended schools in which teachers had no knowledge of the program or its goals.

Training Agents and Recipients

Year 1: Teacher-training; nursery. Of 219 black inner-city 4-year-olds (mean age, 4.3) attending federally funded day-care programs, 113 were trained. Equated in sex distribution, IQ, ICPS scores, and behavioral adjustment level, the remaining 106 youngsters served as controls.

Year 2: Teacher-training; kindergarten. Of the original Year 1 nursery children, 131 remained available for both pre- and postkindergarten testing, and were divided into four groups: Group 1

($n = 39$) were trained both years; Group 2 ($n = 30$), who were trained in nursery, were not trained in kindergarten; Group 3 ($n = 35$) were nursery controls who were trained in kindergarten; and Group 4 ($n = 27$) served as controls both years.

Year 3: Mother-training; nursery (pilot). Twenty inner-city mothers and their 4-year-old children (7 boys and 13 girls) were trained, compared to 113 youngsters previously trained by nursery teachers, and compared to 106 nursery youngsters not trained at all. Youngsters attended federally funded day-care centers, but the centers were different from those in which teachers had been trained.

Year 4: Mother-training; nursery. Inner-city mother–child pairs (40) were tested before and after intervention. Of these pairs, 20 received training, and 20 matched pairs served as controls. Children in both groups consisted of 10 boys and 10 girls, and again, were from federally funded day-care centers.

Pre-Post Measures: Children

All cognitive tests were administered individually by the research staff. Teacher-trained children and their controls (studied over 2 years) received the test battery a total of four times: prior to and immediately following nursery training, and prior to and immediately following kindergarten training. Any possible warm-up effects were negated because all children received an equal number of test exposures. Mother-trained children and controls received the test battery before and after training. Scores obtained on the pilot mother-trained group were compared to the nursery teacher-trained group and controls after they had received the same number of testing sessions (two). Teachers' behavior ratings, obtained for both school- and home-trained children, were completed during the administration of the cognitive tests, and for teacher-trained youngsters, again at the end of first grade. All measures used in the 4-year period are described in detail in Shure and Spivack (1975a). Those maintained throughout are described briefly, below.

PRESCHOOL INTERPERSONAL PROBLEM-SOLVING (PIPS) TEST

PIPS measures the child's ability to conceptualize relevant *alternative solutions* to two types of problems: (1) one child wants a toy another child has, and (2) a child wants to avert mother's anger after having damaged something of value. Supplemented with pictures, the child was shown two child characters, one of whom was depicted as playing with a toy. The child was then asked: "What can [A] do so [B] will let [him or her] have a chance to play with this [drum]?" After one solution was given, such as "Ask him," two new child characters and a new toy were shown, and the procedure repeated. Each child was shown at least seven different toys, but if seven different solutions were given, new toys were added until no further ideas could be offered. Shifting child characters and toys was employed to maintain the child's interest. Each new toy appeared to be a new story, but in fact, the child was being asked to name different solutions to the same basic problem. The mother-problem stories followed the same procedure, shifting from a child character having broken a flower pot to having scratched a table, and the like. With each child having been given four opportunities per toy and per object broken or damaged, all repetitions or enumerations of earlier solutions and irrelevant responses were recorded to control for test verbosity. A child's PIPS score consisted of the total number of different, relevant solutions given to the peer- and mother-type problems, correlated at the .01 level. (A complete manual is available in Shure & Spivack, 1974b.)

WHAT HAPPENS NEXT GAME (WHNG)

WHNG measures the child's ability to conceptualize potential consequences to two types of acts: (1) grabbing a toy from another child, and (2) taking an object from an adult without first asking permission. The procedure was the same as that of the PIPS test, in that toys grabbed and objects taken were switched after each new consequence, or four repetitions or irrelevant responses were given. A child's WHNG score consisted of the total number of consequences given to the two types of stories, correlated at the .01 level.

HAHNEMANN PRE-SCHOOL BEHAVIOR (HPSB)
RATING SCALE

HPSB measures overt behaviors as rated by teachers in school. The scale has been shown to validly classify children into one of three behavioral categories: (1) *impulsive,* defined by items describing nagging and demanding of adults, impatience with children (e.g., grabbing toys), overemotionality in the face of frustration, and/or aggressive/dominating behaviors; (2) *inhibited,* defined as inability to stand up for one's rights, too little expression of feelings, and/or timidity or fear so intense as to not allow for even normal amounts of aggression; (3) *adjusted,* defined by ratings not showing inhibition, and not showing ratings of impulsivity above that of a statistically defined normal range. Other items include the degree to which the child showed overt concern or awareness of others in distress, how well liked the child appeared to be, and the extent to which he or she displayed initiative and autonomy in the classroom.

Pre–Post Measures: Mothers

Each mother was given a 2-hour interview. Measures of particular importance are presented briefly below (and illustrated in full in Shure & Spivack, 1978). Other measures administered in the 2-year period of parent research are detailed in Shure and Spivack (1975a).

CHILDREARING STYLE

Each mother was given six general categories of typical problems that arise during an average day, such as a child wanting something that the mother does not want him or her to have, the child refusing a request, and the like. Once the content of the problem was stated (by the mother), she was asked to relate, as best as she could remember, everything that was said or done by both herself and her child (in dialogue form). While no claim is made that mothers always reported exact details of what actually happened (though that was the stated intent), their reports were still an indication of their capacity to think about handling problems that came up.

A scale was devised to measure the extent to which mothers tended to help their children articulate the problem and explore their own solutions and consequences. Each statement was scored from 0 to 100, at 5-point intervals. Attempts by the mother to guide her child to think of his or her own solutions to the problem or consequences of an act (e.g., "What might happen if you do that?" "What else can you think of to do?") were scored at the highest end of the scale. Also scored very high were attempts to elicit from the child his or her feelings (e.g., "How do you think that makes him [or her] feel when you do that?"). Distinguished from these questions, and scored in the high-middle range, were *offered* solutions or consequences, but accompanied by real explanations and conversation with the child (e.g., "When you take things, she [or he] gets mad." "If you keep snatching toys, someone's going to get hurt.") Suggestions of solutions with no follow-up explanation (e.g., "Why don't you try asking, instead of hitting?") were scored in the middle range. At the lower end of the scale were abstract simple explanations (e.g., "We don't hit friends." "We don't hit friends smaller than we are.") and simply telling the child what to do in a demanding and/or authoritative tone (e.g., "I told you to write on paper.") Still lower were simple commands (e.g., "Wait 'till I'm finished." "Give that toy back!") At the lowest extreme (score 0) were threats, name calling, force, or evidence of a complete lack of communication with the child about the problem (e.g., "I'll talk to the teacher about [your being hit so much].").

A mother's childrearing score consisted of the overall mean of scored statements averaged for each problem.

MEANS–ENDS THINKING: CHILD-RELATED PROBLEM STORIES

Each mother was given the beginning and the end of a story depicting hypothetical problems between a mother and her child, or between two children, and then asked to make up a story connecting the beginning and the end. In one story, for example, a child is depicted as unhappy, and not wanting to go out and play with friends, and ends with the child happy and out playing with the friends. Scored were the number of *means* to the stated goal (e.g., "Get him a toy and he'll want to go out and show it to the kids."); the number of *obstacles* conceptualized (e.g., "But she can't afford a new toy right now"; or "He's afraid the kids would break it."); and the number of statements recognizing that problem resolution might take *time* (e.g., "For three days we talked about it and he finally went out and talked with the kids.").

Based on intercorrelations significant at the .01 level, a mother's score consisted of the total number of *means* (regardless of content) and obstacles for three stories at pretest, and three different ones at posttest. Statements of time occurred too rarely to be scored.

Intercoder reliability met acceptable standards for all cognitive measures, ranging from correlations of .90 (mother's childrearing style) to .96 (child's PIPS solution score). Interrater reliability of the behavior rating scales by teachers and their classroom aides reached 86% agreement (pretest), 88% posttest.

RESEARCH EVALUATION

Three general research issues were of interest: (1) the effects of nursery and/or kindergarten *teacher* training (both practical questions of intervention and the theoretical test of ICPS skills as behavioral mediators); (2) mother's impact on the child's ICPS skills; and (3) the effects of *mother* training, including a replication of the mediational function of ICPS skills on behavior. (Complete details and tables are presented in Shure & Spivack, 1975a.)

Teacher Training

EFFECTS OF NURSERY TRAINING

Project Year 1, nursery-trained youngsters improved significantly more than controls in both PIPS solution score, $F(1, 213) = 106.90$, $p < .001$, and in the number of consequences given from pre- to post-testing, $F(1, 213) = 23.80$, $p < .001$ (see Table 1). Score increases were not a function of willingness to try, as no significant relationships occurred between score change and test verbosity (repetitions, enumerations, irrelevancies). Regarding behavior, 22 of 44 (or 50%) of the initially impulsive youngsters were rated adjusted following training, significantly more than the 8 of 39 (or 21%) of the controls, $\chi^2(1) = 6.56$, $p < .01$. In the initially inhibited group, 21 of 28, or 75%, were rated adjusted at posttest, compared to only 6 of 17, or 35%, of the controls, $\chi^2 = 5.39$, $p < .05$. With no starting point differences, both ICPS and behavioral changes occurred independent of sex, general verbal skills, and IQ (Stanford-Binet).

Having discovered that solution and consequential thinking can be taught, and that trained children's behavior improved, the question of real importance is whether those who improved in the trained ICPS skills were the same as those whose behavior improved (the direct link). As shown in Table 2, this direct link was stronger for PIPS solutions than for consequences. Importantly, improvement in both solution and consequential thinking occurred independently of initial IQ, or IQ change, and within a wide range (70–120+) children were clearly able to benefit from exposure to ICPS training (Shure & Spivack, 1973, 1980; Spivack & Shure, 1974).

In the *kindergarten* (Project Year 2), three questions were asked: (1) Would nursery training effects last throughout kindergarten without further reinforcement? (2) Would training for the first time in kindergarten be effective? (3) What is the optimal amount and timing of training?

LASTING EFFECTS

Six-month follow-up included all still-available Year 1 nursery-trained and control youngsters, because tests and behavior ratings were obtained before new training had begun. One-year follow-up included Group 2 (trained—nursery and control—kindergarten, also called

TABLE 1. Pre- and Posttests of Two ICPS Skills in Three Comparison Groups

| Group | | PIPS solutions[a] | | | | WHNG consequences[a] | | | |
| | | Train | | Control | | Train | | Control | |
		Pre	Post	Pre	Post	Pre	Post	Pre	Post
Nursery–teacher Ss, Year 1	$\bar{x}$	4.74	10.04	5.34	6.09	4.74	6.90	5.28	5.52
	SD	(2.79)	(3.03)	(2.61)	(2.75)	(2.24)	(2.15)	(2.37)	(2.18)
	n	113	113	106	106	113	113	106	106
Kindergarten–teacher Ss, Year 2	$\bar{x}$	7.63	12.34	8.11	8.33	6.46	9.74	6.59	6.59
	SD	(2.20)	(2.75)	(2.33)	(2.08)	(1.60)	(2.06)	(2.36)	(1.74)
	n	35	35	27	27	34[b]	34[b]	26[b]	26[b]
Nursery–mother Ss, Year 4[c]	$\bar{x}$	4.00	8.85	3.95	4.95	4.25	7.30	4.80	5.65
	SD	(2.58)	(3.23)	(2.37)	(2.04)	(1.97)	(2.03)	(2.19)	(1.79)
	n	20	20	20	20	20	20	20	20

Note. At pretest, no significant differences on either measure, either year occurred. Table abstracted from Shure (1979, p. 42).

[a] No ceiling in scores.

[b] One less child received WHNG than PIPS, as that child left school before testing was completed.

[c] Pilot Year 3 mother-trained Ss not included as no matched controls were examined.

TABLE 2. Mean Gain in Two ICPS Skills for Initially Aberrant Training Ss Who Did and Did Not Improve in Behavioral Adjustment

	Behavior improved			Behavior not improved					
ICPS	$\bar{x}$ gain	SD	n	$\bar{x}$ gain	SD	n	t	df	p
PIPS solutions									
Nursery–teacher[a]	7.83	(2.14)	43	4.14	(2.46)	29	6.78	70	.001
Kindergarten–teacher[a]	6.36	(2.87)	14	2.51	(1.64)	6	3.05	18	.01
Nursery–mother[a,b]	5.58	(1.88)	12	3.20	(1.09)	5	2.62	15	.05
WHNG consequences									
Nursery–teacher	3.12	(2.92)	43	1.97	(2.05)	29	1.61	70	.06[d]
Kindergarten–teacher	4.38	(3.18)	13[c]	1.00	(1.26)	6	2.54	17[c]	.05
Nursery–mother	3.85	(1.73)	12	2.60	(1.95)	5	1.03	15	NS

Note. From Shure (1979, p. 44).
[a]Nursery–teacher, trained in school; kindergarten–teacher, trained in school; nursery–mother, trained at home, attended school.
[b]Second group of trained mothers only; first group (pilot group) did not have enough initially aberrant Ss for analyses.
[c]One child did not receive the consequences test.
[d]One-tailed test.

nursery-only—trained) and Group 4 (control—nursery and control—kindergarten, also called never-trained controls). With no significant starting point differences for either measure prior to nursery training (fall, nursery), trained groups were significantly higher than controls immediately following training (spring, nursery), 6 months later (fall, kindergarten), and 1 year later (spring, kindergarten). While controls did gain in solutions over time, youngsters trained in nursery but *not* kindergarten showed no loss over time, and controls never caught up to trained children. (For actual scores, see Shure & Spivack, 1975a; 1979.)

With about 40% of all youngsters having been rated adjusted at fall, nursery, 83% of those trained were judged so immediately following training, 86% 6 months later, and 77% a full year following termination of formal training (no significant decrease). The controls showed no significant increase at any time, with 41% adjusted immediately after training, 42% 6 months later, and 30% (a slight decrease) 1 year following the intervention. Rated by different teachers in kindergarten than in nursery, teachers who were unaware of the nursery experiment and of children's previous behavior, the data clearly indicate that trained youngsters maintained adjusted behaviors significantly more than controls over time.

Analyses of these two groups also revealed that 25 of 27, or 93%, of Year 1 nursery-trained children *not* showing behavioral difficulties remained adjusted 6 months after training, as compared to only 18 of 27, or 67%, of comparable controls, $CR = 2.37, p < .05$. This finding reveals the program's preventive effects in addition to those indicating its ability to help those already displaying behavioral difficulties. Even though n was reduced for full-year follow-up (given attrition and given that about half the remaining Year 1 nursery-trained children were retrained in kindergarten, Year 2), it is encouraging for the prevention issue that of the nine nursery-only–trained-group youngsters who *began* nursery as *adjusted*, eight remained so through the end of kindergarten (89%), compared to five of nine never-trained controls (56%).

EFFECTS OF KINDERGARTEN TRAINING

In these analyses, Group 3 youngsters (control—nursery, trained—kindergarten) were compared to Group 4 youngsters (never-trained controls). Results (in Table 1) revealed that clear benefits could be gained by ICPS exposure in the kindergarten year. Year 2 kindergarten-trained youngsters improved significantly more than controls in

PIPS solution score, $F(1, 58) = 35.11$, $p < .05$, and in their consequences score, $F(1, 57) = 24.44$, $p < .001$. Regarding behavior, 14 of 20 (or 70%) who began the kindergarten year as aberrant (impulsive or inhibited) were judged to be adjusted, compared to only 1 of 16 controls, $\chi^2(1) = 12.36$, $p < .01$. As shown in Table 2, the direct linkage between ICPS and behavioral improvement remained strongest for PIPS solution thinking, though this linkage for consequential thinking was stronger in the kindergarten than in the nursery year. These findings (Shure & Spivack, 1980) suggest that consequential thinking as a behavioral mediator is developmentally more suitable for kindergarten- than for nursery-aged youngsters, and should be especially emphasized in training that age group.

AMOUNT AND TIMING OF TRAINING

Given that ICPS training was effective either year, differential effects of amount and timing of training were examined by comparing ICPS and behavioral adjustment of all four above-described groups.

With appropriate pretest controls, Table 3 shows that at the end of kindergarten, 2-year trained youngsters were significantly superior to all other groups in their PIPS solution and, except for the kindergarten-only—trained, in their consequential scores. The never-trained were significantly more deficient than all other groups in both skills, while no differences occurred between the nursery-only

TABLE 3. Two ICPS Skills at Spring (Kindergarten) in Four Comparison Groups

		Group			
ICPS		Trained Nu + Ki	Trained Nu	Trained Ki	Control Nu + Ki
PIPS	$\bar{x}$	$16.46_{xy}{}^a$	11.53_x	12.34_x	8.33_{xy}
solutions	SD	(4.66)	(3.13)	(2.75)	(2.08)
	n	39	30	35	27
WHNG	$\bar{x}$	10.74_x	9.03_x	9.74_y	6.59_{xy}
consequences	SD	(2.58)	(2.43)	(2.06)	(1.74)
	n	39	30	34^b	26^b

Note. There were no significant pretest differences between any groups at the first measuring period of fall–nursery, 1 year earlier. Table abstracted from Shure (1979, p. 43).

[a]Within each row, means with the same subscripts are significantly different at at least .05, Newman–Keuls.

[b]One less child received WHNG than PIPS.

and kindergarten-only—trained groups. Regardless of starting point, the percentage of adjusted children at the end of kindergarten was similar in all trained groups (77%–88%), and each was significantly greater than the 30% of never-trained youngsters who showed such behavior. Examining those who *began* nursery as either impulsive or as inhibited, only 19% of the never-trained controls improved to the adjusted category, significantly fewer than any of the trained groups (70%–88%). Percentages in behavior classification remained similar at the end of still another year, the first grade (Shure & Spivack, 1975a, 1979, 1980).

For 4- and 5-year-old children, the data suggest that with respect to the ultimate criterion goal—behavioral adjustment—1 year of training is as beneficial as 2, and ICPS exposure is equally effective either year (Shure & Spivack, 1979). Given the evidence of holding power, however, it is clear that youngsters begin kindergarten at a better behavioral vantage point if trained a year earlier, in nursery.

Mother's (Natural) Impact on Child's ICPS Skills

Having learned that ICPS skills can be taught by teachers in school, and that acquisition through those channels can significantly enhance social adjustment, the next question focused on why some children enter nursery school with relatively well-developed ICPS skills and others do not.

In the first study (Spivack & Shure, 1975), it was revealed that girls learn a significant portion of their ICPS skills from their mother. Boys, equal to girls in their ICPS ability, appeared to learn these skills through some other channel. It appeared that a mother's ability to solve adult problems influenced her childrearing style, that is, the extent to which she helped her child solve real problems that came up. It also appeared that her childrearing style in turn affected her daughter's (but not son's) ICPS skills.

To determine whether the differential impact of the mother on sex of the child occurred by chance, the study was repeated with 80 mothers and their 4-year-olds, 40 boys and 40 girls (Shure & Spivack, 1978).

A new measure for mothers was introduced, that of the previously described means–ends ability to solve hypothetical *child*-related problems. We learned that a mother's ability to solve child-related problems (e.g., two kids end up happy after a fight) had more direct impact on how she handled actual problems (childrearing style) than was true of her ability to solve adult-related problems (such as how to keep a friend from being angry after showing up too late to go to a movie). Mother's child-related means–ends problem-solving ability *and* her childrearing style related most to her child's ICPS skills, but again, primarily in daughters, not sons (see Table 4). Partial correlations revealed however, that it was the mother's childrearing style that had the most direct impact on her daughter's ICPS skills.

One might conjecture that boys acquire ICPS skills from their fathers, but in the present samples, nearly 75% of them came from father-absent homes. Flaherty (1978), who studied inner-city 5-year-olds from 30 intact families, found the same significant relationships between mothers and their daughters, but none between fathers and either their daughters or their sons. While it is still not known where boys acquire their ICPS skills (they were not more deficient in such skills than girls), the question became whether mothers could learn to be effective training agents for their children, and whether systematic ICPS intervention at home could equally affect the thinking skills and behavioral adjustment of boys and of girls. (For further discussion of natural parental impact on the child's ICPS skills, see Shure & Spivack, 1978.)

TABLE 4. Relationship of Mother's Childrearing Style and ICPS Skills to Child's ICPS Skills

| | Child's measures | | | |
| | PIPS solutions | | WHNG consequences | |
Mother's measures	Boys ($n = 40$)	Girls ($n = 40$)	Boys ($n = 40$)	Girls ($n = 40$)
Childrearing style	−.03	.68***	.14	.52**
Means–ends (child-related problems)	.03	.61***	.34*	.41**
Means–ends (adult-related problems)	.28	.21	.12	−.02
Alternative solutions (adult problems)	.24	.42**	.30	.33*

*p < .05
**p < .01
***p < .001

Mother Training

In Project Year 3, pilot-group mothers participated in the training for the first time. Their function was to learn the formal program script (via weekly meetings), and then to administer the formal games to their child at home on a daily 20-minute schedule for a 3-month period. The mothers were also taught how to apply informal problem-solving dialogues when real problems came up, and were encouraged to allow the child to generate his or her own solutions and consequences when possible.

Behavior gain (as observed by teachers in school) was encouraging, as 6 of 8 (75%) of the initially aberrant youngsters were rated adjusted following training, about the same as 43 of 72 (60%) of nursery-, teacher-trained youngsters, and both were greater than the 14 of 56 (25%) of nursery controls. Both teacher-trained and mother-trained 4-year-olds improved in PIPS solutions and consequential thinking more than their controls: $F(2, 233) = 27.30, p < .001; F(2, 232) = 10.10, p < .001$, respectively. Encouragingly, boys and girls improved equally. However, the overall improvement of PIPS scores, reflecting the most important of the behavioral mediators, was shown by Newman–Keuls to be significantly *less* among initially aberrant mother-trained than among comparable teacher-trained children.

Given the above-described findings of the pilot year (Shure & Spivack, 1975a), we decided to train mothers' ICPS skills and ask how (and if) change in mothers' ICPS skills and childrearing style would affect their children's ICPS skills and/or behavior (Shure & Spivack, 1978).

Before training, many mothers were just as preoccupied with their own needs ("You must learn to share your toys.") as their children were with theirs ("But I did share, now I want it back!"). Given this, goals for each mother in Project Year 4 were (1) to increase sensitivity that the child's point of view may differ from her own; (2) to help her recognize that there is more than one way to solve a problem; (3) to increase sensitivity that *thinking* about what is happening may, in the long run, be more beneficial than immediate action to stop it; and (4) to help her provide a model of problem-solving thinking—a thinking parent might inspire a child to think. Exercises for parents were strategically interspersed throughout the program script, designed to parallel skills they would be transmitting to their child. As parents learned to problem solve, they also developed an appreciation for the learning process their child was experiencing.

Relative to matched controls, trained mothers improved in both ability to solve hypothetical child-related problems, $F(1,36) = 25.32$, $p < .001$, and in childrearing style, $F(1, 36) = 51.22$, $p < .001$, with equal increase occurring in mothers of boys and mothers of girls. Here is how a trained mother created a means–ends story about a hypothetical child who has been saying no a lot lately.

> Michelle told her mother the kids tease her 'cause she was too fat. She (the mother) knew Michelle was too fat, but it took something like this to do something about it. So she said she'd take her to the doctor (*mean*). Michelle screamed, "No, I don't like doctors" (*obstacle*). "Do you want to get thin so your friends will play with you?" (*mean*). Michelle, very upset, screamed again, "I don't want to go to the doctor!" After Michelle calmed down, her mother asked her what she could do to get thin (*mean*). She said she wouldn't eat candy and cookies (*mean*). Her mother said that was good. "Now, what are you going to do about your friends?" (*mean*). Michelle told her friends she was going to get thin. She (Michelle) made a game of it with the kids (*mean*), and they all played happy again. (Shure & Spivack, 1978, p. 176)

This subject mother recognized a potential obstacle that could interfere with reaching the goal, but did not portray the story mother as insisting on "going to the doctor." Waiting for the child to calm down, conceptualizing time delay, the story mother allowed the child to think it through, and accepted the solutions the child chose. Importantly, mothers who best learned to plan step-by-step means to solve a child-related problem, who were most likely to anticipate potential obstacles (that problem solving is not always smooth sailing), and who allowed a hypothetical child to generate solutions and consequences, were also most likely to apply the earlier-illustrated problem-solving (dialogue) techniques of communication (i.e., increase childrearing style score) when real problems would arise, $r(18) = .54$, $p < .05$. Together, these newly acquired skills of the mother had significant impact on the child's ICPS skills, especially PIPS solution scores: childrearing, $r(18) = .45$, $p < .05$; child-related means–ends problem solving, $r(18) = .53$, $p < .05$.

Not only did the school behavior of trained youngsters significantly improve over the controls, $CR = 2.26$, $p < .05$, but as is true of the teacher-training studies, Table 2 shows that the strongest linkage between ICPS and behavior occurred for alternative-solution thinking as measured by the PIPS test. Again, boys and girls benefited equally in both ICPS and behavior change when trained by their mothers at home. But most importantly, children trained by mothers taught ICPS skills of their own improved in PIPS solution scores more than did those trained by mothers who were not (Shure & Spivack, 1978), suggesting maximum benefits of home training when both mother and child are taught how to think.

INTERPRETATIONS OF FINDINGS

A new approach to social adjustment and interpersonal competence has been supported by a theoretically based intervention program designed to enhance ability of young children to think through and solve real-life interpersonal problems. Impulsive children became less impatient and demanding, and less likely to explode into emotional outbursts when faced with frustration. Overly inhibited children became more socially outgoing, less fearful, and able to express their feelings appropriately.

Of the ICPS skills measured to date in 4- and 5-year-olds, the process of alternative-solution thinking is most strongly related to measured social adjustment before training, is most affected by it, and emerges as the most powerful behavioral mediator. Consequential thinking appears to play a clearer mediating role in 5- than in 4-year-olds.

We are particularly encouraged that children who showed behavioral difficulties could improve that behavior by learning ICPS skills and how to use them. We are also encouraged that both teachers and inner-city mothers, many of the latter initially ICPS-deficient, could become effective training agents in only 3 months' time. That children trained at home could improve their behavior in school is, we believe, due to having taught the children how and not what to think. Having guided children to solve their own problems, and not telling them what to do each time a conflict or need would arise, the children learned skills that enabled them to generalize when new problems confronted them. Impulsive children learned more effective ways to obtain their wish when it was obtainable, and to cope with the frustration when it was not; inhibited children no longer had to deny their desires and withdraw from interpersonal confrontation. One girl, who played onlooker day after day before training, and shied away when the teacher tried to help her into the group, made a dramatic move during the 11th week of the program. She told a group in the doll corner: "If you need a fireman, I'm right here." A child shouted, "The house is on fire," and the girl, executing her own idea, no longer looked on.

That girls but not boys appear to acquire ICPS naturally from their mothers, yet benefit equally when trained by them, is particularly interesting. Before training, mothers with the highest childrearing-style scores offered suggestions and explained consequences, but very few ever elicited the child's view of the problem or of what to do to solve it. If boys are more resistant to modeling ICPS skills of their mothers before training, perhaps they are less resistant to it when guided, then freed to think for themselves.

The importance of problem-solving communication (dialoguing) has always seemed self-evident to us. If children are encouraged to think through a *hypothetical* problem in the formal training sessions, it seems logical that they should also be guided to think through and solve *real* problems when they occur (Shure, 1979). The plausibility of this assumption appears to be strengthened by recent studies showing that ICPS training of young children that is accompanied by dialoguing (Allen, 1978; Wowkanech, 1978) brings more successful behavior change than those that are not (Durlak & Sherman, 1979; Sharp, 1979). While the Durlak and Sharp studies did show significant PIPS score increase (via implementing the formal ICPS program script), and other factors may account for their lack of behavior change, perhaps dialoguing introduces a new *in vivo* quality by encouraging children to exercise these newly acquired thinking skills in the context of real problems—leading to more effective utilization of ICPS thought when children face real problems on their own.

Is our interpretation of ICPS research valid? That children's behavior objectively improved, and the results are not a function of trained teachers' rating bias is evidenced by the behavior ratings of kindergarten and first-grade follow-up teachers, as well as those by teachers of home-trained children, none of whom, at the time of the rating, were aware of the intervention or its goals. Also, other behaviors related to ICPS skills at pretest with IQ controlled showed a direct change linkage, especially those most interpersonal in nature: the child's awareness or concern for others in distress, and how much the child is liked by his or her peers. Any relationship of behaviors, such as general language skills and comprehension of shapes, colors, and the like, were dependent on IQ before training and did not improve after it. If teacher bias were present, the behaviors shown to have improved would have been less consistent with the strength of relationships between specific ICPS skills and behaviors at pretest. (Further discussion of rating validity is provided in Shure & Spivack, 1980.)

FUTURE DIRECTIONS

The PIPS test, which has met stringent criteria of reliability and validity by Granville, McNeil, Meece, Wacker, Morris, Shelly, and Love (1976) in the lower class (related to both positive and negative social behaviors) has now been found by Schiller (1978) and by Arend, Gove, and Sroufe (1979) to relate to measures of ego-resiliency (Block & Block, 1977) in the middle class. These researchers learned that high PIPS-scorers (who gave a relatively high number of solutions) were more likely than low ones to behave flexibly, persistently, and resourcefully, especially in problem situations. We can, therefore, extend the ICPS approach to behaviors other than those described thus far.

ICPS and Behavioral Flexibility

Measuring behaviors similar to those of Schiller (1978) and of Arend et al. (1979), Wowkanech (1978) has discovered promising applications of ICPS flexibility. Independent raters (unaware of the research hypothesis) observed that middle-class 4-year-olds given the complete ICPS training program (including use of dialoguing) were more likely than a modeling control group to generate their own solutions during actual conflict, and also were more likely to try more than one way to solve it. In contrast, youngsters whose teachers suggested solutions, modeled how to carry them out, and explained why a particular solution was a good one were, in the face of failure, more likely to revert to previously used tactics, which often included hitting, grabbing, and the like. In handling conflict, the important issue is that ICPS-trained children were less likely to give up too soon, perhaps because now they were more ready (and able) to turn to a different (more effective) solution when needed.

The findings of the Wowkanech (1978) study are compatible with an ingenious and creative model of problem-solving research proposed by Krasnor and Rubin (1981). As part of their model, these authors suggest that through natural and/or contrived interpersonal problem situations, the sequenced pattern of actual strategies applied by the child can be observed. The extent to which the child attempts a new strategy to obtain a desired goal when prior strategies do not work can measure flexibility or rigidity in the face of failure—flexibility being an index of social competence. Krasnor and Rubin's additional suggestion to examine the *effectiveness* of those strategies may, however, reflect the eye of the beholder. As Krasnor and Rubin note, a child might view a behavioral strategy as effective if his or her self-initiated goal is satisfied (*success*); a child's strategy may also be judged effective by others' (not negative) reaction to it (*affect*). Some define effectiveness from the viewpoint of social acceptability. With adult agreement, Seaman (1979) identified solutions such as "Look real sad" and "Say, 'you can have more fun if you play with me' " to be inappropriate, whether they be in action or in thought (on the PIPS test). While Seaman and his colleagues judge solutions such as these to be devious, we have consistently found that, empirically, children who conceptualize such unique solutions have relatively high PIPS scores (in quantity) and are generally among the better behaviorally adjusted. The question becomes to what extent any *one* strategy is or is not effective, from *whose* point of view, and how much children's habitual pattern of behavior is associated with and generated by their underlying capacity to problem solve.

In our own studies of behavioral impulsivity and inhibition as measured by the HPSB rating scale, lower-class youngsters displaying either type of aberrance were PIPS-deficient relative to their more-adjusted peers. In the middle class however, we found that impulsive youngsters did not have low PIPS scores; it was the *inhibited* group that made the difference (Shure & Spivack, 1970). Given this, the cognitive findings of Schiller (1978) and Arend *et al.* (1979), and the behavioral observations of Wowkanech (1978), the Krasnor and Rubin (1981) model appears to be particularly inviting for study in this social-class group. Thus, an alternative to our own behavioral observations of children's *general* mode of behavior can be to observe the sequential pattern of strategies in *specific* problem situations. Is a child's behavioral flexibility (trying another way when needed) associated with his or her cognitive flexibility (capacity to generate solutions when asked)? Is a behaviorally flexible child also more likely to carry out solutions that are met with positive affect, and if so, is such a child also more capable of consequential thinking? Is Robin (described earlier), who flexibly and successfully obtained (some) of the seeds from Melissa, a case in point?

The Krasnor and Rubin model can potentially add further to our understanding of how processes of problem-solving thinking extend to behavior in natural, real-world settings because children may not *do* what they *say* can be done when asked about it in an isolated test situation. While Robin, a good problem-solver (high PIPS-scorer) actually carried out several ideas when she wanted something, we also have evidence for inflexibility in low PIPS-scorers. Some inhibited middle-class 4-year-olds repeated the solution "say please" to nearly every toy presented. Whether or not they would actually *use* that particular tactic, still, they would likely try only one way and if refused, would typically pout, watch the other child play, or just walk away. These behavioral observations highlight the relative importance of cognitive process to content, because youngsters able to offer only "say please" (on the PIPS) are just as likely to show behavioral maladaption as those who offer only"hit [the child]" or "grab [the toy]."

General Applicability of the ICPS Approach

Whether the impact of ICPS training on behavior of younger children is greater than that of older ones is not yet known. In fourth- and fifth-graders, Elardo and Caldwell (1979) were able to decrease impatience, and increase respect and concern for others, willingness to share experiences with the group, and self-control. However, these and other behaviors changed only after the program was fully incorporated into the school curriculum and the trainers consistently applied the approach (through dialoguing) when real problems arose (Elardo & Caldwell, in preparation). While Elardo and Caldwell did not include direct link analyses in their 1979 report, the highly statistical contribution of solution scores and both positive and negative behaviors to the discrimination of trained from control youngsters suggests the likelihood of overlap.

While able to help relatively normal youngsters with varying degrees of behavioral difficulties, ICPS programs and techniques have been used with moderate to excellent success with 6- to 12-year-old educable-retarded children (Healey, 1977); with hyperaggressive 7-year-olds (Camp & Bash, 1978), the latter in combination with Meichenbaum and Goodman's (1971) self-instructional techniques (see also Meichenbaum, 1977); with young adult alcoholics (Intagliata, 1978); and with short-term inpatients (Coché & Flick, 1975). Gotlib and Asarnow (1979) have found means–ends thinking to be deficient in mildly and clinically depressed university students, as has Steinlauf (1979) in pregnant teenagers, results that suggest training implications for these populations as well.

We recognize that ICPS training does not account for all of the change in a child's behavior, that other influences (such as temporary emotional blockage) can inhibit thinking capacity at any given point in time, and that other training techniques to enhance behavior can be equally effective (a conviction to which other authors in this volume will attest). But the ICPS approach is one way, a different way, and it works. While not the only way to improve social adjustment and interpersonal competence, it does add to our understanding of behavior, and clearly gives us further appreciation of how the way people think can dramatically affect what they do.

ACKNOWLEDGMENTS

The author's problem-solving research of 4- and 5-year-olds presented in this chapter was supported in part by the Applied Research Branch, National Institute of Mental Health, No. MH-20372, 1971–1975.

REFERENCES

Allen, R. J. *An investigatory study of the effects of a cognitive approach to interpersonal problem solving on the behavior of emotionally upset psychosocially deprived preschool children.* Unpublished doctoral dissertation, Union Graduate School, 1978.

Arend, R., Gove, F. L., & Sroufe, L. A. Continuity of early adaptation: From attachment in infancy to resiliency and curiosity at age five. *Child Development,* 1979, *50,* 950–959.

Block, J., & Block, J. H. *The developmental continuity of ego control and ego resiliency: Some accomplishments.* Paper presented at the meeting of the Society for Research in Child Development, New Orleans, March 1977.

Camp, B., & Bash, M. A. *The classroom "Think Aloud" program.* Paper presented at the meeting of the American Psychological Association, Toronto, August 1978.

Coché, E., & Flick, A. Problem-solving training groups for hospitalized psychiatric patients. *Journal of Psychology,* 1975, *91,* 19–29.

Durlak, J. A., & Sherman, D. Primary prevention of school maladjustment. In J. A. Durlak (Chair), *Behavioral approaches to primary prevention: Programs, outcomes, and issues.* Symposium presented at the meeting of the American Psychological Association, New York, September 1979.

Elardo, P. T., & Caldwell, B. M. The effects of an experimental social development program on children in the middle childhood period. *Psychology in the Schools,* 1979, *16,* 93–100.

Elardo, P. T., & Caldwell, B. M. *Project AWARE: A school program to facilitate the social development of kindergarten–elementary children.* Little Rock: University of Arkansas, in preparation.

Flaherty, E. *Parental influence on children's social cognition* (Final Summary Report, No. 29033). Washington, DC: National Institute of Mental Health, 1978.

Gotlib, I., & Asarnow, R. F. Interpersonal and impersonal problem-solving skills in mildly and clinically depressed university students. *Journal of Consulting and Clinical Psychology,* 1979, *47,* 86–95.

Granville, A. C., McNeil, J. T., Meece, J., Wacker, S., Morris, M., Shelly, M., & Love, J. *Pilot year impact study: Instrument characteristics and attrition trends* (Interim Report 4, Vol. 1, No. 105-75-1114). Washington, DC: Office of Child Development, 1976.

Healey, K. *An investigation of the relationship between certain social cognitive abilities and social behavior, and the efficacy of training in social cognitive skills for elementary retarded-educable children.* Unpublished doctoral dissertation, Bryn Mawr College, 1977.

Intagliata, J. Increasing the interpersonal problem-solving skills for an alcoholic population. *Journal of Consulting and Clinical Psychology,* 1978, *46,* 489–498.

Krasnor, L. R., & Rubin, K. H. The assessment of social problem-solving skills in young children. In T. Merluzzi, C. Glass, & M. Genest (Eds.), *Cognitive assessment.* New York: Guilford Press, 1981.

Meichenbaum, D. *Cognitive-behavior modification: An integrative approach.* New York: Plenum Press, 1977.

Meichenbaum, D. H., & Goodman, J. Training impulsive children to talk to themselves: A means of developing self-control. *Journal of Abnormal Psychology,* 1971, *77,* 115–126.

Schiller, J. D. *Child care arrangements and ego functioning: The effects of stability and entry age on young children.* Unpublished doctoral dissertation, University of California at Berkeley, 1978.

Seaman, J. M. *Cross validation of a cognitive interpersonal problem solving program with kindergarten children.* Unpublished doctoral dissertation, University of Utah, 1979.

Sharp, K. *Impact of interpersonal problem-solving training on preschoolers' behavioral adjustment.* Paper presented at the meeting of the American Psychological Association, New York, September 1979.

Shure, M. B. Training children to solve interpersonal problems: A preventive mental health program. In R. F. Muñoz, L. R. Snowden, & J. G. Kelly (Eds.), *Social and psychological research in community settings: Designing and conducting programs for social and personal well-being.* San Francisco: Jossey-Bass, 1979.

Shure, M. B., Newman, S., & Silver, S. *Problem-solving thinking among adjusted, impulsive and inhibited Head Start children.* Paper presented at the meeting of the Eastern Psychological Association, Washington, DC, May 1973.

Shure, M. B., & Spivack, G. *Problem-solving capacity, social class and adjustment among nursery school children.* Paper presented at the meeting of the Eastern Psychological Association, Atlantic City, April 1970.

Shure, M. B., & Spivack, G. *Solving interpersonal problems: A program for four-year-old nursery school children: Training script.* Philadelphia: Department of Mental Health Sciences, Hahnemann Medical College, 1971.

Shure, M. B., & Spivack, G. *A preventive mental health program for four-year-old Head Start children.* Paper presented at the meeting of the Society for Research in Child Development, Philadelphia, March 1973.

Shure, M. B., & Spivack, G. *A mental health program for kindergarten children: Training script.* Philadelphia: Department of Mental Health Sciences, Hahnemann Medical College, 1974. (a); revised, 1978.
1978.

Shure, M. B., & Spivack, G. *Preschool interpersonal problem solving (PIPS) test: Manual.* Philadelphia: Department of Mental Health Sciences, Hahnemann Medical College, 1974. (b)

Shure, M. B., & Spivack, G. *A mental health program for preschool and kindergarten children, and a mental health program for mothers of young children: An inter-*

personal problem-solving approach toward social adjustment (A Comprehensive Report of Research and Training, No. MH-20372). Washington, DC: National Institute of Mental Health, 1975. (a)

Shure, M. B., & Spivack, G. *Interpersonal cognitive problem-solving intervention: The second (kindergarten) year.* Paper presented at the meeting of the American Psychological Association, Chicago, August 1975. (b)

Shure, M. B., & Spivack, G. *Problem-solving techniques in childrearing: Training script for parents of young children.* Philadelphia: Department of Mental Health Sciences, Hahnemann Medical College, 1975. (c)

Shure, M. B., & Spivack, G. *Problem-solving techniques in childrearing.* San Francisco: Jossey-Bass, 1978.

Shure, M. B., & Spivack, G. Interpersonal cognitive problem solving and primary prevention: Programming for preschool and kindergarten children. *Journal of Clinical Child Psychology,* 1979, *2,* 89–94.

Shure, M. B., & Spivack, G. Interpersonal problem solving as a mediator of behavioral adjustment in preschool and kindergarten children. *Journal of Applied Developmental Psychology,* 1980, *1,* 29–44.

Spivack, G. Problem-solving thinking and mental health. *The Forum* (Department of Mental Health Sciences, Hahnemann Medical College, Philadelphia), 1973, *2,* 58–73.

Spivack, G., Platt, J. J., & Shure, M. B. *The problem-solving approach to adjustment: A guide to research and intervention.* San Francisco: Jossey-Bass, 1976.

Spivack, G., & Shure, M. B. *Social adjustment of young children: A cognitive approach to solving real-life problems.* San Francisco: Jossey-Bass, 1974.

Spivack, G., & Shure, M. B. *Maternal childrearing and the interpersonal cognitive problem-solving ability of four-year-olds.* Paper presented at the meeting of the Society for Research in Child Development, Denver, April 1975.

Steinlauf, B. Problem-solving skills, locus of control, and the contraceptive effectiveness of young women. *Child Development,* 1979, *50,* 268–271.

Wowkanech, N. Personal communication, August 26, 1978.

III

INTERPERSONAL DIAGNOSIS AND SOCIAL COMPETENCE TRAINING WITH INSTITUTIONALIZED POPULATIONS

7

A PSYCHOSOCIAL COMPETENCE CLASSIFICATION SYSTEM

LORNA SMITH BENJAMIN

LORNA SMITH BENJAMIN is Professor in the Department of Psychiatry at the University of Wisconsin Medical Center. Her work on the use of structural analysis of social behavior as a psychiatric diagnostic system began in 1968. Since that time she has continued her research and clinical work on the Structural Analysis of Social Behavior (SASB), and has published her findings in a number of journals, including the *Psychological Review*, the *American Psychologist,* and the *Journal of Abnormal Psychology.* Her work has had considerable impact on the work of researchers and clinicians in this area.

Benjamin equips social competence investigators with a diagnostic system that facilitates the understanding of the psychiatrically diagnosed individual from a social–environmental perspective. Benjamin has examined a large body of research that signals the import of a few basic dimensions of interpersonal behavior, and has developed a diagnostic system that is simplifying. Her chapter escapes many of the criticisms of medical diagnostic systems in that it concerns itself with the transactions of the individual with other people, thus focusing directly on the individual's social environment. In addition, the SASB has the advantages of having clear-cut treatment implications and of reducing the evaluative connotations of diagnosis.

"Competence" has been defined in terms of "positive characteristics, particularly the capacity for coping with life situations" (Sundberg, Snowden, & Reynolds, 1978, p. 180). When one becomes unable to cope with life situations, one is, according to this definition, incompetent, and the probability of becoming a psychiatric patient increases dramatically. It is natural then, that psychiatric diagnostic systems are focused on inadequacies, breakdown, and symptoms such as anxiety, depression, fear, disordered thinking, hallucinations, and so on. Such an emphasis on symptoms is the *modus operandi* of the medical establishment and so when it turned its attention to social behavior, medicine hardly could do anything other than look at symptoms and pathology.

RECENT HISTORY OF PSYCHIATRIC DIAGNOSIS

Within this tradition, diagnosis, which for some purposes can be considered to be the dark side of competence, has had at least three major purposes. These are to provide:

1. Classification for the purpose of communication with professionals and for research.

2. Statements about etiology that have preventative implications. For example, if it could be established that the so-called double-binding communications from the parent to the child do indeed increase the probability of schizophrenia in the child, then the incidence of schizophrenia could be reduced by routinely helping parents learn to avoid double-binds and to develop positive alternatives.

3. A rational understanding that has clear treatment implications. Continuing the example, if double-binds were shown definitively to relate to schizophrenia, then it could be prevented from developing in the first place, and where that failed, stricken families could have the option of learning alternative, more constructive ways of relating to each other.

Recently, psychiatry has been "remedicalizing," which means large numbers of psychiatrists have moved away from social approaches such as family therapy or psychoanalysis toward biochemistry. The new psychiatry holds that major mental illnesses such as schizophrenia and the primary affective disorders have strong genetic input manifest in defective biochemical functioning, which must necessarily be treated pharmacologically. The heat of this dispute about underlying models of mental illness with their differing implications for etiology and treatment has been intensified by economic considerations. At issue is third-party payments, with some physicians arguing that they must preside over treatments of disturbances in behavior because of the presumed biochemical causes and treatments. On the other hand, believers in social causes and treatments argue that the medical model is too mechanistic and overlooks the dynamic and profoundly social nature of the human being.

In addition to squabbling over professional territory, there has been legitimate scientific debate about the adequacy of psychiatric diagnostic systems. Criticisms have come from many quarters and they include the opinions that psychiatric diagnoses lack reliability; are not operationally defined; have no useful implications for etiology; have few implications for treatment planning; overlook the contribution of the environment and milieu; focus too much on pathology; invoke burdensome labels that overgeneralize and negate the individual; and are based on very debatable theoretical notions. A balanced and comprehensive summary of these criticisms along with some reasonable rebuttals are offered by Kendell (1975).

Sociologists have suggested that diagnosis introduces bias by sex and social class, with females and lower-class persons receiving the worst labels. It has also been observed that diagnostic labels can be used for social control, as is allegedly the case in the U.S.S.R. Medical sociologists add that the psychiatric views are strongly tied to the vested interest of pharmaceutical companies. A summary of these concerns is presented by Goldstein (1979).

Kanfer and Saslow (1965) are behavior therapists who recognized the advantages of having a diagnostic system and accepted the challenge to create an alternative nosology. They proposed a functional (behavioral–analytic) approach that involves seven steps: analysis of a problem situation; clarification of the problem situation; motivational analysis; developmental analysis; analysis of self-control; analysis of social relationships; analysis of social, cultural, and physical environment. Although this well-conceived system has been pursued by practitioners and researchers of behavioristic persuasion, a large segment of mental health practitioners have not taken up the functional analytic approach for varying reasons. Among these are the widespread belief that behavior therapies are too concrete, superficial, and mechanistic. It is argued they ignore much of the wisdom of the Freudian heritage.

Psychiatry's own response to the criticisms of its nosology has been to try to improve it. Feighner, Robins, Guze, Woodruff, Winokur, and Muñoz ("St. Louis Group") (1972) carefully developed diagnostic terminology for some mental illnesses that reliably could be identified by independent observers. The terminology of the St. Louis Group was elaborated upon, expanded, and modified by Spitzer, Endicott, and Robins (1975), with the assistance of other participants in the National Institute of Mental Health (NIMH) Clinical Research Branch Collaborative Program on the Psychobiology of Depression. The result of these combined efforts was the Research Diagnostic Criteria (RDC) for a selected group of functional conditions. The RDC criteria focused largely on the major psychiatric disorders and were applied in conjunction with an exhaustive, highly structured interview called Schedule for Affective Disorders and Schizophrenia (SADS). The SADS–RDC combination gave highly reliable results and led to the development of an entirely new diagnostic system (American Psychiatric Association, 1980) called the DSM-III *(Diagnostic and Statistical Manual,* 3rd ed.). As the DSM-III was developed, the SADS interview associated with RDC diagnosis was revised to become the Diagnostic Interview Schedule (DIS) in order to optimize DSM-III diagnoses. Data from DIS can be submitted to a computer program that will directly generate a DSM-III diagnosis. With the DIS–DSM-III technology, psychiatry has become more specific about the diagnostic process, at least for research purposes. However, clinician use of the DSM-III is expected to be less reliable than the research use because usually clinicians do not use SADS or DIS interviews, nor do they use a computer's algorithm to interpret their interview results.

The creation of DSM-III has not silenced the critics of psychiatric diagnosis and a representative statement was offered by McLemore and Benjamin (1979):

> As in the past, diagnosis still rests partly on impressionistic clinical judgment, including, for example, global ratings of the "severity" of the psychosocial stresses and of the patient's highest level of adaptive functioning during the past year. Second, the system still categorizes human beings in terms of illness very broadly defined. Finally, and most importantly, DSM-III shows near total neglect of social psychological variables and interpersonal behavior. We submit that rigorous and systematic description of social behavior is uniquely critical to effective definition and treatment of the problems that bring most individuals for psychiatric or psychological consultation. (p. 18)

Prior to the DSM-III, a psychiatric precedent for including social variables in a formal diagnostic system had been set by Strauss (1973, 1975). In reviewing the shortcomings of psychiatric diagnoses, Strauss noted that assessment of degrees of thought disorder, depression, and social competence (Strauss, 1973, p. 447) would be more appropriate than simple noting of presence or absence of symptoms. Calling the models that work with presence or absence of symptoms "typological," and calling those that work with degrees "dimensional," Strauss concluded the best choice would be a mixed model that took advantage of each. His own suggestion for a multivariate mixed model (Strauss, 1975, p. 1194) was a system that would include measurement of (1) symptoms, (2) circumstances associated with symptoms, (3) previous duration and course of symptoms, (4) quality of personal relationships, and (5) level of work function. The DSM-III is a mixed model since it uses some discrete variables and some dimensional variables; however, it does not develop Strauss's fourth listed dimension: quality of personal relationships.

Despite the increasing specificity and increasing methodological sophistication within psychiatric nomenclature, including the multidimensional approaches proposed by Strauss and by others as reviewed by Mezzich (1979, pp. 128–129), there is still a need to organize the variables within some kind of coherent theoretical framework. Gathering of large amounts of discrete and continuous data and interrelating them by multivariate analytical procedures are improvements, but until such variables can be organized under a reasonable integrative theory there is little hope for a nomenclature that is able to relate meaningfully to etiology and reliably to treatment implications. Moreover, such an integrative theory must include social variables as a major aspect because it is, after all, social behavior that brings people most often to the psychiatric or psychological clinic.

Interpersonal Diagnosis

The implicit presence of interpersonal behaviors in the use of traditional diagnostic labels has been discussed at length by McLemore and Benjamin (1979). They observed that the extensive, but not explicit, overlap between traditional psychiatric nosology and interpersonal behavior has been understood by many, though never incorporated into the nosology itself.

Perhaps the most direct evidence of overlap comes from Plutchik and Platman (1977), who formally showed that in the minds of a group of psychiatrists at the New York State Psychiatric Institute, there were clear expectations for interpersonal behavior associated with traditional diagnostic categories. Using Plutchik's Emotions Profile Index (EPI), based on the work of Schaefer (1965, 1971) and Schaefer and Plutchik (1966), several traditional psychiatric categories were rated on the 12 words in the EPI: adventurous, affectionate, brooding, cautious, gloomy, impulsive, obedient, quarrelsome, resentful, self-conscious, shy and sociable. In the EPI, these traits are paired in all possible combinations for a total of 66 combinations. A rational analysis yields eight EPI scores, called trusting, dyscontrolled, timid, depressed, distrustful, controlled, aggressive, gregarious. Interpersonal aspects of the categories schizoid, paranoid, and compulsive were shown in the Plutchik and Platman study by considering the highest EPI scores. For the schizoid category they were timid (78), depressed (75), distrustful (74), and controlled (72). The paranoid personality was called distrustful (85), aggressive (66), depressed (65), and controlled (63). The compulsive was called timid (85), controlled (66), and distrustful (63). These judgments were made at a very high level of reliability, the correlations between judges generally being over .90.

An earlier, important, and extensive effort to develop an interpersonal nosology and relate it to the traditional psychiatric nosology was offered by Timothy Leary in his classic book, titled *Interpersonal Diagnosis of Personality: A Functional Theory and Methodology for Personality Evaluation* (1957). Leary constructed an Interpersonal Circle around two axes called love–hate and dominance–submission. Reasoning that different social behaviors can be represented in terms of mixes of these underlying dimensions, Leary described the social universe as follows: Beginning with the dominance point, the social behavioral classification is managerial–autocratic; moving stepwise in the direction of the love pole, the next category is responsible–hypernormal, followed by cooperative–overconventional; moving toward what Leary called the opposite of dominance, namely submission, the next category is docile–dependent, followed by self-effacing–masochistic, the category that includes pure submission. Continuing around the circle toward the hate pole, the next category is rebellious–distrustful, followed by aggressive–sadistic, the category that includes the hate pole itself. Finally, the circle is closed by the category located between hate and dominance, and this is called competitive–narcissistic. Leary and his colleagues (Leary & Coffey, 1955) related these interpersonal categories to some traditional psychiatric categories. One example is the schizoid personality, which was said to overlap the rebellious–distrustful category and to be characterized by interpersonal behavior that is "passively resistant, bitter, distrustful." The compulsive personality was tentatively equated with the category managerial–autocratic and described as managing, autocratic, poweroriented. The hysterical personality was related to the category cooperative–overconventional and was described as "naive, 'sweet,' and overconforming."

Use of the interpersonal circle to study the relation between its interpersonal descriptions and traditional psychiatric categories did not stop with Leary. Lorr, Bishop, and McNair (1965) are a distinguished example. After revising Leary's Interpersonal Behavior Checklist, they decided to measure the attributes of dominance, recognition, hostility, mistrust, detachment, inhibition, evasiveness, submissiveness, succorance, deference, agreeableness, nurturance, affection, sociability, and exhibition. Nonpsychotic psychiatric patients in psychotherapy were rated by their therapists in terms of these 15 categories and ratings were then factor-analyzed. In three samples there were four replicated interpersonal types named: (1) inhibited, submissive, evasive; (2) agreeable, nurturant, sociable; (3) hostile, distrustful, detached; (4) dominant, competitive, exhibitionistic. These categories were then compared to psychiatric categories and the findings were (Lorr *et al.*, 1965, p. 471):

> Table . . . presents the therapist's diagnostic impressions grouped by major disorder. A Chi Square test indicated differences among the cells significant at $p < .01$. Type I members (self-inhibited and submissive) compared to other types tend to be diagnosed as psychoneurotic or personality pattern disorders. Diagnosis appears not to differentiate Type I from Type III (withdrawn, hostile, suspicious). Type II members (agreeable, helpful, responsible, friendly) tended to be labeled psychoneurotic or to left undiagnosed. Personality pattern diagnoses (schizoid or paranoid personality) are less frequent for Type II than for others. Type IV members (dominant, competitive, exhibitionistic) compared to other classes are more frequently diagnosed personality trait disturbance, that is, passive–aggressive, aggressive or compulsive.

Clearly, there are promising trends linking interpersonal style with diagnostic category, at least in selected categories, and the promise for an interpersonal nosology seems good.

The Current Need for a Classification System

In conclusion, what is needed is a nosology that will retain the advantages of the medical model's diagnostic system and avoid the disadvantages. A nosology that does classify individuals in a manner useful for research and has etiological and treatment implications would be welcomed by many. Since psychiatry has demonstrated effectiveness with some medications, such as lithium carbonate (Jefferson & Greist, 1977), a reasonable nosology should be able to describe individuals in a fashion that will allow some statement about probable response to medications. There should be a rigorous emphasis on social behavior. The diagnostic description should not be so rigid as to flounder on the so-called trait–state problem (Mischel, 1968). Resolution of that probably could be reached through use of an interactional model (Endler & Magnusson, 1976). Such an interactional model could be implemented by measuring social behavior in specific situations as well as measuring it in more general contexts. The formal interactional logic is also appropriately applied to the question of genetic versus environmental causes. There should be balance between attention given to variables inhering in the individual and those coming from the environment. Certainly there is genetic input to social behavior just as there is to intelligence, musical, athletic, or artistic performance. Individuals differ in their behavioral propensities, and environmental input to what happens to these genetic potentials is very important. Finally, in measuring the social self, the intrapsychic as well as the interpersonal should be included because the wisdom of the psychoanalytic heritage should not be jettisoned. Just as behaviorists have more recently come to consider the introspector a legitimate behavioral observer (Beck, Rush, Shaw, & Emery, 1979), so an interpersonal nosology should legitimately be able to discuss social events if they are represented by an individual observing his or her thoughts and feelings about himself or herself.

In the best of all worlds, an interpersonal nosology ought not to mark off professional territory. Balance and integration are desirable goals for the nosology; the patient, rather than any particular category of health care provider, should be the beneficiary. Thus, potential conflicts such as the biological versus the psychosocial belief systems concerning etiology and appropriate treatment should be set aside; so should the family versus the individual approach, the psychosocial versus the medication, and the warm, humanistic individualistic versus the cold, objective, scientific dichotomies—all should be filed away as early but outmoded views. It is a truism that each of these well-known positions carries a certain amount of truth and validity. The nosology that serves the patient or client the best would be one that makes available the wisdom of each.

STRUCTURAL ANALYSIS OF SOCIAL BEHAVIOR (SASB)

The specific purpose of this chapter is to explore in some detail the possibilities of using SASB to further develop the idea of an interpersonal nomenclature and work toward the goals discussed. The SASB model was developed by starting with Schaefer's (1965, 1971) circumplex for describing parental behavior. Schaefer's model places emancipation in opposition to domination and, in its earlier forms, hate in opposition to love; it has been tested and confirmed in several different cultures. The SASB model started with Schaefer's model, added the concept of submission from Leary's model (in the SASB model, submission is the complement rather than the opposite of dominance), and extended both in the directions of explicitness, precision, and mathematical logic. The SASB is compatible with, and can be viewed as, an integration and extension of these and several other circumplex models (Benjamin, 1974).

There have been many revisions of the SASB model, and construct validity has been tested by several methods, including autocorrelation, circumplex analysis, factor analysis, and a dimensional ratings procedure (Benjamin, 1974, 1977, submitted). Content validity will be illustrated in Figures 3-7. Reliability is measured principally by a coefficient of internal consistency and it will be illustrated in the discussions of those figures.

The current version of the SASB model is presented in Figure 1. It was described efficiently in McLemore and Benjamin (1979):

> As with Leary's circle, the horizontal axis in all three diamonds is affiliation (love–hate). The vertical axis is interdependence, with maximum interdependence at the bottom of each diamond and maximum independence at the top. Because of its detailed structure, the SASB model has desirable versatility on the molar–molecular dimension, in that all 72 interpersonal chart points on the first two surfaces can either be used or be collapsed into two sets of four complementary quadrants (see Figure 2). Note that the top half of each of the top two surfaces represents behavior not saturated with control, either in the sense of dominance (controlling the other) or submission (being controlled by the other). This allows for the charting of a whole range of behaviors not capable of being mapped onto the Leary circle.
>
> Limitations of space preclude explication of the details of the SASB structure and many of its applications. There are, however, four major advantages related to the fact that the model was constructed using mathematical logic and a large number of empirical analyses: (1) Opposite behaviors are defined at 180° angles; for example, the opposite of 114 *(show empathic understanding)* is 134 *(delude, divert, mislead)*. (2) Complementary behaviors, those that tend to draw each other, are defined and can be used to show what interpersonal behavior can be expected to accompany what other interpersonal behavior; for example, 214 *(clearly express oneself)* is the complement of 114 *(show empathic understanding)*, and 234 *(uncomprehending agreement,* a kind of hostile submission) is the complement of being effectively misled by 134 *(delude, divert, mislead)*. (3) Antitheses can be specified; that is, the model prescribes what behavior to enact in order to draw out the opposite of what is at hand, specifically the opposite of its complement. For ex-

INTERPERSONAL

OTHER

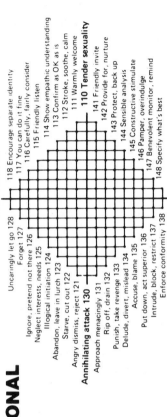

120 Endorse freedom
118 Encourage separate identity
117 You can do it fine
116 Carefully, fairly consider
115 Friendly listen
114 Show empathic understanding
113 Confirm as OK as is
112 Stroke, soothe, calm
111 Warmly welcome
110 Tender sexuality
141 Friendly invite
142 Provide for, nurture
143 Protect, back up
144 Sensible analysis
145 Constructive stimulate
146 Pamper, overindulge
147 Benevolent monitor, remind
148 Specify what's best
Manage, control 140

Uncaringly let go 128
Forget 127
Ignore, pretend not there 126
Neglect interests, needs 125
Illogical initiation 124
Abandon, leave in lurch 123
Starve, cut out 122
Angry dismiss, reject 121
Annihilating attack 130
Approach menacingly 131
Rip off, drain 132
Punish, take revenge 133
Delude, divert, mislead 134
Accuse, blame 135
Put down, act superior 136
Intrude, block, restrict 137
Enforce conformity 138

SELF

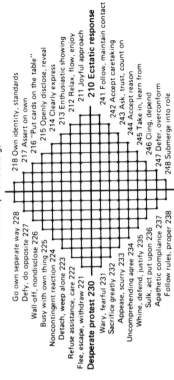

220 Freely come and go
218 Own identity, standards
217 Assert on own
216 "Put cards on the table"
215 Openly disclose, reveal
214 Clearly express
213 Enthusiastic showing
212 Relax, flow, enjoy
211 Joyful approach
210 Ecstatic response
241 Follow, maintain contact
242 Accept caretaking
243 Ask, trust, count on
244 Accept reason
245 Take in, learn from
246 Cling, depend
247 Defer, overconform
248 Submerge into role
Yield, submit, give in 240

Go own separate way 228
Defy, do opposite 227
Wall-off, nondisclose 226
Busy with own thing 225
Noncontingent reaction 224
Detach, weep alone 223
Refuse assistance, care 222
Flee, escape, withdraw 221
Desperate protest 230
Wary, fearful 231
Sacrifice greatly 232
Appease, scurry 233
Uncomprehending agree 234
Whine, defend, justify 235
Sulk, act put upon 236
Apathetic compliance 237
Follow rules, proper 238

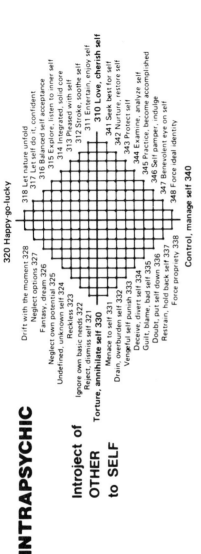

INTRAPSYCHIC

320 Happy-go-lucky

318 Let nature unfold
317 Let self do it, confident
316 Balanced self acceptance
315 Explore, listen to inner self
314 Integrated, solid core
313 Pleased with self
312 Stroke, soothe self
311 Entertain, enjoy self
310 Love, cherish self
341 Seek best for self
342 Nurture, restore self
343 Protect self
344 Examine, analyze self
345 Practice, become accomplished
346 Self pamper, indulge
347 Benevolent eye on self
348 Force ideal identity

Drift with the moment 328
Neglect options 327
Fantasy, dream 326
Neglect own potential 325
Undefined, unknown self 324
Reckless 323
Ignore own basic needs 322
Reject, dismiss self 321
Menace to self 331
Drain, overburden self 332
Vengeful self punish 333
Deceive, divert self 334
Guilt, blame, bad self 335
Doubt, put self down 336
Restrain, hold back self 337
Force propriety 338

Torture, annihilate self 330

Control, manage self **340**

Introject of
OTHER
to SELF

FIGURE 1. Chart of social behavior. The top diamond describes behavior involving focus on the other (transitive action); the second surface describes behavior involving focus on the self (intransitive state). The third surface represents the intrapsychic state resulting when focus on other is turned inward. Each surface is built on an affiliative axis on the horizontal and on an interdependence axis on the vertical. Points between the poles of the axes consist of proportionate amounts of elements described by those poles. For example, the point on the focus-on-other surface located at about 11 o'clock is Forget (127). It is made up of two units of Annihilating attack (130) and seven units of Endorse freedom (120). Opposites appear at 180° angles: Benevolent monitor, remind (147) is the opposite of Forget (127). Complements appear at comparable locations on the first two surfaces. Benevolent monitor, remind (147) is complemented by Defer, overconform (247). Antitheses are the opposite of the complements and represent the interpersonal posture required to draw out an opposite—Defer, overconform (247) is the antithesis of Forget (127). For example, the child can sometimes reengage the forgetful (127) parent by deference (247) and clinging (246). Also, the overcontrolling parent (147) will sometimes become forgetful (127) and let go if the adolescent is defiant (227) enough. From "Structural Analysis of Differentiation Failure" by L. S. Benjamin, *Psychiatry*, 1979, *42*, 1–23. Reprinted by permission.

199

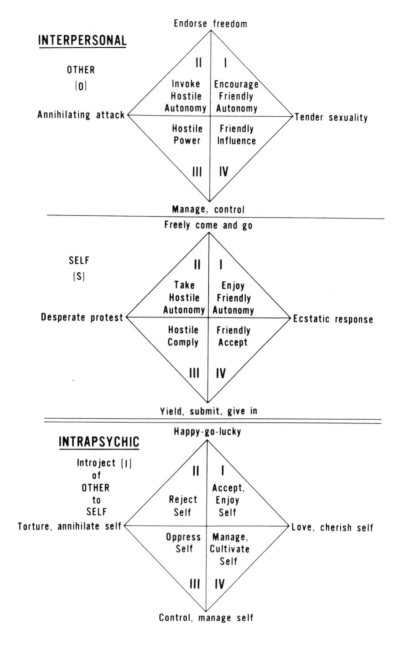

FIGURE 2. The SASB chart reduced to quadrants. From "Structural Analysis of Differentiation Failure" by L. S. Benjamin, *Psychiatry*, 1979, *42*, 1–23. Reprinted by permission.

ample, if someone is diverting and misleading the therapist (a form of hostile power), the antithetical behavior would be 214, such as the statement, "I'd like to believe what you're saying but I'm having a little trouble" (friendly autonomy). In an affiliative relationship, this kind of I statement seems to draw the deceiver toward developing more understanding of the speaker. If the nodal point in the relationship is hostile, however, there would be increasing attempts at deception and hostile control. In terms of the model, augmented deceit is the deceiver's antithesis to the benevolent person's gesture to put the relationship on more respectful and friendly grounds. (4) Finally, the Benjamin model explicitly translates the psychoanalytic idea of introjection into geometric terms and, in so doing, specifies ways in which interpersonal experiences affect one's treatment of oneself. The third (bottom) diamond of Figure 1 thus indicates what happens if the behaviors charted on the top diamond are turned inward. If a child has a parent who routinely uses hostile power, for example, blaming (Chart Point 135), and the child turns the hostile power inward, he or she becomes guilty (Chart Point 335). A constructive encounter with a benevolent therapist who shows empathic understanding (114) may reverse this trend toward self-blame and in time result in the introjection of the therapist's good will (314, integrated, solid core).

The principles of opposites, complements, antitheses, and introjects apply consistently among all 108 points of the model. These features give the model considerable power: in the generation of hypotheses about etiology; in aiding our understanding of how current life situations affect behavior of the person in question, which is relevant to the recent state–trait controversy (Mischel, 1968, 1973); and in therapeutic goal setting (Benjamin, 1977).[1]

APPLICATIONS OF SASB TO THE PROBLEM OF DIAGNOSIS

In NIMH-funded research currently under way, there is an exploration of (1) the possibility of systematically incorporating psychosocial behavior into traditional psychiatric nosology by using SASB to describe persons assigned to diagnostic categories (Interpersonal Description of Diagnostic Categories—IDDC), and/or (2) the possibility of developing an entirely new classification of persons grouped on the basis of interpersonal behavior as described by the SASB (In-

[1]From "Whatever Happened to Interpersonal Diagnosis? A Psychosocial Alternative to DSM-III" by C. W. McLemore and L. S. Benjamin, *American Psychologist*, 1979, *34*, 22–23. Copyright 1979 by the American Psychological Association. Reprinted by permission.

terpersonal Nomenclature—IN). The procedure will be to obtain subjective (by self) and objective (by others) ratings of interpersonal behavior and of psychiatric symptoms (anxiety, depression, thought disorder, etc.) on 200 psychiatric inpatients assigned to eight diagnostic categories defined by the new research DIS and DSM-III procedures. In five diagnostic categories 100 psychiatric outpatients will be defined by a DSM-III algorithm performed on therapist responses to brief interview by computer made available through a project under the direction of Greist and Klein (1980). In addition, a subgroup of 10 inpatients from each diagnostic category will perform a Family Consensus Task, which involves having the family group rate the blaming behavior of the mother, the father, and the significant other in relation to the patient. This judgment process will be videotaped, coded according to the SASB categories, and subjected to Markov Sequential Analyses (Benjamin, 1979b, 1979c).

IDDC analyses will compare and contrast diagnostic categories. IN analyses will define new categories, primarily through cluster analyses, and relate these new categories to symptoms and to a preliminary measure of response to medications.

In Figure 3 there is a presentation of the SASB self-descriptions of a person diagnosed schizoid personality by his hospital staff. The clinical description offered for this patient prior to the analysis of the SASB ratings was "an anxious, socially withdrawn 24-year-old man who suffers from feelings of emptiness. He lives with his parents in a household that he describes as empty. His mother would like him to talk to her and keep her feeling alive and narcissistically adequate, but he feels unable to do so. He is diagnosed as a schizoid personality, but under stress, behavior has been labeled schizophrenic." The SASB description presented in Figure 3 is called a map (Benjamin, 1974, 1977, 1979d). The raw data were patient ratings of applicability on a scale ranging from 0 to 100 with 50 being the marker between "false" and "true." One item representing each chart point was presented in a randomly determined order, and to create the map, the computer program unscrambled the items and printed the numbers assigned to each item in the pattern of the model. In addition, the map shows printed phrases describing the chart points that received endorsements at an above-median level. For the focus-on-other surface, it can be seen in Figure 3 (upper half) that the patient felt he engaged in much hostile rejection of the staff; this is shown by the large number of above-median items occurring in Quadrant II of that surface. Figure 2 shows that quadrant is named Invoking Hostile Autonomy. It is interesting to note that the average profile created by pooling the descriptions of this patient by three judges (a staff nurse, a psychiatrist, and a psychotherapist) showed relatively few above-median items in Quadrant II. This means that the patient's self-description as rejecting the staff was not consistently perceived by the staff.

The focus-on-self portion (lower half) of Figure 3 shows again that the schizoidal person could be characterized mostly in terms of Quadrant II, which, in the case of the focus-on-self surface, represents Taking Hostile Autonomy. In addition to the impression given by scanning the figure for above-median items, a summary score (called the weighted affiliation–autonomy vector) is available to characterize the interpersonal posture. The weighted affiliation score is obtained by multiplying each of the scores assigned to the 36 points of a given surface by weights arranged so that maximal positive weights are given to items theoretically consisting of maximal amounts of affiliation, while maximal negative weights are given to items theoretically near the disaffiliative pole. The same logic is invoked for obtaining the weighted autonomy score, except that the maximal positive weights are around the autonomy poles and the maximal negative weights are assigned to the interdependence pole (dominance–submission). For Figure 3, the affiliation–autonomy vector for the focus on other surface was (− 88, + 63). This means the two-dimensional average of the endorsements for that group can be shown by counting 88 arbitrary units in the negative direction on the horizontal axis, and by counting 63 arbitrary units in the positive vertical direction. This vector located the "center of gravity" for this surface in Quadrant II. By the same method, the patient's self-description for the focus-on-self surface was also located in Quadrant II; the weighted affiliation–autonomy vector here was (− 97, + 42). The very high positive coefficients of internal consistency for both types of focus show that the orientations in Quadrant II were highly stable for this schizoidal individual (for a complete description of the coefficient of internal consistency see Benjamin, 1974, 1979d).

In Figure 4 the self-ratings of a person described by hospital staff as "a single, 29-year-old, paranoid personality who has been diagnosed paranoid schizophrenic during his most difficult times in the past. He's been divorced three times and is generally quite depressed and at times suicidal. He also gets impulsively angry and disruptive." Most of the above-median items for this patient's self-description occurred on the disaffiliative side of the SASB model. Many of the maximal ratings (appearing in the figure as 99 instead of 100 because of the wish to use 1 less column per item when keypunching computer

I FOCUS ON STAFF MEMBERS (TOP) AND ON MYSELF (BOTTOM)
THE SCORE   40 IS MEDIAN

```
                                                    0*  30
                          UNCARINGLY LET GO       90* *  *   90 YOU CAN DO IT FINE
                   FORGET                     50* *     *
             IGNORE,PRETEND NOT THERE     90* *         *       40
          NEGLECT INTERESTS,NEEDS     80* *             *     *   0
        ILLOGICAL INITIATION      90* *                 *   *    0   0
       ABANDON,LEAVE IN LURCH  60* *                    * *    *  0  0
      STARVE,CUT OUT        60* *                       *    *  *   0  20
    ANGRY DISMISS,REJECT  70* *                      * * *  * *  *  0
   ANNIHILATING ATTACK  50* * * * * * * * * * * * * * * *  * *  *   0
  APPROACH MENACINGLY 60*                              *    *    0
                       0*                              *  *  0
                                                       * *    0
   DELUDE,DIVERT,MISLEAD    50*                    *  0
     ACCUSE,BLAME        70*                    * 30
                        30*                   *  30
                      20* *               0* * *  0
                     0*  *             0*
```

WEIGHTED AFFILIATION — AUTONOMY VECTOR=(-.98.. .43..)
COEFFICENT OF INTERNAL CONSISTENCY = .97?
CONTRADICTION COEFFICIENT = .13? RIGHT ANGLES COEFFICIENT = .5?0

GO OWN SEPARATE WAY   0* 60 FREELY COME AND GO
        DEFY, DO OPPOSITE   90* * 90 OWN IDENTITY, STANDARDS
    WALL--OFF, NONDISCLOSE   80* * * 60 ASSERT ON OWN
    AVOID THROUGH ACTIVITIES   90*   * * 90 PUT/CARDS ON TABLE
                             0*   * * 40
                                       *   * 70 CLEARLY EXPRESS
        GRIEVE, MOURN, FEEL ALONE   50*   *   0
    REFUSE ASSISTANCE, CARE   60*   *   *   0
FLEE, RUN AWAY, WITHDRAW   60*   *   *   *   0
DESPERATE PROTEST   70* * * * * * * * * * * * * * * * * *   0
WARY, FEARFUL   90*   *   *   0
SACRIFICE   70*   *   * 30
APPEASE, SCURRY   70*   *   * 30
                                               *
    WHINE, DEFEND, JUSTIFY   30*   *   * 20
        SULK, ACT PUT UPON   90*   *   * 40
                           0*   *   * 40
                          40* * * 60 SUBMERGE INTO ROLE
                         50*

            YIELD, SUBMIT, GIVE IN

WEIGHTED AFFILIATION - AUTONOMY VECTOR=(-.97, .42.)
COEFFICIENT OF INTERNAL CONSISTENCY = .931
CONTRADICTION COEFFICIENT = .298 RIGHT ANGLES COEFFICIENT = .664

FIGURE 3. A schizoidal (sometimes schizophrenic) patient rates himself in relation to staff members. His weighted affiliation–autonomy vectors for both types of focus are located in Quadrant II (see Figure 2), and show a high degree of internal consistency. This means this schizoidal person consistently retains an interpersonal posture of hostile rejection and hostile withdrawal. Data available through the generosity of Professor Leonard Horowitz of Stanford University.

I FOCUS ON STAFF MEMBERS (TOP) AND ON MYSELF (BOTTOM)
THE SCORE   80 IS MEDIAN

```
                                          0*  20
                  UNCARINGLY LET GO     99* *  * 50
                                        90*    * 90
          IGNORE.PRETEND NOT THERE  90*        * 90
                                    90*          * 80
                                    40*            * 30
  ABANDON.LEAVE IN LURCH  99*                        * 40
                          50*                          * 90
  ANGRY DISMISS.REJECT  99* * * * * * * * * * * * * *  * 10
  ANNIHILATING ATTACK   99*                              * 0
  APPROACH MENACINGLY   99*                              * 90
                         0*                              * 50
  PUNISH.TAKE REVENGE   99*                            * 50
                        50*                          * 90
          ACCUSE.BLAME  99*                        * -1
      PUT DOWN.ACT SUPERIOR  99*                  * 90
        INTRUDE.BLOCK.RESTRICT  90*            * 90
                              90* * * * * *  * 50  BENEVOLENT MONITOR.REMI
                                       50*
```

WEIGHTED AFFILIATION -- AUTONOMY VECTOR=(-70.., -4..)
COEFFICIENT OF INTERNAL CONSISTENCY = .45?
CONTRADICTION COEFFICIENT = -.07? RIGHT ANGLES COEFFICIENT = .01?

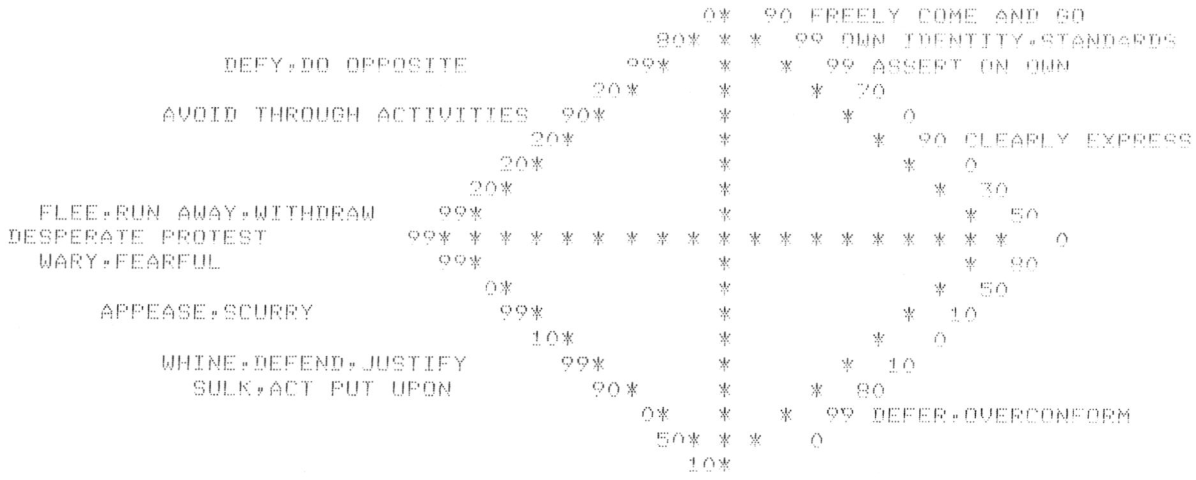

WEIGHTED AFFILIATION - AUTONOMY VECTOR=(-50., 55.)
COEFFICENT OF INTERNAL CONSISTENCY = .179
CONTRADICTION COEFFICIENT = -.010 RIGHT ANGLES COEFFICIENT = .103

FIGURE 4. A paranoid patient (sometimes paranoid–schizophrenic) rates himself in relation to staff members. The weighted affiliation–autonomy vector for focus on other is located very near the attack axis. The interpersonal postures are not internally consistent and behaviors describing focus on self were especially unpredictable. Figures 3 through 7 were generated by computer and there was not always enough room to print the full name of the chart point, as in "Benevolent monitor, remi," here. Data available through the generosity of Professor Leonard Horowitz of Stanford University.

cards) occurred near the maximally disaffiliative poles for both the focus-on-other and the focus-on-self surfaces. The average vector for the focus-on-other surface was (− 70, − 6), placing it near the purely attacking pole. The coefficient of internal consistency was not high (.456), and this suggests that these behaviors were unstable and unpredictable.

The weighted affiliation–autonomy vector for the focus-on-self ratings was (− 50, + 55), placing the center of gravity for this group of behaviors in Quadrant II. The internal consistency for these ratings was quite low (.176), indicating essentially no predictability for focus on self. The patient self-description presented in Figure 4 suggests that in relation to staff he might show a very broad range of interpersonal behaviors, with some contradiction, such as a great degree of deference and overconformity alternating with defiance. In addition, there was a strong tendency to show independence and assertiveness, but, on the other hand, to sulk and appease. Scattered other behavioral propensities also appear, which are neither contradictory nor related to the center of gravity. These include fearfulness and withdrawal, as well as a tendency to clearly and warmly express oneself. Such broad variability is responsible for the low coefficient of internal consistency.

If in a larger sample these trends were confirmed, then it could be said that paranoids can be characterized as likely to engage in blatant attack and hostile control when focusing on others and likely to show strong withdrawal, assertiveness, and defensiveness when focus is on the self. These trends are unpredictable and unstable, especially when the focus is on the self. By contrast, the schizoidal person would be hypothesized to be clearly and consistently oriented around hostile withdrawal whether the focus is on other or on self.

By this methodology, reliability as measured by the coefficient of internal consistency is expected to be low for some categories, and that is pathognomic. To make this statement with any degree of certainty, one would have to find this unreliability reliably. In other words, on test–retest, the same low coefficients of internal consistency should be obtained for the diagnostic groups to be named as unstable.

There is some overlap between the schizoidal and the paranoid individuals represented in Figures 3 and 4. In general, the schizoidal person hypothetically centers in Quadrant II. Another way of describing this would be to say the schizoidal center is theoretically located at 135° from the origin using ordinary geometric conventions. The paranoid person shown in Figure 4 had some above-median items in Quadrant II, but was centered near the disaffiliative pole, and had proportionately more items in Quadrant III. At least for the focus-on-other surface, it could be said that the paranoid personality is centered at about 180° from the origin. These generalized or "ball-park" descriptions of the orientation of these two presumably representative individuals are summarized in Table 1, where hypothetical centers are presented for three DSM-III categories: schizoid, paranoid, and compulsive.

In Table 1 there is an attempt to show how the SASB methodology might characterize these three diagnostic categories and account for the overlap among them in a logical, operationally measurable fashion. Traditional nosology has been faulted for overlap of categories (Zigler & Phillips, 1961), so if overlap exists in practice, the theory must account for it. To provide a frame of reference for reading Table 1, the DSM-III descriptions for these three diagnoses are presented: The schizotypal personality disorder (301.22) appears under the category Introverted Personality Disorder (301.21)—"Few, if any, close friends. A defect in capacity to form social relationships. Introversion (reserved, withdrawn, seclusive, pursues solitary interests, detached). Bland or constricted affect. Diagnosed as schizotypal personality disorder (301.22) if accompanied by eccentricity of communication or behavior." These DSM-III descriptions correspond reasonably to the Quadrant II endorsements discussed in connection with Figure 3 and it should be noted that the patient assigned himself a score of 90 when evaluating the applicability of the item titled "Illogical initiation." On the questionnaires this item reads: "Regardless of what is said or done, I treat them [staff] according to unwarranted, illogical assumptions." This corresponds to DSM-III, "Eccentricity of communication." Moving to the introject surface not shown in Table 1, the schizoidal individual can be expected to neglect personal options, fantasize and dream, and show the other introjected Quadrant II behaviors specified in Figure 1. The DSM-III and SASB descriptions relate also to Leary's suggestion that the schizoid is "passively resistant, bitter, distrustful."

The DSM-III description of paranoid personality mentions "pervasive and unwarranted suspiciousness and mistrust of people. Hypersensitivity (including readiness to counterattack any perceived threat). Restrictive aspect of experience. Perceived by others as cold and unemotional. Lacks humor and softness." The paranoid self-description shown in Figure 4 corresponds quite closely to the interpersonal aspects of this DSM-III description. Moving to the introject surface not shown in Table 1, the paranoid person can be expected to be a

TABLE 1. Comparison of the Categories Schizoid, Paranoid, and Compulsive in Terms of SASB and the Proposed Models for Affect (SAAB) and Cognition (SACB)

DSM-III category	Focus on other			Focus on self		
	SASB behavior	SAAB affect	SACB cognitive style	SASB behavior	SAAB affect	SACB cognitive style
Schizoid (135°)	Forget Ignore	Uncaring Disgusted	Tune-out Illogical	Wall-off Alone Withdraw	Pessimistic Bitter	Oppositional Loose, incoherent
Paranoid (180°)	Reject Attack Punish	Disgusted Enraged Vengeful	Illogical Termination Nihilistic	Withdraw Protest Appease	Bitter Hateful Fearful	Loose, incoherent Closed Ruminative
Compulsive (225°)	Punish Act superior Enforce conformity	Vengeful Arrogant	Nihilistic Judgmental	Appease Put-upon Proper	Fearful Humiliated	Ruminative Constricted, overcautious

menace to himself or herself and show other introjections around the disaffiliative pole. When attacking, the paranoid is identifying with the parental aggressor; when fearful and suicidal, he or she is complementing and introjecting the aggressor.

The compulsive personality disorder in DSM-III (301.40) includes the descriptors "inappropriate preoccupation with trivial details, rules, orders, organization, schedules, lists. Insists that others submit to his ways of doing things. Obsessive devotion to work and productivity to the exclusion of pleasure and value in interpersonal relationships. Indecisiveness and fear of making a mistake." SASB data are not shown from an individual diagnosed obsessive, but in Table 1 it is suggested that the obsessive persons will tend to overlap the paranoid, and be oriented further into the Quadrant of Hostile Power, say at about 225°. Looking back at the SASB model in Figure 1, it can be seen then that the description will include points like *intrude, block, restrict; enforce conformity; manage, control* on the focus-on-other surface; *apathetic compliance; following rules* and being *proper* on the focus-on-self surface. When moving to the introject surface not included in Table 1, one would also expect on the basis of Figure 1 to see high endorsement of guilt, self-doubt, self-restraint, and enforcing propriety in the self as well as in others. The DSM-III and SASB descriptions correspond somewhat to Leary's description of the compulsive as "managing, power-oriented, autocratic."

In summary, it is hypothesized that individuals classified in the three DSM-III categories of Table 1 would show complementary orientations on the two interpersonal surfaces (along with corresponding introjects). Other diagnostic categories may not show this autocomplementarity, which, by the way, rules out complementary relations with another person, but lack of space precludes further examination of these possibilities here. Just to illustrate, however, it could be mentioned that the hysteric (called the histrionic personality disorder in DSM-III) is hypothetically oriented in Quadrant IV of the focus-on-self surface (Friendly Acceptance, Figure 2). This posture compares to Leary's description of the hysteric as naive, sweet, and overconforming. However, when the hysteric starts to "give trouble," she or he can move very effectively into Quadrant III, Hostile Power. Usually the hysteric is accompanied by a significant other person who characteristically complements these two orientations: normally, the kindly significant other accompanying the hysteric functions in Quadrant IV of the focus-on-other surface (showing Friendly Influence, including much protectiveness and nurturance). However, when the hysteric gets "out of control" and into one of her or his irrational outbursts, the significant other moves into the complementary quadrant of Hostile Compliance, Quadrant IV on the focus-on-self surface. The compliance usually is of the form of trying ever harder to meet the hysteric's "needs."

STRUCTURAL MODELS FOR AFFECT AND COGNITION AND THEIR APPLICATION TO DIAGNOSIS

This discussion of the categories schizoid, paranoid, and compulsive began with social behavior shown in just two of the columns of Table 1. The columns were headed "Focus on other, SASB behavior," and "Focus on self, SASB behavior." For each type of focus in Table 1, there is also a column describing affect, and another describing cognitive style. The entries in these columns respectively came from a model for Structural Analysis of Affective Behavior (SAAB) and Structural Analysis of Cognitive Behavior (SACB). These models hypothetically parallel the SASB behavior model and exhibit the same principles of opposition, complementarity, and antithesis. Lack of space and other considerations preclude full exposition of the proposed SAAB and SACB models here, but predictions based on them are included in Table 1 to show what the final diagnostic picture might look like when the logic of structural analysis has been pursued to its conclusion.

To give an idea of the source of the entries in Table 1, the poles of each of the axes for each model will be named. Entries in the Table either include these poles, or are located on the models between them. Poles for the SAAB model are focus on other—enraged (−) and amorous (+) on the horizontal; indifferent (+) and forceful (−) on the vertical; focus on self—hate (−) and love (+) on the horizontal; unconcern (+) and helpless (−) on the vertical. Poles for the SACB model, focus on other, are termination (−) and extension (+) on the horizontal; broad scan (+) and sharp focus on detail (−) on the vertical. For focus on self the poles are: closed to experience (−) and openness to experience (+) on the horizontal; free-thinking (+) and appeal to authority (−) on the vertical. A dimensional ratings procedure completed by five psychiatric residents has supported the general structure of these new models, but further tests for validity are needed and planned. The SAAB and SACB models are expected to require several revisions, as did the SASB during its 10 developmental years.

The current SAAB and SACB models shown in Table 1 suggest

that the schizoid's affects would be uncaring, disgusted, pessimistic, and bitter. The cognitive style would be tune-out, illogical, oppositional, loose, incoherent. These predictions are consistent with clinical experience and can be partially confirmed by reviewing the DSM-III description mentioned above. In addition, they are supported by looking at the self-description mentioned above. They also are supported by looking at the self-descriptions of the schizoidal person in Figure 3 while imagining how he might feel and think.

Inspection of Table 1 suggests the paranoid's affects would center around fearfulness, hatefulness, and bitterness when the focus is on self, and on disgust, rage, and vengefulness when the focus is on others. Thought processes would be ruminative, closed, loose, and incoherent when focus is on self, and they would be nihilistic, terminal, and illogical when focusing on others. Again, the description of table 1 is consistent with DSM-III as presented and with phenomenology expected to accompany behaviors endorsed by the paranoid person presented in Figure 4.

For the compulsive person, the entries in Table 1 suggest the affects would be arrogance, vengefulness, fearfulness, and sensitivity to humiliation. Thought processes would be judgmental, nihilistic, constricted, overcautious, and ruminative. Clinically, compulsive persons are sometimes said to be without affect, and the only affect clearly mentioned in DSM-III is fear of making a mistake. In general, managerial types, who often decompensate in the compulsive direction, have not been intensively studied and labeled in clinics. Leary (1957) has suggested there is a need to create a diagnostic description for the managerial types even though they rarely bring themselves for treatment. An important and long-neglected beginning in this area was offered by Adorno, Frenkel-Brunswick, Levinson, and Sanford (1950). If the SASB, SAAB, and SACB models were to be used to further the study of the authoritarian personality, the specific predictions shown in Table 1 could be empirically checked and/or revised.

There is much more that could be said about Table 1, but for now the discussion must close with three thoughts:

1. The predictions are explicit and testable.

2. Overlap between these three diagnostic categories makes sense if one thinks of a category as centering at a given point and associated behaviors and styles are being normally distributed around it.

3. Transitions between diagnoses can also be described rationally. For example, the observation that compulsives usually de-

compensate in the direction of paranoia can be described as a rotation of about 45° toward the disaffiliative pole. Causes of such a rotation will have to be established by research, but a starting hypothesis might be that such a rotation could be induced by strong disaffiliative messages, such as those sometimes given when a person is up for tenure review, reelection, or otherwise subject to attack and/or rejection in a setting where the stakes are high.

USE OF SASB FOR INPATIENT DIAGNOSIS AND TREATMENT

To illustrate how the SASB methodology might be used for diagnosis and treatment on an inpatient unit, a case labeled a borderline personality disorder will briefly be presented. The patient, a female, had been referred from one hospital to another because of excessively destructive behavior on the first hospital's inpatient ward. The principle presenting symptom was a readiness to carve on herself with any available sharp object; the patient reported that she felt much better when she did this. From time to time there was suicidal thinking, although it was not associated with the carving. The patient's self-concept as measured by the introject part of the SASB model is presented in Figure 5. There, it can be seen that there was a highly consistent introjection of hostile power with a weighted affiliation-autonomy vector of (− 50, − 60). The carving on herself and the accompanying verbalizations certainly correspond to the points in Figure 5: ignore own basic needs; reject, dismiss self; torture, annihilate self; menace to self; drain, overburden self; vengeful self-punishment; and guilt, blame, bad self.

In Figure 6, the patient's SASB ratings of the family as a category are presented. The family's focus on the patient was strongly disaffiliative and represented a highly consistent orientation around attack and rejection. The patient revealed on interview that her father had given her daily beatings and this probably accounts for the strong endorsements around the attack pole; it also probably relates to her report of constantly fearing that a male figure was after her and going to hurt her. She disclosed that she felt her mother was very absorbed with her father, who had a chronic illness, and with her brother. The absorption with the brother and father possibly accounts for the heavy endorsements in the rejecting region of the focus on other surface.

```
PERSON RATES INTROJECT
THE SCORE   40 IS MEDIAN

                                    40*  *  *  20
                                  20*  *  *  30
                                40*  *  *  10
                              20*  *  * 50 EXPLORE, HEAR INNER SEL
                            40*  *  *  30
                          40*  *  *  20          * 50 ENTERTAIN,ENJOY SELF
                        20*  *  *  10            *  40
     IGNORE OWN BASIC NEEDS  80*  *  *           * 50 SEEK BEST FOR SELF
   REJECT, DISMISS SELF  70*  *  *               *  40
 TORTURE, ANNIHILATE SELF  70* * * * * * * * * * *  * 50 PROTECT SELF
MENACE TO SELF  99*  *  *                         *  40
DRAIN, OVERBURDEN SELF  70*  *  *                 *  40
  VENGEFUL SELF PUNISH  80*  *  *                 * 50 PRACTICE, BE ACCOMPLISHE
       GUILT, BLAME, BAD SELF  60*  *  *          * 80 SELF PAMPER,INDULGE
                      40*  *  *  20               * 70 BENEVOLENT EYE ON SELF
       RESTRAIN, HOLD SELF BACK  80*  *  *
             FORCE PROPRIETY  60*  *  *  20
                  CONTROL, MANAGE SELF  70*  *

WEIGHTED AFFILIATION -- AUTONOMY VECTOR=(-50., -60.)
COEFFICIENT OF INTERNAL CONSISTENCY = .968
CONTRADICTION COEFFICIENT = .054  RIGHT ANGLES COEFFICIENT = .604
```

FIGURE 5. A "borderline" rates her introject. The weighted affiliation–autonomy vector centers in the middle of the quadrant of hostile oppression (see Figure 2) and this orientation is maintained with a high degree of internal consistency. Her carving on herself is consistent with this orientation and her internal strengths are shown by the entries on the right-hand side of the figure.

```
FAMILY FOCUSES ON ME (TOP) AND ON THEMSELVES (BOTTOM)
THE SCORE    50 IS MEDIAN
                                                    0*   90 ENDORSE FREEDOM
              UNCARINGLY LET GO                80*  *   50 *
              FORGET                      90*  *    *  80 YOU CAN DO IT FINE
              IGNORE,PRETEND NOT THERE    90*  *    *   20
              NEGLECT INTERESTS,NEEDS     99*  *    *   40
              ILLOGICAL INITIATION    60*  *        *   20
              ABANDON,LEAVE IN LURCH  99*  *        *   10
              STARVE,CUT OUT      80*  *            *   10
                              50*  *                *   30
ANNIHILATING ATTACK      80* * * * * * * * * * * * * *   30   0
              APPROACH MENACINGLY  80*  *           *   20
              RIP OFF,DRAIN    70*  *               *   10
              PUNISH,TAKE REVENGE  90*  *           *   10
              DELUDE,DIVERT,MISLEAD   80*  *        *   10
              ACCUSE,BLAME            99*  *        *   20
              PUT DOWN,ACT SUPERIOR      70*  *     *   50
              INTRUDE,BLOCK,RESTRICT        80*  *  *   50
                                          50* * *  *
                                             30*

WEIGHTED AFFILIATION - AUTONOMY VECTOR=(-129., 35.)
COEFFICENT OF INTERNAL CONSISTENCY = .996
CONTRADICTION COEFFICIENT = .059  RIGHT ANGLES COEFFICIENT =   .611
```

```
               GO OWN SEPARATE WAY              0*  70 FREELY COME AND GO
                                        90*   *  50
                                             40*  *  50
                  WALL-OFF,NONDISCLOSE   90*      *  60 ASSERT ON OWN
                AVOID THROUGH ACTIVITIES   90*        *  50
                  NONCONTINGENT REACTION  80*            *  40
                GRIEVE,MOURN,FEEL ALONE  80*               *  30
                 REFUSE ASSISTANCE,CARE  70*                 *  40
               FLEE,RUN AWAY,WITHDRAW  70*                     *  40
           DESPERATE PROTEST  80* * * * * * * * * * * * *  40
                 WARY,FEARFUL  80*                           *  30
                              20*                         *  70 ACCEPT CARETAKING
                            40*                         *  80 ASK,TRUST,COUNT ON
                          20*                       *  70 TAKE IN,TRY,LEARN FROM
           WHINE,DEFEND,JUSTIFY  60*   10*        *  70 CLING,DEPEND
                                     40*         *  20
                              20*  20*         *  20
                                   10*
```

WEIGHTED AFFILIATION - AUTONOMY VECTOR=(-38., 62.)
COEFFICENT OF INTERNAL CONSISTENCY = .748
CONTRADICTION COEFFICIENT = .636 RIGHT ANGLES COEFFICIENT = .511

FIGURE 6. The "borderline" patient of Figure 5 rates her family as a category. Entries on the focus-on-other surface show that the family was very hostile and rejecting in its orientation toward the patient and this was maintained with a high degree of internal consistency. The focus-on-self surface shows a high degree of hostile withdrawal contradicted by an opposing tendency to accept nurturance and care-giving from the patient. The oppressive aspects of the patient's introject in Figure 5 were related to the oppressive aspects of family input in Figure 6 by program INTERP.

The family's focus on themselves was characterized mostly by hostile withdrawal, as suggested by the block of above-median items in Quadrant II and the vector of (− 38, + 62). However, there was also a contradictory tendency for the family to show Friendly Acceptance, indicated in Figure 6 by the block of above-median items in Quadrant IV with a contradiction coefficient of .636. The family's Friendly Acceptance shown in Figure 6 was complementary to the patient's giving of friendly support, shown in Figure 7.

In Figure 7, the SASB analysis of the patient's ratings of herself in relation to the family are presented and there it is clear that she saw herself as providing many warm, friendly, supportive behaviors in a highly consistent fashion. This is not an unusual presentation for abused children. Moving to the focus-on-self surface of Figure 7, it can be seen the patient described herself as acceptant in a friendly way, but also as quite submissive, appeasing, sacrificing, fearful, and protesting. Her focus-on-self behaviors were not consistent at all (.035); this group of behaviors included friendly approach (characteristic of children) alternating with the hostile compliance (complementing hostile power received from the family).

In summary, the patient's carving on herself could be related to the hostile–oppressive introject shown in Figure 5. That introject theoretically was strengthened by the perception of consistent hostile attack coming from the family. During the initial SASB consultation, it was learned that the patient felt she deserved punishment because of the following incident, which, apparently, was not unusual in the somewhat chaotic family setting. The patient's mother had had an affair and the patient had disclosed this to the father, who then set off in an attempt to murder the other man. The whole family, the patient included, agreed that the murderous attempt was the patient's fault. At the consultation, it was suggested that this myth should be dispelled and everyone should be encouraged to take responsibility for his or her own actions. However, the family conference was conducted by another staff person who worked from a different model, and the incident and the pattern inherent in it were not discussed. The medical student commented on the basis of his observations during the family conference that Figures 6 and 7 were "amazingly accurate."

The SASB ratings were used for treatment planning to the extent that it was possible on a once-a-week consulting basis. Initially the staff was asked to talk with the patient whenever she felt anxious in order to help her learn to figure out why she was feeling like carving on herself as well as to help her learn to develop alternative means of

dealing with that anxiety. The reasoning was that such friendly protectiveness and teaching (Quadrant IV, focus on other) would serve
as an opposite to the family's rejection (Quadrant II, focus on other)
and as an antithesis to their hostile withdrawal (Quadrant II, focus
on self).

The staff attempted to carry out this program, although it was
disruptive of their schedules and they were not specifically trained in
helping her understand herself at a deep level; conversations tended
to be at the symptomatic level. Gradually, however, the acting-out on
the ward decreased and the nursing note entered the night before the
family conference read: "Is more hopeful, still struggles with self-
mutilation. Good control without a contract [to contact staff if feeling self-destructive]." Following the family conference, the first nursing note entry was: "I don't want to talk, I feel talked out. I want to do
something destructive. Maybe I should be in seclusion. I'm feeling
very out of control. I think I should have a shot." Later that day, a
nursing note recorded: "Was unsatisfied with family conference. Felt
family still scapegoats her. They do not own up to their responsibilities in the family dynamics. Later felt the need to punish herself and
was placed in seclusion and given [medications]." In the days that
followed the staff became increasingly frustrated with her decompensation and increasing demands. The medical student was enraged
and wanted to go in and tell her off. Use of the SASB model precluded
this even though the student's reaction was understandable enough.
For the staff to act out anger at the patient would mean that they
would begin to behave like the family as shown in Figure 6 and only
increase the self-punitive behavior and the patient's conviction that
she deserved it. Complementarity like this is otherwise known as self-
fulfilling prophecy or, in Freudian terms, as repetition compulsion.
Ideally there should have been a series of family conferences focusing
on the scapegoating dynamic and helping to change the family input;
if that failed, the patient should have been helped to separate from
that input. In reality no further family conferences were possible, so
for purposes of management in the hospital there was nothing left to
do but switch to a simple behavior program, which provided that the
staff would give attention and concern only if the patient had effectively resisted attempts at self-mutilation for an agreed-upon length
of time. Under this model, staff attention and concern were given as a
reward for constructive rather than destructive behaviors and this
proved effective for inpatient management. The problem with the behavioral program was that it was essentially a model for external control rather than one that involved understanding and learning of self-

I FOCUS ON FAMILY (TOP) AND ON MYSELF (BOTTOM)
THE SCORE   40 IS MEDIAN

```
                              0%  40
                         20* *  50 ENCOURAGE SEPARATE IDEN
                      10*    *  90 YOU CAN DO IT FINE
                    20*      *  80 FAIRLY CONSIDER
                            *  80 FRIENDLY EXPLORE=LISTEN
ILLOGICAL INITIATION  10*   *  50 SHOW EMPATHIC UNDERSTAN
                  10*       *  50 CONFIRM AS OK AS IS
              20*           *  80 STROKE=SOOTHE=CALM
             30*           *  90 WARMLY WELCOME
         30* *  *  *  *  * *  0
          10*              *  99 FRIENDLY INVITE
            20*            *  70 PROVIDE FOR=NURTURE
             30*          *  90 PROTECT=BACK UP
            20*           *  50 SENSIBLE ANALYSIS
          40*             *  80 CONSTRUCTIVE STIMULATE
         20*              *  10
        30* *            *  40
           30*        * *  50 SPECIFY WHAT'S BEST
            30*
```

WEIGHTED AFFILIATION - AUTONOMY VECTOR=(89., 13.)
COEFFICENT OF INTERNAL CONSISTENCY = .965
CONTRADICTION COEFFICIENT = -.028 RIGHT ANGLES COEFFICIENT = .546

220

```
                              0*  50 FREELY COME AND GO
                            20** * 80 OWN IDENTITY, STANDARDS
                         40* * * 90 ASSERT ON OWN
                      10* * * 90 PUT/CARDS ON TABLE''
                    30* * * 70 OPENLY DISCLOSE, REVEAL
                  40* * * 70 CLEARLY EXPRESS
                10* * * 80 ENTHUSIASTIC SHOWING
              10* * * 30
            20* * * 40
          60** * * * * * * * 0
        70* * * 90 FOLLOW, MAINTAIN CONTACT
      70* * * 80 ACCEPT CARETAKING
    80* * * 60 ASK, TRUST, COUNT ON
  60* * * 60 ACCEPT REASON
50* * * 50 TAKE IN, TRY, LEARN FROM
  40* * * 40
    20* * * 60 DEFER, OVERCONFORM
      40** * 60 SUBMERGE INTO ROLE
        50*

DESPERATE PROTEST
WARY, FEARFUL
SACRIFICE
APPEASE, SCURRY
UNCOMPREHENDING AGREE
WHINE, DEFEND, JUSTIFY
        YIELD, SUBMIT, GIVE IN

WEIGHTED AFFILIATION - AUTONOMY VECTOR=( 31., -1.)
COEFFICIENT OF INTERNAL CONSISTENCY = .035
CONTRADICTION COEFFICIENT = .415 RIGHT ANGLES COEFFICIENT = .685
```

FIGURE 7. The "borderline" patient of Figures 5 and 6 rates herself in relation to what she re-
ceived, the patient was quite friendly to the family for both types of focus and, in addition, showed hostile compliance with their attack and demands. The giving of nurturance and high compliance as a response to attack is often the fate of abused children who are
attempting to provide the antithesis and opposite of what they receive. This rating emphasizes her competence.

221

directed self-control. These remarks are not intended to set up a dichotomy between behavioral and SASB approaches; indeed, they can and should be compatible and facilitate each other (Benjamin, 1977, pp. 395, 402). Over a longer period of time, there could have been fading out of the external reward model back toward the procedure that encouraged introjection of a "teacher."

This informally managed case is not a rigorous test or demonstration of the possibilities for the use of SASB on an inpatient service. Consultation was too infrequent; staff was not specifically trained to use SASB, and treatment approaches (e.g., the family conference) were not coordinated; and there was no direct connection with the after-care system to make sure there would be long-range pursuit of the relearning needs outlined by the SASB analysis. Nevertheless, the presentation does serve to show how the SASB model could make specific statements about social dynamics according to an operationally specified procedure. To underscore how totally operationalized the SASB procedures can be, there will be a direct quotation of the essence of the case as generated by computer program INTERP:

> For each clearly defined aspect of self-concept, there will be a report of behaviors from other persons which hypothetically reinforce the listed aspects of self-concept. . . .
>
> Aspect of self concept—self rejecting and destroying. The person rated is described as very hurtful of self. This may include ignoring illness and injuries, enduring great harm for the sake of others; rejecting, depriving and devaluing the self; generally behaving as one's own worst enemy. In its harshest form, this may include senseless torture and annihilation of the self. The possibility of self-destructive behavior should be discussed with a health professional.
>
> This aspect of self-concept may be reinforced by—
>
> The family when . . . [they] show—
>
> Attacking and rejecting. The person rated is described as seriously threatening and/or hurting the other person. Extreme behaviors of this sort would include overt attack, whether physical or mental, with the intent of destroying. Other forms could include starving, "cutting out," angrily rejecting, and/or taking unfair advantage. If this situation is current, it probably should be discussed with a health professional.

The patient's ratings of the staff (not shown) suggested the staff was providing antithetical behavior to the self-destruction. Program INTERP read

> The relationship theoretically needing antithesis is—
>
> The patient's introject

The often undesirable behavior is self-rejection and destroying
Antitheses would be nurturing and comforting exhibited by the other person
Rated relationships theoretically providing antitheses are—
Staff in relation to patient (patient's view)

A COMPARISON OF SASB AND TRADITIONAL DIAGNOSIS

The inpatient case presented in Figures 5–7 shows that the SASB methodology is responsive to a number of the criticisms of traditional diagnosis. The SASB is not based on a hodge-podge of miscellaneous observations of social behavior. Rather, it systematically measures social behavior and offers a strong theoretical base for describing social aspects of etiology. Figure 5 was created and related to Figure 6 in a highly explicit, operationally defined manner; the intrarater reliability of program INTERP is 100%. In addition to considering etiology, the SASB methodology prescribes treatment interventions using the principle of antithesis.

The failure to obtain a miracle cure with the two SASB consultations on this case serves to remind that behavior is complex and that there are no shortcuts to the process of relearning. It requires consistent, expert, focused, patient guidance, a supportive milieu, and will on the part of the patient to learn and practice hard. The SASB is a "living" model and contrasts with the medical and auto-mechanic models, wherein the malfunctioning machine or person is brought in, worked upon, and released when running better. The living model, with its evolutionary heritage (Benjamin, 1979a), compares to a music lesson rather than to a trip to the automobile-repair shop. The SASB analysis corresponds to the expert input from the music teacher to the student. In contrast to auto repair, there is no expectation that the teacher's intervention will suddenly prepare the student for Carnegie Hall. The major responsibility for change lies in the learner whose genetic potential is being developed. Much independent practice with reiterated constructive input from the teacher will be required.

The personal growth orientation of the SASB model means, among other things, that its use is not adversarial. Descriptions such as those presented in Figures 3 through 8 are not appropriate or available for professional self-enhancement of the sort that might be characterized by the phrase "He or she is half and I am whole." As a matter of fact, for best results, SASB ratings require a high degree of patient–doctor mutuality. Patients rate doctors as well as vice versa. The self-descriptions are good faith ratings and are vulnerable to distortion in the direction of social desirability. The questions are straightforward and the analysis is forthright, so one who wished to present a rosy picture according to his or her own values would have little problem doing so. This is a deficit in the methodology according to the people who are concerned about response sets, but it is a strength according to patient-advocates. The patient view is built directly into the diagnostic and treatment process. The self-ratings are most useful to the patient when the patient has motivation for self-discovery and personal growth. In cases where this is lacking, contrast between self-ratings and the staff ratings will show themselves, and the discrepancy will be pathognomic. However, assumptions are not automatically made about who is "right." Recall, for example, that the self-description for Figure 3 was more accurate than the staff description.

The SASB methodology shows the pathology as, for example, in Figure 5, but it also shows strengths or competence as in Figure 7. There the patient's ability to nurture and take care of her family was clearly described. Like many abused children, she had developed the ability to take care of others but not herself. In effect, she gave the family the opposite of what they gave her (compare Figures 6 and 7). Looking at it another way, she provided for them what she needed to have provided for her. A further discussion of pathology and "health" as described by the SASB model appears in Benjamin (1979a).

The illustrative case also showed how the trait–state issue can be handled by taking ratings for different relationships. For example, when the staff rated the patient in relation to patients, the focus-on-self surface, the weighted affiliation–autonomy vector was (− 12, + 9) and there was a very low degree of internal consistency. This suggested an average orientation of hostile withdrawal with much variability. By contrast, the staff ratings of the patient in relation to staff yielded a weighted affiliation–autonomy vector of (+ 78, − 34) with a higher degree of internal consistency (.743). Her orientation to staff was friendly and submissive. In other words, the staff rating of the patient in one context (in relation to patients) was the geometric opposite (see Figure 2) of the staff rating of the patient in another context (in relation to staff). The differences were meaningful; it would be a mistake to characterize the patient either as withdrawn or as compliant. She showed these two different types of focus on self in different contexts. Contextual differences also were found for her focus on others. The SASB method combines interpersonal with the intrapsychic viewpoints along the lines proposed years ago by Harry Stack Sullivan (1953). It is consistent with the psychoanalytic notion of introjection and with the thoughts of G. H. Mead (1934) about the self. Specific links between interpersonal experience and the self-concept as represented by the introject were illustrated by the relation between Figures 5 and 6. This aspect of the model, along with the parallel, cognitive, and affective models, potentially provides an organizing link between observations about social milieu and intrapsychic phenomena.

There are other aspects of SASB methodology not specifically illustrated in Figures 3–7 that also should be mentioned in the context of comparing SASB to traditional psychiatric diagnoses. The SASB methodology may have useful implications for medication. One therapist's rating of a lithium responder in the manic phase contrasted dramatically with the ratings of the same person in the depressive phase. During the manic phase there was a clear orientation around the attack pole for focus on other (the spouse), and an equally clear orientation around the autonomy pole for focus on self. The exact reverse was recorded for the depressed phase—there was a clear orientation around affiliation when the focus was on the spouse, and a consistent orientation around the submissive pole when the focus was on the self. If these trends were confirmed on appropriate larger samples, then SASB would be a clear behavioral measure for predicting who would and who would not be a lithium responder.

The SASB methodology combines the technological strengths usually characteristic of behavioristic approaches and the experiential or phenomenological features that are more characteristic of the so-called humanistic therapies.

The SASB methodology is complex enough to be realistic and yet the use of computers allows the organization of seemingly diverse bits of social information into coherent figures interrelated by operationalized procedures. Patients frequently say when viewing the output: "I *see*, I didn't realize my husband is like my mother. I had no idea there was so much information in those questions." Because the output is directly from patient-generated input, patients do not have difficulty recognizing the face validity of the description. By contrast, patient reaction to traditional psychiatric descriptions and psychological test results are so problematic that complex legal procedures have been set up regarding disclosure of such information to patients and normally disclosure occurs only if the patient insists.

It appears that the unconscious also may be measurable after more experience is gained with use of SASB in tracing patient progress. For example, one patient took and SASB interpersonal history at the beginning of her outpatient therapy and reported a quite positive self-concept as well as an excellent relationship with her lover. In this initial measurement, however, the patient described a great deal of hostile oppression from the mother, nurturance accompanied by some hostile withdrawal from the father, and extensive hostile interdependence between the mother and father. In sum, the initial report suggested the patient had a fairly positive self-concept and a good current relationship, but there was a difficult interpersonal history. The reasons for coming to therapy were numerous, including drug abuse and a tendency to go "far out" when stressed. As the relationship with the lover went on in time, it became clear that he was subject to periods of withdrawal and inaccessability, much like the father. His withdrawal usually was associated with a sharp decompensation in her self-concept and accompanied by the emergence of an oppressive introject that took the form of a voice that behaved in ways similar to the initial SASB descriptions of the parents. The voice had been present off and on during periods of stress since adolescence, but never had been disclosed to anyone, including physicians and preceding therapists. Direct SASB ratings of the voice confirmed its relation with the parents. At this point, the Minnesota Multiphasic Personality Inventory (MMPI) profile had elevations on the *Ma, Pd,* and *Sc* scales, and there was a marked vulnerability to suicide. In retrospect then, the SASB descriptions of the early history had relevance to what was going to unfold when the relationship with the lover lost its ability to provide antitheses for the potentials lying within the unconscious.

The SASB model can accomodate crosscultural differences. A recent factor analysis of a sample of outpatients with many Mexican-Americans showed the hypothesized factor structure, but also showed different average ratings to reflect the different lifestyles. In general, this outpatient Mexican-American sample showed less affiliative feelings about themselves and others than did the middle-class white comparison sample (Cerling, 1979). One might hypothesize that some of this disaffiliation could be related to the lesser degrees of social affirmation received by Mexican-Americans in this culture.

Theoretically the SASB model could be used at a national as well as at a group or individual level. For example, with its high value on individualism, the politics of the United States might be characterized in terms of Quadrant I. Those of the People's Republic of China, currently presented in terms of benevolent control, might be described by Quadrant IV. The oppressive dictatorships prevailing in the news so often seem to function in Quadrant III. They seem especially prone to a punishment and revenge morality. Finally, the anarchists might be described in terms of a desire for Quadrant II.

For purposes of prevention, SASB developmental norms might be useful. Preliminary norms on an earlier version of SASB are available (Benjamin, 1979d), and if confirmed with the newer versions of the SASB on larger, more diversified samples, the resultant developmental norms might be used to monitor the social development of normal pediatric outpatients. The model could be used for prescribing appropriate parental behaviors, especially in terms of varying the degrees of affiliation and autonomy-giving at different developmental stages.

Finally, SASB can provide a rationale for some puzzling clinical phenomena that seemingly defy logic and scientific understanding. In a first example, the SASB model offers a clear technology for defining the common clinical phenomenon of contradiction. The contradiction coefficient represents the extent to which subjects rate or are rated in terms of opposites as specified by the SASB model. When this reaches noticeable levels (.75 or greater according to program INTERP), one can begin to speak of double-binding communications if the domain being described involves focus on other; such a high contradiction coefficient describes ambivalence if the domain being described involves focus on self. There is still another phenomenon that may represent an especially destructive kind of bind; in SASB language this bind might be called a quadruple- rather than a double-bind: When a communication is multiply codable (Estroff & Benjamin, 1979) in terms of opposites, complements, and antitheses, it closes off all possible responses; crazy reverberating among chart points is one likely result. A detailed analysis of this viewpoint was offered in Benjamin (1979a), wherein one of Bateson's classic double-binds was discussed in terms of the SASB codings.

For a second example, the SASB methodology also can explain the effectiveness of some unconventional interventions, such as the ability of children to rehabilitate parents (Midelfort, 1957), or prisoners (*60 Minutes,* 11/4/79). In these cases, the children's friendly dependence upon the abusive parent and/or the prisoner is the antithesis of the hostile rejection (bonding failure) that these adults have experienced heretofore.

A third example is offered by Abramson and Sackeim's (1977) description of an intriguing paradox about depression. Their question was, How can persons who are depressed claim they are helpless, and yet, at the same time, take the familiar omnipotent position inherent in such monumental self-blame? How can the depressed person be so responsible for so many disasters, and at the same time, be so patently helpless? The resolution of that paradox using the SASB model is simple. The discussion of helplessness is relevant when the patient is focusing on self and is summarized mostly by interpersonal postures described by Quadrant III of that surface. The self-blaming is described by Quadrant III of the introject surface. Both Quadrant III focus on self and Quadrant III introject are results of hostile oppression from significant others and are represented by Quadrant III of the focus-on-other surface. Both effects are expected and predicted according to the SASB model: the uneasy helplessness represented by Quadrant III of the focus-on-self surface is the complement of the hostile oppression, and the self-blame represented by Quadrant III of the introject surface is the introjection of the hostile oppression. Resentful compliance and hostile self-oppression scores on SASB both correlate significantly with the pathology scales of the MMPI (Cerling, 1979).

CONCLUSION

Much of what has been said here requires extensive documentation through research. The interpersonal diagnosis project represents a beginning. It is hoped that treatment projects will follow so that interventions will not be sketchy and uncoordinated as they were for the inpatient case discussed here. The research potential for SASB seems infinite, as is appropriate for a valid hypothetical construct (MacCorquodale & Meehl, 1951). The SASB model preserves for the social domain many of the advantages of the traditional medical model, including the ability reliably to classify and operationally to specify hypotheses about etiology and to develop treatment implications with a theoretical rationale. In addition, the model avoids many of the criticisms of traditional diagnosis in that it is operational, valid, reliable, theoretically organized, not adversarial, draws heavily on data coming directly from the patient, measures competence as well as pathology, and is suitably complex and yet usable. In one illustrative sample, SASB was not vulnerable to crosscultural differences, and it may be that SASB can be used to characterize cultures or political orientations. Descriptions of social behavior by SASB may have implications for medications. In addition, the method offers hope for handling difficult and complex, but well-known clinical phenomena, such as the links between the interpersonal and the intrapsychic, the overlap between diagnostic categories, the effectiveness of some unconventional social interventions, the definition of double-bind and ambivalence, and the resolution of a paradox of depression. After further study, SASB may apply to the unconscious as well as to the preconscious. With the addition of the parallel affective and cognitive models (see Table 1), SASB may relate traditional affective and cognitive symptoms to social behavior and vice versa. Moreover, these symptoms themselves may be organized within a coherent theoretical framework, with the overlap between diagnostic categories being explained rationally. In conclusion, the methodology, if applied conscientiously and persistently, might help bring order to the questions of the development or the failure of the development of competence of both the patient and the clinician.

REFERENCES

Abramson, L. Y. & Sackeim, H. A. A paradox in depression: Uncontrollability and self-blame. *Psychological Bulletin,* 1977, *84,* 838–851.

Adorno, T. W., Frenkel-Brunswik, E., Levinson, D. J., & Sanford, R. N. *The authoritarian personality.* New York: Wiley, 1950.

American Psychiatric Association. *Diagnostic and statistical manual of mental disorders* (3rd ed.). Washington, DC: Author, 1980.

Beck, A. T., Rush, A. J., Shaw, B., & Emery, G. *Cognitive therapy of depression.* New York: Guilford Press, 1979.

Benjamin, L. S. Structural analysis of social behavior. *Psychological Review,* 1974, *81,* 392–425.

Benjamin, L. S. Structural analysis of a family in therapy. *Journal of Consulting and Clinical Psychology,* 1977, *45,* 391–406.

Benjamin, L. S. Structural analysis of differentiation failure. *Psychiatry: Journal for the Study of Interpersonal Process,* 1979, *42,* 1–23. (a)

Benjamin, L. S. Use of structural analysis of social behavior (SASB) and Markov chains to study dyadic interactions. *Journal of Abnormal Psychology,* 1979, *88,* 303–319.

Benjamin, L. S. *Social behavior, Markov chains, and development of insight in therapy.* Paper presented at the meeting of the American Psychological Association, New York, 1979.

Benjamin, L. S. *A manual for using SASB questionnaires to measure correspondence among family history, self-concept and current relations with significant others.* (Available from the author at University of Wisconsin Clinical Sciences Center,

Madison, WI 53792, and through ERIC Document Reproduction Service, No. ED 164 137, January 1979.) (d)

Benjamin, L. S. *Validity of structural analysis of social behavior (SASB)*. Submitted for publication.

Cerling, D. C. *Interpersonal dimensions of psychopathology*. Unpublished doctoral dissertation, Fuller Theological Seminary, Pasadena, CA, 1979.

Endler, N. S., & Magnusson, D. Toward an interactional psychology of personality. *Psychological Bulletin,* 1976, *83,* 956-974.

Estroff, S., & Benjamin, L. S. *Manual for using SASB to code videotapes and typescripts*. Unpublished manuscript, 1979.

Feighner, J. P., Robins, E., Guze, S. B., Woodruff, R. A., Winokur, G., & Muñoz, R. Diagnostic criteria in psychiatric research. *Archives of General Psychiatry,* 1972, *26,* 57-63.

Goldstein, M. S. The sociology of mental health and illness. *Annual Review of Sociology,* 1979, *5,* 381-409.

Greist, J. H., & Klein, M. H. *Psychiatric diagnosis by computer interview*. Grant application to NIMH, approved for April 1, 1980 through March 31, 1983.

Jefferson, J. W., & Greist, J. H. *Primer of lithium therapy*. Baltimore: Williams & Wilkins, 1977.

Kanfer, F. H., & Saslow, G. Behavioral analysis: An alternative to diagnostic classification. *Archives of General Psychiatry,* 1965, *12,* 529-538.

Kendell, R. E. *The role of diagnosis in psychiatry*. Edinburgh: Aberdeen University Press, 1975.

Leary, T. *Interpersonal diagnosis of personality: A functional theory and methodology for personality evaluation*. New York: Ronald Press, 1957.

Leary T., & Coffey, H. S. Interpersonal diagnosis: Some problems of methodology and validation. *Journal of Abnormal and Social Psychology,* 1955, *50,* 110-124.

Lorr, M., Bishop, P. F., & McNair, D. M. Interpersonal types among psychiatric patients. *Journal of Abnormal Psychology,* 1965, *70,* 468-472.

MacCorquodale, K., & Meehl, P. Hypothetical constructs in intervening variables. In H. Feigl & M. Brodbeck (Eds.), *Readings in the philosophy of science*. New York: Basic Books, 1951.

McLemore, C. W., & Benjamin, L. S. Whatever happened to interpersonal diagnosis? A psychosocial alternative to DSM-III. *American Psychologist,* 1979, *34,* 17-34.

Mead, G. H. *Mind, self and society from the standpoint of a social behaviorist*. Chicago: University of Chicago Press, 1934.

Mezzich, J. E. Patterns and issues in multi-axial psychiatric diagnosis. *Psychological Medicine,* 1979, *9,* 125-137.

Midelfort, C. F. *The family in psychotherapy*. New York: McGraw-Hill, 1957.

Mischel, W. *Personality and assessment*. New York: Wiley, 1968.

Mischel, W. Toward a cognitive social learning reconceptualization of personality. *Psychological Review,* 1973, *80,* 252-283.

Plutchik, R., & Platman, S. R. Personality connotations of psychiatric diagnoses: Implications for a similarity model. *Journal of Nervous and Mental Diseases,* 1977, *165,* 418-422.

Schaefer, E. S. A configurational analysis of children's reports of parent behavior. *Journal of Consulting Psychology,* 1965, *29,* 552-557.

Schaefer, E. S. From circular to spherical conceptual models for parent behavior and child behavior. In J. P. Hill (Ed.), *Minnesota symposium on child psychology* (Vol. 4). Minneapolis: University of Minnesota Press, 1971.

Schaefer, E. S., & Plutchik, R. Interrelationships of emotions, traits and diagnostic construct. *Psychological Reports,* 1966, *18,* 399–410.

Spitzer, R. L., Endicott, J., & Robins, E. Clinical criteria for psychiatric diagnoses and DSM-III. *American Journal of Psychiatry,* 1975, *132,* 1187–1192.

Strauss, J. S. Diagnostic models and the nature of psychiatric disorder. *Archives of General Psychiatry,* 1973, *29,* 445–449.

Strauss, J. S. A comprehensive approach to psychiatric diagnosis. *American Journal of Psychiatry,* 1975, *132,* 1193–1197.

Sullivan, H. S. *The interpersonal theory of psychiatry.* New York: Norton, 1953.

Sundberg, N. D., Snowden, L. R., & Reynolds, W. M. Toward assessment of personal competence and incompetence in life situations. *Annual Review of Psychology,* 1978, *29,* 179–221.

Zigler, E., & Phillips, L. Psychiatric diagnosis and symptomatology. *Journal of Abnormal and Social Psychology,* 1961, *63,* 69–75.

8

SOCIAL COMPETENCE AND THE INSTITUTIONALIZED MENTAL PATIENT

GORDON L. PAUL

GORDON L. PAUL is presently the Cullen Distinguished Professor of Psychology at the University of Houston, Houston, Texas. He is a highly prolific contributor to the methodological and behavioral intervention literature. His 1966 book, *Insight vs. Desensitization in Psychotherapy: An Experiment in Anxiety Reduction,* was groundbreaking in its demonstration of methodological rigor in the area of psychotherapy and behavior change. The study reported there rapidly became one of the most widely cited standards of methodological excellence in this area.

In the present chapter, Paul expands on work presented in his 1977 book with Lentz, *Psychosocial Treatment of Chronic Mental Patients: Milieu vs. Social-Learning Programs.* In this work he has brought his formidable methodological expertise to bear on an area considered difficult, if not intractable, by many clinical researchers—that is, the assessment of institutionally administered intervention programs with chronic psychiatric patients. His focus on specific overt behaviors required by the severely disabled population stands in marked contrast to the cognitive focus of other contributors in this volume who have dealt with higher-functioning groups, such as Meichenbaum, Butler, and Gruson in Chapter 2, Wrubel, Benner, and Lazarus in Chapter 3, and Shure in Chapter 6.

Without disregard for the importance of a social competence focus in other populations, nowhere is its relevance more established *empirically* than with the institutionalized mental patient—especially the chronically institutionalized. Until very recently (Paul & Lentz, 1977), no intramural treatment programs had been found to show differential long-term effects on resident (patient) behavior, release, or eventual stay in the extramural community. From 40% to 50% of releases from mental institutions are expected to be readmitted within a year (Anthony, Buell, Sharrett, & Althoff, 1972) and 72% of admissions receiving psychotic diagnoses are readmissions (Taube, 1974). With the attempts to purge the mental hospital population through what is euphemistically called "deinstitutionalization," more than half the chronically institutionalized so purged are readmitted in less than a year (Rieder, 1974). Even for those released to community extended-care facilities in which operators benefit financially by keeping them in the community, 30% to 40% are reinstitutionalized within 2 years (Anthony *et al.*, 1972; Kohen & Paul, 1976). After a decade of such practices, nearly half the residents of public mental institutions have been there 5 years or more, and 72% have been institutionalized at least a year and a half (Rieder, 1974). Those who do manage to avoid readmission to mental institutions are typically functioning at a marginal level, at best (Erickson, 1975).

The above statistics provide a sorry commentary on mental health systems at large, given the fact that institutions deal with populations most in need of mental health services and are the most expensive mode of treatment generally available. A further indication of the lack of positive impact of traditional institutional practices may be seen in the predictors of who will become chronically institutionalized: (1) ineffective prehospital adjustment—that is, low social competence, and (2) length and number of previous institutionalizations. These predictors have remained the most consistent for over 20 years and suggest needed changes in both institutional practices and a necessary focus of treatment efforts (Paul & Lentz, 1977).

FACTORS RELATED TO HOSPITALIZATION OR REHOSPITALIZATION

Some years ago I reviewed the available literature on follow-up studies of released mental patients (Paul, 1969). This review was undertaken to see if there were any consistencies in the environment, the individual's behavior, or the interaction between the two in determining the conditions for rehospitalization or continuing community stay. I hoped that such a review would provide the basis for an analysis to focus upon target areas for treatment of institutionalized mental patients that could prepare them for release with continuing tenure in the extramural community.

The act of hospitalization itself is a social action reflecting sanctions for behavior that is distressing (Ullmann & Krasner, 1975). Therefore, it may now come as no surprise that the behaviors associated with hospitalization, empirically, had a social referent and interacted with the expectations, tolerance, and support existent in the community environment.

Deficiencies in the performance of instrumental roles, for example, were found to be associated with hospitalization, but differentially depending upon the setting—absence of employment for a wage-earner; deficits in carrying out household responsibilities for housewives (and, presumably, househusbands, had sufficient numbers existed for inclusion); failures to be on time and on task for important events and activities in nearly any setting. Lack of competence in self-care, communications, and social–interactional skills were regularly associated with hospitalization if the performance deficit was severe enough to create a management problem for others, although less severe deficits were dependent upon the tolerance for deviance of people in the environment. However, the absence of at least one close social relationship—and, by inference, the skills necessary to allow such relationships to develop—was regularly associated with hospitalization, independent of other environmental factors.

Note that all of the factors mentioned above relate to social competence. They have little direct relevance to traditional concepts of psychiatric symptomatology, except as active withdrawal, depression, anxiety, or excess bizarre behavior might result in secondary performance deficits. In fact, indications of withdrawal, depression, anxiety, and mildly bizarre behavior were *not* found to be associated with hospitalization unless self-care, social interaction, and communications skills or instrumental role performance were drastically impaired. Even more severe problematic behavior of the level that typically leads to extramural psychological treatment—including occasional reports of hallucinations—were dependent upon the tolerance for deviance of people in the environment to be cited as a basis for hospitalization.

However, the occurrence of extremes in bizarre cognitive and motoric behavior, including assaultive acts, was most regularly identified as the basis for rehospitalization across studies, time, and no matter what the environmental setting. Indeed, such extreme bizarre behavior appears to be the primary factor for rehospitalization from community extended-care facilities in which preselection for acceptance has been based upon the possession of minimal social competencies (Paul & Lentz, 1977).

TARGETS OF FOCUS (MINIMAL GOALS)
FOR INSTITUTIONAL PROGRAMS

Based upon the analysis of circumstances empirically associated with the act of hospitalization or rehospitalization, four areas of focus were identified for institutional work (Paul, 1969). These four areas are proposed as the minimal necessary focus and goals to be addressed by intramural treatment programs to return institutionalized mental patients to the outside community.

1. *Resocialization*—including development of self-maintenance, interpersonal interaction, and communication skills.

2. *Instrumental role performance*—including provision of salable vocational skills and housekeeping skills—with a minimum of "on task" and "on time" components of performance necessary to freely interact with the local community and participate in future training programs.

3. *Reduction or elimination of extreme bizarre behavior*—including appropriate changes in frequency, intensity, or timing of individual acts or mannerisms consensually identified as distressing.

4. *Provision of at least one supportive "roommate" in the community*—including either a spouse, relative, parent, or friend.

Several points should be clarified with regard to these target areas or goals. Clarification is necessary due to the greater severity of the problems necessarily dealt with in institutionalized populations rather than noninstitutionalized populations, and due to the fact that the setting of treatment is intramural (inpatient) rather than extramural (community or outpatient) at the start.

Problem Behavior versus "Competence-Only" Focus

There is no doubt that nearly any problem can be conceptualized as an absence or deficit of requisite behavior and skill rather than an excess of problematic behaviors. McFall (1976) has been one of the most cogent proponents of this point of view and it is an orientation that I find generally compatible at the point of specifying treatment objectives. McFall, in fact, offers the "dead-man" test (first attributed to Ogden Lindsley) as a means of determining if treatment objectives are properly specified. That is, if a dead man could fulfill the criteria for the treatment objective, that objective is inadequate. Thus, any focus upon reduction or elimination of excess behavior would fail the dead-man test, since a dead man does nothing.

The first two targets for intramural treatment programs—resocialization and instrumental role performance—clearly focus on acquisition of requisite skills in areas of potential deficits in competent performance. They would therefore pass the dead-man test. However, the third target—reduction or elimination of extreme bizarre behavior—explicitly focuses upon the identification of excess problem behaviors to be reduced. As such, the third target would flunk McFall's dead-man test. I agree that the third target without the inclusion of the first two would be incomplete. Nevertheless I do believe that a comprehensive assessment of performance excesses, as well as learning and performance deficits and their functional relationships, is a better strategy, in general, than always attempting to force a "deficit-only" definition of problems, as I have detailed elsewhere (Paul, 1974). For the institutionalized mental patient, in particular, the reduction or elimination of excess bizarre behaviors is empirically more relevant to the prevention of rehospitalization than the absolute level of skill or specific alternative behaviors that might appropriately occur in a variety of situations in place of the bizarre behavior. This is not to say that treatment procedures focused predominantly upon acquisition of competent adaptive behavior will not affect bizarre behavior—they are remarkably effective. It merely emphasizes that the extremes of bizarre behavior are so important for the adequate treatment of the institutionalized that they must be assessed and reduced before community tenure is probable.

Situational Determinism

Excesses and deficits in performance cannot be determined in the abstract, but must be related to the specific situation in which performance is called forth. *Webster's Dictionary* provides a prime definition for "social" as "of or having to do with human beings living together as a group in a situation requiring that they have dealings with one another," and of "competence" as "capacity equal to requirement." Thus, by definition, social competence—in fact, competence of any sort—must be situationally determined. In Western culture, however, the minimum levels of competence in self-care, interpersonal interaction, communication, and instrumental skills required and maximum levels of bizarre behavior allowed for adults to continue to "have dealings with one another," thereby avoiding wholesale institutionalization, appear fairly consistent. Except for a few identifiable subcultures, our society at large is adequately homogeneous across situations in behavioral requirements that the minimal levels of performance required for remaining in the outside community rather than being extruded to an institution can be easily specified. Even so, treatment and assessment operations should ultimately focus upon the specific community of release and the transition from institution to the community to assure that situationally determined requirements are met.

Minimal Goals versus Optimal Goals

Note, also, that the targets of focus are parenthetically referred to as "minimal goals." Elsewhere Lentz and I have discussed minimal goals and optimal goals for treatment and training (Paul & Lentz, 1977). Based upon the expense of institutional treatment and its restrictiveness for clientele, we recommend that intramural treatment programs focus on minimal goals, defined as those that will allow the client to survive safely in less-restrictive community environments without serious burden to self or others; that is, to bring residents to documented performance levels of resocialization and instrumental roles needed to care for themselves and freely interact with available local communities, and to reduce bizarre motoric and cognitive behaviors to the level required for community tolerance and safe interactions—including complete elimination of acts that might cause harm to self or others.

In fact, we further recommend that work beyond minimal goals in publicly supported mental institutions be *limited* to the achievement of instrumental role performance sufficient to achieve financial independence, with social skills adequate to develop an independent supportive social network. "Optimal goals" are defined as further enhancement of social functioning and instrumental role skills and further reductions in distressing maladaptive behaviors to allow greater freedom of choice, autonomy, and satisfactions in the social and economic areas. Focus on optimal goals would be appropriate for work starting or continuing on an extramural basis, not *in* an institution.

MORE SEVERE DISABILITIES REQUIRE COMPREHENSIVE TREATMENT PROGRAMS

The great majority of the literature on social competence, social skills training, and assertiveness training has been directed at optimal goals—and rightly so, given the problems and client populations of focus (Argyle, Trower, & Bryant, 1974; Curran, 1977; Hersen & Eisler, 1976). Only recently have reports begun to appear in which a specific social skills training approach has been applied to institutionalized mental patients (Hersen & Bellack, 1976). Several promising reports have come from the research programs of Goldstein, Hersen, Liberman, McFall, Meichenbaum, and their colleagues, among others. For the most part these reports have been directed toward specific time-limited training procedures for institutionalized persons, either above the level of minimal goals or as an experimental development and evaluation of techniques and principles.

I would like to draw attention to the *more* severely disabled of the institutionalized mental patients, since they are becoming a larger proportion of the residential population as deinstitutionalization of the less severely disabled procedes (Paul & Lentz, 1977). Specifically, the very severity of the problems that require continued institutionalization place *primary* importance on the achievement of minimal goals. In addition, the extent of such problems logically demands a comprehensive, integrated treatment program with assessments appropriate to the targets of focus.

At the time of my earlier review of the literature, from which the above targets of focus were determined, I also reviewed the literature on treatment programs to see if any comprehensive approach offered promise for effecting change in them (Paul, 1969). At that time only two comprehensive approaches to residential treatment offered promise at all, and neither had yet been systematically evaluated for specific effectiveness in improving functioning to the point of allowing community tenure. Interestingly, both of these were psychosocial approaches, implicitly or explicitly placing emphases on positive social competence goals. The two approaches were milieu therapy, based upon a therapeutic community structure, and social learning therapy, based upon a token-economy structure. These approaches existed only as isolated, often experimental programs—not at all typical of what happens in the *great* majority of treatment units in mental institutions. In fact, the only inklings of awareness of the minimal goals required within traditional hospital structures is typically found in the "rehabilitation services" (Anthony, 1977; Becker, 1974) —which remain support services rather than the "real treatment."

Traditional Programs Lack Focus and Comprehensiveness

What is the real treatment in traditional hospital programs? We can get some picture of the comprehensiveness and target focus by looking at published program schedules. As part of an extensive long-term project testing the comparative effectiveness of intramural treatment programs, the Continued Treatment Service of one of the best traditional state hospitals was monitored for nearly 6 years (Paul & Lentz, 1977). In addition to regular checks of the published ward schedules, a full-week's sample of actual moment-to-moment schedules implemented and actual staff behavior was obtained by professional observers on the Staff–Resident Interaction Chronograph—an instrument designed to objectively record ongoing staff behavior in functional relationship to resident behavior (Licht, 1979; Paul, 1979, in preparation).

With few differences, the physicians in charge of each ward listed the treatment modalities of the traditional programs to include chemotherapy, industrial therapy, recreational and activity therapy (including both social and physical activities), individual or group therapy, and ward meetings (or "milieu therapy"). On paper, at least, there were potentially comprehensive treatment efforts. However, inspection of the amount of time scheduled for these activities—presented in the "traditional hospital" column of Table 1—reveals that less than 5% of the average resident's waking hours were even scheduled for *any* of the listed treatment modalities besides chemotherapy, and less than 3% of the resident's waking hours were actually involved. In fact, twice as much time was devoted to receiving drugs as to any formal psychosocial treatment activities. Is it any wonder that changes in severe deficits in competent performance are unrelated to traditional hospital practices when less than 5% of the resi-

TABLE 1. Weekly Program Scheduled for Average Resident (Patient) in Traditional Hospital and Two Psychosocial Programs

Program content	Percentage of waking hours scheduled	
	Traditional hospital	Psychosocial programs
Classes, meetings, focused activities	4.9% (2.9%)	58.9%
Meals	18.8%	14.7%
A.M. and P.M. routines	6.3%	11.6%
Unstructured time	63.8% (65.8%)	11.6%
Drug administration	6.3%	3.1%
Total formal treatment (excluding drugs)	4.9% (2.9%)	85.2%

Note. Figures in parentheses show discrepancy in incidence observed from defined schedules. Adapted from Table 5.1, Paul and Lentz (1977).

dents' time within the program is even scheduled for formal psychosocial focus?

Alternative Psychosocial Programs Provide Focus and Comprehensiveness

As the reader may have anticipated, there are better alternatives. Based upon the empirical promise suggested by the early literature on therapeutic communities and token economies, two explicit, comprehensive psychosocial programs were constructed for comparative testing with the severely disabled institutionalized mental patient (Paul & Lentz, 1977). The principles and technology of the two programs differed. The milieu therapy program based structure, verbal content, and staff–resident interactions on communication theory and therapeutic community principles. The social learning program based structure, verbal content, and staff–resident interactions on social learning theory and principles of instrumental and associative learning. However, both programs were constructed to maintain an equal therapeutic focus with scheduled times and procedures explicitly directed to the identified target areas and minimal goals.

Comparison of the amount of time scheduled for the average resident in the psychosocial programs (see Table 1) with traditional programs shows that *a lot* more treatment can be accomplished with the same staff-to-patient ratios and an equal number of waking hours. Meals and morning and evening routines became scheduled as part of comprehensive treatment, rather than just a necessary task to move patients from one place to another and provide nourishment. What better place to train self-care skills than during that time when we all normally engage in such activity? Meals also provide an excellent opportunity for training in interpersonal and communication skills—all of which should directly generalize to the extramural community. Therefore, assessments of competence and individualized programmatic interactions were given detailed focus in those activities.

Nearly 60% of the residents' time was explicitly scheduled for classes, meetings, and other focused activities. Three to four periods each day and evening were scheduled for assessment and training in interpersonal and communication skills in the context of informal interaction around recreational facilities. At lowest levels of functioning, two activity periods each weekday used physical exercise, arts and crafts, and practical self-care training as a means to activate residents and to train them to focus on external stimuli. Three periods of formal classes each weekday focused upon functional arithmetic, reading, writing, speaking, home-making, and grooming or the minimal attentional skills necessary to participate in those content areas. Large and small group meetings during days and evenings were scheduled for practice in problem identification and solution as well as further social skills training. Individual component behaviors were monitored for each resident, with a step system increasing responsibilities such that higher levels of performance resulted in more time devoted to prevocational and vocational training. Increasingly greater exposure to the outside world was systematically introduced as competence was demonstrated in each lower-level component. Thus, the focus on skill acquisition was specifically programmed with explicit times and subgoals provided for each area of possible deficit. In contrast, maladaptive and bizarre behaviors were consistently dealt with by specific principles at *all* times.

Staff Activities Differ Drastically among Treatment Programs

The scheduled content of treatment programs and supporting organizational structure provides the opportunity for treatment and training to occur with focus on particular objectives. Specific treatment techniques within that structure and schedule then functionally reduce to the interpersonal interaction of staff with residents. Although both psychosocial programs shared common objectives and identified focus as comprehensive treatment programs, the principles and nature of staff–resident interactions were constructed to differ systematically.

Space limitations prohibit a detailed presentation of components of the treatment programs, staff training and monitoring procedures, and particulars of staff performance. A global picture of differences in staff activities in the two psychosocial programs and traditional hospital programs may be gained by study of the average hourly instances of staff activity presented in Table 2. The data presented in Table 2 are based upon 10 consecutive minutes of observation, approximately every hour, for a full 7-day sample in traditional hospital programs, and over nearly 4½ years of continuous assessment in the psychosocial programs. Staffing levels and staff-to-resident ratios were the same in all three programs. In fact, the *identical* staff conducted both psychosocial programs concurrently, counterbalancing time between programs by specified daily rotations.

Note first the drastic differences in total staff activity between traditional programs and psychosocial programs. In addition to the

TABLE 2. Nature of Resident (Patient) Behavior to Which Staff Responded in Traditional Hospital and Two Psychosocial Treatment Programs

Class of resident behavior	Average instances of staff activity per hour		
	Traditional hospital	Milieu therapy	Social learning
Appropriate	41.86 (25.6%)	107.78 (27.1%)	168.85 (53.9%)
Inappropriate—failure	25.05 (15.2%)	184.46 (46.4%)	60.33 (19.2%)
Inappropriate—crazy	1.94 (1.2%)	17.39 (4.4%)	2.25 (.7%)
Request	6.97 (4.2%)	4.51 (1.1%)	1.73 (.6%)
Neutral (staff-initiated) Interactions with residents	26.74 (16.3%)	34.76 (8.7%)	31.56 (10.1%)
No interaction (job-relevant)	47.22 (28.7%)	48.70 (12.2%)	48.74 (15.5%)
No interaction (job-irrelevant)	14.69 (8.9%)	.08 (0%)	.06 (0%)
Total staff activity	164.47 (100%)	397.67 (100%)	313.51 (100%)

Note. Data from Staff–Resident Interaction Chronograph. Adapted from Table 5.4, Paul and Lentz (1977).

differential amount of time scheduled for formal treatment in comprehensive programs as compared to traditional programs, staff activity was sustained at remarkably higher rates as well. This was a direct function of ongoing staff assessment and feedback procedures. Examination of the "no-interaction" rows in Table 2 reveals that the higher levels of staff activity in psychosocial programs were a result of increased rates of staff–resident interaction rather than other activities. In fact, staff in traditional programs averaged nearly 15 instances each hour, or nearly 9% of total activities, simply "screwing off" (job-irrelevant activities), while psychosocial staff averaged 8 or less instances per *100* working hours for such activities. Particularly important to note is the near-perfect equation of the amount of activity devoted to job-relevant, noninteractive behavior—about 48 instances per hour in all three programs. This reflects nearly equal amounts of paperwork, attending to residents without interacting, and job-relevant contacts with other staff members. The importance of the equation in this category of staff activity is that it documents the fact that ongoing assessments and recordings by clinical staff in the psychosocial programs—to be described below—and highly structured, comprehensive program schedules do not result in an added burden of paperwork and administration. What is notable for traditional programs is that noninteractive staff activities account for a larger proportion of staff effort than any class of contact with patients.

Turning briefly to interactive staff behaviors, the great majority of staff focus in the social learning program was clearly upon appropriate resident behavior, while focus in the milieu therapy program was more upon resident failures. These are both in keeping with the principles of the respective treatment programs. Details of specific types of staff behavior and the contingencies between staff behavior and resident functioning are very interesting, but too complex for presentation here (see Paul & Lentz, 1977). The major points for present purposes are that traditional institutional programs do not provide the focus identified as necessary for treatment of the institutionalized mental patient, the comprehensiveness of programming logically required for the severely disabled, or efficient utilization of staff to provide psychosocial interaction as a treatment modality. Psychosocial programs demonstrate that the same amount of resources available in public institutions can be directed toward the identified targets of focus, can provide comprehensive programming, and can, in fact, increase the amount of psychosocial attention received by the institutionalized by a factor of nearly 4:1. However, within such comprehensive programs with identical focus and goals, and identical staff, the interactional treatment techniques can differ markedly. These differences turn out to be the crucial ones for effective treatment.

DIRECT ASSESSMENT SYSTEMS ARE NECESSARY FOR EFFECTIVE PROGRAMS

One of the psychosocial programs did emerge as a remarkably effective treatment program on an absolute level. It was also significantly more effective than the others on every target area as well as on release and community-stay criteria. Before presenting some of those findings and providing specific information on the severity of problems posed by the chronically institutionalized, some familiarity with the assessment systems employed will be required. In addition to the ongoing assessment of staff behavior noted above, continuous assessment of resident behavior is also necessary to identify areas of excesses and deficits, monitor progress within comprehensive treatment programs, and to evaluate the effectiveness of specific interventions as well as overall treatment programs. Two systems are crucial for these purposes—the Clinical Frequencies Recording System and the Time-Sample Behavioral Checklist (Paul, 1979, in preparation; Power, 1979; Redfield, 1979).

The Clinical Frequencies Recording System (CFRS)

The CFRS is a means of making the paperwork of clinical staff directly relevant to assessment and treatment. Thirty-five parallel forms within each psychosocial program were structured to be time–place–situation-specific such that each resident's behavior could be immediately recorded by a responsible staff member. The time, nature, and incidence of utilization of all facilities, services, and consumable items were recorded.

More important for current purposes is the continuous recording of resident performance within the scheduled areas of treatment focus. Staff recorded the presence or absence of terminal-level performance (i.e., performance indistinguishable from "normal") for each discrete target behavior on each scheduled occasion of focus on particular competencies within the programs. Additionally, successive achievements below terminal levels were recorded, specifying component subtargets of appropriate behavior accomplished, as well as those established as goals for the next occasion. Individualized focus of programmatic procedures was thus automatically maintained for each resident over staff members and occasions. The appearance form, for example, provided for specification of each of 11 component criteria (e.g., clean fingernails, appropriate clothing). Three scheduled checks on appearance occurred daily. Residents meeting terminal-level performance on all 11 criteria on a single check received appropriate programmatic interaction and were recorded as achieving terminal-level performance for appearance on that check. For residents not achieving terminal-level appearance, those discrete components successfully performed were recorded, plus the specific component established as a target for the next check. By reference to the previous appearance check, staff could immediately determine the prior level of achievement, the identified subtarget, and the discrete behavior of focus. Each incidence of intolerable behavior (e.g., physical assault, fire setting) and failure to be at scheduled activities was also recorded as part of the CFRS.

The CFRS forms, thus, were an integral part of the accurate application of the psychosocial treatment programs, providing an ongoing objective specification of situationally defined appropriate and inappropriate behaviors in enough detail for day-to-day use in clinical programming. Weekly computer summarization provided objective scores reflecting the proportion of specific performances at a "normal" level relative to the opportunity to perform. Thus, a Total Inappropriate Behavior Index provided continuous event recording of the proportion of time each resident performed a grossly inappropriate response to minimal expectations for appropriate behavior. The terminal-level performances of 22 specific classes of behavior were summarized to provide index scores directly assessing resocialization and instrumental role treatment targets. A Self-Care Index consists of the proportion of terminal-level performances over six classes of self-maintenance activities (e.g., appearance, meal behavior, bathing) relative to the opportunities to demonstrate each class. An Interpersonal Skills Index consists of the proportion of terminal-level performances over six classes of interpersonal interaction and communication skills (e.g., informal interaction, normal conversations in meetings) relative to the opportunity to demonstrate such skills. The instrumental role performance target was directly assessed by an Instrumental Role Index, consisting of the proportion of terminal-level performances over 12 classes of instrumental role behavior—primarily on-task in classes and job training positions and on time at scheduled meetings, activities, and work—relative to the opportunities to perform each class of behavior.

Due to the nature of staff training procedures, the reliability of recordings of terminal-level performances has regularly produced phi coefficients of .95 or above. Thus, each CFRS index score—whether reflecting the level of adaptive or maladaptive functioning or on-going-process characteristics—provides objective data on resident performance based upon continuous event recordings of actual behavior demonstrated 24 hours per day, 7 days per week.

The Time-Sample Behavioral Checklist (TSBC)

The TSBC is an observational assessment system in which data are obtained by trained technician-level professional observers with computer summarization. Unlike the CFRS, the TSBC is not program-specific, but is designed to measure resident behavior in any residential setting in enough detail to allow individual problem identification and monitoring in clinical work, with higher-level composite scores providing assessment of functioning for determining the specified effectiveness of interventions for individuals as well as overall program evaluation. The TSBC provides the only known means for continuous assessment of clinically relevant bizarre behavior—one of the identified targets of focus for the institutionalized—as well as assessing adaptive interpersonal activities not specifically tied to a particular treatment program.

In practice, professional observers code the presence or absence of 69 specific behavioral classes, or one of three control codes, following a standardized instance of observation each waking hour. Each observation also specifies the time and nature of activity in which the observation occurred. The behavioral codes include the resident's: physical location (17 classes, e.g., bedroom, hallway), position (6 classes, e.g., walking, lying down), whether eyes are open or closed, facial expression (6 classes, e.g., smiling with apparent stimulus, neutral with no apparent stimulus), social orientation (4 classes, e.g., alone, with staff), engagement in normal elective appropriate activities (17 classes, e.g., talking normally to others, personal grooming), and performance of crazy behaviors (17 classes, e.g., talking to self, posturing).

Since the TSBC is a time-sampling instrument, an individual observation has little meaning. Rather, a computer scoring program provides relative frequency scores over a succession of observations—typically, a full week—for each of the 72 codes, plus higher-order composite scores. The higher-order indexes include a Total Inappropriate Behavior Index—a proportional score that reflects the observed incidence of any one of 24 classes of bizarre, maladaptive behaviors—thus directly assessing one of the target areas identified as crucial for the institutionalized mental patient. Component index scores for conceptually different classes of bizarre behavior are also provided. The Schizophrenic Disorganization Index reflects the relative frequency of occurrence of nine classes of bizarre motoric behaviors (e.g., rocking, repetitive movements, blank staring). The Cognitive Distortion Index reflects the relative frequency of occurrence of six classes of bizarre verbal and facial expressions indicative of thought disorder (e.g., delusions and hallucinations, incoherent speech, smiling without apparent stimulus), while the Hostile–Belligerence Index reflects the relative frequency of occurrence of six classes of high-intensity aggressive behaviors (e.g., screaming, cursing, verbal intrusion).

A Total Appropriate Behavior Index reflects the relative frequency of any one of 27 classes of normal behavior, including facial expressions (e.g., smiling with apparent stimulus), positions (e.g., sitting, walking), and elective activities (e.g., grooming, writing). Component index scores for conceptually different classes of adaptive behavior are also provided for identified targets and descriptive purposes (e.g., indexes for social interaction, self-maintenance, instrumental activities, and self-amusement).

Interobserver reliabilities for the TSBC regularly provide product–moment correlations exceeding .90 for individual codes and .97 for higher-level composites for weekly data. Thus, each TSBC index score—whether reflecting adaptive or maladaptive functioning or ongoing process characteristics—provides objective data on concurrent behavior of residents based upon hourly time samples of actual behavior every waking hour, 7 days per week.

THE SEVERITY OF THE PROBLEM FOR THOSE REMAINING INSTITUTIONALIZED

Having some familiarity with the nature of assessments, we may now turn to look at the severity of the problem posed by those individuals who remain in mental institutions after the higher-functioning population has been deinstitutionalized. I'll also remove the suspense with regard to which comprehensive treatment program emerged as the effective one by presenting some illustrative data only for the residents who participated in that program—the social learning program. However, since resident groups were all well equated prior to participation in the different treatment programs, the pretreatment data are representative of the entire institutionalized population studied.

Patients were drawn from those who were rejected for community placement after extensive efforts to deinstitutionalize the hospital population. Selection criteria included an age range of 18 to 55 years, a primary diagnosis of schizophrenia, and 2 or more years of hospitalization. Half were female, one out of seven was black, and over 80% were divorced or never married. All were of low socioeconomic status and well within the process range of the process-reactive continuum. About half had previously received electroconvulsive shock treatments, nearly a third had previously received insulin shock, all had previously received chemotherapy, and about 90% were currently receiving psychotropic drugs before psychosocial programs were introduced. Less than one in six had received any contact—even a letter—from friends or relatives in the previous year. On the average these people had spent about 17 years—nearly two-thirds of their adult lives—in a mental institution.

Social Competence Deficits

The extent to which the targets of focus identified in the literature had relevance for this population may best be seen in the normal levels of competence recorded on the CFRS before programmatic treatment began, presented in Table 3. The *least* deficient performance was in instrumental roles, which at this point reflected, primarily, attendance at scheduled activities. In this area of performance, the average resident did attend scheduled activities about 38% of the time, and the best performance obtained reflected normal on-task and on-time activities on 92% of opportunities. These lower-level instrumental tasks were maintained in traditional hospital programs better than any others. Nevertheless, even this "most competent" area of performance reflected failures on 62% of opportunities, with about a third of the population *never* getting to activities on their own for an entire week when specifically instructed and over half never continuing on-task in scheduled classes, activities, and meetings after they got there.

The importance of the resocialization target is dramatically evident in the Interpersonal Skills and Self-Care Indexes shown in Table 3. Here we see nearly a complete deficit in competent performance, with the average resident failing in interpersonal and communication skills on 95% of opportunities and failing in self-care on 87% of opportunities. Even the best functioning of the group remaining after dein-

TABLE 3. Proportion of Individual Performance at "Normal" Levels of Competence for Severely Disabled Mental Patients Engaged in the Social Learning Treatment Program

Class of performance	Before programmatic treatment		After 120 weeks of treatment	
	Mean	Range	Mean	Range
Total appropriate behavior	.19	(.00–.56)	.62	(.04–1.00)
Interpersonal skills	.04	(.00–.30)	.49	(.03–1.00)
Self-care	.13	(.00–.42)	.51	(.00–1.00)
Instrumental roles	.38	(.00–.92)	.81	(.08–1.00)

Note. Weekly data from Clinical Frequencies Recording System; $n = 28$ in original treatment group (see Paul & Lentz, 1977).

stitutionalization efforts failed at normal performance interpersonally 70% of the time and failed at self-care 58% of the time. Indeed, the majority of the group failed to appropriately feed themselves, clothe themselves, bathe, or carry on a normal conversation on even one occasion during an entire week before programmatic treatment procedures were introduced. Over all social competencies combined (Total Appropriate Behavior), the average resident failed to perform at normal levels on about 81% of opportunities. Clearly, deficiencies in social competence were serious, and required continued institutional control for the residents' survival.

Bizarre Behavior Excesses

The extent to which the extreme bizarre behavior target had relevance for this population may be seen in the actual incidence of crazy behaviors observed on the TSBC before programmatic treatment, presented in Table 4. The Total Inappropriate Behavior Index shows that the average resident was performing at least one observable bizarre behavior on 93% of observations taken every waking hour over a full week! The least bizarre of the group performed at least one crazy act 13% of the time, while the craziest averaged over two and a half separate bizarre behaviors on *every* observation. These excesses in bizarre behavior are all the more notable because about 90% of the population was still receiving the maintenance chemotherapy prescriptions from previous hospital programs when these data were obtained.

The nature of bizarre behaviors can be seen in the component TSBC scores presented in Table 4. For the group as a whole, the most extensive class of clinically maladaptive behaviors were bizarre motoric acts and mannerisms reflected in the Schizophrenic Disorganization Index. These are blatantly crazy acts that draw the attention of nearly anyone in the environment, with the average resident performing at least one such act 62% of the time. Bizarre verbal content and facial expressions reflected in the Cognitive Distortion Index occurred about 25% of the time, on the average, but the worst resident in this regard was displaying such indications of thought disorder nearly all the time. As noted in the footnote to Table 4, the high-intensity aggressive acts reflected in the Hostile–Belligerence Index were relatively low on an absolute level, but this index is less satisfactory for determinations of the absolute incidence of such acts. Because of the critical nature of aggressive behavior, in which even a single incident causes disruption and prevents community tenure, event recording via the CFRS provides a better measure than time

TABLE 4. Average Incidence per Observation of Discrete Clinically Inappropriate (Crazy) Behaviors Occurring over All Waking Hours for Severely Disabled Mental Patients Engaged in the Social Learning Program

	Before programmatic treatment		After 120 weeks of treatment	
Class of concurrent behavior	Mean	Range	Mean	Range
Total inappropriate behavior (all bizarre combined)	.93	(.13–2.63)	.32	(.01–.92)
Schizophrenic disorganization (bizarre motoric behavior)	.62	(.03–1.66)	.23	(.01–.89)
Cognitive distortion (bizarre verbal and facial behavior)	.25	(.01–.98)	.08	(.00–.40)
Hostile–belligerence[a] (high-intensity aggressive behavior)	.004	(.00–.074)	.001	(.00–.008)

Note. Weekly data from Time-Sample Behavioral Checklist; $n = 28$ in original treatment group (see Paul & Lentz, 1977).

[a]Time sampling is less satisfactory for continuous monitoring of low-frequency critical behaviors. Event recording via the Clinical Frequencies Recording System for grossly inappropriate response to minimal expectations yielded ratios of performance to opportunity averaging .19 (range .03–.40) before treatment and .03 (range .00–.25) after 120 weeks.

sampling. Thirty-two separate instances of physical assault occurred during this week before introduction of programmatic procedures, while the average resident failed to meet even minimal expectations 19% of the time.

Data on actual resident performance clearly support the importance of the target areas of focus. Contrary to the traditional clinical lore regarding the "burned-out schizophrenic" who no longer shows psychotic symptomology, those individuals remaining in mental institutions after extensive efforts at deinstitutionalization are remarkably bizarre in moment-to-moment functioning. Over half are so bizarre that they simply frighten others to the extent that they fail to meet the minimum tolerance for deviance of the outside community, in addition to the severe deficiencies in social competence that would preclude their survival.

THE NATURE OF RESPONSIVENESS TO THE MOST EFFECTIVE PROGRAM

As indicated above, the social learning program did emerge as a remarkably effective program on an absolute level, and a significantly more effective program than alternatives—including the milieu therapy program with the same comprehensiveness and psychosocial focus, but different treatment technology. Comprehensive residential treatment programs are complex social systems that are demonstrably responsive to a variety of internal and external events. Any attempt to summarize briefly the process and outcome of even one program from 10 years of investigation must fall short of satisfaction. Therefore, in the remaining space allotted, I shall simply note highlights of what can be accomplished and refer the interested reader to the detailed analyses and presentation that is available elsewhere (Paul & Lentz, 1977).

Intramural Changes in Social Competence and Bizarre Behavior

In addition to indicating the severity of the problem before programmatic treatments were introduced, Tables 3 and 4 also present the levels of performance achieved after 120 weeks of treatment in the social learning program. As shown in Table 3, some of the improvements in social competence were, indeed, remarkable. Some residents had improved to the point of showing performance indistinguishable from normal in every area on every opportunity. Others had shown significant improvement, but were still functioning at a level that required institutional control for their survival. In fact, every resident had shown significant and practical improvement in instrumental roles, interpersonal skills, and total appropriate behavior and all but two had shown significant improvement in self-care. On the average, interpersonal skills and self-care were being performed at levels indistinguishable from normal on about half the opportunities, while instrumental roles had increased to 81% normal performance. Where overall social competence had reflected failures on 81% of opportunities before treatment, by 120 weeks the average resident was succeeding 62% of the time. In contrast to the improvements obtained in the milieu therapy program, the level of social competence achieved by the social learning program was about 23% higher for instrumental roles and about double for all other areas.

The changes in bizarre behavior shown in Table 4 are equally impressive. After 120 weeks of treatment, every resident had shown significant decreases in clinically relevant maladaptive behaviors to a point where even the craziest resident showed no bizarre behaviors at all 8% of the time. On the average, all classes of bizarre behavior had been reduced to about a third of the initial levels. Cognitive distortion was the only class of bizarre behavior for which the milieu therapy program produced an equal amount of improvement. For both schizophrenic disorganization and total inappropriate behavior, the milieu therapy program had produced significant improvement, but the social learning program had reduced such bizarre behavior by an additional third on an absolute level.

Eventually, *every resident* treated by the social learning program—including failures in the milieu therapy program—showed significant improvement in all areas of social competence, and all but one resident showed significant reductions in every class of bizarre behavior. That resident did show improvements in all classes of bizarre behavior, save one. Unfortunately, he had a physical condition that precluded the effort required to participate in the social learning procedures that were known to be effective in eliminating that bizarre behavior. Thus, the social learning program showed significantly greater effectiveness on all target areas identified as crucial for the institutionalized mental patient—and did so in the relative absence of psychotropic drugs (only 10.7% of residents were receiving any drugs at all after systematic withdrawal; see also Paul, Tobias, & Holly, 1972).

The Utility of Improvements in Social Competence and Bizarre Behavior

Clearly, the comprehensive social learning program with focus upon the identified targets did produce improvements. Do these improvements in intramural functioning have utility beyond the moral desirability of allowing residents to function as human beings rather than at the animalistic level shown by the majority before programmatic treatment? This is essentially a question of generalizability and of the practical importance of such improvements in functioning. Several substudies have shown concurrent and discriminative validity of scores from the CFRS and TSBC over other modes of assessment, settings, and times, thereby providing evidence of generalizability (Lentz, 1975; Mariotto, 1979; Mariotto & Paul, 1974; Montgomery, Paul, & Power, 1974; Paden, Himelstein, & Paul, 1974; Paul, 1979, in preparation; Paul et al., 1972; Paul & Lentz, 1977; Paul, Redfield, & Lentz, 1976). Additionally, differential situational specificity has been found for different classes of behavior, which denotes the need for prescriptive focus in other settings for some classes of behavior but does not require it for others (Mariotto, 1978; Mariotto & Paul, 1975).

From a practical as well as moral stance, the most important question of utility for these improvements has to do with whether or not the intramural changes are related to the ultimate goal of institutional programs—namely, achieving release from the institution with continuing community stay. Are the improvements, in fact, to the level of minimal goals presented earlier and is there a relationship between intramural functioning in these target areas and release and community stay?

First, with regard to the level of minimal goals, nearly 11% of the original group treated by the social learning program improved to the point that allowed independent release with self-support and continuing community stay without rehospitalization—that is, improvement to a level above minimal goals. Any such release for this population was remarkable (about 7% achieved such release from the milieu program, and none did from traditional programs). Some ex-residents from the social learning program had been successfully functioning in the community for over 5 years at project termination. The absolute level of improvement was such that about 25% of the treated group was indistinguishable from others of the same social class. Although the remainder were still functioning at marginal levels, over 92% of all residents treated by the social learning program not only achieved minimal goals in functioning, but achieved significant release with continuing stay for a minimum of 18 months in the community (at which time follow-up was terminated). The latter figures compare to 72% continuing releases for the milieu program and 48% for traditional programs. Of course, community stay is dependent upon aftercare and follow-up procedures, and releases from all programs were provided declining contact aftercare consultation following social learning procedures. These procedures were successful in preventing recidivism in over 97% of cases, without differences among those released from the different treatment programs.

Is the level of intramural functioning in the identified target areas related to release and community stay? In fact, the areas of functioning related to continuing community tenure in previous literature were related to achieving release in our work. Since all but one resident treated by the social learning program improved in every target area and achieved significant release, no variance was left to predict. Combining residents across psychosocial programs for the original equated groups, level of functioning during the week prior to release or program termination did predict release ($r = .68$). Even more impressive as an indication of both the importance of the target areas and the relevance of the CFRS and TSBC assessment systems are the data presented in Table 5. That data, based upon successful

TABLE 5. Prediction of Rated Functioning in the Community from Objectively Assessed Behavior during the Week Prior to Release for 46 Releases from Psychosocial Programs

Intramural score prior to release	Months after release		
	6 months	12 months	18 months
Global Functioning Factor Score	75	72	76
TSBC Total Appropriate Index	71	72	72
CFRS Total Appropriate Index	75	70	70
Interpersonal Skills	66	65	62
Self-Care	73	66	67
Instrumental Roles	69	65	67
CFRS Total Inappropriate Index	−47	−47	−56
TSBC Total Inappropriate Index	−74	−68	−71
Schizophrenic Disorganization	−79	−67	−73
Cognitive Distortion	a	a	a
Hostile–Belligerence	a	a	a

Note. Table entries are product–moment correlations, plus signs and decimal points omitted. All correlations significant at p < .01, two-sided test.

[a]Zero-level correlations. All Hostile–Belligerence Indexes zero prior to release.

releases from the original equated groups, shows the only prediction of functioning in the community from intramural assessments of which I am aware. Thus, even for residents who did improve sufficiently to achieve release with continuing stay in the community, the objective data obtained on the CFRS and TSBC were differentially predictive of the level of functioning seen by nonproject raters on standardized scales as long as 18 months after release. Cognitive distortion was the only class of behavior that occurred at all prior to release that did not predict rated functioning in the community. This suggests that the low levels of bizarre verbal and facial expressions achieved by those who were released were below the point where significant others noticed them.

WHERE DO WE GO NOW?

I have attempted to provide an overview of the current sorry status of institutional treatment, and what are logically and empirically the necessary targets of focus for the institutionalized population. The problems posed by residents of our mental institutions are more severe than the great majority of mental health professionals or the public realize—both in deficits in social competency and excesses in bizarre behavior. At a policy level, treatment rather than care needs to become the goal of mental health systems, with *real* evaluation rather than paper criteria and politics as the basis for decision making (Paul, 1978).

In addition to providing a picture of the severity of the problem, I've tried to highlight some significant findings for both assessment systems and treatment programs for the institutionalized. As McFall (1976) appropriately cautions, "Beware of psychologists bearing panaceas—the present author included!" There are no quick and easy procedures. There are seldom even any breakthroughs—although the area seems to have such reports about every 6 months. Rather than a panacea or a breakthrough, I suggest that we now have for use in any residential setting a complex assessment technology that comes closer to providing the kinds of information required for careful problem identification, clinical monitoring, and program evaluation than has been previously available (Paul, in preparation). We also have a complex, comprehensive treatment program of documented effectiveness (Paul & Lentz, 1977). That program is nearly four times as cost-effective as traditional practices, requires the same level and number of staff currently available in public institutions, and—when fully functioning with all components now known to be effective—can reasonably achieve minimal goals for the most severely debilitated mental patient in 26 to 30 weeks. Therefore, it can be recommended as a current treatment of choice. It is clear that both staff and resident behavior must become the primary focus of comprehensive integrated programs rather than being viewed as an epiphenomenon.

REFERENCES

Anthony, W. A. Psychological rehabilitation: A concept in need of a method. *American Psychologist,* 1977, *32,* 658–662.

Anthony, W. A., Buell, G. J., Sharrett, S., & Althoff, M. E. Efficacy of psychiatric rehabilitation. *Psychological Bulletin,* 1972, *78,* 447–456.

Argyle, M., Trower, P., & Bryant, B. Explorations in the treatment of personality disorders and neuroses by social skills training. *British Journal of Medical Psychology,* 1974, *47,* 63–72.

Becker, R. E. The challenge of rehabilitation. In R. Cancro, N. Fox, & L. Shapiro (Eds.), *Strategic intervention in schizophrenia: Current developments in treatment.* New York: Behavioral Publications, 1974.

Curran, J. P. Skills training as an approach to the treatment of heterosexual–social anxiety: A review. *Psychological Bulletin,* 1977, *84,* 140–157.

Erickson, R. C. Outcome studies in mental hospitals: A review. *Psychological Bulletin*, 1975, *82*, 519–540.

Hersen, M., & Bellack, A. S. Social skills training for chronic psychiatric patients: Rationale, research findings, and future directions. *Comprehensive Psychiatry*, 1976, *17*, 559–580.

Hersen, M., & Eisler, R. M. Social skills training. In W. E. Craighead, A. E. Kazdin, & M. J. Mahoney (Eds.), *Behavior modification: Principles, issues and applications*. Boston: Houghton Mifflin, 1976.

Kohen, W., & Paul, G. L. Current trends and recommended changes in extended-care placement of mental patients: The Illinois system as a case in point. *Schizophrenia Bulletin*, 1976, *2*, 575–594.

Lentz, R. J. Changes in chronic mental patients' interview behavior: Effects of differential treatment history and explicit impression management prompts. *Behavior Therapy and Experimental Psychiatry*, 1975, *6*, 192–199.

Licht, M. H. The Staff–Residential Interaction Chronograph: Observational assessment of staff performance. *Journal of Behavioral Assessment*, 1979, *1*, 185–197.

Mariotto, M. J. Interaction of person and situation effects for chronic mental patients: A two-year follow-up. *Journal of Abnormal Psychology*, 1978, *87*, 676–679.

Mariotto, M. J. Observational assessment systems use for basic and applied research. *Journal of Behavioral Assessment*, 1979, *1*, 239–250.

Mariotto, M. J., & Paul, G. L. A multimethod validation of the Inpatient Multidimensional Psychiatric Scale with chronically institutionalized patients. *Journal of Consulting and Clinical Psychology*, 1974, *42*, 497–508.

Mariotto, M. J., & Paul, G. L. Persons versus situations in the real-life functioning of chronically institutionalized mental patients. *Journal of Abnormal Psychology*, 1975, *84*, 483–493.

McFall, R. M. Behavioral training: A skill-acquisition approach to clinical problems. In J. T. Spence, R. C. Carson, & J. W. Thibaut (Eds.), *Behavioral approaches to therapy*. Morristown, NJ: General Learning Press, 1976.

Montgomery, G. K., Paul, G. L., & Power, C. T. Influence of environmental contingency history on acquisition of new discriminations by chronic mental patients. *Journal of Abnormal Psychology*, 1974, *83*, 339–347.

Paden, R. C., Himelstein, H. C., & Paul, G. L. Video-tape vs. verbal feedback in the modification of meal behavior of chronic mental patients. *Journal of Consulting and Clinical Psychology*, 1974, *42*, 623.

Paul, G. L. Chronic mental patient: Current status—future directions. *Psychological Bulletin*, 1969, *71*, 81–94.

Paul, G. L. Experimental–behavioral approaches to schizophrenia. In R. Cancro, N. Fox, & L. Shapiro (Eds.), *Strategic intervention in schizophrenia: Current developments in treatment*. New York: Behavioral Publications, 1974.

Paul, G. L. The implementation of effective treatment programs for chronic mental patients: Obstacles and recommendations. In J. A. Talbott (Ed.), *The chronic mental patient*. Washington, DC: American Psychiatric Association, 1978.

Paul, G. L. (Ed.). *New assessment systems for residential treatment, management, research, and evaluation: A symposium. Journal of Behavioral Assessment*, 1979, *1* (Whole Issue 3).

Paul, G. L. (Ed.). *Observational assessment instrumentation for institutional research and treatment*. Cambridge, MA: Harvard University Press, in preparation.

Paul, G. L., & Lentz, R. J. *Psychosocial treatment of chronic mental patients: Milieu vs. social-learning programs*. Cambridge, MA: Harvard University Press, 1977.

Paul, G. L., Redfield, J. P., & Lentz, R. J. The Inpatient Scale of Minimal Functioning: A revision of the Social Breakdown Gradient Index. *Journal of Consulting and Clinical Psychology,* 1976, *44,* 1021-1022.

Paul, G. L., Tobias, L. T., & Holly, B. L. Maintenance psychotropic drugs in the presence of active treatment programs: A "triple blind" withdrawal study with long-term mental patients. *Archives of General Psychiatry,* 1972, *27,* 106-115.

Power, C. T. The Time-Sample Behavioral Checklist: Observational assessment of patient functioning. *Journal of Behavioral Assessment,* 1979, *1,* 199-210.

Redfield, J. Clinical Frequencies Recording System: Standardizing staff observations by event recording. *Journal of Behavioral Assessment,* 1979, *1,* 211-219.

Rieder, R. O. Hospitals, patients, and politics. *Schizophrenia Bulletin,* 1974, *11,* 9-15.

Taube, C. A. Readmissions to inpatient services of state and county mental hospitals, 1972. *Statistical Note 110,* National Institute of Mental Health, Division of Biometry, Survey and Reports Branch, November 1974.

Ullmann, L. P., & Krasner, L. *A psychological approach to abnormal behavior* (2nd ed.). Englewood Cliffs, NJ: Prentice-Hall, 1975.

IV

BRITISH AND NORTH AMERICAN SOCIAL SKILLS APPROACHES

9

THE CONTRIBUTION OF SOCIAL INTERACTION RESEARCH TO SOCIAL SKILLS TRAINING

MICHAEL ARGYLE

MICHAEL ARGYLE is Reader in Social Psychology at Oxford University and a Fellow of Wolfson College. He has been a Fellow at the Center for Advanced Studies in the Behavioral Sciences, and a visiting professor at universities in the United States, Canada, Europe, Israel, Africa, and Australia. He is the author of *Social Interaction, Bodily Communication, Gaze and Mutual Gaze* (with Mark Cook), *Social Situations* (with Adrian Furnham and Jean Graham), and other books. Since 1963 he has directed a research group at Oxford concerned with various aspects of social interaction, particularly nonverbal communication, social skills training, and the analysis of social situations. Argyle's work is widely known throughout Europe and North America; he was a pioneer in the study of nonverbal behavior, and was one of the first individuals to establish social skills training as a legitimate psychological pursuit.

In this chapter, Argyle overviews the work in social skills training that he and his Oxford research team have been conducting for the last two decades. This work has been notable for the precision and detail of its situational and behavioral analyses. They have characteristically emphasized the acquisition of highly specific overt behaviors, especially the nonverbal components of such interpersonal behaviors, as well as the characteristics of the specific situations in which the behaviors are to be performed. This approach is in marked contrast to the self-focused North American assertion model.

Social skills training (SST) is becoming very widely used in various parts of the world—for shy students and students who don't think they have enough dates; for lonely and isolated adults and for marital therapy; for mental patients who have difficulties with people; for prisoners, alcoholics, and disturbed adolescents; as well as for teachers, doctors, managers, interviewers, salesmen, and others. In North America SST most often takes the form of some kind of assertiveness training. In other parts of the world, assertiveness training is less popular: in Britain a more common problem is wanting to make friends. So I am a little critical of assertiveness training since it deals with only one aspect of social competence, and also because of its failure to take account of social psychology research.

Some SST derives from group therapy. Again little use is made of the now-extensive body of research in social psychology, particularly in the field of social interaction. In this chapter I want to discuss some basic processes of social interaction, consider how they can go wrong, and suggest the forms of training necessary to correct them. In the behavior therapy tradition there are two main forms of failure of social competence—social phobias and lack of assertiveness. From the social interaction perspective there are many more kinds of social inadequacy—each of them easily recognizable, and each requiring a special form of training.

We have been developing methods of SST at Oxford for a number of years (Trower, Bryant, & Argyle, 1978), in close connection with a program of research into nonverbal communication, social interaction, and allied topics. It began with our social skills model, which pointed to the analogies between the performance of motor skills and social skills. Even this simple model suggests that social performance may go wrong in several different ways—inaccurate perception and feedback, unskilled production of social signals, inappropriate goals, and deficient planning.

When we say that a person has inadequate social skills, this may be because he or she does not know what the most effective behavior is, or doesn't know the rules; or he or she may know but be unable to produce effective social responses. Someone might in some sense "know" how to do a back somersault off a springboard, but not be able to carry it out.

The conceptual model we have of the role of social competence in mental health is as follows. Some people, by college age, have failed to acquire some aspects of everyday social skills, either through exposure to unskilled models (e.g., in parents), or through lack of experience and practice (e.g., with the opposite sex), or in other ways. This results in their becoming socially rejected and isolated, which in turn leads to anxiety and depression. Or, more widespread disturbance of affect or cognition leads to ineffective social behavior, which has the same consequences.

There are two alternative views here. Unskilled behavior might be due to anxiety or lack of self-confidence, rather than lack of skill. And it is found that desensitization and relaxation therapy are quite effective forms of therapy for the socially inadequate. Another theory is that there must be a dynamic basis to interpersonal difficulties— such as fear of or hostility toward people, in which case SST would not be expected to help. However, we now know that it does help, so I am inclined to reject this theory, for the majority of socially incompetent patients at least.

THE EXTENT AND NATURE OF SOCIAL DIFFICULTY IN THE POPULATION

The Normal Population

There is no doubt, from common experience and social surveys, that various kinds of social difficulty are very common: anxiety in different situations, assertiveness problems, difficulty in making friends and in forming relationships with the opposite sex. It is, however, difficult to decide on a cutoff point, beyond which a person is said to suffer from social behavior problems. Possible criteria are (1) seeking SST, or accepting it when it is available—though this will depend on how readily available it is and how attractively presented; (2) reporting avoidance of everyday situations, or "great difficulty," etc., or reporting that loneliness, social anxiety, etc., is one of the greatest problems; (3) behavioral evidence of social inadequacy, such as not having any friends, being unsuccessful as a salesperson, teacher, and so forth, or the object of complaints from others.

Zimbardo (1977) reported surveys of 2500 American students, of whom 42% reported that they were shy now and 62% reported that it had been a serious problem. Similar results were obtained in other cultures.

Bryant and Trower (1974) surveyed a 10% sample of Oxford undergraduates and found that a high proportion reported great difficulty or avoidance of common social situations. Of first-year students, 42% reported moderate to great difficulty, or avoidance of parties; this fell to 25% for second-year students, showing the benefit of university education. Comparable figures for dealing with the opposite sex were 38% and 21%. Nine percent of the sample reported "great difficulty" or avoidance of 6 common situations out of 30, and could be regarded as suffering from serious social problems. From this and various other surveys, it seems likely that at least 7% of the normal adult population have fairly serious difficulties with social behavior.

Other studies have been directed toward finding out which situations are the most difficult. From factor analyses the most commonly obtained factors are

1. fear of performing in public, being the focus of attention

2. fear of rejection, disapproval, or conflict

3. anxiety over intimacy, heterosexual or otherwise

4. problems over meeting strangers, going to parties, making new friends

5. problems over assertiveness

Other situations that can cause trouble are

6. formal situations with complex or unknown rules

7. dealing with difficult subordinates (e.g., Richardson & Tasto, 1976; Stratton & Moore, 1977)

Neurotics

Bryant, Trower, Yardley, Urbieta, and Letemendia (1976) found that 28% of a sample of neurotic outpatients were regarded as socially unskilled by clinical psychologists and psychiatrists. They were low in components of both control (assertiveness) and rewardingness, and were extremely bad conversationalists. They often suffered acutely from social anxiety, and avoided many situations altogether. A distinction can be drawn, however, between patients who have social phobias and those who have inadequate social skills, though the two groups overlap. Neurotic patients suffer from all of the main kinds of social inadequacy. Their behavior can also be described in terms of the mechanisms described later—deficient production of nonverbal communication (NVC) such as smiling and looking, disruption of skilled behavior by anxiety, inappropriate goals (as in the case of Berne's socially destructive patients), low rewardingness, egocentricity, and inability to take the role of the other. Henderson, Duncan-Jones, McAuley, and Ritchie (1978) found that a sample of neurotic patients had far fewer friends than a matched control group, and that the friends they had did not form a social network. Some neurotic conditions may be mainly due to lack of social skills: social inadequacy leads to rejection and isolation, which in turn leads to anxiety, depression, and other symptoms. There is some evidence that SST can result in the remission of such symptoms as anorexia and amenorrhea. However, for many neurotic patients, social behavior difficulties are neither the only symptom nor the sole factor in the etiology.

Delinquents and prisoners have been found deficient in a variety of social skills (Freedman, Rosenthal, Donahoe, Schlundt, & McFall, 1978). Aggressive people and sexual offenders lack ordinary persuasive skills and therefore resort to violence. Lack of perceptual sensitivity results in men not realizing how much they are annoying people, resulting in fights. Others have employment difficulties, since they do not have the social skills to obtain or keep a job. Similar deficits have been found in alcoholics.

Psychotics

Psychotics are all deficient in social competence. Schizophrenics are socially withdrawn, do not form social relationships, and have difficulty in conducting conversations. Their deficiencies can be described in terms of the processes described later—for example, inappropriate use of NVC (especially face, gesture, and posture), failure in the production of verbal messages, and poor synchronizing, low rewardingness, poor perception of others, etc. (Argyle, 1969). Depressives are also socially inadequate, in quite different ways, and are unable to elicit positive responses from others, since their level of social activity, initiation of behavior and rewardingness is so low (Lewinsohn, 1975). However, the social inadequacy of psychotics is more likely to be caused by deeper cognitive, affective, or other disturbances; but their lack of social skills results in rejection and isolation, thus adding to the overall stress and resulting in further deterioration.

COMPONENTS OF SKILLED PERFORMANCE

Perception of Other People

It does not need to be demonstrated that to respond effectively to a stimulus it is first necessary to perceive that stimulus, and to perceive it accurately. If we are going to respond effectively to another person, he or she must be perceived accurately.

Research on social skills shows the importance of attending to particular events at certain points in the sequence—for example, attending to other's reactions at the ends of one's own utterances (see p. 274). This involves gazing at the other's face, and listening carefully to what he or she says: both require paying close attention and taking a keen interest in the other. NVC research has shown that there are great individual differences in decoding nonverbal signals, like tone of voice (Davitz, 1964).

Mental patients and people with inadequate social skills are often deficient in person perception. We have found that socially unskilled neurotics often do not attend to or show much interest in other people, and may not look very much (Trower *et al.*, 1978). Schizophrenics have been found to be poor at decoding nonverbal signals, and do not have personal constructs for persons or emotions (Bannister & Salmon, 1966). Manic and paranoid patients are notorious for the inaccuracy of their perception of events, and delinquents have been found to be very insensitive—failing to recognize either approval or annoyance in others.

Training in the perception of emotions from facial expression can be done using the materials and exercises provided by Ekman and Friesen (1975), showing the range of brow, eye, and mouth positions for each emotion. Training in the perception of emotions from tone of voice can be done as suggested by Davitz (1964), listening to tape recordings of neutral sentences spoken as sad, anxious, etc.

Taking the Role of the Other

As well as perceiving others' reactions accurately, it is also important to perceive their perceptions, sometimes called "metaperception." An interviewer studies the candidate, but the candidate is more interested in the interviewer's perception of him than in the interviewer himself. This is one way in which social performance is different from a motor skill (p. 273). Metaperception is activated in situations like interviews, where the other is evaluating, and in front of audiences. There are many situations where people may regard others as audiences. Duval and Wicklund (1972) called this state "objective self-awareness"—that is, being aware of oneself as an object for others.

There are individual differences in the ability to see another person's point of view, as measured by tests in which subjects are asked to describe situations as perceived by others. Those who are good at it have been found to do better at a number of social tasks (Feffer & Suchotliffe, 1966), and to be more altruistic.

Socially competent performance calls both for the ability to take the role of the other, and the motivation to do it appropriately. If a person performing in front of an audience thought all the time about audience reactions, his or her performance would deteriorate; if an interviewer empathized fully with each candidate, he or she would want to give them all the job. Meldman (1967) found that psychiatric patients were more egocentric (i.e., talked about themselves more) than controls, and it has been our experience that socially unskilled patients have great difficulty in taking the role of the other.

One form of training that is sometimes used here is role reversal, where the trainee takes the role of one of the other people in a situation that he finds difficult. We have also given patients practice at interviewing, since this forces them to take a serious interest in someone else—as well as having to ask questions and take the initiative in interaction.

NVC of Interpersonal Attitudes and Emotions

NVC plays a very important role in communicating interpersonal attitudes, such as friendly–hostile and dominant–submissive, as well as emotional states.

My colleagues and I compared the effects of verbal and nonverbal signals for communicating interpersonal attitudes. It was found that nonverbal signals had a far greater effect than verbal ones on judgments of whether the performer was friendly or hostile, dominant or submissive (Argyle, Salter, Nicholson, Williams, & Burgess, 1970; Argyle, Alkema, & Gilmour, 1971). Manipulation of the nonverbal component of videotaped messages accounted for 10 times as much variance as similar manipulations of verbal contents. Where there was conflict between verbal and nonverbal, the verbal was virtually ignored (Figure 1).

The same is true of emotions. Emotional states can be conveyed by speech—"I am feeling very happy"—but probably such statements will not be believed unless supported by appropriate NVC, and the NVC can convey the message without speech.

This is a sphere in which social performance often fails: if interactors do not send clear facial and vocal signals, others simply do not know what the performer's attitudes or feelings are. Some patients do send such signals, but they are all negative—sarcastic, superior, hostile, and so forth. The training of these cases is quite straightforward: trainees are coached in the use of facial expressions with the aid of a mirror or videotape recorder, and coached in vocal expression with the help of an audiotape recorder.

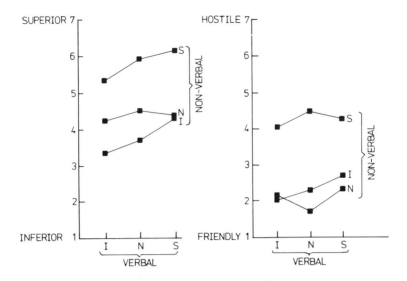

FIGURE 1. Effects of inferior, neutral, and superior verbal and nonverbal signals on semantic ratings. From Argyle, Salter, Nicholson, Williams, and Burgess (1970).

Nonverbal Accompaniments of Speech

Most social behavior involves speech, but this is accompanied and supported by a number of nonverbal signals. To begin with, two (or more) people must be able to hear and preferably see one another, which has clear implications for proximity and orientation. There are three main ways in which NVC supports speech.

COMPLETING AND ELABORATING ON VERBAL UTTERANCES

Some utterances are meaningless or ambiguous unless the nonverbal accompaniments are taken into account. A lecturer may point at part of a diagram: a tape recording of this part of the lecture would be meaningless. Some sentences are ambiguous if printed ("They are hunting dogs") but not if spoken ("They are hunting *dogs*"). Gestural illustrations are used to amplify the meanings of utterances—we found that shapes were more accurately communicated if hands could be used as well as voice. The percentages show the increased accuracy in the hands condition; the effect of adding hands was greater for shapes of low verbal codability, and with Italian subjects (Graham & Argyle, 1975; Figure 2).

The way in which an utterance is delivered "frames" it; that is, the intonation and facial expression indicate whether it is intended to be serious, funny, sarcastic (implying the opposite), rhetorical, or requiring an answer, and so on: The nonverbal accompaniment is a message about the message, which is needed by the recipient in order to know what to do with it. There are finer comments and elaborations too: particular words can be given emphasis, pronounced in a special accent, or in a way suggesting a particular attitude. The most important nonverbal signals are the prosodic aspects of vocalization—the timing, pitch, and loudness of speech.

SENDING FEEDBACK SIGNALS

When someone is speaking he or she needs intermittent but regular feedback on how others are responding, so that the speaker can modify his or her utterances accordingly. He or she needs to know whether the listeners understand, believe or disbelieve, are surprised or bored, agree or disagree, are pleased or annoyed. This information could be provided by sotto voce verbal mutterings, but is in fact obtained by careful study of the other's face: the eyebrows signal surprise, puzzlement, and so forth, while the mouth indicates pleasure and displeasure. When the other is invisible, as in telephone conversation, these visual

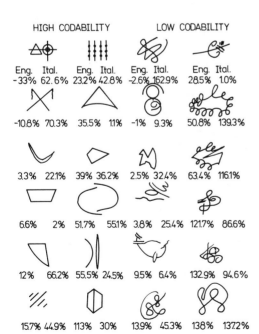

FIGURE 2. Accuracy of communicating shapes. The percentages show improvement when gestures were allowed for English and Italian subjects. From Graham and Argyle (1975).

signals are unavailable and more verbalized, listening behavior is used—"I see," "Really?", "How interesting," etc. Socially inadequate people may fail here in two main ways—they may not send attention signals indicating that they are attending and interested, and they may not send any feedback signals indicating their reactions to the speaker.

MANAGING SYNCHRONIZING

When two or more people are talking they have to take turns to speak. This is achieved mainly by means of nonverbal signals. For example, if a speaker wants to avoid being interrupted, he or she will be more successful if he or she does not look up at the ends of sentences, keeps a hand in midgesture at these points, and if, when interrupted, he or she immediately increases the loudness of his or her speech. The actual contents of speech (e.g., asking a question) are also important. Not only is synchronizing usually successful, but interactors may help each other, by finishing utterances. Some interruptions are mistaken anticipations of the other's ending, rather than attempts to break in. Errors in this general area of nonverbal support of speech are often due to a defective pattern of gaze. The normal pattern of gaze is for the listener to look nearly twice as much as the speaker, and especially at the ends of long utterances (Kendon, 1967; Figure 3); these "terminal gazes" also act as full stop signals. At grammatical pauses in long utterances, the speaker looks up—for feedback and for "backchannel" signals from the listener giving him or her permission to continue speaking. At speech disturbance pauses on the other hand, the speaker looks away, as at the beginning of utterances, in order to plan or replan the utterance (Kendon, 1967; Figure 4).

The training for failures of social competence in this area consists of first identifying the problem, and then of showing trainees the videotape, so that they can see what is happening.

Reinforcement and Rewardingness

Studies of operant verbal conditioning show that the delivery of small, mainly nonverbal signs of approval and disapproval, have a rapid and sizeable effect on another person's behavior. In ordinary conversation, participants are simply reacting positively or negatively to what pleases or displeases them in the other's behavior. And the effect works in both directions: while A is influencing B, B is also influencing A. This is one of the main processes whereby people are

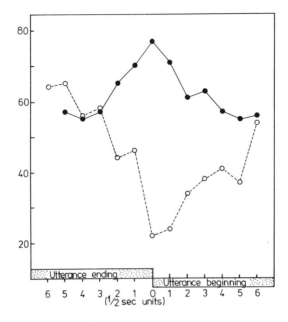

FIGURE 3. Direction of gaze at the beginning and ending of long utterances. From Kendon (1967).

able to modify each other's behavior in the desired direction. Obviously, if people do not give clear, immediate, and consistent reinforcements, positive and negative, they will not be able to influence others in this way, and social encounters will be correspondingly more frustrating and difficult for them. This appears to be a common problem with many psychiatric patients, who characteristically fail to control or try to overcontrol others.

If an individual provides rewards, interaction with such a person is enjoyable and he or she is liked. If he or she fails to provide sufficient rewards, others will leave. In a celebrated study of girls at a reformatory, Helen Jennings (1950) found that the popular girls helped and protected the others, encouraged and cheered them, made them feel accepted and wanted, and controlled their own moods so as not to inflict anxiety or depression on others, and were concerned with the needs and feelings of others. In other words, the popular girls were rewarding in a variety of ways. The unpopular girls did just the opposite—they were boastful, demanded attention, and tried to get others to do things for them—they were trying to extract rewards, at a cost to others. There are a number of different sources of popularity and

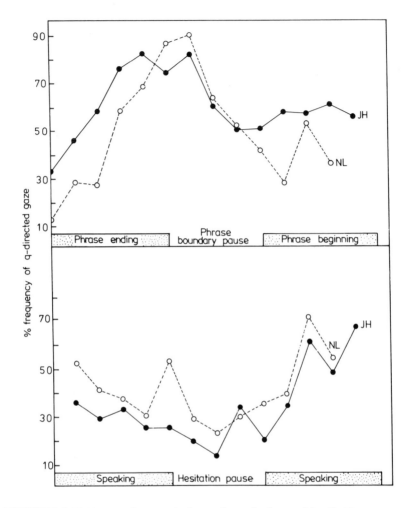

FIGURE 4. Patterns of gaze at phrase boundaries and hesitation pauses. From Kendon (1967).

unpopularity, but there is little doubt that being a source of rewards is one of the most important (Rubin, 1973). One of the most common characteristics of socially unskilled patients is their low rewardingness; this is particularly the case with chronic schizophrenics, who have been described as "socially bankrupt" (Longabaugh, Eldred, Bell, & Sherman, 1966).

A person may be rewarding because the interaction with him or her is enjoyable (e.g., making love, playing squash); interactions may be rewarding because the person is kind, helpful, interesting, and so forth; and people are rewarding just by being attractive or of high status.

How can people be trained to be more rewarding? It must be admitted that this is rather difficult; all one can do is to work away at the instructions, modeling, and video playback. However, once the process starts, trainees will begin to receive reinforcement in the outside world and a positive upward spiral of reinforcement may set in.

Plans and Feedback in Skilled Performance

Competent social performance is similar to performance of a motor skill (Argyle & Kendon, 1967), as we have seen (Figure 5). In each case the performer is pursuing certain goals, makes continuous response to feedback, and emits hierarchically organized motor responses. This analogy emphasizes the motivation, goals, and plans of interactors. It is postulated that every interactor is trying to achieve some goal, whether he or she is aware of it or not. These goals may be, for example, to get another person to like him or her, to obtain or convey information, to modify the other's emotional state, and so on. Such goals may be linked to more basic motivational systems. Goals have subgoals: for example, a doctor must diagnose the patient before he or she can give treatment.

Patterns of response are directed toward goals and subgoals, and have a hierarchical structure—large units of behavior are composed of smaller ones, and at the lowest levels these are habitual and automatic.

FIGURE 5. The motor skill model. From Argyle (1969).

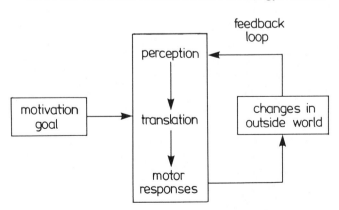

Harré and Secord (1972) have argued persuasively that much human social behavior is the result of conscious planning, often in words, with full regard for the complex meanings of behavior and the rules of situations. This is an important correction to earlier social psychology views, which often failed to recognize the complexity of individual planning and the different meanings that may be given to stimuli, for example, in laboratory experiments. However, it must be recognized that much social behavior is *not* planned in this way: The smaller elements of behavior and longer automatic sequences are outside conscious awareness, though it is possible to attend, for example, to patterns of gaze, shifts of orientation, or the latent meanings of utterances. The social skills model, in emphasizing the hierarchical structure of social performance, can incorporate both kinds of behavior.

The social skills model also emphasizes feedback processes. A person driving a car sees at once when it is going in the wrong direction, and takes corrective action with the steering wheel. Social interactors do likewise—if another person is talking too much, they interrupt, ask closed questions or no questions, and look less interested in what he has to say. Feedback requires perception, looking at and listening to the other person's reactions to one's behavior. It requires the ability to take the appropriate corrective action, referred to as "translation" in the model—not everyone knows that open-ended questions make people talk more, and closed questions make them talk less. And it depends on a number of two-step sequences of social behavior, whereby certain social acts have reliable effects on another. This analysis of social performance is most applicable to asymmetrical social situations, such as interviewing and teaching, where the performer is in charge.

Competence at specific skills like assertiveness and making friends, as well as interviewing and chairmanship, come under this heading, though each involves some of the other processes we have discussed, such as use of NVC, rewardingness, and so on.

The skill system may go wrong in a number of ways: (1) the plans may be inappropriate—as in the case of Berne's patients who wanted to make other people feel uncomfortable or look foolish (Berne, 1966); (2) an interactor may have no persistent plans; some socially inadequate neurotic patients take the subordinate side of encounters and leave other people to take all the initiative; (3) some individuals are very unresponsive to feedback, either because they don't notice the effect their behavior has on others, or because they don't know what corrective action to take.

What is the appropriate training here? Where a person fails to plan or to take the initiative he is given simple social tasks, such as an interview, where he must take the initiative, and needs to plan the encounter beforehand, including making written notes.

Self-Presentation

This refers to the signals that are sent to indicate a person's role, status, or other aspects of his or her identity. This is a normal and important component of social performance. From these signals others know what to expect, including what rewards are likely to be forthcoming, and how to deal with the person. Self-presentation is also needed for professional skills—teachers teach more effectively if their pupils think they are well informed, for example. If people tell others how good they are in words, this is regarded as a joke and disbelieved, in Western cultures at least. E. E. Jones (1964) found that verbal ingratiation is done with subtlety—drawing attention to assets in unimportant areas, for example. Most self-presentation is done nonverbally—by clothes, hairstyle, accent, badges, and general style of behavior. Social class is very clearly signaled in these ways, as is membership of rebellious social groups (Argyle, 1975).

Goffman (1956) maintained that social behavior involves a great deal of deceptive self-presentation, by individuals and groups, often in the interest of observers, as in the work of undertakers and doctors. In everyday life, deception is probably less common than concealment. Most people keep quiet about discreditable events in their past, and others don't remind them. Goffman's theory gives an explanation of embarrassment—this occurs when false self-presentation is unmasked. Later research has shown that this is the case, but that embarrassment also occurs when other people break social rules, and when social accidents are committed—unintentional gaffes, and forgetting names, for example (Argyle, 1969).

Self-presentation can go wrong in a number of ways: (1) by presenting bogus claims that are unmasked; (2) by being too "gray," that is, sending too little information; (3) by sending too much—overdramatizing, as hysterical personalities sometimes do; (4) by presenting an inappropriate self, as, for example, with a bank manager who dresses like a criminal, a female graduate student who looks and sounds like a retired professor. The training in these cases is done simply by showing trainees videos of themselves or by letting them hear their voices.

A related area is that of self-disclosure. When getting to know someone, it is important to keep to the rules—gradual disclosure, starting with safe topics, moving to more important ones, each reciprocating the other's disclosures. Neurotic patients often get this wrong by moving either too fast or too slowly.

Situations and Their Rules

The traditional trait model supposed that individuals possess a fixed degree of introversion, neuroticism, and so forth, and that it is displayed consistently in different situations. This model has been abandoned by most psychologists following an increased awareness of the great effect of the situation on behavior (e.g., people are more anxious when exposed to physical danger than when asleep in bed), and the amount of personality–situation interaction (e.g., A is more frightened by heights, B by cows), resulting in low intersituational consistency (Mischel, 1968).

It is found that neurotic and especially psychotic patients are *more* consistent across situations than normals—they do not accommodate to the special requirements of situations (Moos, 1968). We find that a proportion of clients for SST are mainly troubled by quite specific situations—dates, parties, interviews, etc.

In order to carry out SST for such people it has been necessary to analyze the main features of situations, and to find out where these people are going wrong. Just as a newcomer might be baffled by, say, American football, so a newcomer might be baffled by certain social situations. What does he need to know in order to be able to perform competently? In order to understand a new game one would need to know such things as the goals (how to score and win), the moves allowed, the rules, the roles, and the physical setting and equipment. Similar information is needed to a social situation—the goals, rules, roles, physical setting, repertoire of moves, concepts used, and special skills.

GOALS

In all situations there are certain goals that are commonly obtainable. It is often fairly obvious what these are, but socially inadequate people may simply not know what parties are for, for example, or may think that the purpose of a selection interview is vocational guidance.

We have studied the main goals in a number of common situations by asking samples of people to rate the importance of various goals, and then carrying out factor analyses. The main goals are usually (1) social acceptance, etc.; (2) food, drink, and other bodily needs; (3) task goals specific to the situation. We have also studied the relations between goals, within and between persons, in terms of conflict and instrumentality. This makes it possible to study the "goal structure" of situations. An example is given in Figure 6, showing that the only conflict between nurses and patients is between the nurses' concern for the bodily well-being of the patients and of themselves (Graham, Argyle, & Furnham, 1980).

RULES

All situations have rules about what may or may not be done in them. Socially inexperienced people are often ignorant or mistaken about the rules. It would obviously be impossible to play a game without knowing the rules and the same applies to social situations.

We have studied the rules of a number of everyday situations. There appear to be several universal rules—be polite, be friendly, don't embarrass people. There are also rules that are specific to situations, or groups of situations, and these can be interpreted as functional, since they enable situational goals to be met. For example, when seeing the doctor one should be clean and tell the truth; when going to a party one should dress smartly and keep to cheerful topics of conversation (Argyle, Graham, Campbell, & White, 1979).

SPECIAL SKILLS

Many social situations require special social skills, as in the case of various kinds of public speaking and interviewing, but such everyday situations as dates and parties also require special skills. A person

FIGURE 6. The goal structure for nurse and patient.

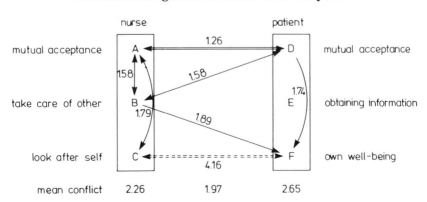

with little experience in a particular situation may find that he or she lacks the special skills needed for it (Argyle, Furnham, & Graham, 1981).

REPERTOIRE OF ELEMENTS

Every situation defines certain moves as relevant. For example, at a seminar it is relevant to show slides, make long speeches, draw on the blackboard, etc. If moves appropriate to a cricket match or a Scottish ball were made, they would be ignored or regarded as totally bizarre. We have found the 65 to 90 main elements used in several situations, like going to the doctor; we have also found that the semiotic structure varies between situations. We found that questions about work and about private life were sharply contrasted in an office situation, but not on a date (Argyle *et al.,* 1981).

ROLES

Every situation has a limited number of roles; for example, a classroom has the roles of teacher, pupil, janitor, and school inspector. These roles carry different degrees of power, and the occupant has goals peculiar to that role.

COGNITIVE STRUCTURE

We found that the members of a research group classified each other in terms of the concepts *extroverted* and *enjoyable companion* for social occasions, but in terms of *dominant, creative,* and *supportive* for seminars. There are also concepts related to the task (e.g., "amendment," "straw vote," "nem con") for committee meetings.

ENVIRONMENTAL SETTING AND PIECES

Most situations involve special environmental settings or props. Cricket needs bat, ball, stumps, etc.; a seminar required blackboard, slide projector, and lecture notes.

Sequences of Interaction

Social behavior consists of sequences of utterances and nonverbal signals. For such a sequence to constitute an acceptable piece of social behavior, the moves must fit together in order. Social psychologists have not yet discovered all the principles or "grammar" underlying these sequences, but some of the principles are known, and can explain common forms of interaction failure.

CONTINGENCIES

Jones and Gerard (1967) distinguished between asymmetrical contingency (where one person directs the sequence, as in interviewing and teaching), mutual contingency (where both parties can initiate interaction, as in negotiation and discussion), and two other types. Our social skills model fits the dominant partner in asymmetrical contingency. However, socially inadequate people often adopt the subordinate asymmetrical role, do not pursue any plans, and simply respond passively to others.

TWO-STEP SEQUENCES AND REPEATED CYCLES

Conversational sequences are partly constructed out of certain basic building blocks, like the question–answer sequence, and repeated cycles characteristic of the situation. Socially inadequate people are usually very bad conversationalists and this appears to be due to a failure to master some of these basic sequences. Here is a common way of stopping a conversation:

A: Where do you come from?

B: Swindon.

(End of conversation.)

B should have used a double, or proactive, move, of the type, "I come from Swindon; where do *you* come from?" Here is another example:

A: I went to Swindon yesterday.

B: Oh yes.

(End of conversation.)

Person A should have added a handing-over phrase, such as, "I was in Swindon yesterday; have you been there recently?", or "I went to Swindon yesterday; an extraordinary thing happened."

EPISODE SEQUENCE

Most social encounters consist of a number of distinct episodes, which may have to come in a particular order. We have found that encounters usually have five main episodes or phases:

1. greeting
2. establishing relationship
3. presenting the central task
4. reestablishing relationship
5. parting

The task in turn may consist of several subtasks; for example, a doctor has to conduct a verbal or physical examination, make a diagnosis, carry out or prescribe treatment. Often, as in this case, the subtasks have to come in a certain order. At primarily social events, the task seems to consist of eating or drinking, accompanied by the exchange of information.

Some unskilled people are incapable of conducting a conversation; probably they have not mastered these rules of sequence. Here are some of the ways a person may fail to sustain a conversation:

1. no initiation, only responds to other
2. poor responsiveness in nonverbal sphere
3. failure to reciprocate
4. produces uninteresting information about self
5. can't start or end encounter properly
6. omits phase of establishing the relationship

METHODS OF SST

The most widely used form of SST at the present time is role playing, with videotape recorder playback, and we include this in our battery of methods. (Our lab looks something like Figure 7.)

It includes split-screen video, and an ear microphone to communicate with the trainee during the role playing. The "stooges" (role partners) are carefully selected, and trained, to provide graded degrees of difficulty (e.g., reluctance to be dated). The instructions that are given before the role playing proper usually include modeling of the skill to be taught, done by one of the trainers or shown on video.

The transfer of laboratory-based skills to the real world is effected by means of homework—trainees are exhorted to practice what they have learned several times before the next session. Falloon, Lindlay, McDonald, and Marks (1976) found that much better results were obtained with neurotic patients when homework was used.

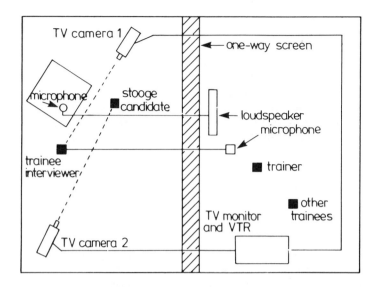

FIGURE 7. An SST laboratory.

We always use video playback. There has been some disagreement over the effectiveness of this, but in fact nearly all studies that have compared the effectiveness of SST with and without the videotape recorder have obtained clearly better results when it was used (Bailey & Sowder, 1970; Maxwell, 1976).

We have used both individual and group methods of training. Group therapy increases productivity and provides a source of role partners, but there is a danger in having so many unskilled models in the group. We usually start people in groups, working on common social behavior problems, and then shift to individual training for specific difficulties.

While we use role playing in much the same way as other trainers, we make more use of social psychological analysis in designing the contents of what is trained. For example, a trainee might be a very poor conversationalist, and the reason for this might be diagnosed as failure to provide feedback to synchronizing signals; he or she would then be given specialized instruction and training in these matters.

Some forms of SST have drawn heavily on the results of research in social psychology, and this is particularly the case with the Oxford form of SST. Here are some examples, related to the processes described earlier.

Expression of NVC. Patients who are unable to express emotions and interpersonal attitudes can be given training in the use of the face and voice. Facial expression can be taught with the help of a mirror, and then a videotape recorder; vocal expression needs an audiotape recorder.

Planning and initiating. Patients who fail to pursue persistent goals, and react passively to others, can be given special exercises. Simple interviewing is useful: the trainee makes notes beforehand, and directs the encounter; an ear microphone can be used to coach him or her during the role playing.

Self-presentation. In addition to the usual role playing exercises, trainees can be given advice over clothes, hair, and other aspects of appearance. Their voices can be trained to produce a more appropriate accent or tone of voice.

Situational analysis. For patients who have difficulty with particular situations, situational analysis is useful. The goals, rules, repertoire, roles, and other features of the situation are established, the difficulties located, and the best solutions are discussed and practiced.

Analysis of conversational sequences. Many patients cannot sustain a simple conversation. Study of their social performance in role-playing sessions makes it possible to discover exactly what it is they are doing wrong (e.g., failure to reciprocate or hand over conversation, failure of nonverbal accompaniments, etc.). Coaching is then directed toward these deficits.

THE EFFECTIVENESS OF SST

Neurotics

Several British and American studies have been carried out on outpatients, using experimental control-group designs and a 6-month follow-up. The patients selected for these studies have been neurotics judged to be socially inadequate. The target behaviors have been general social skills, heterosexual skills, assertiveness, verbal and nonverbal behavior, as well as removal of clinical symptoms. The criterion measures used have included role-played tests, but also self- and other-ratings of behavior in real-life situations. Methods used have included the usual role playing, modeling, and coaching, but also more specialized methods based on social psychological analysis. In all studies SST had positive effects on the behavior of patients, but so did psychotherapy, desensitization, and relaxation therapy.

Trower, Yardley, Bryant, and Shaw (1978) found that SST led to more improvement on social skills, and specifically social anxieties, than did desensitization. Vitalo (1971) found that SST had more effect on warmth, empathy, and genuineness than did traditional group therapy. On the other hand, group therapy had more effect on clinical measures. Argyle, Bryant, and Trower (1974) found that SST based on social psychology analysis did somewhat better than twice as much psychotherapy. Maxwell (1976), using similar methods in New Zealand, and with emphasis on homework, found that this form of SST produced much better results than group therapy or a control condition (see Marzillier, 1978, and Twentyman & Zimering, 1979, for a review of these studies).

I conclude that SST, of various kinds, is useful for neurotics, especially those with social behavior problems, and I believe that it will be most effective if use is made of the principles of social interaction. A valuable recent development, especially in North America, is the administration of SST by nurses, social workers, probation officers, and so on, as well as by psychologists.

Psychotics

Goldstein (1973) recommends SST as an alternative to psychotherapy for uneducated people, though there is no evidence yet for such differential effects. A number of studies by Hersen, Eisler, Gutride, and others, have shown that psychotic patients' social behavior *in the hospital* can be improved by SST, but there is little evidence that they improve to the extent of leaving the hospital (see Marzillier, 1978). However, intensive studies on individual patients, using a multiple-baseline method and at least 30 hours of training, have had some success with depressives and schizophrenics, some of whom have been discharged (Hersen, 1979).

Professional Social Skills Performers

SST has been found to be successful, and has become firmly established as part of the regular training of teachers, salesmen, interviewers, police, managers, and others, and is becoming more widely used in the training of doctors. Microteaching for teachers has been the most extensively developed. However, much more use could be made of knowledge about social interaction—for example, in analyzing the main situations involved, and in helping those who have special deficiencies in social performance. For example, a number of teachers leave the profession because they can't keep order. Research is needed into the most effective skills here, together with additional training in these skills for those who need it.

Normal Adults and Children

We have seen that many normal individuals suffer greatly from shyness, can't make friends, or can't cope with various social situations. It is fairly easy to train people to deal with those problems, but the training is not widely available. And it is not really appropriate to define these problems as medical or psychiatric, or those concerned as patients. I would greatly welcome the establishment of SST as one of the regular activities of community centers, or evening classes, along with tennis lessons and square dancing.

I would also greatly welcome the inclusion of SST as part of the school curriculum. A certain amount of such training is going on already, and McPhail (1972; McPhail, Middleton, & Ingram, 1978) has produced two textbooks and related classroom materials, mainly directed toward increasing awareness of the point of view of other people. So far, however, no follow-up studies have been done.

CONCLUSION

SST has been used with a wide range of patients, professional social skills performers, and others. Follow-up studies have shown considerable success with most of these groups. The most effective method is role playing, combined with coaching, modeling, videotape recorder playback, and homework, conducted in groups.

Social psychological research has revealed the main processes and skills underlying social competence, each of which can go wrong in various ways. Research on different groups of clients has found special deficits in particular groups. This has made possible forms of SST that are specially designed to deal with particular difficulties, such as NVC, conversational sequences, self-presentation, and particular situations.

REFERENCES

Argyle, M. *Social interaction.* London: Methuen, 1969.

Argyle, M. *Bodily communication.* London: Methuen, 1975; New York: International Universities Press.

Argyle, M., Alkema, F., & Gilmour, R. The communication of friendly and hostile attitudes by verbal and non-verbal signals. *European Journal of Social Psychology,* 1971, *1,* 385–402.

Argyle, M., Bryant, B., & Trower, P. Social skills training and psychotherapy: A comparative study. *Psychological Medicine,* 1974, *4,* 435–443.

Argyle, M., Furnham, A., & Graham, J. A. *Social situations*. Cambridge, England: Cambridge University Press, 1981.

Argyle, M., Graham, J. A., Campbell, A., & White, P. The rules of different situations. *New Zealand Psychologist*, 1979, *8*, 13–22.

Argyle, M., & Kendon, A. The experimental analysis of social performance. In L. Berkowitz (Ed.), *Advances in experimental social psychology*. New York: Academic Press, 1967.

Argyle, M., Salter, V., Nicholson, H., Williams, M., & Burgess, P. The communication of inferior and superior attitudes by verbal and non-verbal signals. *British Journal of Social and Clinical Psychology*, 1970, *9*, 221–231.

Bailey, K. C., & Sowder, W. T. Audiotape and videotape confrontation in psychotherapy. *Psychological Bulletin*, 1970, *74*, 127–137.

Bannister, D., & Salmon, P. Schizophrenic thought disorder: Specific or diffuse? *British Journal of Medical Psychology*, 1966, *39*, 215–219.

Berne, E. *Games people play*. London: Deutsch, 1966.

Bryant, B., & Trower, P. Social difficulty in a student population. *British Journal of Educational Psychology*, 1974, *44*, 13–21.

Bryant, B., Trower, P., Yardley, K., Urbieta, H., & Letemendia, F. J. J. A survey of social inadequacy among psychiatric outpatients. *Psychological Medicine*, 1976, *6*, 101–112.

Davitz, J. R. *The communication of emotional meaning*. New York: McGraw-Hill, 1964.

Duval, S., & Wicklund, R. A. *A theory of objective self-awareness*. New York: Academic Press, 1972.

Ekman, P., & Friesen, W. V. *Unmasking the face*. Englewood Cliffs, NJ: Prentice-Hall, 1975.

Falloon, I. R., Lindlay, P., McDonald, R., & Marks, I. M. Social skills training of outpatient groups: A controlled study of rehearsal and homework. *British Journal of Psychiatry*, 1977, *131*, 599–609.

Feffer, M., & Suchotliffe, L. Decentering implication of social interactions. *Journal of Personality and Social Psychology*, 1966, *4*, 415–422.

Freedman, B. J., Rosenthal, L., Donahoe, C. P., Schlundt, D. G., & McFall, R. M. A social–behavioral analysis of skill deficits in delinquent and non-delinquent adolescent boys. *Journal of Consulting and Clinical Psychology*, 1978, *46*, 1448–1462.

Goffman, E. *The presentation of self in everyday life*. Edinburgh: Edinburgh University Press, 1956.

Goldstein, A. J. *Structured learning therapy: Toward a psychotherapy for the poor*. New York: Academic Press, 1973.

Graham, J. A., & Argyle, M. A cross-cultural study of the communication of extra-verbal meaning by gestures. *International Journal of Psychology*, 1975, *10*, 57–67.

Graham, J. A., Argyle, M., & Furnham, A. The goal structure of situations. *European Journal of Social Psychology*, 1980, *10*, 345–366.

Harré, R., & Secord, P. *The explanation of social behaviour*. Oxford: Blackwell, 1972.

Henderson, S., Duncan-Jones, P., McAuley, H., & Ritchie, K. The patient's primary group. *British Journal of Psychiatry*, 1977, *131*, 599–609.

Hersen, M. Modification of skill deficit in psychiatric patients. In A. S. Bellack & M. Hersen (Eds.), *Research and practice in social skills training*. New York: Plenum, 1979.

Jennings, H. H. *Leadership and isolation*. New York: Longman Green, 1950.

Jones, E. E. *Ingratiation: A social psychological analysis*. New York: Appleton-Century-Crofts, 1964.

Jones, E. E., & Gerard, H. B. *Foundations of social psychology*. New York: Wiley, 1967.

Kendon, A. Some functions of gaze direction in social interaction. *Acta Psychologica*, 1967, *28*(1), 1–47.

Lewinsohn, P. M. The behavioral study and treatment of depression. In M. Hersen, R. M. Eisler, & P. M. Miller (Eds.), *Progress in behavior modification* (Vol. 1). New York: Academic Press, 1975.

Longabaugh, R., Eldred, S. H., Bell, N. W., & Sherman, L. J. The interactional world of the chronic schizophrenic patient. *Psychiatry*, 1966, *29*, 319–344.

Marzillier, J., Outcome studies of social skills training: A review. In P. Trower, B. Bryant, & M. Argyle (Eds.), *Social skills and mental health*. London: Methuen, 1978.

Maxwell, G. M. *An evaluation of social skills training*. Unpublished manuscript, University of Otago, Dunedin, New Zealand, 1976.

McPhail, P. *In other people's shoes*. London: Longman, 1972.

McPhail, P. Middleton, D., & Ingram, D. *Moral education in the middle years*. London: Longman, 1978.

Meldman, M. J. Verbal behavior analysis of self-hyperattentionism. *Diseases of the Nervous System*, 1967, *28*, 469–473.

Mischel, W. *Personality and assessment*. New York: Wiley, 1968.

Moos, R. H. Situational analysis of a therapeutic community milieu. *Journal of Abnormal Psychology*, 1968, *73*, 49–61.

Richardson, F. C., & Tasto, D. L. Development and factor analysis of a social anxiety inventory. *Behavior Therapy*, 1976, *7*, 453–462.

Rubin, Z. *Liking and loving*. New York: Holt, Rinehart & Winston, 1973.

Stratton, T. T., & Moore, C. L. Application of the robust factor concept to the fear survey schedule. *Journal of Behavior Therapy and Experimental Psychiatry*, 1977, *8*, 229–235.

Trower, P., Bryant, B., & Argyle, M. (Eds.). *Social skills and mental health*. London: Methuen, 1978.

Trower, P., Yardley, K. M., Bryant, B. M., & Shaw, P. H. The treatment of social failure: A comparison of anxiety-reduction and skills acquisition procedures on two social problems. *Behaviour Modification*, 1978, *2*, 41–60.

Twentyman, C. T., & Zimering, R. T. Behavioral training of social skills: A review. *Progress in Behavior Modification*, 1979, *7*, 319–400.

Vitalo, R. Teaching improved interpersonal functioning as a preferred mode of treatment. *Journal of Clinical Psychology*, 1971, *22*, 166–171.

Zimbardo, P. G. *Shyness: What it is, what to do about it*. Reading, MA: Addison-Wesley.

10

PERSPECTIVES ON ASSERTION AS A SOCIAL SKILLS MODEL

JOHN P. GALASSI
MERNA DEE GALASSI
MARILYN J. VEDDER

JOHN P. GALASSI is Professor at the University of North Carolina at Chapel Hill. Merna Dee Galassi is Visiting Assistant Professor at North Carolina State University. Marilyn J. Vedder is a doctoral student in counseling psychology at the University of North Carolina at Chapel Hill. The Galassis have been involved with assertion/social skills training for the past decade and have authored over two dozen publications in the area.

Galassi, Galassi, and Vedder have provided in their chapter an extremely thorough, thoughtful, and searching review of the recent assertion literature. For researchers working in this area, this chapter is an invaluable reference. They have not only reviewed the assessment and intervention research, they have thoroughly examined existing definitions and theoretical formulations, noting their vagueness and outmoded nature. In keeping with Wine's discussion of assertion in Chapter 1, these contributors conclude that "the assertion construct is outmoded and should be relinquished."

By the time that this chapter appears, we will have marked the end of a decade of almost feverish activity in assertion training, both in clinical application and empirical investigation. Prior to this time, there was, of course, some clinical (Salter, 1949; Wolpe, 1958) and research (Lazarus, 1966; Wagner, 1968) interest in assertion and other closely related treatment approaches. However, the publication of the first edition of Alberti and Emmons's (1970) *Your Perfect Right* and the appearance of McFall's (McFall & Marston, 1970) first treatment study seemed to trigger developments in the applied and research areas or, at least, to signal what was to come.

Since that time, interest in assertion training, or AT, as it has been popularly abbreviated, has grown to what some authors have called almost social movement proportions (Heimberg, Montgomery, Madsen, & Heimberg, 1977). In many ways, assertion training has left behind its behavior therapy beginnings to the point that it is not uncommon to hear it being identified as developing from the women's movement. Undoubtedly, interest in assertion training reflects perceived personal and social needs of the 1970s in much the same way as interest in sensitivity–encounter groups mirrored those concerns in the '60s.

In the professional arena, fascination has been almost as intense. Assertion training has been used as a treatment with such varied populations and concerns as adult offenders (Bornstein, Winegardner, Rychtarik, Paul, Naifeh, Sweeney, & Justman, 1978), job interviewing skills (Onoda & Gassert, 1978), junior high school students (Rashbaum-Selig, 1976), management personnel (Shaw & Rutledge, 1976), rehabilitating the disabled (Dunn, Van Horn, & Herman, 1977; Jung, 1978), teachers in training (Piercy & Ohanesian, 1976), veterans (Moffett & Stoklosa, 1976), the visually handicapped (Ryan, 1976, 1977), and working women (Pilla, 1977). It also has been incorporated as part of a treatment package for anorexia nervosa (Hauserman & Lavin, 1977), families in crisis (Kinney, Madsen, Fleming, & Haapala, 1977), long-standing eye closure reactions (Norton, 1976), migraine headache sufferers (Lambley, 1976), narcotic users (Lesser, 1976), and premature ejaculation (Yulis, 1976). In addition, attempts have been made to relate assertion to a host of other constructs, such as conflict-handling behavior (Ruble & Thomas, 1976), drug abuse (Lindquist, Lindsay, & White 1979), extraversion (Averett & McManis, 1977; Vestewig & Moss, 1976), dating and depression (Phibbs & Arkowitz, in press), occupational prestige (More & Suchner, 1976), ordinal position and family size (Hall & Beil-Warner, 1977), prosocial behavior and social inferential ability in children (Barrett & Yarrow, 1977), and sex differences, aggression, and openness to experience (Wyrick, Gentry, & Shows, 1977).

This chapter reviews the recent developments in assertion training research and attempts to place them within the broader context of social skills training. Specifically, it is a review of assertion training for approximately the second half of the decade. As such, it serves as an update of findings and conclusions discussed in review articles by the authors (Galassi & Galassi, 1978a) and others (Heimberg *et al.*, 1977; Hersen & Bellack, 1976; Rich & Schroeder, 1976), all of which were completed about 1975 or 1976.[1] It is important to note that such a review is considerably more difficult to write at this time for at least two reasons. First, the number of published and unpublished articles and the number of investigators in the field have increased dramatically. Secondly, the boundaries of the area have been even more difficult to identify as some investigators (Eisler, Blanchard, Fitts, & Williams, 1978) have now chosen to identify their work as social skill rather than assertion training, even though the dependent variables are labeled assertion and the treatment procedures include behavior rehearsal. Others have extended the use of assertion training procedures to social skill areas (e.g., job interviews) not traditionally defined as assertion (Onoda & Gassert, 1978). To cope with this situation, the following decisions were made in preparing the chapter: (1) to focus on published, in press, and readily accessible unpublished reports (papers presented at professional meetings as opposed to doctoral dissertations); (2) to focus on behavioral and cognitive–behavioral research reports as opposed to studies relating assertion to other constructs; (3) to emphasize data-based as opposed to opinion-based articles; and (4) to focus primarily on articles that specifically mention assertion as an independent or dependent variable and not on all other related social skill articles. Finally, because there is another chapter in this volume concerned with women and assertion (Kahn, Chapter 11), we will not emphasize that area.

DELIMITING ASSERTION

Defining Assertion

As noted in our earlier review (Galassi & Galassi, 1978a), the lack of a commonly accepted definition of assertion or assertive behavior has constituted a major problem for researchers and clinicians alike. This unresolved definitional problem has affected developments in a variety of areas from the construction of paper-and-pencil assessment instruments to the selection of target behaviors and treatment

[1]For a more recent review of the assertion and social skills literature, the reader may want to consult Twentyman and Zimering (1979).

techniques. Although a number of investigators have addressed the problem, we agree with Skatsche and Skatsche-Depisch (1979) that the unresolved definitional issues remain. They continue to hamper developments in this area of behavior therapy. If anything, definitional uncertainties may even have increased as new definitions of assertion have been proposed.

To date, there have been at least six basic approaches to defining assertive behavior. An approach used by many popular books is to define it in terms of basic human rights abstracted from democratic traditions, for example, "You have the right to judge your own behavior, thoughts, and emotions, and to take responsibility for their initiation and consequences upon yourself" (Smith, 1975, p. 28). Recently, however, definitions of this type have been criticized for their failure to take account of functionally related antecedent and consequent obligations (Rakos, 1979).

A second approach is to define assertion as honest and/or appropriate emotional expression. "Assertive behavior is defined as the proper expression of any emotion other than anxiety towards another person" (Wolpe, 1973, p. 81). This last example incorporates theoretical notions (reciprocal inhibition) as well by linking assertive behavior with the absence of anxiety. Lange and Jakubowski's (1976) definition combines the rights and emotional expression elements without theoretical attachments. "Assertion involves standing up for personal rights and expressing thoughts, feelings and beliefs in direct, honest, and appropriate ways which do not violate another person's rights" (p. 71). Still a fourth approach (Alberti & Emmons, 1978) has combined personal rights, honest and appropriate emotional expression, and theoretical assumptions. "Behavior which enables a person to act in his or her own best interests, to stand up for herself or himself without undue anxiety, to express honest feelings comfortably, or to exercise personal rights without denying the rights of others we call assertive behavior" (p. 2).

A more behavioral approach to the definitional problem is demonstrated by linking assertive behavior to clearly delineated response classes. For example, Lazarus (1973) defined it as "the ability to say 'no,' the ability to ask for favors or to make requests; the ability to express positive and negative feelings; the ability to initiate, continue, and terminate general conversation" (p. 697). Similarly, M. D. Galassi and Galassi (1977) proposed that assertion includes the following response classes: giving and receiving compliments, making requests, expressing liking, love, and affection, initiating and maintaining conversations, standing up for rights, refusing requests, expressing personal opinions, expressing justified annoyance and displeasure, and expressing justified anger with the ability to express these responses being influenced by the person to whom they are directed as well as by other situational and cultural context factors.

A final approach is represented by definitions that stress content-free, functional properties of assertive behavior: "We suggest that assertive behavior be conceptualized as 'effective problem solving' " (Heimberg et al., 1977, p. 954). "Assertive behaviors may be defined as skills that (a) are concerned with seeking, maintaining, and enhancing reinforcements and (b) occur in interpersonal situations involving the risk of reinforcement loss or the possibility of punishment" (Rich & Schroeder, 1976, p. 1083).

Of course, there are unique problems with each definitional approach. Definitions based on rights are open to questions about subjectivity, arbitrariness, and validity of those rights. Emotional expressiveness definitions suffer from vagueness. Theory-based definitions are overly dependent on available research supporting predictions derived from those theories. Although response-class definitions offer the advantage of specificity, they are open to questions about the arbitrariness of those classes and disputes about whether those classes have completely defined the construct. As noted by Rakos (1979), functional definitions are unspecific and fail to differentiate assertive from aggressive responses. Finally, definitions based on combinations of individual definitional elements suffer from the same problems as definitions based on the individual elements themselves.

Differentiating Assertion, Aggression, and Nonassertion

Differentiating assertion from aggression and from nonassertion (or submission) and the question of the interrelationships among these constructs represent still other facets of the definitional problem. A method for systematically distinguishing between assertive and aggressive behavior was first introduced by Alberti and Emmons (1970), who found these distinctions to be useful clinically. Such distinctions, however, have proven difficult to draw (Hewes, 1975; Lazarus, 1973) and, for the most part, the constructs have been confounded in the research literature (DeGiovanni & Epstein, 1978).

The criteria offered for these distinctions have varied considerably. Alberti and Emmons (1970), for example, relied on the likely feelings and consequences experienced by the person expressing the behavior and by the person acted upon. Another early criterion was the differential social acceptability of assertive and aggressive behavior (Wolpe, 1973).

Hollandsworth (1977b) criticized these distinctions because of the nonbehavioral criteria they invoked or the problems encountered by defining a response in terms of its consequences. He offered a distinction based on the verbal and nonverbal characteristics of the response itself. Aggressive responses employ coercion, and assertive responses do not. Coercion is defined behaviorally as the use of punishment and threats to gain compliance with threats specifying the future delivery of punishment. Punishment includes noxious stimulation, deprivation of existing resources or expected gains, ridicule, disparagements, name calling, expressions of dislike, and other forms of negative evaluation and social rejection.

Expressing concern about the reductionistic nature of Hollandsworth's criterion, Alberti (1977) suggested that the distinctions should be based not only on the characteristics of the behavior itself, but also on its effects, the social-cultural context, and on intent. Using Alberti's criteria, it is possible for the same responses to be judged assertive on one criterion, aggressive on another, and nonassertive on still another.

In rejecting consequences as a criterion, Rakos (1979) called for a distinction based on rights and obligations (social responsibilities). Aggressiveness involves the simple expression of rights, whereas assertiveness includes not only the expression of rights but also the consideration and emission of antecedent and subsequent obligation behaviors.

Related to which characteristics differentiate nonassertive (submissive), assertive, and aggressive behavior is the question of whether the differences are primarily in degree or in kind. That is, do the constructs vary along a single dimension in terms of intensity, or do they represent more than one separate and distinct dimension? It is apparent that investigators have been operating on different assumptions. Rose and Tryon (1979) have assumed a single nonassertive-assertive-aggressive continuum. In validating the College Self-Expression Scale (CSES), Galassi and Galassi (1975) assumed that an assertion—nonassertion continuum was relatively independent from an aggression continuum and that scores on the CSES would be minimally correlated with scores on an aggression measure. McFall and Lillesand (1971) appear to have assumed separate continua for nonassertion and assertion in constructing the Conflict Resolution Inventory (CRI), although subsequent research (Galassi, Galassi, & Westefeld, 1978; Rodriguez, Nietzel, & Berzins, 1980) indicated that the two subscales are highly correlated, in part due to the ipsative scoring system of the CRI. MacDonald (1974, 1978) seems to have assumed separate submission, assertion, and aggression continua for the College Women's Assertion Sample, although intercorrelations suggest that they are by no means mutually exclusive. Finally Rathus (1973) and Wolpe (1969) in their earlier work linked assertion closely with aggression and in opposition to nonassertion. One validational datum for the Rathus Assertiveness Schedule (RAS) is that it is correlated highly with semantic differential ratings of aggressiveness. Wolpe noted that "assertiveness usually involves more or less aggressive behavior" (1969, p. 61).

Regardless of the effort expended by professionals to differentiate assertion from aggression, some recent data indicate that the lay population not only fails to distinguish between them (Hess, Bridgewater, Bornstein, & Sweeney, 1980) but also evaluates both of them negatively (Rathus, Fox, & De Cristofaro, 1979). For instance, when Rathus et al. (1979) subjected teachers' ratings of high school students on an adjective checklist to factor analysis, assertiveness and aggressiveness loaded highly and at about the same level on a factor concerned with negative evaluation judgments. Further, assertiveness failed to load significantly on factors concerned with openness and social facility.

Conceptualizing Assertion

In addition to the definitional issues and the problems of differentiating assertion from aggression, the conceptual underpinnings of assertion have also been debated without clear resolution. Two major positions exist: assertion as a generalized disposition, person variable, or trait, and assertion as a situation-specific behavior. It is our contention that both of these positions are oversimplifications. In addition, reliance on them reflects the fact that the entire area has been shaped more by the early developments and influences in behavior therapy than by recent and more sophisticated conceptualizations.

To be sure, assertion has been strongly influenced by a trait conception of personality that attributes consistency of behavior to relatively enduring personality dispositions. The influence of this position is evident in both the historical antecedents of assertion and in the early statements of assertion theory. Salter's (1949) work on the excitatory and inhibitory personality markedly affected Wolpe's (1958) early statements about assertion. Skatsche and Skatsche-

Depisch (1979) believe that both Wolpe and Salter implicitly seem to favor a trait concept of assertiveness as they appear to assume high correlations between different response classes of assertion. More recently, the influence of the trait position is reflected in the frequent use of the terms "assertive," "aggressive," and "nonassertive" to describe individuals and in the construction of global self-report measures of assertion. "Although behavior therapists have paid lip service to situational determinants of behavior, they have treated assertiveness as a trait" (Rich & Schroeder, 1976, p. 1094).

Correspondingly, there have been a variety of attempts to demonstrate whether assertion is more adequately conceptualized in terms of a trait or situation-specific view of personality, or, stated differently, whether assertive behavior primarily reflects the influence of personological or situational variables. Situation-specificity attributes consistency in behavior to situational similarities rather than personal dispositions. Evidence supporting a situational view has been marshaled from at least three different research areas: treatment studies, factor analyses of self-report measures, and role-playing behavior.

If assertion is situation-specific, then treatment of one response class or situation should not result in improvement (generalization) in untreated response classes or situations. Although generalization will be discussed more extensively in a later section, results (Kirschner, 1976; McFall & Lillesand, 1971; Young, Rimm, & Kennedy, 1973) demonstrating limited generalization effects have been offered as support for a situation-specific conceptualization. However, caution should be exercised in forming strong conclusions based on such studies given that the separate question of the effectiveness of these programs has not been answered unequivocally.

A second form of support is provided by factor analytic studies of responses to self-report measures. If assertion is situation-specific, then factor analyses should reveal a number of discrete factors rather than a single general factor. The results of such studies (Bates & Zimmerman, 1971; Galassi & Galassi, 1979a; Gambrill & Richey, 1975; Lawrence, 1970; Nevid & Rathus, 1979) reveal a number of factors, each accounting for a modest proportion of total common variance rather than a single factor accounting for a large amount of variance.

Perhaps the most direct evidence concerning situational specificity comes from studies of role-playing behavior in diverse situations. Before summarizing these data, however, a few comments are needed about interactionism, a third conceptual approach. This model appears to have been almost ignored by investigators in assertion training even though it is receiving a great deal of attention in both behavior therapy (Bandura, 1977; McReynolds, 1979; Mischel, 1973) and personality research (Endler & Magnusson, 1976; Magnusson & Endler, 1977). Interactionism assumes that behavior is a function of person variables, situation variables, and person × situation interactions. The basic elements of an interactionist model are (Magnusson & Endler, 1977, p. 4):

1. Actual behavior is a function of a continuous process of multidirectional interaction or feedback between the individual and the situations he or she encounters.

2. The individual is an intentional, active agent in this interaction process.

3. On the person side of the interaction, cognitive and motivational factors are essential determinants of behavior.

4. On the situation side, the psychological meaning of situations for the individual is the important determining factor.

There have been a number of studies with hospitalized patients (Eisler, Hersen, Miller, & Blanchard, 1975; Hersen, Bellack, & Turner, 1978; Zielinski, 1978) and college students or other nonhospitalized persons (Bourque & Ladouceur, 1979; Burchardt-Pharr & Serbin, 1977; Edinberg, Karoly, & Gleser, 1977; Pitcher & Meikle, 1980; Rodriguez *et al.,* 1980; Skillings, Hersen, Bellack, & Becker, 1978; Zeichner, Pihl, & Wright, 1977; Zeichner, Wright, & Herman, 1977) relevant to the trait versus situation-specific issue and, in most instances, to an interactionist position as well. In these studies, subjects are divided on trait or person variables (e.g., high–low assertion, male–female, self-reported sex-role orientation) and then asked to role play a variety of situations. In many instances, these situations are divided into positive and negative, depending upon whether they require hostile or commendatory assertion.[2] They often are divided further based on such variables as the sex and degree of familiarity of the stimulus person. A variety of verbal, nonverbal, paralanguage, and physiological reactions are subsequently assessed for the subjects across the situations. Although the results from individual studies are too complex to summarize, the general pattern has been interpreted to support a situation-specific view. This conclusion is surprising given that a number of the studies (Eisler *et al.,* 1975; Skillings *et al.,* 1978) clearly demonstrate effects due to persons,

---

[2]We consider this division to be one of response classes rather than situations.

situations, and person × situation interactions. At least one study (Edinberg *et al.*, 1977), concluded that assertion is situation-specific while, at the same time, reporting that the estimated variance component attributable to the interaction of individuals and situations was the highest of the three.

There are several points that we are trying to make. First, the trait–situation debate is a pseudo issue based on a limited conceptualization of behavior (Haynes, 1979). Results from the above studies clearly indicate that some reactions or response components (verbal, nonverbal, paralanguage, and physiological) may be consistent across response and situation classes, whereas others may not. More importantly, however, the influence of persons, situations, response classes, response components, and their interactions in interpersonal behavior all need to be clearly acknowledged.

Identifying the Components of Assertion

Still another important unresolved issue is specifying the effective verbal, nonverbal, and paralanguage components or content of assertive behavior. Without knowledge of these components, assessment of individual clients and evaluation of treatment effects are impeded. Moreover, to the extent that assertion training should be skill-based, a question that is presently unresolved, progress in that area is retarded as well.

There have been several approaches to identifying the effective components of assertive behavior. One common method, the known-groups approach (McFall, 1976), has been to compare subjects identified as high and low or high, moderate, and low in assertion for differential role-playing performance on a variety of verbal, nonverbal, and paralanguage measures. If the groups differ on a particular measure, then the performance of the high-assertive group is assumed to reflect effective behavior. Studies contrasting highs and lows can be subdivided based on whether assertive behavior was investigated (1) across a variety of response and/or situation classes, (2) for negative and positive response classes, or (3) for a single response or situation class. Within each of these categories, it is important to differentiate studies (Curran, 1979) of hospitalized adults from those with college students and other nonhospitalized individuals. Findings from a few representative studies are summarized below.

Studies using a variety of situations and response classes with college students have been conducted by Galassi, Hollandsworth, Radecki, Gay, Howe, and Evans (1976) and Bourque and Ladouceur

(1979). The former, for example, reported that highs and lows were differentiated on eye contact and verbal content but not on response latency. The latter reported significant correlations between self-reported assertiveness, measures of verbal content, and global judgments of assertiveness. However, high and low scorers were not differentiated by eye contact, length or response, response latency, tone of voice, or affect.

A number of studies with both hospitalized (Eisler, Miller, & Hersen, 1973; Eisler *et al.*, 1975) and nonhospitalized subjects (Pitcher & Meikle, 1980; Reardon, Hersen, Bellack, & Foley, 1979; Skillings *et al.*, 1978) have investigated the behavior of high- and low-assertive subjects in negative and positive situations. Negative situations were described as requiring expressions of anger, displeasure, and disappointment, whereas positive situations involved praise, appreciation, and liking.[3] In several of these studies, situational variables such as sex and degree of familiarity of the stimulus person were also varied. A sampling of the results from two of the studies illustrates the type of information to be derived from this approach.

Eisler, Miller, and Hersen (1973), who studied male psychiatric patients in negative situations, reported that high-assertives had louder speech, shorter latency, more pronounced affect, and exhibited less compliance and more requests for behavior change than low-assertives. Eisler *et al.* (1975) found that, in negative as compared to positive situations, the responses involved generally longer replies, increased eye contact, greater affect, more speech volume, and longer latency. Significant effects on the verbal, nonverbal, and paralanguage components were also contributed by the sex and familiarity of the role player and by various combinations of the situation factors.

Still others (Bourque & Ladouceur, 1979; Schwartz & Gottman, 1976) have investigated differences between highs and lows for single response classes. Surprisingly the Bourque and Ladouceur study failed to find differential performance for highs and lows as a function of response class (positive feelings, legitimate rights, negative feelings, refusing unreasonable requests) even though significant main effects were found for both level of assertiveness and response class alone.

At this point, some comments are in order about the adequacy of the known-groups approach in general and about the ways in which it has been employed in particular. Unfortunately, users of the ap-

[3]See Footnote 2.

proach often are prone to assume that whatever differences are found between the groups are necessarily relevant to the issue of effective components of assertive behavior. However, the question of which components to contrast groups on initially is a somewhat separate issue. The assumption also precludes the possibility that, even though an individual is regarded as assertive, some parts of his or her behavior may not be effective, either in the long or short run. Moreover, the behavioral components of an assertive response are inextricably determined by cultural and subcultural norms and values (Furnham, 1979; Galassi & Galassi, 1979a; Jenkins, 1979).

With respect to specific applications of the known-groups approach to assertion, difficulties arise in pooling verbal, nonverbal, or paralanguistic components across a variety of situations and response classes. The assertive response topography for refusing an unreasonable request is likely to be quite different from that for expressing affection. If that is the case, then pooling is inappropriate, ill-advised, and misleading. Dichotomizing situation (really response) classes into positive and negative does little to ameliorate the problem unless it can be shown empirically, for example, that the particular representatives of positive assertion belong together. Studies of high-and low-assertives with individual situation or response classes are also not without their difficulties. No taxonomy of response classes and situations has been accepted to date.

A second approach has been to determine whether components selected on a nonempirical basis are in fact related to or affect global judgments of assertiveness. In a factor analytic study of psychiatric patients' performance in vocationally related interpersonal scenes, Pachman, Foy, Massey, and Eisler (1978) reported that eye contact, duration of reply, compliance, and requests for new behavior, but not latency, all loaded on a common factor with global judgment of assertiveness. For college students, Bordewick and Bornstein (1979) found that duration, loudness, affect, latency, compliance, requests, and global assertiveness loaded together. Rose and Tryon (1979) reported that, in a restaurant and a breaking-in-line situation, variations in voice loudness, latency to reply, speech content, gestures, and voice inflection by male and female actors altered judgments on a subassertive–assertive–aggressive continuum. Differences were also reported between the situations and for the sex of the responder. Research by McFall, Winnett, Bordewick, and Bornstein (1979) also employed actors in an attempt to have subjects identify the influence of body parts in judgments of assertiveness.

A third approach has been to construct an overall assertive re-

sponse, consisting of verbal, nonverbal, and/or paralanguage components, based on preconceived distinctions such as those by Alberti
and Emmons (1974). The effects of the assertive response are then
contrasted with those of an aggressive and/or a nonassertive response (Ford & Hogan, 1978; Hollandsworth & Cooley, 1978; Hull &
Schroeder, 1979; Woolfolk & Dever, 1979) in written, taped, or live
presentations. Regardless of whether an assertive response achieves
desired goals, these studies report that assertion results in more
negative reactions in comparison to nonassertion than previously
thought. For example, assertion is viewed as dominant, unsym-
pathetic, and aggressive (Hull & Schroeder, 1979); more hostile, less
polite, and less satisfying (Woolfolk & Dever, 1979); and less cooperative, less friendly, and more aggressive and hostile (Ford & Hogan,
1978) than nonassertion. In comparison to an aggressive response, it
generally elicits less anger (Hollandsworth & Cooley, 1978; Hull &
Schroeder, 1979), is regarded as more polite, less neurotic, more satisfying (Woolfolk & Dever, 1979), and is judged more pleasant, fair,
sympathetic, nonrevengeful, friendly (Hull & Schroeder, 1979), and
more positive (Bordewick & Bornstein, 1979).

Although some useful information has been derived from this
last approach, it has several shortcomings. First, it serves to maintain our trait emphasis, and it assumes the existence of commonly accepted definitions. Second, the studies employing it often fail to
specify the exact verbal, nonverbal, and paralanguage differences involved. In addition, the results of these studies as well as those mentioned next indicate that we need to take an even more systematic
account of a variety of situation and response class variables in identifying effective content.

Among the situational variables, there are data suggesting that
gender of the target person (Bean, 1977; Burchardt-Pharr & Serbin,
1977; Eisler et al., 1975; Ford & Hogan, 1978; Hess & Bornstein,
1979; Hess et al., 1980; Hull & Schroeder, 1979; Skillings et al., 1978),
perceived masculinity or feminity of the target person (Hess & Bornstein, 1979), the target person's role or status (Bean, 1977), and the
setting (Brummage, 1976; Rose & Tryon, 1979) all may be influential.

With respect to gender, Hess et al. (1980), for example, investigated observers' perceptions of assertion as delivered by a taped
typical male, typical female, or ambiguous voice. Female observers
perceived all voices as significantly more assertive, aggressive, and
masculine in their response style. Burchardt-Pharr and Serbin (1977)
reported that both sexes appeared to be more assertive to the same-
sex partner, particularly in traditional sex-role situations. At pres-

ent, the results for gender differences do not show a clear pattern, a state of affairs that may partially be a function of the population and the response and situation classes investigated.

Considering gender and target person, Bean (1977) found that males considered assertion more appropriate than nonassertion for standing up for rights with peers and professors, whereas females considered it appropriate toward a peer but inappropriate toward a professor. With respect to setting, Brummage (1976) noted that males perceived assertive women as behaving less appropriately at work than at home. Effects attributable to response-class differences have been reported by Hull and Schroeder (1979), who found that refusals are rated as more unfair and result in more resistance than requests for behavior change. Of course, interactions among situational and response class influences also occur (Bean, 1977; Hess *et al.*, 1980).

Resolving the Issues

Throughout this section, we have discussed a number of problems in defining, conceptualizing, and identifying assertion. A major question then is how do we resolve these issues. Our position, which seems to be shared by others (Rathus *et al.*, 1979), is that even if it is possible to resolve these dilemmas, it may not be advantageous to do so. For a variety of reasons, it seems more valuable to discontinue referring to the assertiveness construct (Galassi, 1978; Mullinix & Galassi, 1981) and to integrate what has been investigated in this area of research with the social skills–social competence literature more generally. There would be several distinct advantages of doing so.

From a training perspective, it seems clear that most clinicians teach their clients to be more socially competent in a given situation rather than to be more assertive overall. To know that loudness is one characteristic of highly assertive persons provides little helpful information to the clinician who is trying to teach a client to express love and affection more effectively. The loudness criterion would seem to be of relatively limited value (except if taken to extremes) in either training or evaluating effective behavior in this area. Thus reliance on statements about assertiveness in general can provide irrelevant or misleading information in training clients to be more effective with particular response classes or in particular situations. Divesting ourselves of the assertiveness construct eliminates our definitional problems as well as the notion that all interpersonal behavior can be reduced to three mutually exclusive categories, two of which, aggressive and nonassertive, are totally undesirable and the other, assertive, which is desirable. As we have seen, even assertive behavior can have a variety of effects, and classification based on a three-category system is overly simplistic. Still another advantage is the likelihood that we might reduce the heavy emphasis on trait assumptions and increase the emphasis on situation-specific and interactionist conceptions of behavior. Further, a reduction in unnecessary literature duplication should follow from studying only social skills rather than the related assertion area as well.

Obviously, there would need to be changes in our research strategies. Regardless of whether we subscribe to a situation-specific or interactionist perspective, we need to develop a taxonomy of situations. Investigators in both assertion and social skills training and more basic personality research have devoted relatively little effort to identifying important situational parameters. Situations have usually been selected by fiat or consensus rather than empirically. As noted by Endler and Magnusson (1976) and by Magnusson and Endler (1977), situations may be categorized based on the way they are perceived and classified by judges (Kolotkin, 1980) or by the reactions they elicit. Most assertion research has focused on dyadic interaction. To date, the following variables have influenced the meaning of dyadic situations or the behaviors elicited: gender, degree of familiarity, and status or role of the target person, as well as somewhat less clearly specified social characteristics of the setting (e.g., home–work setting, restaurant, waiting in line). To be sure, determining the primary situational influences is not an easy task. In the process, the issue of utility must be considered in conjunction with the number of possible situational parameters. Using too few parameters can result in confusion or vague generalities; too many would lead to unnecessary and spurious specificity.

Likewise, there is a need to develop a taxonomy of response classes. In the past, the role of response classes has often been minimized as examples from different response classes (Galassi, Galassi, & Litz, 1974) have been lumped together under the global assertiveness category. Similarly, they have often been confounded with situations (Eisler et al., 1975). At this point in social skills research, it is most important to employ scaling and other statistical techniques to identify homogeneous response and situation classes. Once these classes have been identified, we believe that research in assessment and training can proceed more systematically, that results will have more direct clinical applications, and that some of the confusion and contradictions in the literature will be reduced. To date, the work by

McFall and his associates (McFall & Lillesand, 1971; McFall & Twentyman, 1973) on refusal behavior represents one of the few systematic efforts with a well-defined response class.

Two additional changes in our research strategies are needed.
First, being careful to avoid swapping one set of traitlike assumptions for another (e.g., assertiveness for social competence), we need
to specify the criteria for evaluating interpersonal behavior. Those
criteria need to be developed recognizing response- and situation-
class influences and the fact that behavior can produce multiple and,
at times, conflicting effects depending on which dependent variables
are assessed. Second, we need to determine or at least validate empirically which verbal, nonverbal, and paralanguage components of a
response influence interpersonal behavior. This latter effort must
recognize that response components may vary in their importance
across response and situation classes. Of course, the question of which
response components are important is necessarily related to the criteria we adapt for evaluating interpersonal behavior.

Two recent studies (Mullinix & Galassi, 1981; Romano & Bellack,
1980) provide suggestive approaches to the criteria and response
components issues. In an approach that is related but developed independently from social validation (Kazdin, 1977; Wolf, 1978), Galassi
(1978) and Mullinix and Galassi (1981) proposed that the content of
social skills training be selected in accordance with three criteria reflecting its social impact. First, what are the immediate behavioral
consequences produced by the content? For example, does it produce
compliance if that is the intention? How likely is it to produce un-
wanted consequences (e.g., hostile reactions)? Second, how socially
appropriate is it as perceived by others? Third, how much comfort/
discomfort is engendered in the parties by the content? Confining
their investigation to an empirically derived situation for a specific
response class in which one coworker consistently took advantage of
another at work, Mullinix and Galassi demonstrated that a verbal
message could be divided into combinations of commonly used, additive verbal subcomponents (e.g., conflict statement, behavior
change request, empathy statement, threat). These combinations
produced different effects, as measured by the three criteria of response consequences, appropriateness, and comfort. Contrary to
what is often assumed, adding a behavior change request to a statement identifying the presence of a conflict did not increase the likelihood of that conflict being resolved. In general, the conflict statement
appeared to be the most important verbal component. An empathy
statement did not add to the impact of a message containing a behav-

ior change request and a conflict statement, and a threat increased hostility and discomfort while decreasing appropriateness. The Mullinix and Galassi approach can be used to determine effective combinations of verbal, nonverbal, and paralanguage components for given response and situation classes.

Romano and Bellack (1980) videotaped role plays of women refusing unreasonable requests. Subsequently, male and female adults judged the scenes for social skill and listed the cues they believed influenced their judgments. Trained raters also scored the videotapes on a standard set of dependent variables plus those generated by the judges. Romano and Bellack found that the derived component model, as opposed to the standard set of variables, incorporated more complex verbal categories—statement of position and feelings, empathic statements, offering alternatives, compliance, apologies, hostility, reasons for behavior, and humor. These categories accounted for a significant amount of the criterion variance, and thus, Romano and Bellack believe that, within the component of verbal behavior, more complex categories need to be assessed in order to derive the necessary content of socially skilled responses. However, they found that most of the variance for refusing requests was due to nonverbal and paralinguistic components. Finally, the authors reported that males and females differed in the number, pattern, and valence of cues used and the adequacy with which components accounted for their ratings.

Still another aspect of validating response components is reflecting the interactive nature of interpersonal interactions. As we have discussed elsewhere (Galassi & Galassi, 1979b), there is increasing recognition (Fischetti, Curran, & Wessberg, 1977; Glasgow & Arkowitz, 1975) that many of the standard behavioral measures, such as simple frequency counts or percentage of eye contact, alone do not adequately capture the natural give and take in social situations. Single-response role-playing situations and the associated dependent variables can not reflect how individuals adjust their behavior in accordance with the responses they receive from each other during a dyadic interaction. As we have advocated previously (Galassi & Galassi, 1979b), social skills researchers might do well to give consideration to the structural approach of Duncan and Fiske (1977). This approach assumes that dyadic interaction is an organized, rule-governed phenomenon and attempts to capture the moment-to-moment flow of that interaction using variables that reflect the ongoing reciprocity between the participants. In an example of that approach, Duncan and Fiske (1977) identified behaviorally defined verbal and nonverbal signals and rules by which speaking turns are smoothly exchanged. Identifying the rules and signals governing particular response classes and situations might provide extremely useful information for social skills training.

THEORETICAL FORMULATIONS

The theoretical formulations guiding assertion research are fundamentally the same as those in other areas of social skills research (Galassi & Galassi, 1979b). With respect to nonassertive behavior, they have emphasized the role of anxiety, skill deficits, or cognitions with an increasing emphasis on cognitions since our earlier review (Galassi & Galassi, 1978a). Clearly, each theoretical formulation implies a correspondingly different intervention focus—anxiety reduction, skill acquisition, and cognitive change.

The earliest formulations by Wolpe (1958, 1969, 1973) viewed anxiety and assertion as occupying a reciprocally inhibitory relationship. High levels of conditioned anxiety in social situations block the expression of assertive behavior. Similarly, strong assertive tendencies can inhibit weaker conditioned anxiety responses. Operant conditioning, modeling, and restricted learning opportunities occupy secondary roles in anxiety-based explanations.

A more recent formulation proposed by McFall and his colleagues (McFall, 1976; McFall & Lillesand, 1971; McFall & Marston, 1970; McFall & Twentyman, 1973) is that nonassertive behavior is the result of a skill deficit. If an individual fails to behave assertively, it is because the skills necessary for competent performance are absent from his or her behavioral repertoire. If anxiety is present, it is a consequence rather than a cause of behavior.

Some of the most recent research (Schwartz & Gottman, 1976) has been concerned with the role of cognitions in mediating nonassertive behavior. From a cognitive perspective, nonassertion is neither the result of the effects of conditioned social anxiety nor a deficit in performance capability. Rather, it is a function of excesses or deficits in certain cognitive behaviors. It may result from negative self-statements, irrational beliefs, an incorrect prediction of behavioral consequences, a failure to discriminate when assertive behavior is required, faulty problem-solving or decision-making skills, limited ability to read and process social cues, lack of knowledge about appropriate behavior, and so forth.

An important question, then, is what data support the predictions of these three alternative formulations. Before answering this question, however, it must be stated that data from successful treatment studies purporting to employ anxiety reduction, behavioral, or cognitive interventions can not be cited in this regard. The mechanisms underlying effective treatment are generally unknown, and treatment may effect change in a target behavior in a manner unrelated to the way the target behavior developed initially (Bandura, 1969; Davison, 1968; McFall, 1976).

In general, anxiety-based formulations have been the subject of increasing criticism in behavior therapy in recent years (Bandura, 1977; Mahoney, 1974; Rachman, 1977). More important, however, is the lack of direct evidence that assertion physiologically inhibits anxiety (Rimm & Masters, 1974). The evidence that does exist consists of mainly correlational data between overall scores on global, self-report measures of assertiveness and social fear/anxiety with adults (Hollandsworth, 1979) or college students (Hollandsworth, 1976; Morgan, 1974; Orenstein, Orenstein, & Carr, 1975) and between behavioral measures of assertion and self-report measures of social anxiety with male inpatient alcoholics (Pachman & Foy, 1978) and psychiatric patients (Eisler, Miller, & Hersen, 1973). With the exception of Eisler *et al.* (1973), results have consistently shown a statistically significant and inverse relationship between social fear and assertiveness regardless of population. However, the strength of that relationship has varied markedly with correlations of − .17 (Morgan, 1974) to − .81 (Orenstein *et al.*, 1975). Such correlational data support an inverse, but not necessarily a reciprocally inhibitory, relationship. In a study involving a self-report measure of assertion (CRI) and a physiological measure, Twentyman, Gibralter, and Inz (1979) failed to find differences between the heart rates of high- and low-assertives in role-playing situations.

Evidence for skill-based formulations may be derived from studies demonstrating that subjects identified as nonassertive are deficient in relevant observable skills as compared to assertive subjects. At this time, we are aware of only a few studies that directly test this formulation (Eisler, Miller, & Hersen, 1973; Schwartz & Gottman, 1976). In addition, suggestive evidence comes from test validation studies, studies on situational determinants, and studies on assertive response classes. A number of the studies are weakened by classifying subjects on the basis of global rather than specific measures of assertion and by using the same sample of behavior to classify subjects and to score dependent variables. Nevertheless, unlike some social skill areas (e.g., heterosocial skills), differences between assertive and nonassertive subjects, which were discussed in an earlier section, have been found on a variety of behavioral variables regardless of whether the population is college students (Bourque & Ladouceur, 1979; Galassi *et al.*, 1976; McFall & Twentyman, 1973; Skillings *et al.*, 1978), college students and subjects from a more general adult population (Pitcher & Meikle, 1980), or psychiatric patients (Eisler, Miller & Hersen, 1973; Eisler *et al.*, 1975). However, caution must be exercised in concluding from these studies that low-assertive subjects do not possess the skills necessary for successful performance in their behavioral repertoires. It should be noted that these differences were obtained in role-playing tests, and several studies (Nietzel & Bernstein, 1976; Rodriguez *et al.*, 1980; Westefeld, Galassi, & Galassi, 1980) have shown that altering the instructional and performance demands of these tests can result in significantly more skillful performance, at least by nonassertive college students.

With respect to a cognitive conceptualization, Schwartz and Gottman (1976) have shown that low-assertive (refusal behavior) college students did not differ from moderate- and high-assertives in knowledge of assertive skills or in performance ability in a "safe" situation. However, they did differ from high-assertives in a role-playing assessment. No significant differences were found in heart rate, even though self-perceived tension was significantly higher for low-assertives. The results suggested that the skill differences in role playing did not constitute skill deficits. Rather, the skill differences were considered to be a function of cognitive differences as low-assertives reported significantly more negative and fewer positive self-statements than the other groups. The self-statements best distinguishing the highs and lows fell into the following categories: (1) concern about negative self-image and fear of being disliked and (2) other-directed versus self-directed concern for the other's position, feelings, and needs. Pitcher and Meikle (1980) present additional data on the potential role of self-statements in mediating assertive behavior. Bruch (in press), however, reported a partial failure to replicate Schwartz and Gottman's (1976) results in that lows were less proficient than highs in both knowledge and the informal delivery of refusal statements.

At least three other studies (Alden & Safran, 1978; Eisler, Frederiksen, & Peterson, 1978; Fiedler & Beach, 1978) provide suggestive evidence for the role of different cognitive variables. Alden and Safran (1978) found that high versus low scorers on a measure of irrational beliefs (mainly perfectionistic standards and overconcern for others) were less assertive on a variety of measures even though they did not differ on knowledge of appropriate behavior. Fiedler and Beach (1978) reported that high and low scorers on intention to refuse a request differed in their assessment of the probabilities that good and bad consequences would occur but not in their evaluations of the favorableness of those consequences. Working with psychiatric patients, Eisler, Frederiksen, and Peterson (1978) found that high-assertives expected more favorable consequences, chose more socially appropriate alternatives, and had less discrepancy between their choices and actual responses than low-assertives.

Unfortunately, the *ex post facto* nature of the above studies makes it premature to conclude that cognitive variables play *the* causal role in assertion problems. A number of the studies (e.g., Eisler, Frederiksen, & Peterson, 1978) present data that could as easily be interpreted to mean that the differences in expected consequences and so forth were a function of preexisting differences in assertion skills. Even the innovative study by Schwartz and Gottman (1976) does not provide an unequivocal basis for causal inference. Thus, at this time, the data seem to suggest that conditioned anxiety, skill deficits, and cognitive distortions may play a role either singly or in combination in the causation and/or maintenance of assertion difficulties. Accordingly, each of these three areas merits systematic assessment, à la Schwartz and Gottman, in order to develop effective and efficient intervention programs for clients.

ASSESSMENT

Not surprisingly, there has been a substantial amount of assessment research since our previous review (Galassi & Galassi, 1978a). This section presents a selective review of recent developments in the two areas, self-report and behavioral assessment, in which there has been the most activity. For other recent reviews of instruments and issues in assertion and social skills assessment, the reader is referred to Bellack, (1979a, 1979b), Curran (1979), and Van Hasselt, Hersen, Whitehill, and Bellack (1979).

Self-Report Assessment

Our previous reviews of self-report measures (J. P. Galassi & Galassi, 1977, pp. 307–325; Galassi & Galassi, 1978a) of assertiveness revealed at least 17 of these measures. In addition, we concluded that measurement in this area has been hampered due to unresolved definitional issues, confounding of assertion with aggression and assertion with anxiety, the failure to develop situation- and response-class-specific rather than global measures, and the absence of psychometric data (see also Bellack, 1979a, 1979b; DeGiovanni & Epstein, 1978). Although the first three problems still remain, psychometric data have increased. Below, we have compiled some of the studies that can be viewed as providing data relevant to the reliability and validity of the most frequently used global measures. Although we have come to prefer a more response- and situation-specific assessment of social skills rather than assertiveness, these instruments have utility as general screening and outcome measures. Our comments focus primarily on the studies concerned with behavioral validation of the measures.

Studies by Eisler, Miller, and Hersen (1973), Eisler *et al.* (1975), and Eisler, Frederiksen, and Peterson (1978) may be interpreted as providing validity data on the Wolpe–Lazarus Assertiveness Questionnaire (WLAQ) (Wolpe & Lazarus, 1966). Psychiatric patients differentiated as high- and low-assertives based on a behavioral test also were discriminated on the WLAQ. A more recent study by Hersen, Bellack, Turner, Williams, Harper, and Watts (1979) with psychiatric patients investigated both test–retest and split-half reliability, factor analytic structure, and external validity against behavioral performance in the Behavioral Assertiveness Test—Revised (BAT-R) (Eisler *et al.*, 1975). Unfortunately, low to moderate reliability and only limited validational support were found even when factor scores for the WLAQ were correlated with positive and negative situations for males and females separately. Psychometric data for the Assertion Inventory (AI) (Gambrill & Richey, 1975) also remain limited, with Pitcher and Meikle (1980) reporting differential role-playing performance of low, moderate, and high AI scorers, and Rock (1977) reporting significant correlations with other assertion measures.

By far, the greatest amount of psychometric data have been generated for the RAS (Rathus, 1973) and the CSES (Galassi, DeLo, Galassi, & Bastien, 1974). A number of investigations have focussed on the RAS (Anchor, Cherones, & Broder, 1977; Appelbaum, 1976; Appelbaum, Tuma, & Johnson, 1975; Blanchard, 1979; Burkhart, Green, & Harrison, 1979; Chandler, Cook, & Dugovics, 1978; Futch & Lisman, 1977; Green, Burkhart, & Harrison, 1979; Heimberg & Harrison, 1980; Heimberg, Harrison, Goldberg, Desmarais, & Blue, 1979; Hollandsworth, Galassi, & Gay, 1977; Hull & Hull, 1978; Law, Wilson, & Crassini, 1979; Mann & Flowers, 1978; Nevid & Rathus, 1978, 1979; Orenstein *et al.*, 1975; Quillin, Besing, & Dinning, 1977;

Rathus, 1973; Rathus & Nevid, 1977; Vestewig & Moss, 1976). Four of the studies (Burkhart *et al.*, 1979; Futch & Lisman, 1977; Green *et al.*, 1979; Heimberg *et al.*, 1979) reported on the correspondence between RAS scores and behavioral performance. The Futch and Lisman study, for example, investigated the relationship between total RAS scores and role-play performance and between RAS factor scores and performance in corresponding role-play situations. Results generally indicated the females' self-reports were related to behavioral performance but that little relationship existed between males' self-reports and behavior. Overall, these four studies reported low to moderate correlations between scores on the RAS and role playing. As will be noted later, however, the validity of behavioral role-playing tests is itself in question, and, thus, the lack of higher correlations between self-report and role-playing measures may not reflect the absence of strong validity data for self-report scales. It is clear that more direct validation against actual *in vivo* performance is needed.

Considerable data are also available for the CSES (Burkhart *et al.*, 1979; Cummins, Holombo, & Holte, 1977; Galassi, DeLo, Galassi, & Bastien, 1974; Galassi & Galassi, 1974, 1975, 1979a; Galassi *et al.*, 1976; Green *et al.*, 1979; Kipper & Jaffe, 1976, 1978; Langone, 1979; Schwartz & Gottman, 1976; Skillings *et al.*, 1978; Stebbins, Kelly, Tolor, & Power, 1977; Wyrick *et al.*, 1977). Six of these studies (Burkhart *et al.*, 1979; Cummins *et al.*, 1977; Galassi *et al.*, 1976; Green *et al.*, 1979; Skillings *et al.*, 1978; Stebbins *et al.*, 1977) provided data on the relationship between total and/or partial scores on the CSES and behavioral performance in laboratory situations. For example, Green *et al.* (1979) and Skillings *et al.* (1978) found moderate (.43 and .42) but significant correlations between CSES scores and behavioral ratings of overall assertiveness. Burkhart *et al.* (1979) reported significant correlations between positive and negative CSES items and ratings of corresponding positive and negative role-playing situations. Some additional data (Averett & McManis, 1977; Bourque & Ladouceur, 1979; Hollandsworth, 1977a; Hollandsworth, *et al.*, 1977; Hollandsworth & Wall, 1977) have also been generated for the related Adult Self-Expression Scale (ASES) (Gay, Hollandsworth, & Galassi, 1975). Bourque and Ladouceur (1979), for example, reported significant correlations between item combinations on the ASES and behavioral measures of role-playing performance.

There have been several studies that have compared self-report assertion measures with each other. Many of these have reported correlations between the measures—for example, CSES with AI, .59 (Rock, 1977); CSES with ASES, .88, .79 (Gay *et al.*, 1975); CSES with

CRI, .72 (Schwartz & Gottman, 1976), .51 (Hartwig, Dickson, & Anderson, 1977); CSES with RAS, .84 (Norton & Warnick, 1976), .80 (Galassi & Galassi, 1980), .79, .74 (Tolor, Kelly, & Stebbins, 1976) .79 (Hartwig et al., 1977), .68 (Burkhart et al., 1979; Green et al., 1979), .58 (Rock, 1977), .52 (Weiskott & Cleland, 1977); ASES with AI, − .78 (Hollandsworth, 1979); RAS with AI, − .38 (Rock, 1977); RAS with ASES, .84, .86 (Hollandsworth, 1976), .78 (Hollandsworth et al., 1977); RAS with CRI, .38 (Hartwig et al., 1977). Undoubtedly, the strength of these relationships is due in part to shared method variance (Cone, 1979).

Studies by Burkhart et al. (1979) and Green et al. (1979) compared the CSES and RAS with behavioral performance criteria. The Green et al. (1979) study, for example, reported that subjects' total scores form the CSES correlated somewhat higher than RAS totals with general assertiveness, verbal, and nonverbal measures in a role-playing test. The conclusion of these two studies and that of Jakubowski and Lacks (1975) is that the CSES is the instrument of choice if a global measure of assertiveness is to be used with college student.

Studies by Galassi and Galassi (1980) and Norton and Warnick (1976) have employed factor analysis or cluster analysis to compare the CSES and RAS. Although some similarity was demonstrated by the measures in each study, the Galassi and Galassi (1980) study indicated that a factor analysis of the combined CSES and RAS items yielded factors appearing more response- and situation-class-specific than for either instrument alone. The study underlined the importance of constructing instruments composed of response- and situation-specific subscales relevant to the population of interest and validated against behavioral performance criteria. Furthermore, given the situational specificity of interpersonal behavior (Kazdin, 1979c), it seems important that the behavioral performance situations mirror the response and situation classes of the self-report measures as closely as possible (Bellack, Hersen, & Turner, 1979). In addition, if the self-report measure primarily taps a verbal response component, one should expect strong correlations only with verbal response components in actual behavioral performance situations and not with nonverbal response components.

Of the early measures, the CRI (McFall & Lillesand, 1971) was the only single response-class-specific instrument. It tapped refusal behavior. Although data have been presented concerning external validity as determined by role-play performance (Loo, 1972; McFall & Lillesand, 1971; McFall & Twentyman, 1973; Twentyman et al.,

1979), other psychometric data have not been available. In a recent study, Galassi *et al.* (1978) found that the global-difficulty item used in screening has low (.56) 3-week, test–retest reliability and the non-assertion score has only moderate (.70) reliability. In addition, use of both the assertion and nonassertion scores is redundant because they are highly correlated, that is, $-.91$ (Galassi *et al.*, 1978) and $-.84$ (Rodriguez *et al.*, 1980). In addition, Schroeder and Rakos (1978) found that scores on the CRI have increased in recent years, perhaps in response to public knowledge about assertiveness, a fact that may affect the other self-report measures as well (e.g., RAS; Chandler *et al.*, 1978).

At least eight new self-report measures of assertion have been developed since our earlier reviews. These measures include: an Assertion Questionnaire (Callner & Ross, 1976), an Assertiveness Scale (McLachlan & Walderman, 1976), the Bakker Assertiveness–Aggressiveness Schedule (Bakker, Bakker-Rabdau, & Breit, 1978), the Children's Action Tendency Scale (Deluty, 1979), the Dating and Assertion Questionnaire (Levenson & Gottman, 1978), the Interpersonal Behavior Survey (IBS) (Mauger, Firestone, Hernandez, Hook, & Adkinson, 1979), a modified Rathus Assertiveness Schedule (Vaal & McCullagh, 1977), the Self-Report Assertiveness Test for Boys (SRAT-B) (Reardon *et al.*, 1979), and the Social Reaction Inventory (Adinolfi, McCourt, & Geoghegan, 1976). In our view, the newer instruments do not represent significant advances over the earlier measures. In most cases, they lack the extensive validity data of some of the earlier measures. In other instances, they seem to have been constructed with even less regard for the assumptions of a behavioral approach to assessment than the earlier measures.

However, they do make strides in some areas, such as assessing assertion in more homogeneous populations; for example, drug addicts (Callner & Ross, 1976), alcoholics (Adinolfi *et al.*, 1976; McLachlan & Walderman, 1976), and elementary- and junior-high-school-aged children (Deluty, 1979; Reardon *et al.*, 1979; Vaal & McCullagh, 1977). Yet only a few (Callner & Ross, 1976; Mauger & Adkinson, 1979; Reardon *et al.*, 1979) attempted to assess more delimited response classes. Four of the instruments (Bakker *et al.*, 1978; Deluty, 1979; Mauger, Firestone, Hernandez, Hook, & Adkinson, 1979; Reardon *et al.*, 1979) attempted to differentiate assertion from aggression or submission, although Bakker *et al.* (1978) seem to define aggressive behavior in a positive manner in contrast to the other researchers. Validation against behavioral performance was investigated for only two of the measures (Callner & Ross, 1976; Reardon *et al.,* 1979), but the findings of both studies are somewhat tautological given that the behavioral tests were concomitantly derived and tested.

Of the recently developed self-report measures, the most extensive test construction efforts have been conducted for the IBS (Mauger & Adkinson, 1979; Mauger, Adkinson, Hook, & Hernandez, 1979; Mauger, Adkinson, & Simpson, 1979; Mauger, Firestone, Hernandez, Hook, & Adkinson, 1979; Mauger, Firestone, Hernandez, & Hook, 1978; Mauger, Simpson, & Adkinson, 1979). The IBS consists of 314 true–false items comprising 20 scales. The items were drawn from other instruments or written for the IBS. The 20 scales are divided into four categories: validity (3), aggressiveness (7), assertiveness (8), and relationship (2). The scales were constructed by rational, empirical, or factor analytic procedures and vary in the breadth of the response classes they sample. Mauger and his colleagues present extensive data on psychometric properties, norms for a variety of adult populations, and construct validity with a number of assertion and other personality inventories. There appear to be little or no data concerning validation of the subscales against behavioral performance. In many ways, the IBS seems to be similar in test construction and interpretation assumptions to more traditional personality measures such as the CPI and Minnesota Multiphasic Personality Inventory (MMPI) rather than reflecting the newer procedures and assumptions of behavioral assessment. For example, even a number of the most specific assertion and aggression subscales (e.g., self-confidence, frankness, hostile stance) still seem to tap general dispositions rather than response and situation-specific behaviors.

Given the interest in cognitive explanations and cognitively based assertion treatments, a rather surprising oversight is the lack of systematic efforts devoted to designing and validating measures tapping cognitive variables that affect interpersonal interactions. Most of the measures employed were borrowed from other areas (e.g., Ellis's irrational beliefs in Alden & Safran, 1978) or were designed for use in a particular study and not subjected to independent test construction and validational procedures. Even Schwartz and Gottman's (1976) Assertiveness Self-Statement Test appears to have been the subject of only minimal validational efforts. Obviously, to develop effective cognitively based interventions, we must be able to rely on well-developed cognitive assessment procedures. Although there has been limited research in this area, Bellack (1979a, 1979b) has reported on preliminary work by Morrison, Bellack, and Hersen to develop a measure of social perception. The procedure involves showing videotapes of various interpersonal interactions to subjects and asking them to identify the effectiveness of the responses and the emotions of the actors. In addition, J. P. Galassi and Galassi (1977) have employed an Assertion Self-Assessment Table that assesses whether subjects believe they know what an effective response is and what their rights are in a particular situation. Other preliminary work in this area includes the Assertion Information Form (Alden, Safran, & Weideman, 1978) and the Assertiveness Knowledge Inventory (Schwartz & Gottman, 1976). Clearly, more efforts are needed to develop measures of cognitive variables assumed to affect response- and situation-class-specific social interactions.

Behavioral Assessment

Much of the assertion research has relied on investigating subjects' behavior in role play rather than naturalistic interactions. Naturalistic assessment in the form of phone calls, staged interactions, or *in vivo* assignments has been relatively infrequent (Burkhart *et al.,* 1979; Galassi, 1973; Green *et al.,* 1979; Kazdin, 1974; King, Liberman, Roberts, & Bryan, 1977; McFall & Twentyman, 1973; Weinman, Gelbart, Wallace, & Post, 1972). In fact, many of the claims concerning the effectiveness of assertion training have been founded on significant differences between treatment and control groups only in role-play situations. Obviously, the strength of those claims are partially a function of the adequacy of role playing to represent performance in more naturalistic interactions. As noted by Kazdin (1979c), if behavior is situation specific, then behavior changes demonstrated under restricted laboratory or clinic conditions may not reflect changes in the natural environment, where a number of conditions are different. In addition, to the extent that role-playing performance inaccurately reflects *in vivo* performance, then assessing clients' assertion problems through role playing can provide misleading information on which to focus treatment interventions.

With the exception of MacDonald's (1974, 1978) work, not a great deal of attention has been focused on the psychometric properties of behavioral role playing tests. The majority of such tests (1) have been developed on an *ad hoc* rather than an empirical basis, (2) have been concerned with heterogeneous rather than homogeneous response and situation classes, and (3) have devoted little attention to the issue of external validity. Even among the newer tests, the Behavioral Assertiveness Tests for Boys (BAT-B) (Reardon *et al.,* 1979) and for Children (BAT-C) (Bornstein, Bellack, & Hersen, 1977), a behavioral test for older adults (Edinberg *et al.*, 1977), and the Behavioral Test of Tenderness Expression (BTTE) (Warren & Gilner, 1978) only two (the Edinberg *et al.*, 1977, measure and the BTTE) have been concerned with test–retest or split-half reliability. All of the newer measures except the BAT-C devote attention to empirical derivation. However, little or no validity data have been presented for these tests, and only the BTTE and BAT-B make any attempt to tap more homogeneous response and/or situation classes, with the former being concerned with positive assertion among dating or married couples and the latter with both positive and negative assertion.

Recently, however, attention has been focused on the more general issues of the validity of role playing as an assessment strategy in assertion research (Bellack, Hersen, & Lamparski, 1979; Bellack, Hersen, & Turner, 1978a, 1978b, 1979; Curran, 1978; Higgins, Alonso, & Pendleton, 1979). In the Bellack, Hersen, and Lamparski (1979) study, for example, the performance of psychiatric patients was compared on identical behavior measures in identical situations presented via structured interviews, role plays, and naturalistic interactions. In general, significant but moderate correlations were found for only some of the behaviors across only some of the presentation modes. With college students, Higgins *et al.* (1979) reported that role playing as compared to *in vivo* interaction in a staged waiting-room situation enhanced subjects' assertiveness. Overall, the existing data do not provide a strong case for the external validity of behavioral role-play tests of assertion.

In addition, a variety of factors appear to affect role-playing performance. These factors include: pretesting effects (Galassi, Galassi, & Litz, 1974; Mungas & Walters, 1979); variations in the mode of presentation (live or tape-recorded confederate) and the number of responses required from the subject (single or multiple) (Galassi & Galassi, 1976); role-taking ability (Reardon *et al.*, 1979); social desirability (Kiecolt & McGrath, 1979); demand characteristics (Derry & Stone, 1979; Nietzel & Bernstein, 1976; Rodriguez *et al.*, 1980); and amount of information provided about the assessment task (Westefeld *et al.*, 1980).

Clearly, conclusions and implications drawn from research using role-play tests must be approached with some caution. Overall, relatively little progress seems to have been made in behavioral assessment methodology in the 5-year period since our earlier review. There seems to be a better understanding of the limitations of role playing. However, we have not witnessed attempts to modify role-playing procedures so that they yield performance that more closely parallels *in vivo* performance. Finally, we have witnessed almost no efforts to develop unobtrusive, nonreactive assessment procedures that improve on the classic phone-call approach developed by McFall. Clearly, such efforts are sorely needed.

ASSERTION TRAINING RESEARCH

In our previous review (Galassi & Galassi, 1978a), we noted that variation in a number of factors made direct comparison of treatment studies difficult. These factors include the populations sampled, subjects' initial difficulties with assertion, length of treatment, components of treatment, the response classes investigated, the type of study (analogue or clinical), and the assessment procedures used. Our preference for research on clearly defined response classes and for discontinuing the use of the assertion construct further complicate the comparison task. Nevertheless, we have tried to maintain a format similar to the previous review and, in this section, we discuss the effectiveness of assertion training packages, the components of those packages, and generalizability of results. Our purpose is not only to summarize the results obtained but also to identify some of the major methodological shortcomings hampering assertion/social skills research.

Assertion Training Packages

The studies in this section are concerned with the effectiveness of assertion training as compared to no-treatment, waiting-list, placebo, or alternate-treatment control groups. The assertion training packages are by no means equivalent, but usually consist of instructions, behavior rehearsal, modeling, coaching and/or audio- or videotape feedback. Individual studies in this section may have been concerned with questions beyond effectiveness of the package; however, it was our judgment that they are most appropriately mentioned here. Finally, although college students and psychiatric patients continue to provide an important focus for research in this area, the reader will find that assertion training has been extended to a wider variety of target behaviors and populations than considered by the studies in our previous review.

There have been a number of recent studies with outpatient populations (mostly college students) providing additional data concerning the effectiveness of assertion training. These studies have included a single pre–post treatment group design (Rose, 1975) as well as comparisons with no-treatment or waiting-list controls (Janda & Rimm, 1977; Weiskott & Cleland, 1977), with placebo controls (Gormally, Hill, Otis, & Rainey, 1975; Schinke, Gilchrist, Smith, & Wong, 1979; Schinke & Rose, 1976; Winship & Kelley, 1976), with alternative treatments (Rakos & Schroeder, 1979) or alternate-treatment formats (Holmes & Horan, 1976; Linehan, Walker, Bronheim, Haynes, & Yevzeroff, 1979), and a comparison of assertion and rehearsal (simple practice) treatments with and without verbalization during posttesting (Rimm, Snyder, Depue, Haanstad, & Armstrong, 1976).

Despite the favorable results obtained, these studies suffer from the following methodological weaknesses with respect to subject selection: failure to screen subjects on self-report and/or behavioral measures of assertion, screening on measures tangentially related to assertion, failure to report the results of screening, or the use of overly liberal screening criteria (subjects scoring at or above the mean on global assertion measures). These weaknesses make it difficult to know to which populations the results of these studies are generalizable and, more importantly, make it unlikely that the results are relevant to clinical subjects. These weaknesses are regretable because several of the studies (e.g., Linehan, Walker, Bronheim, Haynes, & Yevzeroff, 1979; Rakos & Schroeder, 1979) present interesting and potentially valuable data. The former study failed to find differences between group and individually administered assertion training. The latter indicated that an empirically developed, self-administered, audiotaped assertion training program produced results on self-report and behavioral measures of refusal superior to self-administered relaxation training, an equally credible alternative. Incidentally, similar research on other self-instructional and self-management approaches has also been reported by Stevens (submitted) and Sherman, Barone, and Turner (1977).

Still another study (Janda & Rimm, 1977) investigated effectiveness of male and female therapists with females using assertion for making complaints, increasing small talk, and saying no to unreasonable requests. At first glance, the results appear to suggest the following important conclusions: (1) assertion training results in significantly greater improvement for making complaints than for saying no; and (2) training for female subjects is significantly more effective when provided by male than by female counselors. These sex differences are uncommon in assertion research. In addition to subject-selection limitations, the study suffers from two methodological weaknesses, brevity of treatment and analogue therapists. These weaknesses epitomize some of the unnecessary problems hampering social skills research. Clearly, the first weakness is the more common of the two in social skills training. The authors reported that subjects received treatments of approximately 12–14 minutes duration for each of the three response classes, and, second, treatment was administered by two male and two female undergraduate psychology majors, none of whom had prior behavioral counseling experience but each of whom received 4 hours of "intensive" training. Concerning the trainers, the authors report that one male was very effective; one female was relatively ineffective; and the other two were about equal. Over all, the study exemplifies the fact that much of assertion/social skills research asks clinically important questions but all too frequently employs inadequate methodology to provide satisfactory and meaningful answers.

There have also been several studies providing data about effectiveness with psychiatric patients. (For recent reviews of social skills and social competence with psychiatric patients, the reader is referred to Paul, Chapter 8, this volume, and Hersen, 1979.) Among these studies are two with substantial methodological limitations (Field & Test, 1975; King et al., 1977), one involving a multiple-baseline design across response components (Williams, Turner, Watts, Bellack, & Hersen, 1977), one comparison with a no-treatment control group (Finch & Wallace, 1977), and two comparisons with placebo or alternate-treatment controls (Goldsmith & McFall, 1975; Monti, Fink, Norman, Curran, Hayes, & Caldwell, 1979). Two of the studies (Finch & Wallace, 1977; Goldsmith & McFall, 1975) are noteworthy because they used empirically derived training procedures and/or empirically derived training situations and measures. Both studies provide strong support for the superiority of assertion training as compared to no-treatment and placebo controls on self-report and behavioral measures within the laboratory, although the Goldsmith and McFall study involved only 3 hours of treatment. The Monti et al. (1979) study indicated the ineffectiveness of a bibliotherapy program with psychiatric patients as compared to a control group and a social-skills-plus-bibliotherapy treatment.

As noted by Florin (1977), however, there is a need for more detailed information on the psychopathological characteristics of psychiatric patients if we are to compare results meaningfully across studies. Moreover, lumping together patients from different diagnostic categories (Kiesler, 1966), as is commonly the case in assertion and social skills research, as well as the absence of widely accepted, standardized measures of pretreatment assertion deficits, also hamper comparisons.

In addition to being used as a treatment for lack of assertive behavior, assertion training has frequently been touted (Alberti & Emmons, 1970) as an appropriate intervention for aggressive behavior.[4] Relatively little research has appeared on this application. With psychiatric patients, the studies appear to be limited to a few single-subject designs (Foy, Eisler, & Pinkston, 1975; Frederiksen, Jenkins, Foy, & Eisler, 1976; Matson & Stephens, 1978; McKinlay, Pachman, & Frederiksen, 1977) for patients exhibiting verbally abusive outbursts and explosive rages. In general, the findings from these studies indicate that assertion training (behavior rehearsal, instructions, modeling, and coaching) can produce changes in such behaviors as hostile comments and inappropriate and appropriate requests in trained and untrained situations. Some of these changes have been maintained for up to 6 months, and some have generalized to on-ward behavior.

Two studies (Galassi & Galassi, 1978b; Rimm, Hill, Brown, & Stuart, 1974) were concerned with modifying aggressive behavior of college students. In the Rimm *et al.* (1974) study, the behavioral ratings confounded assertion with aggression. This confounding limits the study's results to differences between the treatment and placebo groups on behavioral ratings of comfort and on subjective ratings of how angry and uptight the subjects felt. The Galassi and Galassi study reported that assertion training was effective in modifying assertive behavior but ineffective, except for one self-report measure, with aggressive behavior. However, difficulties were experienced in eliciting aggression in role plays and from peer reports, both of which reflect some of the assessment problems encountered with the aggression constructs. In an analogue study of couples (Epstein, DeGiovanni, & Jayne-Lazarus, 1978) with unspecified deficit levels in interpersonal skills, a 2-hour assertion training workshop resulted in increases in verbal assertion and decreases in aggressive behavior in a 10-minute communication task as compared to a minimal-treatment control group.

Several attempts have been made to modify aggressive behavior in adolescents. Lee, Hallberg, and Hassard (1979) and Pentz (1980) employed assertion training with ninth-graders and replicated Galassi and Galassi's (1978b) finding of increases in assertion without

---

[4]The reader is reminded of the earlier discussion about the problems involved in differentiating these constructs and in developing adequate assessment procedures.

concomitant decreases in aggression. In addition, the Pentz (1980) study suffered from confounding of assertion and aggression in some of the measures. Unfortunately, all three studies (Galassi & Galassi, 1978b; Lee *et al.*, 1979; Pentz, 1980) lacked the precise response component measurement that tends to characterize the intensive design studies of aggression discussed in this section.

The effects of assertion/social skills training also have been studied for clearly specified response components (e.g., hostile comments, inappropriate responding to negative communication) using multiple-baseline designs with delinquents (Goldsworthy & Zegiob, 1978) and adolescent psychiatric patients (Bornstein, Bellack, & Hersen, 1980; Elder, Edelstein, & Narrick, 1979). Results from these studies have generally been positive, with changes in trained and untrained role-playing situations and some generalization over time or to onward behavior.

With the exception of the studies on aggressive behavior, there has been relatively little interest in investigating the effectiveness of assertion training with children. Our review revealed only three research applications with children (Barone & Rinehart, 1978; Bower, Amatea, & Anderson, 1976; Bornstein *et al.*, 1977). The Barone and Rinehart (1978) study involved a comparison of group assertion training with four junior-high youths and group human relations training with a similar number of subjects. The Bower *et al.* (1976) study consisted of an uncontrolled pre–post design with four fourth-grade females. In contrast, the Bornstein *et al.* (1977) study involved a multiple-baseline design across response components with four 8- to 11-year-olds. Although Bornstein *et al.* (1977) were concerned with assertion toward peers, undergraduate rather than peer role-players were used for assessment. The study also lacked a measure of behavior change in the classroom.

Even though we would not encourage the development of research centering around assertion with children, it is interesting to speculate about why such a body of research has not evolved. At least two explanations have occurred to us. First, assertion training research with children has been impeded by the lack of assessment instruments in much the same way as similar research with adults was impeded 10–15 years ago. Second, judging from a recent literature review (Van Hasselt *et al.*, 1979), social skills research with children has tended to develop and center on social isolation and aggressive behavior. In many ways, these two areas might be considered to overlap with assertion. As a result, it seems doubtful that a separate body of assertion training research is needed.

Assertion training has also been extended to a variety of other target behaviors and populations. For example, there have been a number of studies (Hamilton & Maisto, 1979; Miller, & Eisler, 1977; Miller, Hersen, Eisler, & Hilsman, 1974; Sturgis, Calhoun, & Best, 1979) suggesting that interpersonal encounters, particularly those involving expressions of anger or other negative feelings, constitute a major source of tension for some alcoholics who lack the necessary interpersonal skills to cope with the demands of these situations. Correspondingly, several studies (Adinolfi *et al.*, 1976; Chaney, O'Leary, & Marlatt, 1978; Ferrell & Galassi, in press; Foy, Massey, Duer, Ross, & Wooten, 1979; Foy, Miller, Eisler, & O'Toole, 1976; Hirsch, von Rosenberg, Phelan, & Dudley, 1978) have attempted to modify interpersonal skills of alcoholics using assertion training procedures. The Chaney *et al.* (1978) and Ferrell and Galassi (in press) studies, for example, demonstrated significant gains in assertion on role-playing tests, coupled with significant decreases in drinking by the assertion training as opposed to alternate treatment, placebo, or no-treatment controls. In an analogue, multiple-baseline study, Foy *et al.* (1979) reported gains on role-playing tasks in interpersonal skills related to difficult on-the-job situations.

Similarly, assertion deficits have been viewed as influential in depression (Langone, 1979; Sanchez & Lewinsohn, 1976; Youngren & Lewinsohn, 1978), and studies by Rehm, Fuchs, Roth, Kornblith, and Romano (1979) and Zeiss, Lewinsohn, and Muñoz (1979) have investigated the effectiveness of assertion training in treating depression. Zeiss *et al.* (1979) reported that interpersonal skills, cognition, and pleasant events training were equally effective in alleviating depression. No treatment modality had specific effects on variables directly relevant to its treatment format. In contrast, Rehm *et al.* (1979) found that self-control subjects (training in self-monitoring, self-evaluation, and self-reinforcement skills) improved significantly more on measures of self-control, and assertion-skill subjects improved more on assertion-skill measures. Self-control subjects showed significantly greater improvement on both self-report and behavioral measures of depression. It should be noted that in neither study were subjects selected for treatment based on particular types or degrees of interpersonal skill deficits.

Assertion training has also been extended to meet the needs of a variety of other populations. There has been considerable research interest in assertion training for women (Adams & Wukasch-Williamson, 1976; Brockway, 1976; DeLange, 1978; Hartsook, Olch, & deWolf, 1976; see Kahn, Chapter 11, this volume). Mishel (1978) presented data for handicapped persons indicating that training was related to increases in assertive behavior and activity levels. Studies by Duehn and Mayadas (1976) and Russell and Winkler (1977) were concerned with facilitating homosexual functioning and teaching assertive behaviors in problematic situations encountered by homosexuals. Research by Bornstein, Bach, McFall, Friman, and Lyons (1980), Turner, Hersen, and Bellack (1979), and Wortmann and Paluck (1979) applied assertion training to problems of the retarded. Hautzinger (1979) experimented with assertive training to help obese clients to refuse pressures to eat in social situations, and Callner and Ross (1978) reported preliminary efforts in applying assertion training with drug addicts. One final application is the use of assertion in predicting (Shelton & Mathis, 1976) or improving (Flowers & Goldman, 1976; Jansen & Litwack, 1979; Layne, Layne, & Schoch, 1977) the skills of a variety of professional and paraprofessional mental health workers.

Although the applications of assertion training to other populations and target behaviors are interesting, a number of the studies share some common weaknesses. First, they often assume rather than demonstrate that there is a causal relationship between deficits in assertion and a particular target behavior. Similarly, they frequently assume rather than demonstrate that the members of the particular target population are deficient in assertive behavior and therefore may profit from assertion training. Finally, although the studies often report gains in self-report or role-played assertion, it is not uncommon for them to fail to assess changes in the target behavior of primary interest. That is, a study with alcoholics, for example, will report gains in assertion but fail to assess whether concomitant changes in drinking behavior are forthcoming.

Components of Assertion Training

Considerable interest has continued to center around comparisons of various components and combinations of components of assertion training packages. Unfortunately, many of the problems encountered in earlier component studies are still present. Same-named components are defined differently from one study to another or differently from clinical practice. In research, behavior rehearsal, for example, may be operationalized as simple practice without a guiding rationale or as some combination of instructions, rehearsal, modeling, and coaching. In clinical practice, however, it usually involves all of these components and often role reversal as well. In addition, similar components are given different names (e.g., instructions, corrective feedback, and coaching) from study to study. Marginally significant results and results demonstrating that one component is superior only to a control group, and not to another component, are inappropriately touted as evidence for the greater effectiveness of one component over another.

Nevertheless, there have been some interesting developments in the component studies. In our previous review, we noted that the majority of component research was predicated on behavior rehearsal as the basic technique of assertion training. We also commented that it was equally plausible to build upon a modeling base and that such studies may yield very different results. Interestingly, the majority of recent component studies have involved modeling.

MODELING

In an impressive series of studies with outpatient college students and adults that routinely include 3- to 6-month follow-up self-report data, Kazdin (1975, 1976a, 1976b, 1979a, 1979b) has presented evidence concerning the effectiveness of covert modeling and the additive effects of several other components. This research builds on his earlier work (Kazdin, 1974). Kazdin (1975, 1976b), for example, found that imagining several models engaging in assertive behavior led to greater changes than imagining a single model; favorable model consequences enhanced performance; the gains transferred to novel role-playing situations; and the gains were maintained on self-report follow-up measures 4 months later. In subsequent studies, Kazdin (1979a) reported that generating verbal summary codes of imagined assertive responses enhanced modeling effects and that allowing subjects to elaborate the imagery of the modeling scenes also enhanced those effects (Kazdin, 1979b). In related work, Nietzel, Martorano, and Melnick (1977) found that covert modeling with model reinforcement and reply training produced greater assertion on a posttest and more generalization than the covert modeling with model reinforcement, placebo, and no-treatment control groups. Reply training consisted of the model having to respond effectively to noncompliance following his or her initial assertion.

Two studies (Hersen, Kazdin, Bellack, & Turner, 1979; Rosenthal & Reese, 1976) involved direct comparisons of overt and covert modeling. The Rosenthal and Reese (1976) study provided a weak comparison, as it used college students with unspecified levels of assertion deficits, provided less than 1 hour of training, and failed to include a control group that would have provided a means for assessing if there were any effects due to treatment. The study failed to find differences between overt modeling with a standard hierarchy of situations, covert modeling with a standard hierarchy, and covert modeling with a self-tailored hierarchy. Hersen, Kazdin, Bellack, and Turner (1979) found that both live and covert modeling effected improvements over the test–retest group in the assertive behavior of psychiatric patients and that the two forms of modeling were not differentially effective. The modeling treatments included instructions orienting the patients to attend to key aspects of the model's behavior. Interestingly, the addition of rehearsal to both types of modeling generally did not enhance treatment effects. However, on the eye contact generalization measure, the covert-modeling plus rehearsal group significantly outperformed all groups except covert modeling without rehearsal. The effects that the orienting instructions had independent of modeling is unclear and worthy of further investigation. Moreover, the finding from Edelstein and Eisler's (1976) single-subject study indicating superior effects for modeling plus instructions and feedback as compared to modeling alone also underlines the importance of more clearly identifying the key variables in modeling treatments.

MODELING AND COACHING

Eisler, Blanchard, Fitts, and Williams (1978) investigated the effects of adding modeling to social skills training (behavior rehearsal, coaching, feedback) with schizophrenic and nonpsychotic (unspecified) patients. A social skills training and a behavior-rehearsal (practice only) group served as comparison groups. Results indicated that modeling was necessary for improving the performance of schizophrenics, particularly with respect to style of delivery, but was unnecessary and, at times, even detrimental for nonpsychotics. Interestingly, and unlike results from their previous studies (Eisler, Hersen, & Miller, 1973; Hersen, Eisler, Miller, Johnson, & Pinkston, 1973), Eisler, Blanchard, Fitts, and Williams (1978) reported that practice alone produced some significant improvements in the social skills of nonpsychotics.

Two studies with college students (Turner & Adams, 1977; Voss, Arrick, & Rimm, 1978) compared the effects of groups employing behavior rehearsal plus coaching, behavior rehearsal plus modeling, and behavior rehearsal plus coaching and modeling to a placebo group. In addition, the Voss et al. (1978) study included the dimension of simple (refusal) and complex (initiation) situations. The studies arrived at somewhat different conclusions. Turner and Adams

(1977) found that the two treatments that included coaching tended to outperform the placebo group, whereas Voss *et al.* (1978) found that modeling was important in complex but not in simple situations. However, no effects due to treatment beyond those of the placebo group were found in the simple situations. Coaching did not contribute significantly to the results. Unfortunately, it is difficult to compare the two studies because a definition of coaching was not provided by Turner and Adams.

REHEARSAL

The effects of different forms of rehearsal—exaggerated rehearsal, role reversal, behavior rehearsal—were compared to a treatment consisting of behavior rehearsal, modeling, and coaching and to a no-treatment control group in an analogue (50-minute treatment) study (Twentyman *et al.*, 1979). The exaggerated-rehearsal and full-treatment groups differed primarily from the no-treatment controls on a few measures. However, it is difficult to know whether the gains made by the exaggerated-rehearsal group represent actual improvement or merely the effects of greater demands on this group to act superassertively (Westefeld *et al.*, 1980).

FEEDBACK

Three studies have presented data indicating that neither audio- (Melnick & Stocker, 1977) nor videotape feedback (Gormally *et al.*, 1975; Scherer & Freedberg, 1976) augment the effects of assertion training. Although the results of these studies are consistent with others reported in our earlier review, it must be noted that the Gormally *et al.* (1975) and Melnick and Stocker (1977) studies involved only one or two treatment sessions. As pointed out by Gelso (1974), the effects of recording may initially have negative effects that do not dissipate over a two-session period.

COGNITIVE COMPONENTS

Recently, there have been a number of studies concerned with cognitive interventions. For the most part, these studies reflect the influence of Ellis's and Meichenbaum's work in that the treatments have been concerned with identifying and disputing irrational beliefs or with substituting positive, coping self-statements for negative self-statements. The studies have included a comparison of a cognitive intervention with a delayed-treatment and a placebo control group (Craighead, 1979), comparisons of cognitive and behavioral interventions (Alden *et al.,* 1978; Thorpe, 1975), the effects of adding a cognitive intervention to a more traditional behavioral intervention package (Carmody, 1978; Derry & Stone, 1979; Wolfe & Fodor, 1977), or the effects of a cognitive, behavioral, or combined intervention (Linehan, Goldfried, & Goldfried, 1979; Tiegerman & Kassinove, 1977). All of the studies are marred by important methodological flaws, which include failure to screen subjects on measures of assertion (Alden *et al.,* 1978; Carmody, 1978), inclusion of subjects who score at or above the mean on such measures (Linehan, Goldfried, & Goldfried, 1979; Tiegerman & Kassinove, 1977; Wolfe & Fodor, 1977), failure to demonstrate the presence of cognitive deficits relevant to assertion prior to training (all studies), failure with a few exceptions (Craighead, 1979; Derry & Stone, 1979) to measure cognitions directly tied to assertion, absence of a behavioral measure (Tiegerman & Kassinove, 1977), and brevity of treatment (70 minutes; Derry & Stone, 1979).

The results of the Craighead (1979) study indicated that a cognitive treatment was superior to a delayed treatment and placebo control on self-report measures and a behavioral test in which none of the items were part of training. As compared to the control groups, the cognitive treatment also produced changes in cognitive measures, some of which were directly related to assertion refusal behavior. However, generalization to behavior in two nonlaboratory measures was not found. The last results are particularly disappointing because cognitive interventions are frequently touted as having great potential to increase generalization and enhance maintenance of treatment effects.

The Alden *et al.* (1978) and Thorpe (1975) studies produced an inconclusive and opposite pattern of results concerning the effectiveness of cognitive and behavioral treatments. Although the studies by Carmody (1978) and Wolfe and Fodor (1977) revealed that a cognitive component added little to the effects of an assertion training program containing behavior rehearsal, the Derry and Stone (1979) study found that adding a cognitive self-statement component resulted in gains on a role-playing test and on self-report measures. Unfortunately, the study lacked no-treatment and placebo control conditions.

With respect to a combined treatment versus separate cognitive and behavioral treatments, results from the Linehan, Goldfried, and Goldfried (1979) study suggest that the combined group is superior.

However, this superiority often was a function only of significantly greater improvement relative to the control groups. Interestingly, on a number of the behavioral measures, the rational restructuring group failed to differ from the controls or performed significantly less well than either the behavior rehearsal or combined group. On similar self-report measures, results by Tiegerman and Kassinove (1977) generally parallel those of Linehan, Goldfried, and Goldfried (1979) in revealing few significant differences among treated groups.

As suggested above, the cognitive treatment studies have a number of methodological shortcomings that have retarded progress in this area. Perhaps the most significant of these shortcomings is the failure to demonstrate that assertion deficits are related to cognitive deficits prior to treatment. If we believe that cognitive treatments produce their effects through cognitive routes, then identifying the existence of such relationships is critical. In future research, it would seem necessary to establish that subjects' interpersonal deficits are related to cognitive variables prior to instituting cognitive treatments. Similarly, at posttest and follow-up, it is important to assess whether changes have occurred in both the interpersonal deficits and the associated cognitive variables.

It is encouraging that researchers have continued to investigate the contribution of a variety of treatment components in assertion and social skills interventions. Unfortunately, however, relatively little attention seems to have been devoted to selecting components designed to accomplish specific objectives. In both the component and the more general treatment studies, the emphasis continues to be on locating the single most effective treatment. To continue to search for the one best treatment for all subjects rather than to tailor treatments to the needs of more homogeneous subject groupings (Kiesler, 1966) and task requirements seems ill-advised.

Organismic Variables and Generalization of Results

The role of organismic (person) variables in mediating the effects of assertion training has been infrequently investigated. Studies in this area by Frankel, Reilly, and Lert (1978) and Schwartz and Higgins (1979) involved analogue treatments and investigated cognitive-style variables. Frankel *et al.* (1978) reported that improvement was related to scores on a hypnotic susceptibility measure. High-susceptibility subjects demonstrated significantly greater improvement on refusal behavior as compared to low-susceptibility subjects, and low-susceptibility subjects showed significantly more change on requests for new behavior. Schwartz and Higgins (1979) predicted and found significantly greater generalization of treatment (an automated approach) effects to untrained social skill role-playing situations for external as opposed to internal locus of control subjects. Also, as expected, internals felt significantly more uncomfortable in treatment than externals and perceived it as taking too much control away from them. Although it seems likely that person variables may very well mediate the effects of social skills treatments, the results of these and other studies (Eisler, Blanchard, Fitts, & Williams, 1978) concerning the role of particular person variables must be tentative at this time. Clearly, considerable effort could be focused on developing a theory and taxonomy of organismic variables that influence the effectiveness of social skills and other behavioral techniques.

The issue of generalization of treatment results continues to be of concern in behavior therapy. Recently, considerable effort has been devoted to developing a conceptual framework for classifying different types of generalization effects (Drabman, Hammer, & Rosenbaum, 1979) and a technology for increasing the probability of obtaining such effects (Stokes & Baer, 1977). Generalization has been defined as "the occurrence of relevant behavior under different, nontraining conditions (i.e., across subjects, settings, people, behaviors, and/or time) without the scheduling of the same events in those conditions as had been scheduled in the training conditions" (Stokes & Baer, 1977, p. 350).

With respect to assertion training, we have previously identified and reviewed the research for four types of generalization. These types are (1) within-laboratory generalization to similar situations for which training has not been received (intraresponse- or situation-class generalization); (2) within-laboratory generalization across response or situation classes; (3) generalization of treatment effects to extralaboratory behavior; and (4) generalization of changes across time as measured by self-report or behavioral measures. Since our previous review, it has become increasingly common for training studies to include measures of generalization. The most typical measures are those tapping generalization to untrained situations within the same response-class within the laboratory and self-report assessments of maintenance over time.

The purpose of the present section is not to review all the data generated since our last review concerning these four types of generalization. Rather, it is to identify some of the methodological problems hampering our efforts to facilitate generalization effects and to restructure some of our current expectations about generalization. In the process, we will concentrate on some of the studies whose primary focus was generalization of treatment effects.

For example, a study by Kirschner (1976) demonstrated that the effects of assertion training generalized only to situations highly similar (intraresponse-class) to those used during training. These effects were not maintained at a 3-week follow-up, although effects on trained situations were maintained. In addition, the effects of training failed to generalize (extraresponse-class) to situations of dissimilar response classes (from positive-affect situations to displeasure–wronged situations or vice versa). Moreover, a procedure specifically designed to facilitate generalization, extensive training, failed to do so. Extensive training involved exposing subjects to a wide variety of different assertive situations during training.

Several important methodological issues are raised by this study. First, the results may be interpreted to indicate that assertion training produces limited generalization. However, given that total treatment time was 40 minutes, they also may be attributable to the equally or more plausible rival hypothesis of insufficient treatment duration. Unfortunately, it is all too common to encounter conclusions about generalization in assertion training based on as little as 1 to 3 hours of treatment. Particularly with chronic psychiatric patients, such limited treatments lend little credibility to the results of research studies. Second, a meaningful assessment of the value of the study is impossible because no data are presented about the initial levels of subjects' assertion deficits either in the trained or generalization scenes. Lack of comparative data on subjects' initial skill deficits and brevity of treatment continue to be two major weaknesses in assertion/social skills research. Third, the failure to effect generalization even after incorporating procedures intended to produce such effects is not uncommon. It has been encountered with the cognitive treatments discussed earlier and in studies by Hersen, Eisler, and Miller (1974) and Rosenthal and Reese (1976). As noted by Bandura (1969), the processes and methods involved in the induction of behavior change may differ from those in generalization and maintenance. To date the primary focus in assertion and social skills training has been on change induction rather than on empirically developing a generalization technology (Stokes & Baer, 1977).

In a multiple-baseline study that employed treatments of clinically relevant duration (25–31 sessions) with three chronic schizophrenics, Bellack, Hersen, and Turner (1976) demonstrated generalization from trained-to-untrained and trained-to-novel role-played interactions (of the same response class) with most of the effects persisting over an 8–10-week posttreatment period. The fact that it was important to distinguish between trained situations (used in all baseline sessions, used for training, and in assessment sessions during posttest and follow-up), untrained situations (used only for assessment purposes during all baseline treatment, posttest, and follow-up assessments), and novel untrained situations (used only for assessment purposes during infrequent probe sessions) is another indication (in addition to brevity of treatment) of the change induction rather than generalization emphasis characterizing assertion training research. It has been all too common for the effectiveness of assertion training to be documented based on studies demonstrating significant pre–post changes in role-play behavior with the same situations used for training and assessment purposes and with training consisting of two 40-minute sessions. At this point, it seems necessary for social skills research to begin to employ treatments of more clinically relevant length and to emphasize effects obtained in untrained and novel rather than trained situations.

Unlike the Kirschner (1976) study, a study by Kelly, Frederiksen, Fitts, and Phillips (1978) investigated generalization across response classes but employed multiple measures rather than a single, global, dependent measure. Although only a single subject was involved, the results probably exemplify what we can expect in terms of extraresponse-class generalization. Specifically, Kelly *et al.* (1978) trained the subject on commendatory assertion and tested generalization to refusal behavior in role-playing situations. Overall, generalization was quite limited and confined to general (eye contact and affect) rather than specific (praise, reciprocal positive behavior, noncompliance, requests for new behavior) response components. The points to be made about this study are, first, that the level of generalization obtained is consistent with what would be expected based on the situation and interactionist perspectives described earlier, and that extraresponse-class generalization is not the most important type of generalization to study in social skills research at this time.

One final investigation meriting comment is by Longin and Rooney (1975). This study reported that chronic hospitalized patients maintained gains in trained refusal situations for 2 years. These results are certainly impressive and together with the studies cited in our previous review suggest that present social skills technology is capable of producing generalization across time. However, generalization across time is not the most important form of generalization to be studying at this point.

From our perspective, the most pressing need in social skill outcome research is for demonstrations of generalization of laboratory gains to behavior in the natural environment based on unobtrusive behavioral measures of known reliability and validity. Much of the support for assertion and social skills training has been built around behavioral role-playing tests. To the extent that those tests continue to be shown to possess limited validity, then data generated from them will continue to build only an analogue case for the effectiveness of assertion and social skills training. Clearly, our efforts need to be directed to developing the type of measures that will permit sophisticated studies of generalization to behavior in the natural environment.

CONCLUDING REMARKS

We have concluded a decade of vigorous research activity in assertion training. Although we have learned a great deal from that research, some redirection of efforts is in order. First and foremost, the assertion construct is outmoded and should be relinquished. The construct has proven to be vague, difficult to define, and to be laden with assumptions reflecting traditional rather than more contemporary views of personality and behavior change. In the future, we need to concentrate more on response- and situation-specific behaviors falling under the rubric of social skills–social competence and retire the assertiveness (assertion) construct.

In order to expedite progress in social skills training, primary research efforts must be focused on assessment rather than treatment issues. Among the most pressing assessment needs are to develop a taxonomy of interpersonal response and situation classes, to identify criteria for socially skilled or competent performance, and to isolate the verbal, nonverbal, and paralanguage response components representing skillful performance in those classes. Identifying cognitive variables mediating behavior in interpersonal situations represents still another important concern. With respect to specific assessment instruments, the clearest need is for reliable and valid measures of response- and situation-class-specific *in vivo* behavior. Developing response- and situation-specific paper-and-pencil measures and improving the validity of our role-playing tests represent additional areas of concern.

Although progress in treatment research undoubtedly will be facilitated by greater sophistication in assessment procedures, specific improvements in the methodology of treatment research are also in order. Greater attention should be focused on identifying personological and task-related variables moderating treatment effects and on incorporating these variables into outcome studies. Comparisons of skills training with alternative treatments and equally credible placebo controls are still important. Finally, treatment research would profit from a shift away from a change induction and toward a generalization emphasis. This shift involves the use of treatments of clinically relevant duration with subjects demonstrating specified levels of deficits. It also means emphasizing results showing generalization to *in vivo* behavior and changes in similar but untrained situations. We expect that incorporating these modifications into social skills–social competence research in the next decade will allow future reviewers to draw stronger conclusions about the contributions of this area to clinical practice.

REFERENCES

Adams, K. A., & Wukasch-Williamson, L. *Assertion training, androgeny, and professional women.* Paper presented at the annual meeting of the American Psychological Association, Washington, DC, September 1976.

Adinolfi, A. A., McCourt, W. F., & Geoghegan, S. Group assertiveness training for alcoholics. *Journal of Studies on Alcohol,* 1976, *37,* 311–320.

Alberti, R. E., Comments on "Differentiating assertion and aggression: Some behavioral guidelines." *Behavior Therapy,* 1977, *8,* 353–354.

Alberti, R. E., & Emmons, M. L. *Your perfect right: A guide to assertive behavior.* San Luis Obispo, CA: Impact, 1970.

Alberti, R. E., & Emmons, M. L. *Your perfect right: A guide to assertive behavior.* (2nd ed.). San Luis Obispo, CA: Impact, 1974.

Alberti, R. E., & Emmons, M. L. *Your perfect right: A guide to assertive behavior.* (3rd ed.). San Luis Obispo, CA: Impact, 1978.

Alden, L., & Safran, J. Irrational beliefs and nonassertive behavior. *Cognitive Therapy and Research,* 1978, *2,* 357–364.

Alden, L., & Safran, J., & Weideman, R. A comparison of cognitive and skills training strategies in the treatment of unassertive clients. *Behavior Therapy,* 1978, *9,* 843–846.

Anchor, K. N., Cherones, J., & Broder, S. Strategies for measurement of different aspects of self-disclosure. *Psychological Reports,* 1977, *41,* 173–174.

Applebaum, A. S. Rathus Assertiveness Schedule: Sex differences and correlation with social desirability. *Behavior Therapy,* 1976, *7,* 699.

Applebaum, A. S., Tuma, J. M., & Johnson, J. H. Internal–external control and assertiveness of subjects high and low in social desirability. *Psychological Reports,* 1975, *37,* 319–322.

Averett, M., & McManis, D. L. Relationship between extraversion and assertiveness and related personality characteristics. *Psychological Reports,* 1977, *41,* 1187–1193.

Bakker, C. B., Bakker-Rabdau, M. K., & Breit, S. The measurement of assertiveness and aggressiveness. *Journal of Personality Assessment*, 1978, *42*, 277-284.

Bandura, A. *Principles of behavior modification.* New York: Holt, 1969.

Bandura, A. *Social learning theory.* Englewood Cliffs, NJ: Prentice-Hall, 1977.

Barone, D. F., & Rinehart, J. M. *Assertive training vs. group counseling for junior-high youth.* Paper presented at the annual meeting of the Association for the Advancement of Behavior Therapy, Chicago, November 1978.

Barrett, D. E., & Yarrow, M. R. Prosocial behavior, social inferential ability, and assertiveness in children. *Child Development*, 1977, *48*, 475-481.

Bates, H. D., & Zimmerman, S. F. Toward the development of a screening scale for assertive training. *Psychological Reports*, 1971, *28*, 99-107.

Bean, L. D. *Interpersonal perception among college students as a function of sex and level of assertiveness.* Unpublished doctoral dissertation, University of Pennsylvania, 1977.

Bellack, A. S. A critical appraisal of strategies for assessing social skill. *Behavioral Assessment*, 1979, *1*, 157-176. (a)

Bellack, A. S. Behavioral assessment of social skills. In A. S. Bellack & M. Hersen (Eds.), *Research and practice in social skills training.* New York: Plenum, 1979. (b)

Bellack, A. S., Hersen, M., & Lamparski, D. Role-play tests for assessing social skills: Are they valid? Are they useful? *Journal of Consulting and Clinical Psychology*, 1979, *47*, 335-342.

Bellack, A. S., Hersen, M., & Turner, S. M. Generalization effects of social skills training in chronic schizophrenics: An experimental analysis. *Behaviour Research and Therapy*, 1976, *14*, 391-398.

Bellack, A. S., Hersen, M., & Turner, S. M. Comments on the utility of suggestive versus definitive data: A reply to Curran. *Behavior Therapy*, 1978, *9*, 469-470. (a)

Bellack, A. S., Hersen, M., & Turner, S. M. Role-play tests for assessing social skills: Are they valid? *Behavior Therapy*, 1978, *9*, 448-461. (b)

Bellack, A. S., Hersen, M., & Turner, S. M. Relationship of role playing and knowledge of appropriate behavior to assertion in the natural environment. *Journal of Consulting and Clinical Psychology*, 1979, *47*, 670-678.

Blanchard, E. B. A note on the clinical utility of the Rathus Assertiveness Scale. *Behavior Therapy*, 1979, *10*, 571-574.

Bordewick, M. C., & Bornstein, P. H. *Perception, likelihood, comfort, and valence of assertive, nonassertive, and aggressive responses.* Paper presented at the annual meeting of the Association for the Advancement of Behavior Therapy, San Fransisco, December, 1979.

Bornstein, M. R., Bellack, A. S., & Hersen, M. Social skills training for unassertive children: A multiple-baseline analysis. *Journal of Applied Behavior Analysis*, 1977, *10*, 183-195.

Bornstein, M., Bellack, A. S., & Hersen, M. Social skills training for highly aggressive children in an inpatient psychiatric setting. *Behavior Modification*, 1980, *4*, 173-186.

Bornstein, P. H., Bach, P. J., McFall, M. E., Friman, P. C., & Lyons, P. D. Application of a social skills training program in the modification of interpersonal deficits among retarded adults: A clinical replication. *Journal of Applied Behavior Analysis*, 1980, *13*, 171-176.

Bornstein, P. H., Winegardner, J., Rychtarik, R. G., Paul, W. P., Naifeh, W. P. Sweeney, T. M., & Justman, A. *Interpersonal effectiveness training: Effects upon an adult offender population.* Paper presented at the annual meeting of the Association for the Advancement of Behavior Therapy, Chicago, November 1978.

Bourque, P., & Ladouceur, R. Self-report and behavioral measures in the assessment of assertive behavior. *Journal of Behavior Therapy and Experimental Psychiatry*, 1979, *10*, 287-292.

Bower, S., Amatea, E., & Anderson, R. Assertiveness training with children. *Elementary School Guidance and Counseling*, 1976, *10*, 236-245.

Brockway, B. S. Assertive training for professional women. *Social Work*, 1976, *21*, 498-505.

Bruch, M. A. A task analysis of assertive behavior revisited: Replication and extension. *Behavior Therapy*, in press.

Brummage, M. D. The influence of sex role expectations on observers' perceptions and evaluations of persons behaving assertively (Doctoral dissertation, University of Texas at Austin, 1975). *Dissertation Abstracts International*, 1976, *36*, 5338B. (University Microfilms No. 76-8002, 186)

Burkhart, B. R., Green, S. B., & Harrison, W. H. Measurement of assertive behavior: Construct and predictive validity of self-report, role playing, and in vivo measures. *Journal of Clinical Psychology*, 1979, *35*, 376-383.

Burchardt-Pharr, C. ., & Serbin, L. A. *The relationship of sex-role identity to personality adjustment*. Paper presented at the annual meeting of the Association for Advancement of Behavior Therapy, Atlanta, December 1977.

Callner, D. A., & Ross, S. M. The reliability and validity of three measures of assertion in a drug addict population. *Behavior Therapy*, 1976, *7*, 659-667.

Callner, D. A., & Ross, S. M. The assessment and training of assertive skills with drug addicts: A preliminary study. *International Journal of the Addictions*, 1978, *13*, 227-239.

Carmody, T. P. Rational-emotive, self-instructional, and behavioral assertion training: Facilitating maintenance. *Cognitive Therapy and Research*, 1978, *2*, 241-253.

Chandler, T. A., Cook, B., & Dugovics, D. A. Sex differences in self-reported assertiveness. *Psychological Reports*, 1978, *43*, 395-402.

Chaney, E. F., O'Leary, M. R., & Marlatt, G. A. Skill training with alcoholics. *Journal of Consulting and Clinical Psychology*, 1978, *46*, 1092-1104.

Cone, J. D. Confounded comparisons in triple response mode assessment research. *Behavioral Assessment*, 1979, *1*, 85-95.

Craighead, L. W. Self-instructional training for assertive refusal behavior. *Behavior Therapy*, 1979, *10*, 529-542.

Cummins, D. E., Holombo, L. K., & Holte, C. S. Target specificity in a self-report measure of assertion. *Journal of Psychology*, 1977, *97*, 183-186.

Curran, J. P. Comments on Bellack, Hersen, and Turner's paper on the validity of role-play tests. *Behavior Therapy*, 1978, *9*, 462-468.

Curran, J. P. Pandora's box reopened? The assessment of social skills. *Journal of Behavioral Assessment*, 1979, *1*, 55-71.

Davison, G. C. Systematic desensitization as a counterconditioning process. *Journal of Abnormal Psychology*, 1968, *73*, 91-99.

DeGiovanni, I. S., & Epstein, N. Unbinding assertion and aggression in research and clinical practice. *Behavior Modification*, 1978, *2*, 173-192.

DeLange, J. *A comparison of the effects of assertive skill training and desensitization in increasing assertion and reducing anxiety in groups of women*. Paper presented at the fourth annual convention of the Midwestern Association of Behavior Analysis, May 1978.

Deluty, R. H. Children's Action Tendency Scale: A self-report measure of aggressiveness, assertiveness, and submissiveness in children. *Journal of Consulting and Clinical Psychology*, 1979, *47*, 1061-1071.

Derry, P. A., & Stone, G. L. Effects of cognitive-adjunct treatments on assertiveness. *Cognitive Therapy and Research,* 1979, *3,* 213–221.

Drabman, R. S., Hammer, D., & Rosenbaum, M. S. Assessing generalization in behavior modification with children: The generalization map. *Behavioral Assessment,* 1979, *1,* 203–219.

Duehn, W. D., & Mayadas, N. S. The use of stimulus/modeling videotapes in assertive training for homosexuals. *Journal of Homosexuality,* 1976, *1,* 373–381.

Duncan, S., Jr., & Fiske, D. W. *Face to face interaction: Research methods and theory.* Hillsdale, NJ: Erlbaum, 1977.

Dunn, M. E., Van Horn, E., & Herman, S. H. *A comparison of three training procedures for spinal cord injury social skills.* Paper presented at the American Congress of Rehabilitation Medicine Meeting, Miami Beach, November 1977.

Edelstein, B. A., & Eisler, R. M. Effects of modeling and modeling with instructions and feedback on the behavioral components of social skills. *Behavior Therapy,* 1976, *7,* 382–389.

Edinberg, M. A., Karoly, P., & Gleser, G. C. Assessing assertion in the elderly: An application of the behavioral–analytic model of competence. *Journal of Clinical Psychology,* 1977, *33,* 869–874.

Eisler, R. M., Blanchard, E. B., Fitts, H., & Williams, J. G. Social skill training with and without modeling for schizophrenic and non-psychotic hospitalized psychiatric patients. *Behavior Modification,* 1978, *2,* 147–172.

Eisler, R. M., Frederiksen, L. W., & Peterson, G. L. The relationship of cognitive variables to the expression of assertiveness. *Behavior Therapy,* 1978, *9,* 419–427.

Eisler, R. M., Hersen, M., & Miller, P. M. Effects of modeling on components of assertive behavior. *Journal of Behavior Therapy and Experimental Psychiatry,* 1973, *4,* 1–6.

Eisler, R. M., Hersen, M., Miller, P. M., & Blanchard, E. B. Situational determinants of assertive behaviors. *Journal of Consulting and Clinical Psychology,* 1975, *43,* 330–340.

Eisler, R. M., Miller, P. M., & Hersen, M. Components of assertive behavior. *Journal of Clinical Psychology,* 1973, *29,* 295–299.

Edler, J. P., Edelstein, B. A., & Narrick, M. M. Adolescent psychiatric patients: Modifying aggressive behavior with social skills training. *Behavior Modification,* 1979, *3,* 161–178.

Endler, N. S., & Magnusson, D. Toward an interactional psychology of personality. *Psychological Bulletin,* 1976, *83,* 956–974.

Epstein, N. DeGiovanni, I. S., & Jayne-Lazarus, C. Assertion training for couples. *Journal of Behavior Therapy and Experimental Psychiatry,* 1978, *9,* 149–155.

Ferrell, W. L., & Galassi, J. P. Assertion training and human relations training in the treatment of chronic alcoholics. *International Journal of the Addictions,* in press.

Fiedler, D., & Beach, L. R. On the decision to be assertive. *Journal of Consulting and Clinical Psychology,* 1978, *46,* 537–546.

Field, G. D., & Test, M. A. Group assertive training for severely disturbed patients. *Journal of Behavior Therapy and Experimental Psychiatry,* 1975, *6,* 129–134.

Finch, B. E., & Wallace, C. J. Successful interpersonal skills training with schizophrenic inpatients. *Journal of Consulting and Clinical Psychology,* 1977, *45,* 885–890.

Fischetti, M., Curran, J. P., & Wessberg, H. W. Sense of timing: A skill deficit in heterosexual-socially anxious males. *Behavior Modification,* 1977, *1,* 170–194.

Florin, I. Comment to M. T. Williams *et al.*: Group social skills training for chronic psychiatric patients. *European Journal of Behavioural Analysis and Modification,* 1977, *1,* 230–232.

Flowers, J. V., & Goldman, R. D. Assertion training for mental health paraprofessionals. *Journal of Counseling Psychology,* 1976, *23,* 147–150.

Ford, J. D., & Hogan, D. R. *Assertiveness and social competence in the eye of the beholder.* Paper presented at the annual meeting of the Association for the Advancement of Behavior Therapy, Chicago, December 1978.

Foy, D. W., Eisler, R. M., & Pinkston, S. Modeled assertion in a case of explosive rages. *Journal of Behavior Therapy and Experimental Psychiatry,* 1975, *6,* 135–137.

Foy, D. W., Massey, F. H., Duer, J. D., Ross, J. M., & Wooten, L. S. Social skills training to improve alcoholics' vocational interpersonal competency. *Journal of Counseling Psychology,* 1979, *26,* 128–132.

Foy, D. W., Miller, P. M., Eisler, R. M., & O'Toole, D. H. Social-skills training to teach alcoholics to refuse drinks effectively. *Journal of Studies on Alcohol,* 1976, *37,* 1340–1345.

Frankel, A. S., Reilly, S., & Lert, A. A style variable in assertion training. *Cognitive Therapy and Research,* 1978, *2,* 289–292.

Frederiksen, L. W., Jenkins, J. O., Foy, D. W., & Eisler, R. M. Social skills training to modify abusive verbal outbursts in adults. *Journal of Applied Behavior Analysis,* 1976, *9,* 117–125.

Furnham, A. Assertiveness in three cultures: Multidimensionality and cultural differences. *Journal of Clinical Psychology,* 1979, *35,* 522–527.

Futch, E. J., & Lisman, S. A. *Behavioral validation of an assertiveness scale: The incongruence of self-report and behavior.* Paper presented at the annual meeting of the Association for the Advancement of Behavior Therapy, Atlanta, December 1977.

Galassi, J. P. *Assertive training in groups using video feedback* (Final report of NIMH Small Research Grant MH22392-01). Chapel Hill, NC: University of North Carolina, 1973.

Galassi, J. P. Review of *Achieving assertive behavior: A guide to assertive training,* by H. H. Dawley, Jr., & W. W. Weinrich. *Behavior Therapy,* 1978, *9,* 132–133.

Galassi, J. P., DeLo, J. S., Galassi, M. D., & Bastien, S. The College Self-Expression Scale: A measure of assertiveness. *Behavior Therapy,* 1974, *5,* 165–171.

Galassi, J. P., & Galassi, M. D. Validity of a measure of assertiveness. *Journal of Counseling Psychology,* 1974, *21,* 248–250.

Galassi, J. P., & Galassi, M. D. Relationship between assertiveness and aggressiveness. *Psychological Reports,* 1975, *36,* 352–354.

Galassi, J. P., & Galassi, M. D. Assessment procedures for assertive behavior. In R. E. Alberti (Ed.), *Assertiveness: Innovations, applications, issues.* San Luis Obispo, CA: Impact, 1977.

Galassi, J. P., & Galassi, M. D. A comparison of the factor structure of an assertion scale across sex and population. *Behavior Therapy,* 1979, *10,* 117–129. (a)

Galassi, J. P., & Galassi, M. D. Modification of heterosexual skills deficits. In A. S. Bellack & M. Hersen (Eds.), *Research and practice in social skills training.* New York: Plenum, 1979. (b)

Galassi, J. P., Galassi, M. D., & Litz, M. C. Assertive training in groups using video feedback. *Journal of Counseling Psychology,* 1974, *21,* 390–394.

Galassi, J. P., Galassi, M. D., & Westefeld, J. S. The Conflict Resolution Inventory: Psychometric data. *Psychological Reports,* 1978, *42,* 492–494.

Galassi, J. P., Hollandsworth, J. G., Radecki, J. S., Gay, M. L., Howe, M. R., & Evans, C. L. Behavioral performance in the validation of an assertiveness scale. *Behavior Therapy*, 1976, *7*, 447–452.

Galassi, M. D., & Galassi, J. P. The effects of role playing variations on the assessment of assertive behavior. *Behavior Therapy*, 1976, *7*, 343–347.

Galassi, M. D., & Galassi, J. P. *Assert yourself! How to be your own person.* New York: Human Sciences Press, 1977.

Galassi, M. D., & Galassi, J. P. Assertion: A critical review. *Psychotherapy: Theory, Research and Practice*, 1978, *1*, 16–29. (a)

Galassi, M. D., & Galassi, J. P. Modifying assertive and aggressive behavior through assertion training. *Journal of College Student Personnel*, 1978, *19*, 453–456. (b)

Galassi, M. D., & Galassi, J. P. Similarities and differences between two assertion measures: Factor analysis of the College Self-Expression Scale and the Rathus Assertiveness Schedule. *Behavioral Assessment*, 1980, *2*, 43–57.

Gambrill, E. D., & Richey, C. A. An assertion inventory for use in assessment and research. *Behavior Therapy*, 1975, *6*, 550–561.

Gay, M. L., Hollandsworth, J. G., Jr., & Galassi, J. P. An assertiveness inventory for adults. *Journal of Counseling Psychology*, 1975, *22*, 340–344.

Gelso, C. J. Effects of recording on counselors and clients. *Counselor Education and Supervision*, 1974, *14*, 5–12.

Glasgow, R. E., & Arkowitz, H. The behavioral assessment of male and female social competence in dyadic heterosexual interaction. *Behavior Therapy*, 1975, *6*, 488–498.

Goldsmith, J. B., & McFall, R. M. Development and evaluation of an interpersonal skill-training program for psychiatric inpatients. *Journal of Abnormal Psychology*, 1975, *84*, 51–58.

Goldsworthy, R. J., & Zegiob, L. *Social skills training in modification of aggressive behavior in incarcerated adolescents.* Paper presented at the annual meeting of the Association for the Advancement of Behavior Therapy, Chicago, November 1978.

Gormally, J., Hill, C. E., Otis, M., & Rainey, L. A microtraining approach to assertion training. *Journal of Counseling Psychology*, 1975, *22*, 229–303.

Green, S. B., Burkhart, B. R., & Harrison, W. H. Personality correlates of self-report, role-playing, and in vivo measures of assertiveness. *Journal of Consulting and Clinical Psychology*, 1979, *47*, 16–24.

Hall, J. R., & Beil-Warner, D. Ordinal position, family size, and assertiveness. *Psychological Reports*, 1977, *40*, 1083–1088.

Hamilton, F., & Maisto, S. A. Assertive behavior and perceived discomfort of alcoholics in assertion-required situations. *Journal of Consulting and Clinical Psychology*, 1979, *47*, 196–197.

Hartsook, J. E., Olch, D. R., & deWolf, V. A. Personality characteristics of women's assertiveness training group participants. *Journal of Counseling Psychology*, 1976, *23*, 322–326.

Hartwig, W. H., Dickson, A. L., & Anderson, H. N. *Locus of control and assertiveness.* Paper presented at the annual meeting of the Southeastern Psychological Association, Hollywood, Florida, 1977.

Hauserman, N., & Lavin, P. Post-hospitalization continuation treatment of anorexia nervosa. *Journal of Behavior Therapy and Experimental Psychiatry*, 1977, *8*, 309–313.

Hautzinger, M. Assertive training procedure in the treatment of obesity. *The Behavior Therapist*, 1979, *2*(1), 23–24.

Haynes, S. N. Behavioral variance, individual differences, and trait theory in a behavioral construct system: A reappraisal. *Behavioral Assessment*, 1979, *1*, 41–49.

Heimberg, R. G., & Harrison, D. F. Use of the Rathus Assertiveness Schedule with offenders: A question of questions. *Behavior Therapy*, 1980, *11*, 278–281.

Heimberg, R. G., Harrison, D. F., Goldberg, L. S., Desmarais, S., & Blue, S. The relationship of self-report and behavioral assertion in an offender population. *Journal of Behavior Therapy and Experimental Psychiatry*, 1979, *10*, 283–286.

Heimberg, R. G., Montgomery, D., Madsen, C. H., & Heimberg, J. S. Assertion training: A review of the literature. *Behavior Therapy*, 1977, *8*, 953–971.

Hersen, M. Modification of skill deficits in psychiatric patients. In A. S. Bellack & M. Hersen (Eds.), *Research and practice in social skills training*. New York: Plenum Press, 1979.

Hersen, M., & Bellack, A. S. Social skills training for chronic psychiatric patients: Rationale, research findings, and future directions. *Comprehensive Psychiatry*, 1976, *17*, 559–580.

Hersen, M., Bellack, A. S., & Turner, S. M. Assessment of assertiveness in female psychiatric patients: Motor and autonomic measures. *Journal of Behavior Therapy and Experimental Psychiatry*, 1978, *9*, 11–16.

Hersen, M., Bellack, A. S., Turner, S. M., Williams, M. T., Harper, K., & Watts, J. G. Psychometric properties of the Wolpe-Lazarus Assertiveness Scale. *Behaviour Research and Therapy*, 1979, *17*, 63–69.

Hersen, M., Eisler, R. M., & Miller, P. M. An experimental analysis of generalization in assertive training. *Behaviour Research and Therapy*, 1974, *12*, 295–310.

Hersen, M., Eisler, R. M., Miller, P. M., Johnson, M. B., & Pinkston, S. G. Effects of practice, instructions, and modeling on components of assertive behavior. *Behaviour Research and Therapy*, 1973, *11*, 443–451.

Hersen, M., Kazdin, A. E., Bellack, A. S., & Turner, S. M. Effects of live modeling, covert modeling, and rehearsal on assertiveness in psychiatric patients. *Behaviour Research and Therapy*, 1979, *17*, 369–377.

Hess, E. P., & Bornstein, P. H. Perceived sex-role attitudes in self and others as a determinant of differential assertiveness in college males. *Cognitive Therapy and Research*, 1979, *3*, 155–159.

Hess, E. P., Bridgwater, C. A., Bornstein, P. H., & Sweeney, T. M. Situational determinants in the perception of assertiveness: Gender-related influences. *Behavior Therapy*, 1980, *11*, 49–58.

Hewes, D. D. On effective assertive behavior: A brief note. *Behavior Therapy*, 1975, *6*, 269–271.

Higgins, R. L., Alonso, R. R., & Pendleton, M. G. The validity of role-play assessments of assertiveness. *Behavior Therapy*, 1979, *10*, 655–662.

Hirsch, S. M., von Rosenberg, R., Phelan, C., & Dudley, H. K. Effectiveness of assertiveness training with alcoholics. *Journal of Studies on Alcohol*, 1978, *39*, 89–97.

Hollandsworth, J. G., Jr. Further investigation of the relationship between expressed social fear and assertiveness. *Behaviour Research and Therapy*, 1976, *14*, 85–87.

Hollandsworth, J. G., Jr. The Adult Self-Expression Scale: Criterion-related validity and utility in a community mental health center setting. *Newsletter of the Association for the Advancement of Behavior Therapy*, 1977, *4*(6), 19–20. (a)

Hollandsworth, J. G., Jr. Differentiating assertion and aggression: Some behavioral guidelines. *Behavioral Therapy*, 1977, *8*, 347–352. (b)

Hollandsworth, J. G., Jr. Self-report assessment of social fear, discomfort, and assertive behavior. *Psychological Reports*, 1979, *44*, 1230.

Hollandsworth, J. G., Jr., & Cooley, M. L. Provoking anger and gaining compliance with assertive versus aggressive responses. *Behavior Therapy,* 1978, *9,* 640–646.

Hollandsworth, J. G., Jr., Galassi, J. P., & Gay, M. L. The Adult Self-Expression Scale: Validation by the multitrait–multimethod procedure. *Journal of Clinical Psychology,* 1977, *33,* 407–415.

Hollandsworth, J. G., Jr., & Wall, K. E. Sex differences in assertive behavior: An empirical investigation. *Journal of Counseling Psychology,* 1977, *24,* 217–222.

Holmes, D. P., & Horan, J. J. Anger induction in assertion training. *Journal of Counseling Psychology,* 1976, *23,* 108–111.

Hull, D. B., & Hull, J. H. Rathus Assertiveness Schedule: Normative and factor-analytic data. *Behavior Therapy,* 1978, *9,* 673.

Hull, D. B., & Schroeder, H. E. Some interpersonal effects of assertion, nonassertion, and aggression. *Behavior Therapy,* 1979, *10,* 20–28.

Jakubowski, P. A., & Lacks, P. B. Assessment procedures in assertion training. *The Counseling Psychologist,* 1975, *5*(4), 84–90.

Janda, L. H., & Rimm, D. C. Type of situation and sex of counselor in assertive training. *Journal of Counseling Psychology,* 1977, *24,* 444–447.

Jansen, M. S., & Litwack, L. The effects of assertive training on counselor trainees. *Counselor Education and Supervision,* 1979, *19,* 27–34.

Jenkins, J. O. *A black perspective of assertive behavior.* Unpublished manuscript, University of Georgia, Athens, 1979.

Jung, H. F. Assertiveness training: A new tool for rehabilitation. *Psychosocial Rehabilitation Journal,* 1978, *2,* 24–29.

Kazdin, A. E. Effects of covert modeling and model reinforcement on assertive behavior. *Journal of Abnormal Psychology,* 1974, *33,* 240–252.

Kazdin, A. E. Covert modeling, imagery assessment, and assertive behavior. *Journal of Consulting and Clinical Psychology,* 1975, *43,* 716–724.

Kazdin, A. E. Assessment of imagery during covert modeling of assertive behavior. *Journal of Behavior Therapy and Experimental Psychiatry,* 1976, *7,* 213–219. (a)

Kazdin, A. E., Effects of covert modeling, multiple models, and model reinforcement on assertive behavior. *Behavior Therapy,* 1976, *7,* 211–222. (b)

Kazdin, A. E. Assessing the clinical or applied importance of behavior change through social validation. *Behavior Modification,* 1977, *1,* 427–452.

Kazdin, A. E. Effects of covert modeling and coding of modeled stimuli on assertive behavior. *Behaviour Research and Therapy,* 1979, *17,* 53–61. (a)

Kazdin, A. E. Imagery elaboration and self-efficacy in the covert modeling treatment of unassertive behavior. *Journal of Consulting and Clinical Psychology,* 1979, *47,* 725–733. (b)

Kazdin, A. E. Situational specificity: The two-edged sword of behavioral assessment. *Behavioral Assessment,* 1979, *1,* 57–75. (c)

Kelly, J. A., Frederiksen, L. W., Fitts, H., & Phillips, J. Training and generalization of commendatory assertiveness: A controlled single subject experiment. *Journal of Behavior Therapy and Experimental Psychiatry,* 1978, *9,* 17–21.

Kiecolt, J., & McGrath, E. Social desirability responding in the measurement of assertive behavior. *Journal of Consulting and Clinical Psychology,* 1979, *47,* 640–642.

Kiesler, D. J. Some myths of psychotherapy research and the search for a paradigm. *Psychological Bulletin,* 1966, *65,* 110–136.

King, L. W., Liberman, R. P., Roberts, J., & Bryan, E. Personal effectiveness: A structured therapy for improving social and emotional skills. *Behavioural Analysis and Modification,* 1977, *2,* 82–91.

Kinney, J. M., Madsen, B., Fleming, T., & Haapala, D. A. Homebuilders: Keeping families together. *Journal of Consulting and Clinical Psychology*, 1977, *45*, 667-673.

Kipper, D. A., & Jaffe, Y. The College Self-Expression Scale: Israeli data. *Psychological Reports*, 1976, *39*, 1301-1302.

Kipper, D. A., & Jaffe, Y. Dimensions of assertiveness: Factors underlying the College Self-Expression Scale. *Perceptual and Motor Skills*, 1978, *46*, 47-52.

Kirschner, N. M. Generalization of behaviorally oriented assertive training. *Psychological Record*, 1976, *26*, 117-125.

Kolotkin, R. A. Situational specificity in the assessment of assertion: Considerations for the measurement of training and transfer. *Behavior Therapy*, 1980, *11*, 651-661.

Lambley, P. The use of assertive training and psychodynamic insight in the treatment of migraine headache: A case study. *Journal of Nervous and Mental Disease*, 1976, *163*, 61-64.

Lange, A. J., & Jakubowski, P. *Responsible assertive behavior: Cognitive/behavioral procedures for trainers.* Champaign, IL: Research Press, 1976.

Langone, M. Assertiveness and Lewinsohn's theory of depression: An empirical test. *The Behavior Therapist*, 1979, *2*(2), 21.

Law, H. G., Wilson, E., & Crassini, B. A principal components analysis of the Rathus Assertiveness Schedule. *Journal of Consulting and Clinical Psychology*, 1979, *47*, 631-633.

Lawrence, P. S. The assessment and modification of assertive behavior (Doctoral dissertation, Arizona State University, 1970). *Dissertation Abstracts International*, 1970, *31*, 1B-1601B. (University Microfilms No. 70-11, 888)

Layne, R. G., Layne, B. H., & Schoch, E. W. Group assertive training for resident assistants. *Journal of College Student Personnel*, 1977, *18*, 393-398.

Lazarus, A. A. Behavioral rehearsal vs. non-directive therapy vs. advice in effecting behavior change. *Behaviour Research and Therapy*, 1966, *4*, 209-212.

Lazarus, A. A. On assertive behavior: A brief note. *Behavior Therapy*, 1973, *4*, 697-699.

Lee, D. Y., Hallberg, E. T., & Hassard, H. Effects of assertion training on aggressive behavior of adolescents. *Journal of Counseling Psychology*, 1979, *26*, 459-461.

Lesser, E. Behavior therapy with a narcotics user: A case report: Ten-year follow-up. *Behaviour Research and Therapy*, 1977, *14*, 381.

Levenson, R. W., & Gottman, J. M. Toward the assessment of social competence. *Journal of Consulting and Clinical Psychology*, 1978, *46*, 453-462.

Lindquist, C. U., Lindsay, J. S., & White, G. D. Assessment of assertiveness in drug abusers. *Journal of Clinical Psychology*, 1979, *35*, 676-679.

Linehan, M. M., Goldfried, M. R., & Goldfried, A. P. Assertion therapy: Skill training or cognitive restructuring. *Behavior Therapy*, 1979, *10*, 371-388.

Linehan, M. M., Walker, R. O., Bronheim, S., Haynes, K. F., & Yevzeroff, H. Group versus individual assertion training. *Journal of Consulting and Clinical Psychology*, 1979, *47*, 1000-1002.

Longin, H. E., & Rooney, W. M. Teaching denial assertion to chronic hospitalized patients. *Journal of Behavior Therapy and Experimental Psychiatry*, 1975, *6*, 219-222.

Loo, R. M. Y. The effects of projected consequences and overt behavior rehearsal in assertive behavior (Doctoral dissertation, University of Illinois, 1971). *Dissertation Abstracts International*, 1972, *32*, 5448B. (University Microfilms No. 72-6988)

MacDonald, M. L. *A behavioral assessment methodology applied to the measurement of assertion.* Unpublished doctoral dissertation, University of Illinois, Urbana, 1974.

MacDonald, M. L. Measuring assertion: A model and method. *Behavior Therapy,* 1978, *8,* 889–899.

Magnusson, D., & Endler, N. S. Interactional psychology: Present status and future prospects. In D. Magnusson & N. S. Endler (Eds.), *Personality at the crossroads: Current issues in interactional psychology.* Hillsdale, NJ: Erlbaum, 1977.

Mahoney, M. J. *Cognition and behavior modification.* Cambridge, MA: Ballinger, 1974.

Mann, P. J., & Flowers, J. V. An investigation of the validity and reliability of the Rathus Assertion Schedule. *Psychological Reports,* 1978, *42,* 632–634.

Matson, J. L., & Stephens, R. M. Increasing appropriate behavior of explosive chronic psychiatric patients with a social-skills training package. *Behavior Modification,* 1978, *2,* 61–76.

Mauger, P., & Adkinson, D. The Interpersonal Behavior Survey. *Assert 28: The Newsletter of Assertive Behavior and Personal Development,* October 1979, pp. 2–3.

Mauger, P., Adkinson, D., & Simpson, D. G. *The interpersonal behavior survey: The manual.* Unpublished manuscript, 1979.

Mauger, P. A., Adkinson, D., Hook, J. D., & Hernandez, S. K. *Mapping the domains of assertive and aggressive behavior classes.* Paper presented at the annual meeting of the American Psychological Association, New York, September 1979.

Mauger, P. A., Firestone, G., Hernandez, S. K., & Hook, J. D. *Can assertiveness be distinguished from aggressiveness using self-report data?* Paper presented at the annual meeting of the American Psychological Association, Toronto, August 1978.

Mauger, P. A., Firestone, G., Hernandez, S. K., Hook, J. D., & Adkinson, D. R. *The interpersonal behavior survey.* Unpublished manuscript, Georgia State University, 1979.

Mauger, P. A., Simpson, D., & Adkinson, D. *The assertiveness and aggressiveness of affirming Christian versus nonreligious persons.* Paper presented at the annual meeting of the American Psychological Association, New York, September 1979.

McFall, M. E., Winnett, R. L., Bordewick, M. C., & Bornstein, P. H. *Nonverbal components of assertive behavior.* Paper presented at the annual meeting of the Association for the Advancement of Behavior Therapy, San Fransisco, December 1979.

McFall, R. M. Behavioral training: A skill-acquisition approach to clinical problems. In J. T. Spence, R. C. Carson, & J. W. Thibaut (Eds.), *Behavioral approaches to therapy.* Morristown, NJ: General Learning Press, 1976.

McFall, R. M., & Lillesand, D. B. Behavior rehearsal with modeling and coaching in assertion training. *Journal of Abnormal Psychology,* 1971, *77,* 313–323.

McFall, R. M., & Marston, A. R. An experimental investigation of behavior rehearsal in assertive training. *Journal of Abnormal Psychology,* 1970, *76,* 295–303.

McFall, R. M., & Twentyman, C. T. Four experiments on the relative contributions of rehearsal, modeling, and coaching to assertion training. *Journal of Abnormal Psychology,* 1973, *81,* 199–218.

McKinlay, T., Pachman, J. S., & Frederiksen, L. W. *Coaction: An innovative approach in the treatment of explosive behavior.* Paper presented at the annual meeting of the Association for the Advancement of Behavior Therapy, Atlanta, December 1977.

McLachlan, J. F., & Walderman, R. L. Brief scales for evaluating assertiveness, marital communication, and work satisfaction. *Journal of Community Psychology*, 1976, *4*, 303–305.

McReynolds, P. The case for interactional assessment. *Behavioral Assessment*, 1979, *1*, 237–247.

Melnick, J., & Stocker, R. B. An experimental analysis of the behavioral rehearsal with feedback technique in assertiveness training. *Behavior Therapy*, 1977, *8*, 222–228.

Miller, P. M., & Eisler, R. M. Assertive behavior of alcoholics: A descriptive analysis. *Behavior Therapy*, 1977, *8*, 146–149.

Miller, P. M., Hersen, M., Eisler, R. M., & Hilsman, G. Effects of social stress on operant drinking of alcoholics and social drinkers. *Behaviour Research and Therapy*, 1974, *12*, 67–72.

Mischel, W. Toward a cognitive social learning reconceptualization of personality. *Psychological Review*, 1973, *80*, 252–283.

Mishel, M. H. Assertion training with handicapped persons. *Journal of Counseling Psychology*, 1978, *25*, 238–241.

Moffett, L. A., & Stoklosa, J. M. Group therapy for socially anxious and unassertive young veterans. *International Journal of Group Psychotherapy*, 1976, *26*, 421–430.

Monti, P. M., Fink, E., Norman, W., Curran, J., Hayes, S., & Caldwell, A. Effect of social skills training groups and social skills bibliotherapy with psychiatric patients. *Journal of Consulting and Clinical Psychology*, 1979, *47*, 189–191.

More, D. M., & Suchner, R. W. Occupational situs, prestige, and stereotypes. *Sociology of Work and Occupations*, 1976, *3*, 169–186.

Morgan, W. G. The relationship between expressed social fears and assertiveness and its treatment implications. *Behaviour Research and Therapy*, 1974, *12*, 255–257.

Mullinix, S. B., & Galassi, J. P. Deriving the content of social skills training with a verbal response components approach. *Behavioral Assessment*, 1981, *3*, 55–66.

Mungas, D. M., & Walters, H. A. Pretesting effects in the evaluation of social skills training. *Journal of Consulting and Clinical Psychology*, 1979, *47*, 216–218.

Nevid, J. S., & Rathus, S. A. Multivariate and normative data pertaining to the RAS with the college population. *Behavior Therapy*, 1978, *9*, 675.

Nevid, J. S., & Rathus, S. A. Factor analysis of the Rathus Assertiveness Schedule with a college population. *Journal of Behavior Therapy and Experimental Psychiatry*, 1979, *10*, 21–24.

Nietzel, M. T., & Bernstein, D. A. Effects of instructionally mediated demand on the behavioral assessment of assertiveness. *Journal of Consulting and Clinical Psychology*, 1976, *44*, 500.

Nietzel, M. T., Martorano, R. D., & Melnick, J. The effects of covert modeling with and without reply training on the development and generalization of assertive responses. *Behavior Therapy*, 1977, *8*, 183–192.

Norton, G. R. Biofeedback treatment of long-standing eye closure reactions. *Journal of Behavior Therapy and Experimental Psychiatry*, 1976, *7*, 279–280.

Norton, R., & Warnick, B. Assertiveness as a communication construct. *Human Communication Research*, 1976, *3*, 62–66.

Onoda, L., & Gassert, L. Use of assertion training to improve job interview behavior. *The Personnel and Guidance Journal*, 1978, *56*, 492–495.

Orenstein, H., Orenstein, E., & Carr, J. E. Assertiveness and anxiety: A correlational study. *Journal of Behavior Therapy and Experimental Psychiatry*, 1975, *6*, 203–207.

Pachman, J. S., & Foy, D. W. A correlational investigation of anxiety, self-esteem and depression: New findings with behavioral measures of assertiveness. *Journal of Behavior Therapy and Experimental Psychiatry,* 1978, *9,* 97–101.

Pachman, J. S., Foy, D. W., Massey, F., & Eisler, R. M. A factor analysis of assertive behaviors. *Journal of Consulting and Clinical Psychology,* 1978, *46,* 347.

Pentz, M. A. W. Assertion training and trainer effects on unassertive and aggressive adolescents. *Journal of Counseling Psychology,* 1980, *27,* 76–83.

Phibbs, J. A., & Arkowitz, H. Minimal dating, assertiveness, and depression. *Behavioral Counseling Quarterly,* in press.

Piercy, F. D., & Ohanesian, D. L. Assertion training in teacher education. *Humanist Educator,* 1976, *15,* 41–47.

Pilla, B. A. Women in business. *Training and Development Journal,* 1977, *31,* 22–25.

Pitcher, S. W., & Meikle, S. The topography of assertive behavior in positive and negative situations. *Behavior Therapy,* 1980, *11,* 532–547.

Quillin, J., Besing, S., & Dinning, D. Standardization of the Rathus Assertiveness Schedule. *Journal of Clinical Psychology,* 1977, *33,* 418–422.

Rachman, S. The conditioning theory of fear-acquisition: A critical examination. *Behaviour Research and Therapy,* 1977, *5,* 375–388.

Rakos, R. F. Content consideration in the distinction between assertive and aggressive behavior. *Psychological Reports,* 1979, *44,* 767–773.

Rakos, R. F., & Schroeder, H. E. Development and empirical evaluation of a self-administered assertiveness training program. *Journal of Consulting and Clinical Psychology,* 1979, *47,* 991–993.

Rashbaum-Selig, M. Assertive training for young people. *School Counselor,* 1976, *24,* 115–122.

Rathus, S. A. A 30 item schedule for assessing assertive behavior. *Behavior Therapy,* 1973, *4,* 398–406.

Rathus, S. A., Fox, J. A., & De Cristofaro, J. Perceived structure of aggressive and assertive behaviors. *Psychological Reports,* 1979, *44,* 695–698.

Rathus, S. A., & Nevid, J. S. Concurrent validity of the 30-item assertiveness schedule with a psychiatric population. *Behavior Therapy,* 1977, *8,* 393–397.

Reardon, R. C., Hersen, M., Bellack, A. S., & Foley, J. M. Measuring social skill in grade school boys. *Journal of Behavioral Assessment,* 1979, *1,* 87–105.

Rehm, L. P., Fuchs, C. Z., Roth, D. M., Kornblith, S. J., & Romano, J. M. A comparison of self-control and assertion skills treatments of depression. *Behavior Therapy,* 1979, *10,* 429–442.

Rich, A. R., & Schroeder, H. E. Research issues in assertiveness training. *Psychological Bulletin,* 1976, *83,* 1084–1096.

Rimm, D. C., Hill, G. A., Brown, N. N., & Stuart, J. E. Group-assertion training in treatment of expression of inappropriate anger. *Psychological Reports,* 1974, *34,* 791–798.

Rimm, D. C., & Masters, J. C. *Behavior therapy: Techniques and empirical findings.* New York: Academic Press, 1974.

Rimm, D. C., Snyder, J. J., Depue, R. A., Haanstad, M. J., & Armstrong, D. P. Assertive training versus rehearsal and the importance of making an assertive response. *Behaviour Research and Therapy,* 1976, *14,* 315–321.

Rock, D. L. Interscale variance analysis of three assertiveness measures. *Perceptual and Motor Skills,* 1977, *45,* 246.

Rodriguez, R., Nietzel, M. T., & Berzins, J. I. Sex-role orientation and assertiveness among female college students. *Behavior Therapy,* 1980, *11,* 353–366.

Romano, J. M., & Bellack, A. S. Social validation of a component model of assertive behavior. *Journal of Consulting and Clinical Psychology,* 1980, *48,* 478–490.

Rose, S. D. In pursuit of social competence. *Social Work*, 1975, *20*, 33–39.

Rose, Y. J., & Tryon, W. W. Judgments of assertive behavior as a function of speech loudness, latency, content, gestures, inflection, and sex. *Behavior Modification*, 1979, *3*, 112–123.

Rosenthal, T. L., & Reese, S. L. The effects of covert and overt modeling on assertive behavior. *Behaviour Research and Therapy*, 1976, *14*, 463–469.

Ruble, T. L., & Thomas, K. W. Support for a two-dimensional model of conflict behavior. *Organizational Behavior and Human Performance*, 1976, *16*, 142–155.

Russell, A., & Winkler, R. Evaluation of assertive training and homosexual guidance service groups designed to improve homosexual functioning. *Journal of Consulting and Clinical Psychology*, 1977, *45*, 1–13.

Ryan, K. A. Assertive training: Its use in leisure counseling. *New Outlook for the Blind*, 1976, *70*, 351–354.

Ryan, K. A. Assertive therapy: An applied approach for use in leisure counseling. *Journal of Leisurability*, 1977, *4*, 7–13.

Salter, A. *Conditioned reflex therapy*. New York: Capricorn Books, 1949.

Sanchez, B., & Lewinsohn, P. M. *Assertion in depressed versus nondepressed samples*. Unpublished manuscript, University of Oregon, 1976.

Scherer, S. E., & Freedberg, E. J. Effects of group videotape feedback on development of assertiveness skills in alcoholics: A follow-up study. *Psychological Reports*, 1976, *39*, 983–992.

Schinke, S. P., Gilchrist, L. D., Smith, T. E., & Wong, S. E. Group interpersonal skills training in a natural setting: An experimental study. *Behaviour Research and Therapy*, 1979, *17*, 149–154.

Schinke, S. P., & Rose, S. D. Interpersonal skill training in groups. *Journal of Counseling Psychology*, 1976, *23*, 442–448.

Schroeder, H. E., & Rakos, R. F. Effects of history on the measurement of assertion. *Behavior Therapy*, 1978, *9*, 965–966.

Schwartz, R. D., & Higgins, R. L. Differential outcome from automated assertion training as a function of locus of control. *Journal of Consulting and Clinical Psychology*, 1979, *47*, 686–694.

Schwartz, R. M., & Gottman, J. M. Toward a task analysis of assertive behavior. *Journal of Consulting and Clinical Psychology*, 1976, *44*, 910–920.

Shaw, M. E., & Rutledge, P. Assertiveness training for managers. *Training and Development Journal*, 1976, *30*, 8–14.

Shelton, J. L., & Mathis, H. V. Assertiveness as a predictor of resident assistant effectiveness. *Journal of College Student Personnel*, 1976, *17*, 368–370.

Sherman, A. R., Barone, D. F., & Turner, R. D. *Behavioral self-management of social-effectiveness skills: Assertion and involvement*. Paper presented at the annual meeting of the Association for the Advancement of Behavior Therapy, Atlanta, December 1977.

Skatsche, R., & Skatsche-Depisch, R. Assertive training: Some critical aspects of research and clinical application. *Behavioural Analysis and Modification*, 1979, *3*, 117–125.

Skillings, R. E., Hersen, M., Bellack, A. S., & Becker, M. P. Relationship of specific and global measures of assertion in college females. *Journal of Clinical Psychology*, 1978, *34*, 346–353.

Smith, M. J. *When I say no, I feel guilty*. New York: Dial, 1975.

Stebbins, C. A., Kelly, B. R., Tolor, A., & Power, M. E. Sex differences in assertiveness in college students. *Journal of Psychology*, 1977, *95*, 309–315.

Stevens, T. G. *The effects of self-instructional videotapes on interpersonal and self-*

management skills: Evaluating an alternative method for delivering psychological services. Manuscript submitted for publication, 1979.

Stokes, T. F., & Baer, D. M. An implicit technology of generalization. *Journal of Applied Behavior Analysis,* 1977, *10,* 349-368.

Sturgis, E., Calhoun, K. S., & Best, C. L. Correlates of assertive behavior in alcoholics. *Addictive Behaviors,* 1979, *4,* 193-197.

Thorpe, G. L. Desensitization, behavior rehearsal, self-instructional training and placebo effects on assertive-refusal behavior. *European Journal of Behavioural Analysis and Modification,* 1975, *1,* 30-44.

Tiegerman, S., & Kassinove, J. Effects of assertive training and cognitive components of rational therapy on assertive behaviors and interpersonal anxiety. *Psychological Reports,* 1977, *40,* 535-542.

Tolor, A., Kelly, B. R., & Stebbins, C. A. Assertiveness, sex-role stereotyping, and self-concept. *Journal of Psychology,* 1976, *93,* 157-164.

Turner, S. M., & Adams, H. E. Effects of assertive training on three dimensions of assertiveness. *Behaviour Research and Therapy,* 1977, *15,* 475-483.

Turner, S. M., Hersen, M., & Bellack, A. S. Social skills training to teach prosocial behaviors in an organically impaired and retarded patient. *Journal of Behavior Therapy and Experimental Psychiatry,* 1979, *9,* 253-258.

Twentyman, C. T., Gibralter, J. C., & Inz, J. M. Multimodal assessment of rehearsal treatments in as assertion training program. *Journal of Counseling Psychology,* 1979, *26,* 384-389.

Twentyman, C. T., & Zimering, R. T. Behavioral training of social skills: A critical review. In M. Hersen, R. M. Eisler, & P. M. Miller (Eds.), *Progress in behavior modification* (Vol. 7). New York: Academic Press, 1979.

Vaal, J. J., & McCullagh, J. The Rathus Assertiveness Schedule: Reliability at the junior high school level. *Adolescence,* 1977, *12,* 411-419.

Van Hasselt, V. B., Hersen, M., Whitehill, M. B., & Bellack, A. S. Social skill assessment and training for children: An evaluative review. *Behaviour Research and Therapy,* 1979, *17,* 413-437.

Vestewig, R. E., & Moss, M. K. The relationship of extraversion and neuroticism to two measures of assertive behavior. *Journal of Psychology,* 1976, *93,* 141-146.

Voss, J. R., Arrick, M. C., & Rimm, D. C. Behavior rehearsal, modeling, and coaching in assertive training. *Behavior Therapy,* 1978, *9,* 970-971.

Wagner, M. K. Comparative effectiveness of behavioral rehearsal and verbal reinforcement for effecting anger expressiveness. *Psychological Reports,* 1968, *22,* 1079-1080.

Warren, N. J., & Gilner, F. H. Measurement of positive assertiveness behaviors: The Behavioral Test of Tenderness Expression. *Behavior Therapy,* 1978, *9,* 178-184.

Weinman, B., Gelbart, P., Wallace, M., & Post, M. Inducing assertive behavior in chronic schizophrenics: A comparison of socioenvironmental, desensitization, and relaxation therapies. *Journal of Consulting and Clinical Psychology,* 1972, *39,* 246-252.

Weiskott, G. N., & Cleland, C. C. Assertiveness, territoriality, and personal space behavior as a function of group assertion training. *Journal of Counseling Psychology,* 1977, *24,* 111-117.

Westefeld, J. S., Galassi, J. P., & Galassi, M. D. Effects of role-playing instructions on assertive behavior: A methodological study. *Behavior Therapy,* 1980, *11,* 271-277.

Williams, M. T., Turner, S. M., Watts, J. G., Bellack, A. S., & Hersen, M. Group social skills training for chronic psychiatric patients. *European Journal of Behavioral Analysis and Modification,* 1977, *1,* 223-229.

Winship, B. J., & Kelley, J. D. A verbal response model of assertiveness. *Journal of Counseling Psychology,* 1976, *23,* 215-220.

Wolf, M. M. Social validity: The case for subjective measurement or how applied behavior analysis is finding its heart. *Journal of Applied Behavior Analysis,* 1978, *11,* 203-214.

Wolfe, J. L., & Fodor, I. G. Modifying assertive behavior in women: A comparison of three approaches. *Behavior Therapy,* 1977, *8,* 567-574.

Wolpe, J. *Psychotherapy by reciprocal inhibition.* Stanford, CA: Stanford University Press, 1958.

Wolpe, J. *The practice of behavior therapy.* New York: Pergamon Press, 1969.

Wolpe, J. *The practice of behavior therapy* (2nd ed.). New York: Pergamon Press, 1973.

Wolpe, J., & Lazarus, A. A. *Behavior therapy techniques: A guide to the treatment of neuroses.* New York: Pergamon Press, 1966.

Woolfolk, R. L., & Dever, S. Perceptions of assertion: An empirical analysis. *Behavior Therapy,* 1979, *10,* 404-411.

Wortmann, H., & Paluck, R. J. Assertion training with institutionalized severely retarded women. *The Behavior Therapist,* 1979, *2*(1), 24-25.

Wyrick, L. C., Gentry, W. D., & Shows, W. D. Aggression, assertion, and openness to experience: A comparison of men and women. *Journal of Clinical Psychology,* 1977, *33,* 439-443.

Young, E. R., Rimm, D. C., & Kennedy, T. D. An experimental investigation of modeling and verbal reinforcement in the modification of assertive behavior. *Behaviour Research and Therapy,* 1973, *11,* 317-319.

Youngren, M. A., & Lewinsohn, P. M. *Depression and problematic interpersonal behavior.* Paper presented at the annual meeting of the Western Psychological Association, San Francisco, April 1978.

Yulis, S. Generalization of therapeutic gain in the treatment of premature ejaculation. *Behavior Therapy,* 1976, *7,* 355-358.

Zeichner, A., Pihl, R. O., & Wright, J. C. A comparison between volunteer drug abusers and non-drug abusers on measures of social skills. *Journal of Clinical Psychology,* 1977, *33,* 585-590.

Zeichner, A., Wright, J. C., & Herman, S. Effects of situation on dating and assertive behavior. *Psychological Reports,* 1977, *40,* 375-381.

Zeiss, A. M., Lewinsohn, P. M., & Muñoz, R. F. Nonspecific improvement effects in depression using interpersonal skills training, pleasant activity schedules, or cognitive training. *Journal of Consulting and Clinical Psychology,* 1979, *47,* 427-439.

Zielinski, J. J. Situational determinants of assertive behavior in depressed alcoholics. *Journal of Behavior Therapy and Experimental Psychiatry,* 1978, *9,* 103-107.

11

ISSUES IN
THE ASSESSMENT
AND TRAINING
OF ASSERTIVENESS
WITH WOMEN

SHARON E. KAHN

SHARON E. KAHN is Associate Professor of Education in the Department of Counseling Psychology at the University of British Columbia, Vancouver, British Columbia. Her research has been in counseling women and in counselor education, specifically in training counselors in feminist and nonsexist counseling and active discovery methods to promote client experience and discovery. She has presented her research on counseling women and assertiveness training at a number of conferences, and has published her findings in such journals as the *Canadian Counsellor, Personnel and Guidance Journal, Journal of College Student Personnel,* and *Counselor Education and Supervision.*

Kahn addresses in her chapter the literature on the definition, assessment, and training of assertiveness in women. As she notes, women have been the major consumers of the widely available assertiveness training programs in North America during the last decade. The editors suggest that this surge in the definition of women as in need of assertion enhancement by women and trainers alike is largely a function of assertiveness being stereotyped as a masculine trait, and masculinity being overvalued socially. The reader is cautioned against equating assertion with competence. Kahn concludes her chapter with a thoughtful discussion of women's social competencies from a broader perspective, valuing feminine sex-typed traits and attending to masculine deficits.

Interest in liberation for social minorities, political openness and public responsibility, and primary prevention of disease and individual responsibility for health and fitness have helped create a great public demand for assertiveness training. Women have been a large nonclinical group recipient, and perhaps the major consumer, of assertiveness training (Shoemaker & Satterfield, 1977). Over the past decade women have explored their social, political, and economic powerlessness through consciousness raising while psychology and psychotherapy have investigated the etiology and remediation of women's psychological problems. Assertiveness training has been popularized as "the answer" for women seeking skills to share in the rewards available for work outside the home and/or to demand rewards for work inside the home.

In attempts to understand assertiveness in relation to the sexes it has been assumed that assertiveness is unidimensional, varying only in intensity, and that the experience of assertive behavior is equivalent across the sexes. These assumptions have enabled researchers and writers to discuss issues such as whether women or men are more assertive and whether women have unique problems in being assertive (Jakubowski-Spector, 1973).

Galassi, DeLo, Galassi, and Bastien (1974) found that males tended to be more assertive than females in openly expressing positive and negative feelings on the College Self-Expression Scale. Hollandsworth and Wall (1977) concluded that males reported higher frequencies of assertive behavior than females on all sex-related data from self-report measures of assertion. Tolor and his associates (Stebbins, Kelly, Tolor, & Power, 1977; Tolor, Kelly, & Stebbins, 1976), however, found women to be significantly more assertive than men on the College Self-Expression Scale. On a self-report measure of social skill (Lowe & Cautela, 1978) females rated themselves as higher in social performance than did males. Similarly, on a measurement of positive assertive behaviors (Warren & Gilner, 1978) female subjects outperformed male subjects. In an examination of sex differences in aggression, assertion, and openness to experience, Wyrick, Gentry, and Shows (1977) concluded that aggression and assertion are related to different personality variables for females and males and may be experienced differently by women and men.

Among female psychiatric patients, assertiveness has been associated with personality disorders (Rathus & Nevid, 1977), lower levels of anxiety, and with self-acceptance (Percell, Berwick, & Beigel, 1974). Among university women assertiveness also has been positively correlated with favorableness of self-concept and to the rejection of traditional sex-role patterns (Tolor *et al.*, 1976). Assertive behaviors and personality traits in women, furthermore, have been positively related to physical attractiveness (Greenwald, 1977; Jackson & Huston, 1975) and sexual satisfaction (Whitley & Poulsen, 1975).

Much has been written about women and assertiveness and a great many studies have been undertaken to describe and measure assertiveness in women, yet the literature on assessment and training of assertiveness has suffered from a lack of systematic, controlled research (McFall & Marston, 1970; Rich & Schroeder, 1976). In this chapter the conceptualization of assertiveness as it relates to women is examined through a critical review of research and theory on assertiveness training and assessment. Specifically, four questions are raised:

1. What is assertiveness in women?
2. What are the components of assertive behavior in women?
3. How is assertiveness in women assessed?
4. How is assertiveness training done for women?

Implications for change in assertiveness training for women are explored in an attempt to enhance interpersonal interactions for and with women.

WHAT IS ASSERTIVENESS IN WOMEN?

Sex differences in personality have been associated both with genetic determinants and with differential socialization experiences. Until recently a major assumption of psychological research on sex differences in personality has been that there is a strong relationship between the degree to which an individual is sex-typed in personality characteristics and the degree to which that individual exhibits appropriate gender-role preferences and behaviors. This assumption of personality differences between the sexes also is associated with the beliefs that masculinity and femininity are opposites and that individuals who conform to normative expectations for their gender-role are better adjusted than those whose preferences and behaviors are not sex-typed. Males have been associated with the instrumental characteristics of masculinity, females with the expressive attributes of femininity. Assertiveness and aggression have been considered masculine traits, whereas passivity has been viewed as a feminine characteristic (Broverman, Broverman, Clarkson, Rosen-krantz, & Vogel, 1970). Thus, Melnick (1973) described certain male subjects as displaying more "masculine assertiveness."

The concepts of sex-linked aggression and passivity are being challenged actively by some members of the psychiatric profession. Symonds (1976) responded to the myth that aggression is associated with masculinity while the essence of femininity is passivity. He argued that aggression is necessary for human survival and growth and is an innate human trait; that specific patterns of response to provocation are learned and culturally determined; and that the dependent solutions to conflict that women have adopted result in particular forms of aggression, such as criticism, envy, and hurt.

The psychological construct of learned helplessness has been suggested in an effort to understand how women learn to be passive and unassertive (Walker, 1978). When human subjects experience helplessness, interference occurs with later learning, motivation lags, and the ability to perceive success is undermined, while emotionality is heightened. Because many females learn effectiveness through their ability to elicit help and protection from others (Hoffman, 1972), they also learn the belief, expectation, or cognitive set that how they respond will have little, if any, effect on what happens. Females have been restricted to indirect, personal, and helpless modes of influence (Johnson, 1976), and thus, their style of interaction may be more compliant and submissive, less direct and forceful than that of males.

Simple dichotomous explanations seldom are adequate to account for complex human behaviors. Males and females overlap greatly on all psychological characteristics and variability within each sex often is more impressive than differences between the sexes. Yet both men and women believe in numerous psychological differences between the sexes and these beliefs and attitudes guide males and females toward gender-role stereotypic behaviors (Unger, 1979).

People expect women to behave unassertively. Women may not only accept this judgment of others and behave so as to fulfill prophecies based on stereotyped beliefs, but also women may find themselves deserving of these judgments.Thus, women may avoid behaviors that do not fit "the feminine role," and when they do engage in "masculine assertiveness," they are likely to encounter disbelief or even hostility from others, which further serves to influence women's behaviors. A common attack against females is the labeling of women who assert themselves as aggressive. Darley (1976) has suggested that, for women, success in achieved roles (e.g., career) may imply failure in ascribed roles (e.g., parent); while the opposite is true for men—success as workers may imply success as spouses and parents. Similarly, assertive behavior in women may be viewed by others and by women themselves as jeopardizing their chances for satisfying emotional experiences as lovers, wives, and mothers.

Gender-related effects of assertive behavior are both personal and in the social system. Women incorporate nonassertiveness into their affective, cognitive, and behavioral repertoires. Concurrently, the characteristics of the situation and the meaning ascribed to those situations by men and women determine the amount and type of interaction in which a woman will engage. Deviancy from cultural norms for gender-appropriate behavior may result in both negative psychological consequences and in punishment in interpersonal situations.

Grady (1979) posited two loci of sex differences: subject sex differences (differences within the individual) and stimulus sex differences (differences that arise in response to the sex of the stimulus person). Broverman and her colleagues (1970) found that practicing therapists believed in sex differences in females and males and that these therapists utilized client sex and normative gender-role expectations as criteria for mental health. Therapists have been criticized for encouraging dependency and passivity in female clients, and thereby discouraging assertiveness in women (American Psychological Association, 1975; Chesler, 1972; Hare-Mustin, 1978; Jakubowski-Spector, 1973).

Given the same social situation, the same reinforcement contingencies, and the same expectancies, both sexes will react similarly (Grady, 1979); but women and men encounter different types of situations and different societal standards for appropriate or effective behavior. Goldfried and D'Zurilla (1969) stated that there has been little attention paid to the importance of the situation in which the behavior in question is expected to occur. They chose a male population for their large-scale study of social competence, arguing that the transition from dependency to independence was different and more salient for males than for females, male experience and female experience being very different.

The question as to whether personality characteristics can be studied outside the individual's environment was raised in 1939 by Lewin and continues today (Mischel, 1977). In definitions of assertiveness the outcome or effectiveness of assertive behavior may be stressed (Rich & Schroeder, 1976; Weiss, 1968), or the social and cultural context of assertive behavior may be emphasized (Alberti, 1977; Wolpe, 1973). In Bandura's (1973) discussion of aggressive behaviors, he focused on the effect of the social context:

> Physical assertiveness is more likely to be defined as aggressive if performed by a female than a male because such behavior departs more widely from common expectations of appropriate female conduct. Conversely, similar assertiveness by boys in a delinquent gang would in all probability be underrated with respect to aggressiveness. (p. 8)

Although the cultural stereotype is that women are unassertive, passive, and submissive (Broverman *et al.,* 1970) there have been no findings over a large and representative sample of studies to evidence this belief. The alleged passivity of women is in sharp contrast to the activity of women in the labor force and at home. At present 50% of married women work (U.S. Department of Labor, 1976). Women as a group make up approximately 40% of the labor force and retain most of their traditional domestic responsibilities.

To answer the question "What is assertiveness in women?" gender-role expectations of women's genetic passivity or socialized nonassertiveness must be understood in relation to societal power and status differentials among women and men. The need to assert oneself in the pursuit of individual goals is not a sex-typed characteristic, but modes of self-assertion are learned in a social context, which polarizes the sexes. Assertiveness involves the effective maintenance of self-esteem and the response to provocation that may be displayed by women and men in different kinds of situations.

WHAT ARE THE COMPONENTS OF ASSERTIVE BEHAVIOR IN WOMEN?

Assertive behaviors vary across many individual and interactional dimensions. Assertiveness requires the components of verbal and nonverbal skills to enable effective interpersonal relations, perceptual and cognitive discriminations of performance and consequences, and facilitative levels of anxiety and feelings of self-esteem. Schwartz and Gottman (1976), in a study on the components of assertive behavior, focused on the refusal of unreasonable requests. They reported that nonassertive females and males, although they knew the competent response, had higher self-perceived tension levels and made more negative self-statements than did assertive women and men. Eisler, Frederiksen, and Peterson (1978) found cognitive differences between male psychiatric patients who were high or low in assertive behaviors. Behaviorally assertive males expected more favorable consequences from others in social situations than did relatively unassertive men.

The interpretation and expectation of one's impact on others depends upon cognitive and perceptual structures. In women these structures often are associated with feelings of guilt about gender-role deviancy and fears of loss of approval from significant others. Women must discriminate not only their skills to be assertive, and contextual issues such as whether other individuals are hostile and/or wield power over them, but also their feelings and beliefs about assertiveness.

MacDonald (1975) stated that those people who need assertiveness training are frequently in ambiguous social roles where role rights are either ill-defined or in cultural flux. Hartsook, Olch, and deWolf (1976) concluded that women seeking assertiveness experienced problems in asserting themselves that were by no means very crippling, severe, or even pervasive, and that in many respects these women functioned in assertive ways. Nonetheless, those women who sought assertiveness training reported high levels of anxiety. In a study of professional women, Brockway (1976) found that professional women were assertive by objectively determined measures, but that their self-report anxiety levels were high.

Anxiety about producing interpersonal conflict and fears of one's suppressed anger or eventual loss of femininity may inhibit assertive behavior in women. Shainess (1977) described women's conflict: "The lack of equitable treatment, especially at the hands of those professing to love and care about them, has led to envy of male privilege, but more often to great anxiety about self-assertion" (p. 116).

In role-played responses to simulated social situations, middle-class adolescent females were more assertive than their male peers. However, in their cognitions, these young women were likely to deny their impact on others (Wine, Smye, & Moses, 1980b). Wine and her colleagues concluded that adolescent females had appropriate assertive skills in their response repertoires but appeared to be inhibited by gender-role expectations and social barriers from believing in their interpersonal competence.

The components of social anxiety and behavioral deficits have been investigated in males and females with problematic low-frequency dating patterns. Men who dated infrequently have been found to be anxious and negative in their self-evaluations (Arkowitz, Lichenstein, McGovern, & Hines, 1975; Rehm & Marston, 1968).

Greenwald (1977) found that female nondaters could accurately predict their performance in role-played heterosexual encounters, and that these women were not overly critical of their performance. These women were, however, less attractive than their peers who dated more frequently. Greenwald labeled this difference a skills deficit in grooming. Jackson and Huston (1975) also found a positive relationship between physical attractiveness in females and assertiveness. Women rarely direct or initiate dates even with men who are well known to them. Societal norms concerning power and status, and even physical attractiveness, interact with feelings about self to determine the opportunities for men and women to engage in social interactions.

Kahn and Greenberg (1980) argued that a capacity for self-assertion extends beyond cognitive or behavioral skills training and includes the capacity to discover one's authentic feelings. Wyrick and her colleagues (1977) found that for women, assertive behavior may result from a high level of openness to a variety of experiences and be motivated by strong and highly personal and subjective emotions. Women high in assertiveness were inclined to respond subjectively, emotionally, and viscerally, and they reported that they enjoyed their feelings, images, and emotions.

Variations in nonverbal or paralinguistic behaviors, such as eye contact, voice loudness, affect, and expressiveness, which accompany the delivery of the verbal content of assertiveness, have been found (Eisler, Miller, & Hersen, 1973). Henley (1977) explained nonverbal communication as the link between the internalized and the externalized control of women. The internalization of "feminine" gender-role norms may occur in moments of response to gestures of dominance. Women's self-limiting behavior may be the end of a sequence in which assertive behavior was attempted and surpressed on the nonverbal level.

The gestures associated with women are those of submission, whereas the gestures associated with men are often indicative of dominance and status. These gestures are learned and may be explained as the acting out of cultural traits that do not reflect individual difference in sexism (Unger, 1979). Because of their nonconscious nature, these nonverbal differences are particularly resistant to change through verbal means (Frieze & Ramsey, 1976). The nonverbal maintenance of gender roles can be seen in the male display of touching, staring, taking up extensive space, and looseness of demeanor. For women the nonverbal maintenance of gender roles is displayed in smiling, tilting the head, averting the eyes, condensing the body, and general body tension.

The confusing interaction of intimacy and power or status in nonverbal behaviors between female and male has been clarified by Henley (1977). She pointed out the privileged nature of male gestures of dominance. A woman who protests the touching, space invasion, or staring by a male may be told that she is reacting unkindly to "friendliness." The woman, however, may experience these nonverbal gestures as provocation or threat to her self-esteem.

The habitual nonverbal patterns of women make it difficult for women to sound matter-of-fact, assertive, or forceful (McConnell-Ginet, 1978). Women's paralinguistic patterns, which include high pitches, extreme shifts in pitch, and the rising in pitch at the end of an utterance, may be interpreted as emotionality, hesitancy, insecurity, or shyness on the part of women. Women's emotional expressiveness may be considered unstable, unpredictable, and unassertive, although other explanations for women's paralinguistic styles are possible, such as the need to hold another's attention or behavior, learned in contact with young children. McMillan, Clifton, McGrath, and Gale (1977) have reinterpreted women's linguistic patterns in terms of a feminine subculture that emphasizes emotional involvement and interpersonal sensitivity.

Women learn to dismiss their anger early, as parents and teachers strongly discourage aggression in girls (Sears, Maccoby, & Levin, 1957). The more aggressive a woman is, the more likely she is to be labeled gender-role deviant, mentally ill, even schizophrenic (Chesler, 1972). In discussing female aggression, Oakley (1972) noted, "In confronting aggression either in their own behaviour or in somebody else's, they are less able to accept and recognize it, and this inability is accompanied by feelings of guilt, conflict, and anxiety" (p. 65). Women who feel guilt, conflict, and anxiety may behave passively in a situation in which some form of self-assertion would be appropriate.

Assertiveness involves the ability to confidently express one's rights interpersonally and to interact with others competently, both acknowledging one's own wants and respecting the rights of others. The components of assertive behavior for women appear to be closely related to the response of others to female verbal and nonverbal behaviors, cognitions concerning the appropriate female role, and feelings of self-esteem and power to affect one's situation.

HOW IS ASSERTIVENESS IN WOMEN ASSESSED?

Methodological difficulties in the assessment of assertiveness in women include a lack of well-validated written measures and in vivo behavioral measures. Low interrelationships among measures of assertiveness support a situation-specific phenomenon (Holmes & Horan, 1976; Skillings, Hersen, Bellack, & Becker, 1978). Assertiveness scales have not reflected unitary traits or dispositions. The endorsement of one's typical degree of assertive behavior has not been predictive of personality-correlated behavior.

Correlations between assertive behaviors and attributes appear more often to be weak than strong and to reflect complex rather than simple associations. Assertiveness, passivity, and aggression may be conceptually similar to femininity and masculinity (Bem, 1974; Spence & Helmreich, 1978); that is, these constructs may be separate orthogonal dimensions that vary independently. Thus, assertiveness, aggression, and passivity may be measurable in varying amounts in the same individual.

Males reported themselves to be more assertive than females with bosses and supervisors, more outspoken when stating opinions (Hollandsworth & Wall, 1977), and less likely than females to ask if they had offended someone (Gambrill & Richey, 1975). Women, on the other hand, reported themselves more assertive than men in the expression of love, affection, and compliments; in the expression of anger to parents (Hollandsworth & Wall, 1977); and less likely than men to question someone's criticism of their work (Gambrill & Richey, 1975). As societal norms predict, men reported taking the initiative in heterosexual contacts (Hollandsworth & Wall, 1977; Gambrill & Richey, 1975).

Gambrill and Richey (1975) reported that subjects, on the basis of a self-report inventory where ratings were obtained for both degree of discomfort and response probability for a given assertive behavior, fell into three categories. Some respondents consistently reported high discomfort ratings coupled with low probability or response ratings. A second category of subjects tended to report low ratings of discomfort in conjunction with high ratings of response probability. A third category of subjects consistently reported high level of discomfort together with high probability of performance. These three categories of subjects may correspond to unassertive people, assertive individuals, and those individuals who perform assertively with a great deal of anxiety.

Other studies in which the social context was manipulated also have revealed variations in assertive behavior. Even high-assertive females were less assertive with men than with other women. These female subjects deferred to men and were significantly more compliant and hesitant in role play with men than with women in an uncomfortable social situation (Skillings et al., 1978). In situations requiring hostile assertion, male psychiatric patients were significantly more assertive with females than with other men (Eisler, Hersen, Miller, & Blanchard, 1975). Studies that have attempted to specify assertiveness training procedures that give rise to a global enhancement of assertiveness (Lawrence, 1970; McFall & Lillesand, 1971; McFall & Marston, 1970; Young, Rimm, & Kennedy, 1973) similarly support a stimulus-specific conception of assertiveness. The individual who is assertive in one context has not been found necessarily to be assertive in another context.

In a survey of almost 200 assertiveness trainers across Canada, MacIsaac (1979) found separate construct clarification for assertiveness and aggression. Characteristics rated with high internal consistency by assertiveness trainers were verbal, behavioral, and personality characteristics of assertion and aggression. This finding contradicts other findings in which it was not possible to study assertion and aggression outside of a situational context (Eisler *et al.*, 1975; Gambrill & Richey, 1975). It may be that researchers and practitioners of assertiveness training agree more easily on the definition and components of assertiveness than do other populations, especially those who seek assertiveness training.

Since assertive behavior is vulnerable to interaction with the situational context, interpersonal perceptions and attributional responses are important in the assessment of assertiveness. The interaction and reciprocal influence over time of phenomenal and behavioral realms is important also and suggests the possibility of latent effects of assertiveness training. To date, there has been inadequate follow-up to determine the generalization and the maintenance of assertiveness training gains. Another difficulty in assessing assertiveness training results has been that short-term treatments may produce changes in assertive behavior that are too small to measure.

Another concern in the assessment of assertiveness is how assertive behavior is conceptualized and operationalized. Examples of how assertiveness has been defined in studies include response to impolite behavior (Jackson & Huston, 1975), response to the solicitation of a stranger (Holmes & Horan, 1976; Kwiterovich, 1977; Winship & Kelley, 1976), and correcting the experimenter's error (Stebbins *et al.*, 1977).

The variety of ways in which assertiveness has been measured is further confounded by the relationship of analogue measures of assertiveness to assertive behavior in the natural environment. With regard to gender differences, it may be that females and males respond more alike in the laboratory, where everyday-life power differentials are equalized, than they do in the natural environment (Eagly,

1978). Taking on the role of subject in an experiment, a female subject may feel more equal to the women and men who also are thought to be experimental subjects than she feels in her daily life. Thus, a woman may feel free to act in assertive ways when performing in a laboratory experiment or filling out a self-report form. Then, too, self-report and observation may yield similar results, since both women and men believe in the same stereotyped differences between males and females (Unger, 1979).

The degree and direction of assertive behavior expressed may depend upon a variety of perceptual and situational variables, including expectancies for success, desires to please self and others, real or perceived behavioral skills, perceived status of others, and degree of intimacy. In an investigation of the relationships between self-reported assertiveness and measures of overt assertive behaviors, Wine, Smye, and Moses (1980a) found that the self-reports of adolescent females were more highly correlated with assertive behaviors than were the self-reports of their male peers. The researchers explained that females are not expected to be assertive. Therefore, female self-descriptions of assertiveness may be more valid than the responses of males, who, according to gender-role norms, are expected to say they are assertive even when they are not.

HOW IS ASSERTIVENESS TRAINING
DONE FOR WOMEN?

The assertiveness literature contains several descriptions of assertiveness training programs for women (Kahn & Greenberg, 1980; Lange & Jakubowski, 1976; Osborn & Harris, 1975; Phelps & Austin, 1975; Wilk & Coplan, 1977). Included in the descriptions of these programs for women is the recognition of the need for skills acquisition and practice, discrimination training for assessing appropriate alternatives in interpersonal situations, and cognitive–affective procedures for lowering anxiety levels and facilitating feelings of self-confidence and self-esteem. A sensitivity to and knowledge of psychological issues particular to female clients also are recommended in assertiveness training for women. Specific practices of therapy with women include mutuality and the sharing of power between therapist and client (DeVoge, 1977; Rawlings & Carter, 1977). Additionally, all-female groups and female leaders have been recommended (Lange & Jakubowski, 1976).

Assertiveness training has been suggested for a variety of problems, including issues in sexuality (Carlson & Johnson, 1975; Liss-

Levinson, Coleman, & Brown, 1975) and depression (Jakubowski, 1977), although most research on assertiveness training for women has employed a university, nonclinical population. Recently assertiveness training has been described for couples and families (Lehman-Olson, 1976). Assertive behavior is viewed as the operationalization of the differentiation concept used in marital and family therapies.

Shoemaker and Satterfield (1977) described a three-level model of assertiveness training that includes nonspontaneous and situation-specific verbal assertive techniques, differentiated assertive beliefs and responses, and awareness and responsibility in an assertive life-style. These three levels of assertiveness training can be seen to relate to behavioral skill training, discrimination among response alternatives, and procedures incorporating self-management and self-discovery processes.

Most treatments have been designed on the basis of the researcher's or the practitioner's judgments of what is important. Cooley (1979) surveyed individuals as to their interests in assertiveness training. Eighty percent of the sample were women. Interests that received highest ratings were being assertive in the face of another's aggression or personal attack; expressing feelings of hurt, anger, and disappointment to people close to one; asserting one's opinion in a group; and asking for help in making requests of others. These findings reveal a gap in packaged assertiveness training treatments. Many assertiveness training programs focus solely, or spend considerable time on, practicing the skill of refusing unreasonable requests (Schwartz & Gottman, 1976).

Assertiveness training programs differ in the amount of time spent practicing scripted versus spontaneous problem situations and the components of assertive behavior emphasized. Two studies have involved individualized training in the clients' own examples of problem situations (Gormally, Hill, Otis, & Rainey, 1975; Lehman-Olson, 1976). One assertiveness training research program emphasized anger induction (Holmes & Horan, 1976); another, rational emotive therapy for hostility toward men (Lehman-Olson, 1976). Winship and Kelley (1976) trained female nursing students in a verbal response model. The model focused upon a three-part verbal response that included empathy, conflict, and action statements.

Modeling has been found to be an effective treatment component (Rosenthal & Reese, 1976; Young et al., 1973), as has coaching plus behavior rehearsal (Turner & Adams, 1977). Kwiterovich and Horan (1977) used a commercial assertiveness training film by Pearlman,

Coburn, and Jakubowski-Spector (1973) as a stimulus for group discussion of assertive behavior. She found no effects of training with the film–discussion program recommended by the leader's guide. Kwiterovich recommended that modeling, rehearsal, and feedback of appropriately assertive responses augment the stimulus film.

Using a larger than usual sample for these effectiveness of treatment studies ($n = 64$), incorporating three treatment conditions, as well as both self-report and behavioral measures, Wolfe and Fodor (1977) investigated the modification of assertive behavior in women. Women in two of the groups—modeling plus behavior rehearsal, and modeling and behavior rehearsal plus rational therapy—showed significant improvement on the ratings of response to a laboratory behavioral test and to nonpracticed scenes. The group trained in rational therapy also showed reduction in situational anxiety. Consciousness raising proved effective only on the paralinguistic scale of the behavioral measure; that is, participants in the consciousness-raising group sounded more confident and less hesitant than individuals who were wait-listed as control subjects, though there were no differences in the content of their assertive responses.

A subjective experience of benefit reported by subjects who do not perform assertively by "objective" measures suggests the difference between one's perceptions and cognitions concerning assertiveness and the overt expression of assertive behavior, as well as the difference between the real power and status differentials between women and men and ideal nonsexist situations. Horrocks and Jackson (1972) differentiated role taking and role playing. In role taking one's behavior is congruent with one's self-concept. The person who is role playing, on the other hand, is performing a set of behaviors specified by a set of role expectations (Kahn & Greenberg, 1980).

One of the problems with research on training in assertiveness has been the lack of specific detail concerning the treatment procedures under review and their interaction with subject characteristics. Although most women have been socialized to know themselves through relying on others' protection and guidance, many women are experiencing personal strength and assertiveness in personal and business relations. Feminine roles vary across particular social groups. Relationships among assertiveness, gender roles, and personality attributes are weak. It is undoubtedly the case that many nonassertive women work and provide for their families; many assertive women marry, have children, and assume traditional feminine-role responsibilities. The conflicts experienced by women who are involved in uncomfortably dependent relationships and those who are mastering independence may require different training procedures.

When adaptive responses exist within a woman's behavioral repertoire, behavior rehearsal, discrimination training, and conflict resolution seem warranted. Anxious performers may need an approach that focuses on cognitive and affective conflicts. A traditional skills training approach may be effective for highly anxious individuals who are unlikely to perform assertively. For those women who do not have intact behaviors, either as a result of psychiatric disturbance or social constriction associated with institutionalization or uninterrupted contact with small children or long-term dependency on parents, husband, or other authority figures, modeling of assertive behaviors may be important.

IMPLICATIONS FOR CHANGE IN ASSERTIVENESS TRAINING FOR WOMEN

Women may experience conflict in asserting themselves either because of the difficulty in changing a long-term investment in a traditional wife- and mother-role or as the result of a determined effort to become self-sufficient such that the expression of legitimate needs is inhibited (Baruch & Barnett, 1979). It is clear that a great deal of attention has been paid to helping women acquire the skills associated with self-assertion. That these behaviors have been thought of as masculine, sex-typed traits has hindered the effective learning of these behaviors by women and the acceptance by others of these behaviors in women. Labeling women passive and men aggressive forms expectations and attributions that perpetuate stereotypic and problematic interpersonal encounters.

An emerging area of assertiveness training includes significant others in the education or therapy process. Results have been equivocal as to the positive and negative effects on husbands and wives when one partner is treated (Eisler, Miller, Hersen, & Alford, 1974; Lehman-Olson, 1976; Muchowski & Valle, 1977; Shoemaker & Paulson, 1976), yet it seems change in communication and interaction styles for women inevitably must involve men as well.

If assertiveness training is understood in relation to the devaluation and discrimination of women in our society such training can be a growth-enhancing strategy for dealing with social oppression. Factors in the social environment are central to how women perceive themselves and are perceived by others, and the socialization and learning experiences of women must be highlighted in assertiveness training programs. The helplessness and powerlessness that many women feel result from social expectations and real events women experience. In order to reduce helplessness and powerlessness, both the social and personal levels of women's lives must be addressed. In education and therapy with women behavioral skill training also should include both cognitions and emotions. In order for the technical skills of assertive behavior to make a difference in female experience, women must feel able to act with confidence and their efforts at self-assertion must be supported by others' beliefs about women's roles.

One way to achieve equal power with males is to know how to adopt masculine forms of status and power. The learning of verbal and nonverbal expressions of assertive behavior is one effort toward acquiring equal status. Other ways to create an egalitarian society are to increase the value of feminine forms or to redefine the forms of social power.

Henley (1977) argued that assertiveness training is education for the victims of sexism and that such training blames women for their behaviors rather than confronting social oppression. The association of trait theories of personality with assertive behavior has victimized women and implied that treatment is necessary for change. As Henley pointed out, the use of the symbols of power by women does not guarantee the acceptance of power in women by society. Then, too, the availability of assertiveness training for middle- and upper-class women provides a vehicle for women to oppress other women whose power and status may be even more limited than that of women who seek assertiveness training (Schneidt, 1977). The problems of sexism loom large and are carried in both conscious and nonconscious forms of interpersonal interaction.

Baker-Miller (1976) defined women's strength as the ability to admit vulnerability yet not remain weak. New definitions of strength for women are based on female life experiences rather than by taking on the attributes of men. Assertiveness training for women may obscure the power and strength of women's authentic anger. Baker-Miller described the strength of women's anger: "Anger can be one of the first authentic reactions. While it is not pleasant in the traditional sense, it may give its own kind of pleasure because of its undeniable hard reality. It can be a mobilizing and strengthening factor, although eventually women can add others to it" (1976, p. 109).

Harragan (1977) encouraged women to understand the gamesmanship in corporate management and to play in an aggressive, nonhostile way, as in some competitive sports. Fierce competition can be admired and respected; niceness, even though labeled "assertiveness," will have little effect in the business world according to Harragan.

Goodchilds (1979) and Johnson (1979) have called for a task-oriented approach that emphasizes a collaborative, open, nonaggressive interaction style to enhance women's values and power. Getting one's way and getting along with others may seem to be in conflict for many women. A shift in focus to getting things done might ease the female burden to smooth out relationship problems and defuse the male struggle to have his way. This focus on competence and effectiveness is reflected in the trend in psychological research to establish androgyny as a gender role that describes females and males who are flexible in situations that require effective interpersonal behavior (Bem, 1974).

A broad conceptualization of assertive behavior that values feminine sex-typed traits and attends to masculine deficits in such behaviors as the expression of emotions, the nurturance of others, and empathic communication (Eisler et al., 1975; Warren & Gilner, 1978) would include social skills in the expression of positive feelings. Valuing these skills associated with women and encouraging men to learn them may facilitate the social acceptance of assertive behaviors in females and enhance feelings of confidence in women. When assertive behaviors are placed in the broad framework of social competence, women exhibiting these behaviors may be viewed as more effective. Weiss (1968) defined social competence as "the individual's ability to communicate understanding, interest, or rapport to the speaker." By this definition, many women perform well. The maintenance of relationships, which women do for both men and women, eventually may come to be as valued as the maintenance of self-esteem through self-assertion. Assertiveness is a multidimensional complex of behavioral, cognitive, and emotional expressions of self and reactions to provocation that rewards both the instigator and recipient(s) in the interaction.

Research problems often reflect the interest of the researcher and available populations. Open, honest communication and the nonviolation of others' rights among professional women, university students, and psychiatric patients may or may not reflect the way other people or specific groups of women interact. The possibility that what has already been found out about assertiveness training for women is biased by gender expectation and attribution suggests that there is much more that can be learned about assertive behaviors in all individuals. One area that might be explored is the relationship of assertiveness to family violence and rape.

Change in gender-role norms for both sexes will reduce the meaning of gender-role deviance and mitigate the need to fault one sex or the other for their behaviors. Gender-role norms are interdependent for males and females such that change in one requires change in the other. Spence and Helmreich (1978) have suggested that in situations that specifically demand interpersonal skills a high degree of expressivity may be likely to facilitate performance when it is combined with instrumentality. Opening up new options for women requires more than merely redirecting females into traditionally masculine ways of behaving and perceiving. Training women to be assertive, valuing "womanly" skills for both sexes, supporting women's positive self-interest, and emphasizing effectiveness for both sexes may be a beginning of much larger changes in assertive response to provocation and self-expression for all individuals.

REFERENCES

Alberti, R. E. (Ed.). *Assertiveness innovations, applications, issues.* San Luis Obispo, CA: Impact, 1977.

American Psychological Association Task Force on Sex Bias and Sex Role Stereotyping in Psychotherapeutic Practice. *American Psychologist,* 1975, *30,* 1169–1178.

Arkowitz, H., Lichenstein, E., McGovern, K., & Hines, P. The assessment of social competency in males. *Behavior Therapy,* 1975, *1,* 3–14.

Baker-Miller, J. *Toward a new psychology of women.* Boston: Beacon, 1976.

Bandura, A. *Aggression: A social learning analysis.* Englewood Cliffs, NJ: Prentice-Hall, 1973.

Baruch, G. K., & Barnett, R. C. Implications and applications of recent research on feminine development. In J. H. Williams (Ed.), *Psychology of women: Selected readings.* New York: Norton, 1979.

Bem, S. L. The measurement of psychological androgyny. *Journal of Consulting and Clinical Psychology,* 1974, *42,* 155–162.

Brockway, B. S. Assertive training for professional women. *Social Work,* 1976, *21,* 498–505.

Broverman, I. K., Broverman, D. M., Clarkson, F. E., Rosenkrantz, P. S., & Vogel, S. R. Sex-role stereotypes and clinical judgments of mental health. *Journal of Consulting and Clinical Psychology,* 1970, *34,* 1–7.

Carlson, N. R., & Johnson, D. A. Sexual assertiveness training: A workshop for women. *The Counseling Psychologist,* 1975, *5,* 53–59.

Chesler, P. *Women and madness.* Garden City, NY: Doubleday, 1972.

Cooley, M. L. Interests of assertiveness trainees. *Journal of Counseling Psychology,* 1979, *26,* 173–175.

Darley, S. A. Big-time careers for the little woman: A dual-role dilemma. *Journal of Social Issues,* 1976, *32,* 85–98.

DeVoge, S. Use of hypnosis for assertive training and self-concept change in women: A case study. *American Journal of Clinical Hypnosis,* 1977, *19,* 226–230.

Eagly, A. H. Sex differences in influenceability. *Psychological Bulletin,* 1978, *85,* 86–116.

Eisler, R. M., Frederiksen, L. W., & Peterson, G. L. The relationship of cognitive variables to the expression of assertiveness. *Behavior Therapy,* 1978, *9,* 419–427.

Eisler, R. M., Hersen, M., Miller, P. M., & Blanchard, E. B. Situational determinants of assertive behaviors. *Journal of Consulting and Clinical Psychology,* 1975, *43,* 330–340.

Eisler, R. M., Miller, P. M., & Hersen, M. Components of assertive behavior. *Journal of Clinical Psychology,* 1973, *29,* 295–299.

Eisler, R. M., Miller, P. M., Hersen, M., & Alford, H. Effects of assertive training on marital interaction. *Archives of General Psychiatry,* 1974, *30,* 643–649.

Frieze, I. H., & Ramsey, S. J. Nonverbal maintenance of traditional sex roles. *Journal of Social Issues,* 1976, *32,* 133–141.

Galassi, J. P., DeLo, J. S., Galassi, M. D., & Bastien, S. The College Self-Expression Scale: A measurement of assertiveness. *Behavior Therapy,* 1974, *5,* 165–171.

Gambrill, E. D., & Richey, C. A. An assertion inventory for use in assessment and research. *Behavior Therapy,* 1975, *6,* 550–561.

Goldfried, M. R., & D'Zurilla, T. J. A behavioral–analytic model for assessing competence. In C. D. Spielberger (Ed.), *Current topics in clinical and community psychology* (Vol. 1). New York: Academic Press, 1969.

Goodchilds, J. D. Power: A matter of mechanics? *The Society for the Advancement of Social Psychology Newsletter,* 1979, *5,* 3.

Gormally, J., Hill, C. E., Otis, M., & Rainey, L. A microtraining approach to assertion training. *Journal of Counseling Psychology,* 1975, *22,* 229–303.

Grady, K. E., Androgyny reconsidered. In J. H. Williams (Ed.), *Psychology of women: Selected readings.* New York: Norton, 1979.

Greenwald, D. P. The behavioral assessment of differences in social skill and social anxiety in female college students. *Behavior Therapy,* 1977, *8,* 925–937.

Hare-Mustin, R. T. A feminist approach to family therapy. *Family Process,* 1978, *17,* 181–194.

Harragan, B. L. *Games mother never taught you: Corporate gamesmanship for women.* New York: Warner, 1977.

Hartsook, J. E., Olch, D. R., & deWolf, V. A. Personality characteristics of women's assertiveness training group participants. *Journal of Counseling Psychology,* 1976, *23,* 322–326.

Henley, N. M. *Body politics: Power, sex, and nonverbal communication.* Englewood Cliffs, NJ: Prentice-Hall, 1977.

Hoffman, L. W. Early childhood experiences and women's achievement motives. Journal of Social Issues, 1972, *28,* 129–156.

Hollandsworth, J. G., Jr., & Wall, K. E. Sex differences in assertive behavior: An empirical investigation. *Journal of Counseling Psychology,* 1977, *24,* 217–222.

Holmes, D. P., & Horan, J. J. Anger induction in assertion training. *Journal of Counseling Psychology,* 1976, *23,* 108–111.

Horrocks, J. E., & Jackson, D. W. *Self and role: A theory of self-process and role behavior.* Boston: Houghton Mifflin, 1972.

Jackson, D. J., & Huston, T. L. Physical attractiveness and assertiveness. *Journal of Social Psychology,* 1975, *96,* 79–84.

Jakubowski, P. A. Assertive behavior and clinical problems of women. In E. I. Raw-lings & D. K. Carter (Eds.), *Psychotherapy for women.* Springfield, IL: Charles C Thomas, 1977.

Jakubowski-Spector, P. Facilitating the growth of women through assertive training. *The Counseling Psychologist,* 1973, *4,* 75–86.

Johnson, P. Women and power: Toward a theory of effectiveness. *Journal of Social Issues,* 1976, *32,* 99–109.

Johnson, P. B., Feminist people and power: Are we copping out? *The Society for the Advancement of Social Psychology Newsletter,* 1979, *5,* 3–4.

Kahn, S. E., & Greenberg, L. S. Beyond a cognitive/behavioral approach: Congruent assertion training. In C. Stark-Adamec (Ed.), *Sex roles: Origins, influences, and implications for women.* Montreal: Eden, 1980.

Kwiterovich, D. K., & Horan, J. J. Solomon evaluation of a commercial assertiveness program for women. *Behavior Therapy,* 1977, *8,* 501–502.

Lange, A. J., & Jakubowski, P. *Responsible assertive behavior: Cognitive/behavioral procedures for trainers.* Champaign, IL: Research, 1976.

Lawrence, P. S. *The assessment and modification of assertive behavior.* Unpublished doctoral dissertation, Arizona State University, 1970.

Lehman-Olson, D. Assertiveness training: Theoretical and clinical implications. In D. Olson (Ed.), *Treating relationships.* Lake Mills, IA: Graphic, 1976.

Lewin, K. Field theory and experiment in social psychology: Concepts and methods. *American Journal of Sociology,* 1939, *44,* 868–896.

Liss-Levinson, N., Coleman, E., & Brown, L. A program of sexual assertiveness train-ing for women. *The Counseling Psychologist,* 1975, *5,* 74–78.

Lowe, M. R., & Cautela, J. R. A self-report measure of social skill. *Behavior Therapy,* 1978, *9,* 535–544.

MacDonald, M. L. Teaching assertion: A paradigm for therapeutic intervention. *Psychotherapy: Theory, Research and Practice,* 1975, *12,* 60–67.

MacIsaac, H. M. *A construct clarification study: Identification of the verbal, behav-ioral and personality components of assertion and aggression.* Unpublished master's thesis, University of British Columbia, 1979.

McConnell-Ginet, S. Intonation in a man's world. *Signs,* 1978, *3,* 541–559.

McFall, R. M., & Lillesand, D. B. Behavior rehearsal with modeling and coaching in assertive training. *Journal of Abnormal Psychology,* 1971, *77,* 313–323.

McFall, R. M., & Marston, A. R. An experimental investigation of behavior rehearsal in assertive training. *Journal of Abnormal Psychology,* 1970, *76,* 295–303.

McMillan, J. R., Clifton, A. K., McGrath, D., & Gale, W. S. Women's language: Uncer-tainty or interpersonal sensitivity and emotionality. *Sex Roles,* 1977, *3,* 545–559.

Melnick, J. A comparison of replication techniques in the modification of minimal dating behavior. *Journal of Abnormal Psychology,* 1973, *82,* 51–59.

Mischel, W. On the future of personality measurement. *American Psychologist,* 1977, *32,* 246–254. ·

Muchowski, P. M., & Valle, S. K. Effects of assertive training on trainees and their spouses. *Journal of Marriage and Family Counseling,* 1977, *3,* 57–62.

Oakley, A. *Sex, gender and society.* New York: Harper & Row, 1972.

Osborn, S., & Harris, G. *Assertive training for women.* Springfield, IL: Charles C Thomas, 1975.

Pearlman, J., Coburn, K., & Jakubowski-Spector, P. *Assertive training for women: A stimulus film.* Washington, DC: American Personnel and Guidance Associa-tion, 1973.

Percell, L. P., Berwick, P. T., & Beigel, A. The effects of assertive training on self-concept and anxiety. *Archives of General Psychiatry,* 1974, *31,* 502–504.

Phelps, S., & Austin, N. *The assertive woman.* San Luis Obispo, CA: Impact, 1975.

Rathus, S. A., & Nevid, J. S. Concurrent validity of the 30 item assertiveness schedule with a psychiatric population. *Behavior Therapy,* 1977, *8,* 393–397.

Rawlings, E. I., & Carter, D. K. (Eds.). *Psychotherapy for women.* Springfield, IL: Charles C Thomas, 1977.

Rehm, L. P., & Marston, A. R. Reduction of social anxiety through modification of self-reinforcement. *Journal of Consulting and Clinical Psychology,* 1968, *32,* 565–574.

Rich, A. R., & Schroeder, H. E. Research issues in assertiveness training. *Psychological Bulletin,* 1976, *83,* 1081–1096.

Rosenthal, T. L., & Reese, S. L. The effects of covert and overt modeling on assertive behavior. *Behaviour Research and Therapy,* 1976, *14,* 463–469.

Schneidt, M. Challenging assertiveness training. *Quest: A Feminist Quarterly,* 1977, *4,* 76–84.

Schwartz, R. M., & Gottman, J. M. Toward a task analysis of assertive behavior. *Journal of Consulting and Clinical Psychology,* 1976, *44,* 910–920.

Sears, R. R., Maccoby, E. E., & Levin, H. *Patterns of child rearing.* Evanston, IL: Row & Peterson, 1957.

Shainess, N. The equitable therapy of women in psychoanalysis. In E. I. Rawlings & D. K. Carter (Eds.), *Psychotherapy for women.* Springfield, IL: Charles C Thomas, 1977.

Shoemaker, M. E., & Paulson, T. C. Group assertion training for mothers: A family intervention strategy. In E. J. Mash, L. C. Handy, & L. A. Hamerlynck (Eds.), *Behavior modification approaches to parenting.* New York: Brunner/Mazel, 1976.

Shoemaker, M. E., & Satterfield, D. O. Assertion training: An identity crisis that's coming on strong. In R. E. Alberti (Ed.), *Assertiveness innovations, applications, issues.* San Luis Obispo, CA: Impact, 1977.

Skillings, R. E., Hersen, M., Bellack, A. S., & Becker, M. P. Relationship of specific and global measures of assertion in college females. *Journal of Clinical Psychology,* 1978, *34,* 346–353.

Spence, J. T., & Helmreich, R. L. *Masculinity and femininity.* Austin: University of Texas Press, 1978.

Stebbins, C. A., Kelly, B. R., Tolor, A., & Power, M. Sex differences in assertiveness in college students. *Journal of Psychology,* 1977, *95,* 309–315.

Symonds, M. Psychodynamics of aggression in women. *The American Journal of Psychoanalysis,* 1976, *36,* 195–203.

Tolor, A., Kelly, B. R., & Stebbins, C. A. Assertiveness, sex-role stereotyping, and self-concept. *The Journal of Psychology,* 1976, *93,* 157–164.

Turner, S. M., & Adams, H. E. Effects of assertive training on three dimensions of assertiveness. *Behaviour Research and Therapy,* 1977, *15,* 475–483.

Unger, R. K., *Female and male: Psychological perspectives.* New York: Harper & Row, 1979.

U.S. Department of Labor, Wage and Labor Standards Administration, Women's Bureau. *Women workers today.* Washington, DC: Author, 1976.

Walker, L. E. Battered women and learned helplessness. *Victimology,* 1978, *2,* 525–534.

Warren, N. J., & Gilner, F. H. Measurement of positive assertive behaviors: The behavioral test of tenderness expression. *Behavior Therapy,* 1978, *9,* 178–184.

Weiss, R. L. Operant conditioning technique in psychological assessment. In P. Mc-Reynold (Ed.), *Advances in psychological assessment.* Palo Alto, CA: Science & Behavior, 1968.

Whitley, M. P., & Poulsen, S. B. Assertiveness and sexual satisfaction in employed professional women. *Journal of Marriage and the Family,* 1975, *37,* 573-581.

Wilk, C., & Coplan, V. Assertive training as a confidence-building technique. *Personnel and Guidance Journal,* 1977, *55,* 460-464.

Wine, J. D., Smye, M. D., & Moses, B. Assertiveness: Sex differences in relationships between self-report and behavioural measures. In C. Stark-Adamec (Ed.), *Sex roles: Origins, influences, and implications for women.* Montreal: Eden, 1980.(a)

Wine, J. D., Smye, M. D., & Moses, B. Sex differences in assertiveness: Implications for research and treatment. In C. Stark-Adamec (Ed.), *Sex roles: Origins, influences, and implications for women.* Montreal: Eden, 1980.(b)

Winship, B. J., & Kelley, J. D. A verbal response model of assertiveness. *Journal of Counseling Psychology,* 1976, *23,* 215-220.

Wolfe, J. L., & Fodor, I. G. Modifying assertive behavior in women: A comparison of three approaches. *Behavior Therapy,* 1977, *8,* 567-574.

Wolpe, J. *The practice of behavior therapy* (2nd ed.). New York: Pergamon, 1973.

Wyrick, L. C., Gentry, W. D., & Shows, W. D. Aggression, assertion, and openness to experience: A comparison of men and women. *Journal of Clinical Psychology,* 1977, *33,* 439-443.

Young, E. R., Rimm, D. C., & Kennedy, T. D. An experimental investigation of modeling and verbal reinforcement in the modification of assertive behavior. *Behaviour Research and Therapy,* 1973, *11,* 317-319.

AUTHOR INDEX

Bromley, D. B., 106, 120n., 138, 145, 155n.
Bronheim, S., 316, 339n.
Broverman, D. M., 92, 95n., 349, 363n.
Broverman, I. K., 349–351, 363n.
Brown, L., 358, 365n.
Brown, N. N., 318, 342n.
Bruch, M. A., 306, 333n.
Brummage, M. D., 299, 300, 333n.
Bryan, E., 313, 338n.
Bryant, B., 38, 60n., 108, 122n., 238, 255n., 262–264, 282, 283, 284n.–286n.
Buell, G. J., 233, 255n.
Buell, J. S., 136, 152n.
Burchardt-Pharr, C., 295, 299, 333n.
Burgess, P., 267, 268, 285n.
Burkhardt, B. R., 308–310, 313, 333n., 336n.
Burnstein, E., 72, 98n.
Busk, P. L., 128, 153n.
Buss, A. H., 106, 118n.
Butler, L. J., x, 26, 32, 36–60, 42, 45, 56n., 58n., 106, 148, 153n., 232
Byers, S. D., 70, 96n.

Cacioppo, J., 42, 56n.
Caldwell, A., 317, 341n.
Caldwell, B. M., 182, 183n.
Calhoun, K. S., 320, 344n.
Callner, D. A., 311, 321, 333n.
Camp, B., 112, 118n., 182, 183n.
Campbell, A., 277, 285n.
Campbell, J. D., 48, 56n., 144, 145, 157n.
Carlson, N. R., 357, 363n.
Carlson, P. M., 108, 110, 120n.
Carmody, T. P., 324, 325, 333n.
Carr, J. E., 305, 341n.
Carter, D. K., 357, 366n.
Cartledge, G., 109, 118n.
Cassel, J., 88, 95n., 97n., 98n.
Cassem, H., 68, 96n.
Cautela, J. R., 347, 365n.

Cerling, D. C., 226, 230n.
Chandler, M. J., 46, 56n., 104, 105, 118n.
Chandler, T. A., 308, 311, 333n.
Chaney, E. F., 320, 333n.
Charlesworth, R., 109, 118n., 119n., 128, 154n.
Chase, W., 47, 56n.
Cherones, J., 308, 331n.
Chesler, P., 17, 22, 33n., 350, 354, 363n.
Chinsky, J., 45, 55n., 113, 120n.
Chodoff, P., 88, 96n.
Christensen, C. M., ix–xi
Clarkson, F. E., 349, 363n.
Clausen, J., 126, 154n.
Cleland, C. C., 310, 316, 344n.
Clifford, E., 136, 137, 153n.
Clifton, A. K., 354, 365n.
Cobb, J. A., 109, 118n.
Cobb, S., 88, 95n.
Coburn, K., 359, 365n.
Coché, E., 182, 183n.
Coe, W., 51, 59n.
Coffey, H. S., 194, 230n.
Cohen, A. S., 130n., 153n.
Cohen, J. B., 65, 68, 71, 72, 93, 95n., 97n.
Coie, J. D., 146, 153n.
Cole, R., x
Coleman, E., 358, 365n.
Cone, J. D., 310, 333n.
Cook, B., 308, 333n.
Cook, M., 261
Cooley, M. L., 299, 338n., 358, 363n.
Cooper, M., 113, 118n.
Coplan, V., 357, 367n.
Coppotelli, H. A., 146, 153n.
Cottrell, L. S., 62, 96n.
Cowen, E. L., 113, 119n., 126, 148, 153n.
Coyne, J. C., 89, 95n.
Craighead, L. W., 324, 325, 333n.
Crassini, B., 308, 339n.
Criswell, J. H., 130, 138, 153n.
Crockett, W. H., 138, 156n.
Crutchfield, R. S., 102, 118n.

SUBJECT INDEX